THE REMINISCENCES OF
Captain Frank A. Manson
U.S. Navy (Retired)

INTERVIEWED BY
Paul Stillwell

U.S. Naval Institute • Annapolis, Maryland

Copyright © 2014

Preface

Three principal strong points make this oral memoir valuable to historians. First is that Manson survived one of the most ferocious kamikaze mass attacks of the World War II while serving on board the destroyer *Laffey* (DD-724) in April 1945. His description of the ship's ordeal led to a specialized career within the Navy's public information/public affairs arm. Shortly after World War II, the Navy established a public information (later public affairs) specialty for restricted line officers; Manson was among the first group of officers so designated.

He was a front-row participant in the Navy's 1949 guerrilla attack as the Army and the newly established U.S. Air Force sought to capture Navy and Marine Corps aviation. He also co-authored books that provided cogent, readable descriptions of Navy operations in World War II and the Korean War. He was a speechwriter and advisor for several Chiefs of Naval Operations and, in the early 1950s, was in on the ground floor of the establishment of the North Atlantic Treaty Organization's military component, designed to counter massive attacks against NATO nations in Europe.

Perhaps most valuable of all were his close personal working relationships with a series of four-star admirals: Louis Denfeld, Forrest P. Sherman, Robert B. Carney, Arleigh A. Burke, Harold Page Smith, Harry Don Felt, Robert L. Dennison, David L. McDonald, John S. McCain Jr., and Claude V. Ricketts. This oral history offers Manson's candid assessments of all of them.

Still another feather in his cap came from his development of the "White Fleet" concept, whereby surplus Navy ships would be used for humanitarian purposes throughout the world. His enthusiastic salesmanship of the concept—though it never came into being—drew a great deal of positive public attention to the Navy.

Captain Manson and I did the interviews for the oral history in 1987-88. I greatly regret that competing priorities prevented me from making the contents of the interviews publicly available far sooner. During the period of the interviews and for several years afterward, I was also the editor-in-chief of *Naval History* magazine; its deadlines had to come first. Captain Manson had the opportunity to review and edit the transcripts of the first two interviews in the series, and I have incorporated his changes in the finished product. While editing the final four interviews for clarity, smoothness, and accuracy, I have used an editing style similar to that of Captain Manson. The interviewee's son, Frank Karig Manson, was most generous and gracious in providing valuable additional information about the family. I am grateful for his generosity in enhancing the legacy his dad recorded. In addition, Captain Manson asked for the inclusion in the finished volume of an article about his World War II service. It is at the end of the volume as an appendix.

As the project finally comes to a close, making available the work that Captain Manson intended for publication, I thank Janis Jorgensen of the Naval Institute staff who coordinated the printing and binding of the finished history.

In completing the volume, the Naval Institute expresses its gratitude to the Tawani Foundation and the Pritzker Military Library of Chicago for their generous financial support of the oral history program that produced this memoir.

Paul Stillwell
U.S. Naval Institute
January 2014

CAPTAIN FRANK ALBERT MANSON
UNITED STATES NAVY (RETIRED)

Frank Albert Manson was born in Drumright, Oklahoma, on 26 December 1920, the son of Asa and May Manson; his mother became May Manson Reynolds after her husband died and she remarried. Frank Manson attended public schools in Tahlequah, Oklahoma, and in 1941graduated from Northeastern State Teachers' College at Tahlequah with a bachelor of science degree. He was employed for a brief period as a schoolteacher at Picher (Oklahoma) High School, where he taught economics, government, and speech. He later served for six months in the State Department, Washington, D.C. Commissioned ensign in the U.S. Naval Reserve on 1 July 1942, he transferred to the regular Navy on 7 May 1947 and subsequently attained the rank of captain, to date from 1 September 1962.

Upon receiving his appointment in 1942, he had indoctrination training at the Naval Training School, Cornell University, Ithaca, New York. Completing the course there in September 1942, he served in the office of the Deputy Chief of Naval Operations for Communications, Navy Department, Washington, D.C. In May 1943, he reported as communications officer and assistant operations officer in the Destroyers Atlantic administrative office, Boston Navy Yard, and remained in that capacity until July 1944.

Ordered to duty afloat, he joined the USS *Laffey* (DD-724), and while on board that destroyer, serving first as assistant communications officer and later communications officer, he participated in the fast carrier strikes on the Philippines, November 1944; defense of Leyte Gulf, early in December; invasions of Ormoc Bay, 7 December 1944; Mindoro, 15 December 1944; and Lingayen Gulf, 9 January 1945; fast carrier strikes on Tokyo and radar picket duty at Okinawa, March-April 1945. For services in the *Laffey* he received a letter of commendation, with authorization to wear the commendation ribbon with combat "V" and was entitled to the ribbon for and a facsimile of the Presidential Unit Citation awarded to the *Laffey*. The citations read in part:

Letter of commendation: "For meritorious conduct . . . as Communications Officer and Public Relations Officer aboard the USS LAFFEY after she was damaged in an engagement with Japanese planes while serving as a radar picket ship off Okinawa on April 16, 1945. He displayed outstanding professional ability and initiative in ascertaining and presenting the facts of this complex engagement to the Public Relations Officers and correspondents while his ship was undergoing emergency repairs at Okinawa and again after the ship returned to Seattle . . . "

Presidential Unit Citation: "For heroism in action . . . during an attack by approximately thirty enemy Japanese planes . . . April 16, 1945. Fighting her guns valiantly against waves of hostile suicide planes plunging toward her from all directions, the USS LAFFEY sent up relentless barrages of anti-aircraft fire during an extremely heavy and concentrated air attack. Repeatedly finding her targets, she shot eight enemy planes clear of the ship and damaged six more before they crashed on board. Struck by two bombs, crash-dived by suicide planes and frequently strafed, she withstood the devastating blows unflinchingly and, despite severe damage and heavy casualties, continued to fight effectively until the last plane had been driven off. . . . "

Detached from the *Laffey* in November 1945, Manson served on the Secretary of the Navy's Committee on Research on Reorganization (SCOROR) and between February and April 1946 had duty as officer in charge of an inspection group that conducted a tour across the Pacific, investigating and reporting on the disposal of surplus property. In May 1946 he returned to the Navy Department and was assigned to the writing of the Navy's World War II history. He collaborated with Captain Walter Karig, USNR (Retired), on the last two volumes of the Navy's *Battle Report* series, *The End of an Empire* and *Victory in the Pacific*. In addition, he wrote a number of articles for periodicals, including *The Saturday Evening Post* and *Life* magazine.

Manson reported for duty in the office of the special assistant to the Chief of Naval Operations in June 1948 and continued to serve there until September 1950, when he was assigned to the Office of Information, Department of the Navy. In September of the same year, he was assigned temporary additional duty in the Far East to gather information on the Korean War for preparation of the sixth volume of *Battle Report*. He participated in the invasion of Wonsan, North Korea, and carrier strikes on the Yalu River that separates North Korea from Communist China. He returned to the United States in mid-December 1950 and collaborated on his third volume in the *Battle Report* series, *War in Korea*. In September 1952 he reported as command historian to Commander in Chief Allied Forces Southern Europe, Admiral Robert B. Carney. When Admiral Carney was appointed Chief of Naval Operations in August 1953, Manson returned with him as his special assistant. He continued in this capacity when Admiral Arleigh A. Burke became Chief of Naval Operations in August 1955. In September 1956 he was assigned as head of Plans and Policies Analysis, Office of Progress Analysis, in the Office of the Chief of Naval Operations.

In July 1958 Manson was detached from the Navy Department and reported to the Naval War College, Newport Rhode Island, as a student. Upon completion of this course, he was ordered to the staff of the Commander in Chief U.S. Naval Forces Eastern Atlantic and Mediterranean, located in London, England. In May 1963, he was ordered to the Office of Information, Department of the Navy, where he served until July 1964, as director, Planning and Evaluation Group. In July 1964, he was ordered to the staff of NATO's Supreme Allied Commander Atlantic as chief of public information.

In June 1957, the U.S. Naval Institute published *The Sea War in Korea*, written by Manson in collaboration with Commander Malcolm W. Cagle. For this comprehensive history of naval operations during the Korean War, he was honored with a letter of appreciation from the Chief of Naval Operations of the Republic of Korea Navy. This letter, presented to him by the Korean naval attaché in Washington on 10 April 1958, read in part " . . . has distinguished himself by his exceptionally outstanding and meritorious service and has made an immeasurable contribution to the development of the Republic of Korea Navy by editing and compiling the great literary work of 'The Sea War in Korea' . . . indeed, his excellent work will greatly assist and encourage the

Republic of Korea Navy in the advancement and progress of its battle readiness and efficiency...."

The book, which distilled the lessons of the Korean War, advocated a concept of balanced military forces as the prevailing strategy of the United States. Giving further emphasis to the importance of this book, the Soviet Government in the fall of 1962 published its own translation of *The Sea War in Korea* with its own changes and modifications, including the deletion of the foreword by Admiral Arleigh Burke, former Chief of Naval Operations. *The Sea War in Korea* was selected for the permanent White House library in 1963.

Manson was one of the winners of the Freedom Foundation Award in 1959 for his prize essay on "Winning Friends for Freedom." He was awarded the U.S. Navy League's Alfred Thayer Mahan Award in 1958 for his literary achievements in writing books and articles on naval tactics and strategy.

In the fall of 1957, Manson originated a plan known as the Great White Fleet concept, which envisioned the use of surplus Navy ships for emergency and technical aid to developing countries. He worked on the logistics feasibility of this plan while attending the Naval War College in Newport, Rhode Island, in 1958-59. Numerous congressional resolutions were submitted over the years, recommending the establishment of such a fleet. The U.S. Senate adopted a resolution in support of the Great White Fleet in 1961. In recognition of the concept for his leadership on people-to-people programs in the U.S. Navy, Manson was awarded the Veterans of Foreign Wars Commander in Chief's Gold Medal in 1963.

In September 1964 Manson was one of ten NATO officers cited for outstanding achievement during NATO's triennial maritime Exercise Team Work, in which seven nations, 30,000 personnel, and 170 ships participated. Manson was commended for his leadership as chairman of the command information bureau with headquarters in Whitehall, London. His commendation from the Supreme Allied Commander Atlantic, Admiral Harold Page Smith, was presented on 22 January 1965 in Norfolk, Virginia. It reads in part: "By his foresight, leadership, and imagination, coupled with his professional utilization of various public information media, a better understanding and appreciation of the importance of seapower to the Alliance was formed in the various NATO countries. Under his effective management, this group of personnel, inexperienced for the most part in such a complex undertaking, were welded together and effectively guided by him in making the public information of 'TEAM WORK' undeniably successful."

In national recognition of his public relations at the NATO command, the National Public Relations Society of America awarded the Silver Anvil of 1964 to Supreme Allied Commander Atlantic for the year's most outstanding achievement in the field of international public relations.

In August 1968, Manson was transferred from the NATO command and became chief of the Magazine and Book Division, Office of the Assistant Secretary of Defense (Public Affairs), Department of Defense, Washington, D.C. On 1 January 1969, he retired from active duty with the Navy.

In addition to the commendation ribbon with combat "V" and the Presidential Unit Citation, Manson earned the American Campaign Medal; the Asiatic-Pacific Campaign Medal with four engagement stars; the World War II Victory Medal; the Philippine Liberation Ribbon with one star; the Navy Occupation Service Medal, Asia clasp; the National Defense Service Medal; the Korean Service Medal; and the United Nations Service Medal. He was also awarded the Korean Presidential Unit Citation.

After his retirement from the Navy, Manson was active in congressional, national security, and foreign affairs. He served as director, National Security and Foreign Affairs for the Veterans of Foreign Wars; legislative assistant to Congressman William R. Anderson; the Reserve Officers Association; and as assistant director for the National Security-Foreign Relations Division of the American Legion.

Manson married the former Orie Lee Pickren of Brunswick, Georgia, in Annapolis, Maryland, on 26 May 1948. They were the parents of five children: Frank Karig Manson, now a financial advisor; Jennifer Joy Wilson Pinninger, who had a long career in politics and industry; Barbara Lynne Wilson, now a high school teacher; Melanie Leigh Manson, who died at age five; and Janice Celeste Manson, who died when she was four days old. The Mansons were married for 56 years.

Captain Manson died 20 January 2005 at Culpepper Regional Hospital in Virginia. Mrs. Manson died 14 March 2006.

Deed of Gift

The U.S. Naval Institute is hereby authorized to make available to individuals, libraries, and other repositories of its choosing the audio recordings and/or transcripts of six oral history interviews concerning the life and naval career of the late Captain Frank A. Manson. The Naval Institute may also, at its discretion, use the material in electronic/digital format, including posting on the Internet. The interviews were recorded on 10 December 1987, 23 February 1988, 8 March 1988, 13 April 1988, 21 April 1988, and 28 April 1988 by Captain Manson in collaboration with Paul Stillwell for the U.S. Naval Institute.

The undersigned does hereby release and assign to the U.S. Naval Institute the rights and title to these interviews, with the exception that the Manson family retains the right to use the material for its own purposes. The copyright in both the oral and transcribed versions shall be the property of the U.S. Naval Institute. The audio recordings of the interviews are and will remain the property of the U.S. Naval Institute.

Signed and sealed this __12th__ day of __December__ 2013.

Frank Karig Manson
on behalf of Frank A. Manson

Interview Number 1 with Captain Frank A. Manson, U.S. Navy (Retired)
Place: U.S. Naval Institute, Annapolis, Maryland
Date: Thursday, 10 December 1987
Interviewer: Paul Stillwell

Paul Stillwell: Captain, to begin at the beginning, could you please tell me something about your parents and your early memories from childhood.

Captain Manson: Well, my parents were sort of pioneers in Oklahoma. My father was county commissioner and built the first bridges and roads in Cherokee County. He was a businessman there, too, and a farmer. They had come from Missouri into Oklahoma around statehood.* So my early childhood was pretty much land oriented.

I never dreamed of going into the Navy. I never even dreamed of a military career. I was more interested in the Foreign Service and a political career. My dad had sort of gotten me into politics, and I'd helped him in his campaigns. I was a Republican, and that was not too good—in Oklahoma, anyway. I won the state oratorical contest sponsored by the Republican Party on the duty of the minority party.

Paul Stillwell: What year was that?

Captain Manson: That would have been in 1940. I was pretty much pointed in that direction. I went to the State Department, taught school for a brief moment.

Paul Stillwell: When did you get your college degree?

Captain Manson: The summer of '41. I was an intercollegiate debater and occasionally won a championship.

Paul Stillwell: You were studying journalism, too, weren't you?

---

* The territory of Oklahoma achieved statehood as part of the United States in 1907.

Captain Manson: I was studying journalism and worked on the paper. I was all over the place, really. I was manager of the football team, member of the varsity tennis team, and if there was anything out there that my size would permit me to get into, I was mixing it up. I was just always involved.

Then I started law school in Washington, preparing also for the Foreign Service when World War II came.[*]

Paul Stillwell: Which school were you going to?

Captain Manson: Southeastern, which was a new one.[†] DePaul University of Chicago had sent some faculty members in here for people like myself who worked. Both in morning and afternoon we went to law school. But the war came in, and that was the end of that.

Paul Stillwell: What job were you working at while you were going to law school on the side?

Captain Manson: I was over in the State Department in chancery work, doing passports and working on fraud and all that stuff that they do in passport work. I was getting acquainted with the diplomatic service, really.

Paul Stillwell: What induced you to join the Navy when the war came along?

Captain Manson: Well, I suppose the biggest incentive was the fact that I could qualify for a commission. I did not want the Army and the dirt and the trenches and all that kind of warfare. I figured the Navy would be a fairly clean existence. That's not a very good basis for making a decision, but that's about the extent of it.

---

[*] The United States entered World War II in response to the Japanese attack on Pearl Harbor in December 1941.
[†] Southeastern University was in Washington, D.C. The school went out of business in 2009 and later merged with Graduate School USA.

Paul Stillwell: What steps did you follow once you'd made the decision?

Captain Manson: I went down to the Navy recruiting station, and they told me that I needed to put on a little bit of weight—I was a little underweight—and that if I did that I could qualify for a commission. So I put on the pounds with bananas and a few other things. That was in the spring of '42. So then three weeks later I was made what they call a probationary officer and was sent to Cornell University.* It was Cornell's first class.

I liked the Navy. The first thing that I learned about the Navy at Cornell was the integrity of the organization. They insisted that people tell the truth, and this really did impress me. It was the first time in my life that I had ever seen any organization that said, "This is of prime importance," and I thought, "Well, I like this."

Paul Stillwell: Was this the V-12 program?

Captain Manson: No. It was called Navy indoctrination. It was basically courses in a little bit of everything, just a smattering of gunnery, seamanship, navigation, but mainly about discipline, I would say.

I became a platoon commander right away, and I stayed in there the entire time as a platoon commander. I thought that was great stuff. Never having been in the military, I sort of liked all that marching.

Paul Stillwell: How did this fit in with Cornell's regular collegiate program?

Captain Manson: It was on the side. Cornell had made some of their residential halls available. Baker Hall and Cascadilla Hall were the two main halls. We had a large group; I'll tell you that.

Paul Stillwell: How many, would you guess?

---

* Cornell University in Ithaca, New York, is a member of the Ivy League.

Captain Manson: I would say nearly 1,000, maybe. I really don't know how many.

Paul Stillwell: How long did the training period last?

Captain Manson: I think we had two battalions. It lasted about eight weeks. Then we were sent off to ships and shore stations. I remember the captain, Captain Chippendale.* He said that before snow flew we'd be in battle, and that was in '42. I guess some were, but I went to Washington, D.C., to be in communications, and I didn't think much of that.

Paul Stillwell: Why not?

Captain Manson: It was too dry and boring, and I was young and aggressive and "up and at 'em." So I wrote a letter to BuPers saying I wanted to get into destroyers and into action. It was a letter I lived to regret, but they accommodated me.

They first sent me to Boston to a destroyers' administrative office. From there I was watching the destroyers and their skippers come and go. By that time I was the ops officer at the administrative office and a boarding officer for all the incoming ships. I had been aboard a lot of ships by that time.

Paul Stillwell: Was Captain Menocal there?

Captain Manson: G. L. Menocal was my boss.†

Paul Stillwell: What do you remember about him?

Captain Manson: Well, I remember that he was very angry with me when I got dispatch

---

* Captain Burton W. Chippendale, USN, commanded the naval training school at Cornell.
† Captain George L. Menocal, USN, Administrative Commander Destroyer Squadron 27/Boston Representative of Commander Destroyers Atlantic Fleet.

orders to go aboard the USS *Laffey*.* And I remember when I wrote a speech for him, for which he was very appreciative. He called me to tell me how much the audience liked it. It was on amphibious warfare. He said it was very well received. I said, "Is that so?"

He replied, "Yes, that's so," in a sarcastic tone. Well, the fact that I still remember it—it was a mixed blessing to do something for somebody and have him thank you and then kick you in the seat of the pants at the same time. But another thing about him, he was a flashy kind of guy. His father was a former governor of Cuba. Captain Menocal had a lovely, gracious wife and a lovely daughter named Suzanne, whom I used to date. But I never would get at all serious with her, because I was really afraid of Captain Menocal. He frightened me. Very unpredictable.

Paul Stillwell: He frightened you in what ways?

Captain Manson: Well, you never knew whether he was going to be with you or against you. Let's see, what's that word that describes weather when it's unpredictable? Well, that's the way he was, anyway. Very emotional. He appeared to harbor supposed anger, which became stormy in a flash.

Paul Stillwell: Did he have a tendency to get very irritated about small things?

Captain Manson: Yes. He'd climb all over people for the smallest thing. This was sort of contrary to my philosophy of life, and so I didn't want to get in trouble by dating his daughter. They would invite me out to their house too. I had to walk a very narrow line, because I did like her; she was a very nice girl. My roommate married her, Lieutenant A. B. Ray. He was Supply Corps.

Paul Stillwell: What sorts of duties did you have in that job?

---

* USS *Laffey* (DD-724) is an *Allen M. Sumner*-class destroyer commissioned 8 February 1944. She had a standard displacement of 2,200 tons, was 376 feet long, 41 feet in the beam, and a maximum draft of 19 feet. Her design speed was 34 knots. She was armed with six 5-inch guns, six 21-inch torpedo tubes, and both 20-millimeter and 40-millimeter antiaircraft guns. The ship is now a museum at Mount Pleasant, South Carolina.

Captain Manson: Well, first off, I was in communications. Then Henry Reck went to join Admiral Morison in researching his history series.* When Reck left, they put me in his job, which was ops officer. Mainly, I had to keep track of the comings and goings of ships and to issue foxer gear, which was ASW-type noise-making gear that you pulled behind ships. I also issued Mark 14, Mod 2 sights to the Atlantic fleet.

Paul Stillwell: These were for the antiaircraft guns?

Captain Manson: Yes, 20 millimeter, and I was in charge of that. I used to go aboard incoming ships as a boarding officer, find out what their needs were, their deficiencies, and put it all down and take it to whomever could respond.

Paul Stillwell: The main ComDesLant was up at Casco Bay, Maine.† What was your function separate from that?

Captain Manson: We were SOPA as ComDesRon 27.‡ We also served as ComDesLant's rep in Boston. We were on the spot with the ships. We saw to it that destroyers got the repairs they needed. We inspected their communications setup to see if they had all they needed for long periods at sea. While ships were in port, we received all their message traffic and delivered it to them each day. Com One also helped us on this.§

Paul Stillwell: So that would be your main job, being on-the-spot representative in Boston?

Captain Manson: Yes, that was it. You're amazing me, though, with your knowledge of that time and that place.

---

* Lieutenant Henry D. Reck, USNR.
Rear Admiral Samuel Eliot Morison, USNR, was a noted civilian historian at Harvard University. He received a Naval Reserve commission as a lieutenant commander in order to collect material for what eventually became the 15-volume *History of United States Naval Operations in World War II*.
† ComDesLant – Commander Destroyers Atlantic Fleet.
‡ SOPA – senior officer present afloat.
§ Com One – Commandant First Naval District, based in Boston.

Paul Stillwell: I wrote a book about the *New Jersey*.* Captain Menocal was the skipper, and he displayed some of the same personality traits on board that ship.†

Captain Manson: Oh, did he? Well, at that point in time, of course, I respected him because he'd come from combat—destroyers—and he'd broken his foot. A table had fallen against him or something or other. I had sympathy for his pain and arthritis and everything. But at the same time I had to beware.

Paul Stillwell: That may well have contributed to your desire to go to sea.

Captain Manson: Well, he said I needed salt in my beard; he told me that. So when I heard from Commander Becton, I told him I'd like to go to sea with him.‡ He said if I had the money for a pay phone, we'd go right over and fix it up. So we went over to a pay phone, and he called his friend Red somebody-or-other at the destroyer desk and told him that he'd like for me to go to sea with him. I had dispatch orders the next day, and Captain Menocal just about went through the roof.

But Commander Nolan, the exec there, and Commander Dancy were both very good friends of mine, and they went in and defended me with Captain Menocal. They said instead of kicking me around he ought to be praising me for my initiative and willingness to go into combat and all this and that. So Menocal was kind of mollified, I guess. I don't whether he said goodbye or not, because I was probably gone the next day.

Paul Stillwell: Why was he upset? Because he was losing your services?

Captain Manson: Yes, and I hadn't asked him to help me or anything.

Paul Stillwell: How had you come across Commander Becton?

---

* Paul Stillwell, *Battleship New Jersey: An Illustrated History* (Annapolis: Naval Institute Press, 1986).
† Captain Menocal commanded the *New Jersey* from 23 May 1947 to 14 February 1948.
‡ Commander F. Julian Becton, USN, was the first commanding officer of the destroyer *Laffey* (DD-724). He was the skipper from the ship's commissioning on 8 February 1944 to 24 June 1945.

Captain Manson: Well, I saw all the skippers as they would come in there. I liked Commander Becton; he had a good sense of humor. He liked to go to the races, and I went with him a few times up there. Our personalities just fit, and at sea it was the same way.

Paul Stillwell: How would you describe Becton's personality?

Captain Manson: Well, I would say that he was a serious person. I mean serious as far as his career was concerned. He had a comprehensive knowledge of destroyers. He'd had a lot of experience, a lot of combat experience. He knew the operational destroyers, and, of course, that's what I was getting into. But I suppose the thing that impressed me the most about him was his attitude, the "cut of his jib," so to speak. He wore his cap at a jaunty sort of a rakish angle, enjoyed a good joke, and dated beautiful women. He was in a way spit and polish, but yet in a way he wasn't.

Paul Stillwell: He was willing to let people have some fun too.

Captain Manson: He was willing to let people have fun, and he liked to join with them and have fun as well. He was blue and gold all the way; there was no doubt about that. By that I mean that he believed in the naval traditions.

Paul Stillwell: But not harshly so.

Captain Manson: But not harsh, that's right. I grew to have a great affection for him as the years went on, and still do.* I just thought he was a tremendous person. He and I talk on the telephone now. I do have a profound regard for him. When we went into action, I still had a regard for him, high regard, to see him handle a ship and the way he did it. My appraisal of him in the first instance was not wrong; he was good.

When we first got into kamikaze action, I was on the bridge with him. He put on flank speed and put our ship into a tight spin. This was when we saw the first two

---

* Becton, who retired as a rear admiral, died on 25 December 1995.

kamikazes come down on two other ships that were not too far away from us, and I said, "Captain, what is this? Anything like this in the South Pacific?"

He said, "No. Hell, no, we've never seen anything like this." But, anyway, he put us in a tight spin while going flank speed.

The commodore of our squadron or division commander, I forget which now, called over and told us to take evasive action. Anyway, all Commander Becton, said was, "We are," or "I am" or whatever. But the planes didn't dive on us. They dived on about everybody else. But I guess because we were in this tight spin, the planes decided not to attack us. That happened in Ormoc Bay, December 7, 1944.[*]

Paul Stillwell: Before we get to that, could you cover some of the work-up period from the time you reported aboard?

Captain Manson: Well, the main thing we did in the *Laffey* from the time I reported aboard was to prepare for the Pacific. She had been to Normandy for a brief interlude over there, sort of a shakedown, and then we went down to Chesapeake Bay for a while to test out some new radars. We remained in there not long, perhaps maybe a week or two. We were needed in the Pacific.

But the main thing we did in the Boston Navy Yard was take on stores, double stores if we could. Double amounts of paint, paint sprayers, and whatever else we thought we needed—ammunition, of course. Mainly our time was spent in making ready not just for sea, but an extended tour in the Pacific. So we were trying to get double and triple supplies of things. Plus electricians were tidying up loose ends after our long new construction.

Paul Stillwell: I'm surprised you could take on extra paint. I would think there would be a concern about the fire hazard.

---

[*] On 7 December 1944, the 77th Infantry Division, commanded by Major General A. D. Bruce, USA, landed unopposed about three miles south of the port of Ormoc on the island of Leyte in the Philippines. Ormoc was secured by U.S. forces on 10 December. Kamikazes were Japanese suicide planes.

Captain Manson: Well, we couldn't, not legally. So we had a young ensign named Jerome Sheets, who got killed in action later on at Okinawa.* We thought there was somebody in the headquarters named "Cumshaw."† During our time in the shipyard, he'd go over in the yard somewhere we were getting this paint and everything else. He wanted to find Cumshaw from among the yard workers.

Anyway, young Sheets eventually went to the captain of the yard. He said that he wanted to meet this fellow Cumshaw. The captain of the Boston Navy Yard took him in and said, "That's very fine. Come in and I'll talk to you about Cumshaw." So then Sheets spilled out the entire thing about what all we were getting from Cumshaw. The captain of the yard then called Commander Becton in to chew him out for these rather unique methods of requisition.

Paul Stillwell: I don't think they were unique, but it's unique to admit that it was "Cumshaw" to the boss. [Laughter]

Captain Manson: Oh, my, yes, yes, that's right. Of course, Sheets spilled the whole beans, but none of us could really be sore at Sheets.

Paul Stillwell: He did it innocently.

Captain Manson: Innocent, you know. All the skipper could do was just smile and take the heat. Becton was always keen on having the ship look sharp. Oh, we had a clean ship. Until we finally got it messed up for real, we had the cleanest ship in the Pacific. I never saw one I thought was as clean as ours.

Paul Stillwell: The exec has a big role in that too. Who was he?

---

* Ensign Jerome B. Sheets, USNR.
† "Cumshaw" is a slang term for a bartering system in which shipyard personnel perform work or provide equipment not officially authorized in exchange for coffee, food, or other considerations.

Captain Manson: His name was Charlie Holovak, and I guess the first lieutenant, too, was pretty good at keeping the ship clean.* But the skipper had an eye for cleanliness. I mean, he kept the heat on. Charlie Holovak was later relieved, and then we had another one. He didn't stay long. He ultimately got his own command.

Paul Stillwell: Did the ship undergo any further training before going to the Pacific?

Captain Manson: Not in the Atlantic. I don't recall us firing any guns while we tested the radars in the Chesapeake off North Beach. The ship had fired during shakedown at Gitmo Bay, Cuba, and at Normandy's big guns.† *Laffey* was hit at Normandy—one German shell in the bow. That was before I joined the ship.

Normally they went down to Bermuda to refresh after yard time, but we went down through the Panama Canal. Then we were in San Diego for a couple of days, then Pearl Harbor, where we did spend perhaps two weeks with all kinds of training drills. They sent us officers and petty officers through various schools if we had time. But it was really intensive. For sea training we'd coordinate with naval air. Airplanes would come in on us in coordinated attacks—fighters, dive bombers, and torpedo planes—and we'd do our best. Then we'd go out on shore bombardment, firing at points on those islands around there. We did that kind of training for about two weeks. I was sent to emergency maneuvering school. Computers were programmed to teach us how to avoid collisions.

Paul Stillwell: Did you do antisubmarine work also?

Captain Manson: Yes, we did, but at that point in the Pacific War we weren't too worried about submarines. I learned how to make an attack on a submarine, but we were more interested in AA.‡ This was, of course, in '44, but we didn't know anything about

---

* Lieutenant Charles Holovak, USN.
† "Gitmo" is the nickname for Guantánamo Bay, on the south coast of Cuba, near the eastern end of the island. For many years provided a fleet anchorage and training area for U.S. Navy ships.
‡ AA – antiaircraft.

suicide planes. They weren't even out yet at this point in time.* But, anyway, that was about the extent of our training—not too much ASW, but more shore bombardment and AA. Those were the big training requirements for Pacific destroyers. Our skipper knew all those Pacific training manuals by heart. He had been in the South Pacific.

Paul Stillwell: What do recall about the quality of the enlisted crew in the *Laffey*?

Captain Manson: I was young at that time myself, but at the same time I'd been around a lot of destroyer crews, and I thought the *Laffey* crew had a lot of spirit. The skipper's attitude was sort of manifest in his crew. They were a happy-go-lucky bunch, but when it got right down to doing their job, they were plenty good. Good with the guns—I mean, very good with radar, signals.

We had about three or four chiefs that were expert at fixing technical breakdowns in radar and radio and electronics. Chief Al Csiszar, Chief Najork—they were all topnotch.† We had a radar technician, Englehardt, a first class.‡ At fire control Ensign Donstrom was very good. We had about, I'd say a half a dozen people aboard ship, five or six, who were excellent at repairing the radars, the radios, the electronics, and that was the name of the game. If you could keep those essentials repaired, you could keep operating and remain on the line. That's what really kept us going. Then, of course, we were at general quarters a lot, so the crew had to have endurance. We also had mostly good cooks, and that seemed to keep the morale up.

Paul Stillwell: What effect did those long hours and frequent GQs have on you physically?§

Captain Manson: Well, you got to the point where you hardly knew whether it was day or night. I remember this one period in Lingayen Gulf when I didn't even take off my

---

* Kamikazes were Japanese suicide aircraft that began showing up in the Philippines campaign in the autumn of 1944. The pilots attempted to crash their bomb-armed aircraft directly into American warships. Hundreds of them successfully hit their targets and inflicted great damage.
† Chief Electrician's Mate Albert Csiszar, USN; Chief Radioman Jack Najork, USN.
‡ Radio Technician First Class August G. Englehardt, USN.
§ GQ – general quarters, in which the ship's crew is at battle stations.

shoes for three weeks and rarely took off my helmet. I never removed my life jacket, for about three weeks. That was in the China Sea.[*]

Paul Stillwell: What period of time was that?

Captain Manson: Early January of '45.

Paul Stillwell: Third Fleet went down there with Halsey.[†] Were you part of that operation?

Captain Manson: Well, we didn't run with the big carriers; we were out there with the jeeps. They were out there, too, and the sea was angry and rough, with kamikazes buzzing around.

Paul Stillwell: When did you have your first encounter with a kamikaze? Was that that Ormoc Bay experience?

Captain Manson: Ormoc, yes. Prior to that we had rescued the destroyer *Hughes* off Mindanao.[‡] She had been hit by a suicider. But then after Ormoc we just had it, well, off and on for the rest of the war, at the most unexpected times sometimes. Even when we were at anchor watching a movie at Ulithi, we had a kamikaze attack.

Paul Stillwell: One of them got the *Randolph*.[§]

---

[*] On 9 January 1945 Navy amphibious forces put Army troops ashore to begin the invasion at Lingayen Gulf, which is north of Manila on the island of Luzon in the Philippines.
[†] Admiral William F. Halsey, Jr., USN, served as Commander Third Fleet from 15 March 1943 to 22 November 1945.
[‡] The *Hughes* (DD-410) was hit by a kamikaze on 10 December 1944 and badly damaged. On board was Rear Admiral Arthur D. Struble, USN. The oral history of Struble is in the Naval Institute collection.
[§] The aircraft carrier *Randolph* (CV-15) was hit by a Japanese kamikaze at 2007 on the evening of 11 March 1945 while anchored at Ulithi Atoll in the Caroline Islands. Casualties included 25 dead and 106 wounded.

Captain Manson: Yes. We were sitting right there and saw the plane hit the *Randolph*. They had a movie going over there, *A Song to Remember*.

Paul Stillwell: They certainly will remember that one.

Captain Manson: Yes. That experience we had in the Philippines in getting the *Hughes* off the rocks at Mindanao is something I'll remember too. She'd been hit, and we had to go down and tow her off. That was my first exposure to just mass death. I'd never seen a lot of people dead and dying before, and it made my physically ill. I was just very ill physically, nauseous. It was so spontaneous. I could never have imagined anything so very tragic. *Laffey* sailors carried the *Hughes*'s dying to our wardroom. They filled our wardroom with bloated and dying people from the steam room of the *Hughes*. They filled up my stateroom. They stacked dying men on top of each other. *Hughes* had a young officer wounded with a lot of shrapnel in his back and all over his body. He lay slowly dying on our wardroom table. Well, it's just one of those times when you see death in the most grotesque way, steamed alive. You see it for the first time, and you don't know how you're going to react. But that's the way I reacted. So did others.

Paul Stillwell: When you see things like that and the kamikaze attacks, what thoughts go through your mind about your own personal safety?

Captain Manson: Your idea is that you think, "Well, this could get me," of course. You realize any one of those planes can take out your ship or take you out. I used to look at it this way and say, "Well, if the plane hits the ship and it doesn't hit me, well, I guess I'm going to be okay. If it hits me and it doesn't kill me, perhaps I don't have anything to worry about. If it eliminates me, I guess I don't have anything to worry about."

Paul Stillwell: You don't have anything to worry about in any case.

Captain Manson: Yes, but that doesn't keep you from worrying. But you run through these processes in your mind. and, of course, you do quite a little bit of praying too. If you've never done any of that, you learn how pretty quickly. But the main thing, I suppose—in my mind, anyway—was the thought, "What in the world is going through these Japanese pilots' minds?" I interrogated one of them one time after we picked him up out of the sea. Actually, he wasn't a suicide pilot; he was just a normal bomber pilot from a Japanese carrier. We found this pilot floating around out there. From the bridge I spotted his black hair bobbing up and down.

Anyway, I kept wondering what sort of a kamikaze training program they had and how they could convince these young people, 18, 19 years old, to do it, give up their lives for sure. I mean, once they took off for the target, there was no turning back. It didn't strike me as being a fair way to conduct a war. It looked to me like warriors from both sides should have a fighting chance. You give it your best shot and see who wins. But this business of suicide attack was very hard for me to comprehend. I knew the destroyers weren't built to fight it, nor were any surface ships.

Paul Stillwell: You say you interrogated him. Did you have facility in Japanese?

Captain Manson: I had a little book that the Navy Department put out, about four inches by four inches, and it had the Japanese and the English. I would point to the Japanese, and right alongside there would be the English. So I would ask him what ship he was from and all the things that we wanted to know in the Japanese, and then he would point out the answers. Then I'd find that in Japanese, and I'd get the English out of it. I did about two or three typed pages of interrogation with him. We sent him to the *Enterprise* the next day, and they never did get a word from him.*

Paul Stillwell: How cooperative was he with you?

Captain Manson: Complete, total. He wanted to stay aboard *Laffey*, and he was wounded. We were giving him a little bourbon and a few cigarettes while Dr. Darnell sewed up his wounds.†

---

* The aircraft carrier *Enterprise* (CV-6) had been in action since the beginning of the war.
† Lieutenant (junior grade) Matthew C. Darnell Jr., Medical Corps, USNR.

Paul Stillwell: What sort of things did you get out of him?

Manson: Well, I got out of him what his rating was; he was an enlisted man, a chief. He'd been flying off of this aircraft carrier, but the carrier, the *Shokaku*, had been sunk, and he'd come out to attack our fleet from the Philippines.* He was flying out of Clark Field, I believe he said, and that the situation with their fleet was getting pretty bad. They were losing a lot of ships. He didn't know anything about the big picture.

Paul Stillwell: Did he know about the kamikaze program?

Captain Manson: No, he didn't. Well, I say he didn't—he never mentioned it and I didn't know about it, so I didn't ask him. This was before we knew about it. We were operating east of the Philippines when we picked up the pilot.†

Paul Stillwell: What kind of a leader was Commander Becton in battle?

Captain Manson: He zeroed in on the battle. He was totally focused. Everything else became absolutely unimportant to him. Only those things that really counted would he even think about. No one ever tried to distract him, mind you, but he was out on the open bridge, always in charge, telling people what to do, I guess you'd say directing traffic. His ability to maneuver the ship and get the ship in the best position for the guns was absolutely incredible, and that's what he concentrated on doing, unmasking the batteries so that the guns could bear. He was superb at it. He was also good, when he found out what the kamikaze game was, on accelerating and changing speeds and maneuvering to avoid their dives. He was a natural ship handler, but mainly he was just a man that you could count on. I remember one time I told him that I thought we were going to have to abandon ship and he said, "Oh, no," that he would never abandon ship as long as a gun would fire. And I thought that was amazing—yet typical.

---

* On 19 June 1944, during the "Marianas Turkey Shoot," the submarine *Cavalla* (SS-244) torpedoed and sank the *Shokaku*, one of the Japanese aircraft carriers that had taken part in the air raid on Pearl Harbor in December 1941.

† The *Laffey* recovered the badly wounded Japanese pilot on 11 November 1944 and transferred him to the *Enterprise* the following day. This was about two and half weeks after the first kamikaze strikes.

Paul Stillwell: What was the occasion for that? What kind of shape was the ship in?

Captain Manson: We were down by the stern; our stern was under the water there, I guess about two feet.* The stern was about two feet under the water, maybe three, I don't know. But the bow was high in the air. It was so steep, to walk from the stern to the bow, you almost had to hold onto something inside the passageway or along a lifeline.

The ship was, to my way of thinking, sinking. This was the first time I'd ever been on one that I thought was about to sink, but I thought at any minute she was going to slide under, stern first. But meanwhile the skipper was right, we still had a gun or two that would shoot, and he said he would never, never abandon ship as long as he had a gun. That's the sort of guy he was.

Paul Stillwell: He's the kind who inspires courage and confidence.

Captain Manson: Oh, definitely, yes. He had some very courageous people working for him. But, believe you me, he was out front.

Paul Stillwell: What were you personally doing during this kamikaze attack?

Captain Manson: Well, for the most part, a lot of us were sort of watching it as much as anything, because the flagship had sent us a special fighter-director team. It included two Air Force officers, I believe, one young Navy type, three altogether. They were especially good at directing our combat air patrol and fighter direction. So the job I had been doing when we were on the fast carrier strikes against Tokyo was done by the experts. I had been keeping track of incoming bogeys from the combat information center.† So here I was, mainly following the action, since we were alone out there with

---

* The *Laffey*'s worst trial by fire was on 16 April 1945 off Okinawa when she was hit by four bombs and five kamikaze hits but survived. During the battle 32 members of her crew were killed and 71 wounded. See the commanding officer's memoir, F. Julian Becton, with Joseph Morschauser III, *The Ship That Would Not Die* (Englewood Cliffs, New Jersey: Prentice Hall, 1980). The book contains lists of those killed in the battle and those who survived.
† "Bogey" is a term used to designate an unidentified air contact.

one LCS.* We hadn't been hit during the first few minutes of action. Our guns were blazing, rapid fire, and we were getting strafed early with no injuries. You could hear the bullets hitting the ship.

Paul Stillwell: Was this on a picket station?

Captain Manson: Yes, we were on radar picket station number one, which was 60 miles north of Point Bolo. Number one was on a direct line from Kyushu to Okinawa. So mainly I was going around the ship, checking gun crews to see if they had any requirements, if they needed something they didn't have or get whatever it might be. Once we started getting hit and getting hurt, I started helping the wounded with the morphine syrettes. Then the doctor had some bourbon and different kinds of liquor aboard for medicinal purposes. I got about four or five bottles of it, and I went around to the gun crews, all of them, and I gave anybody that needed it a good stiff shot. They needed it, drank it like water.

Paul Stillwell: Did they seem to welcome that?

Captain Manson: Oh, yes. Some had put a white cream on their faces as burn protection. Oh, I mean, their eyes were bloodshot. They were really fighting to save their ship. So for quite a long time I was involved in going around the ship from gun to gun with morphine syrettes and liquor. But, of course, we eventually got to the point where we were virtually out of action, and there wasn't much that anybody could do. Except the damage control crews were skilled at putting out fires and saving the ship, dealing with battle damage. They were busy rigging pumps, trying to dislodge the rudder when it was jammed hard left.

Paul Stillwell: Damage control.

---

* LCS – landing craft (support).

Captain Manson: Damage control. They were pumping, trying to get the bilge pumps to work. Finally, two tugs came out there and tied up on either side of us. The tugs were really what saved us.

Paul Stillwell: Were they able to pump out enough to bring the stern back up?

Captain Manson: Yes, with the help from the tugs, they did. It took quite a while.

Paul Stillwell: I've seen pictures of how badly the *Laffey* was damaged, and it is remarkable that she survived.

Captain Manson: Oh, yes, it is. I'd say it's a miracle because so many ships had sunk out there under conditions that were certainly no worse than ours. Kerama Retto looked like a destroyer cemetery—so many mangled ships there.[*]

Paul Stillwell: So where did you go from there?

Captain Manson: We went back to Kerama Retto, or near there, and we stayed there for about six days. They pulled us near or alongside an ammunition ship to put on soft patches and do different things. I thought, "Man, if they could find something besides an ammunition ship or some other type, that would have been just as well with me."

Then I was asked, I believe the first night we were back in the anchorage, to go over to Admiral Turner's flagship, to meet with the flag officers and the press and report on the action.[†]

Paul Stillwell: Was this the *Eldorado*?

---

[*] Kerama Retto is a group of small islands off the southwest coast of Okinawa. It was used as an anchorage and logistics base during the Okinawa campaign.
[†] Vice Admiral Richmond Kelly Turner, USN, served as Commander Task Force 51, the Joint Expeditionary Force, for the Okinawa operation. Captain Manson expanded on describing this briefing about the kamikazes in an article that is an appendix to this volume of oral history.

Captain Manson: Yes. So the skipper and I got into a huddle over the best we could make out what had happened. You might say it was the two of us just back and forth until I thought I had a pretty good grasp of how many planes had come in and how many bombs, how many we had shot down, where we were hit, as many things as we could put together. It's hard to know exactly everything that happens when you're under a massive attack like that. You don't have time or inclination to take notes.

Paul Stillwell: You were too busy getting out of the way.

Captain Manson: Well, sure, and you don't count them. You're just waiting to see where the next one's coming in.

Paul Stillwell: Why were you selected as one of the spokesmen?

Captain Manson: Actually, a few months before that, CinCPac had put out a directive that every ship must have a PR officer, and I was designated.[*] The skipper called me in and said, "See this?"

    I said, "Yes, I've seen it."

    He said, "You're it." So that's how come.

Paul Stillwell: Were you a regular officer of the deck in the watch-standing rotation?

Captain Manson: No. I had been off and on until Lieutenant Runk returned.[†] He had been sick for a few months. When he returned, he became a regular deck watch stander. He was an excellent ship handler. I suppose I could have done all right during the kamikaze attack, because the skipper had the conn. The thing that used to give me trouble on watch standing was anticipating the tactical maneuvers of the carriers. I had not had enough experience to know and to anticipate. Well, I had done it some, but we had others that were better than I. Then, of course, after the action, I went back to

---

[*] CinCPac – Commander in Chief Pacific Fleet.
[†] Lieutenant Theodore W. Runk, USNR. He was awarded the Navy Cross for his role in this battle.

standing regular rotation watches because so many officers had been wounded and had gone from the ship. I did OOD for as long as I remained aboard the ship.* I was usually OOD coming into port and getting under way. But during Commander Becton's tour we didn't enter port all that much. It was more often an anchorage.

Paul Stillwell: How did the press conference go on Turner's flagship?

Captain Manson: Well, we had an air raid aboard at the time I was giving this press conference. I almost got choked, as did everybody, breathing that smog or smoke in the flagship's wardroom. I told them, a hundred or so, as best I could what happened. When the information I gave them was released in Washington, it made headlines in all the newspapers, magazines. Books were written, and it had a fantastic pick-up back in the States, just absolutely unbelievable. We had survived the heaviest aerial attack of World War II against a single ship.

Paul Stillwell: How many hits altogether?

Captain Manson: Well, we actually had five direct hits. We had two that glanced the ship, just grazed it and knocked off a yardarm, one of them did, and I forget what the other one did. Then we had I'm still not sure how many bombs, but it was two, I think, two bombs, one 500-pounder. We had one small bomb land on our deck that Lieutenant Runk just personally rolled off into the ocean before it exploded.

Paul Stillwell: That takes some guts.

Captain Manson: Yes. They gave him a Navy Cross, and he deserved it. It was a fantastic group of people when you got them all together, and to think that—except for a very few—they had all been just a bunch of civilians.

Paul Stillwell: Right. Well, including yourself.

---

* OOD – officer of the deck.

Captain Manson: Yes, me above all else. A lawyer, yes, that's what I had intended and what I could have done well. But all of us had to fit our lives into a combat situation. We had four Naval Academy graduates: the skipper; Lieutenant Paul Smith, the gunnery officer; Ensign Jim Townsley, assistant gunnery; and Ensign Thomsen, the navigator who was killed.[*]

Paul Stillwell: Did that effectively put the *Laffey* out of the war?

Captain Manson: Yes. We were in Seattle for repairs for 83 days, and when we were just about ready to go back for the invasion of Japan, they dropped the A-bombs on the 15th of August.[†]

Paul Stillwell: It was a little earlier than that.

Captain Manson: Was it?

Paul Stillwell: The surrender was on the 15th.

Captain Manson: Okay. Well, then it was earlier than that. But we were preparing, and we were going to be in that invasion, and I was not looking forward to that. I remember the new skipper was a fellow named Odale Waters, and he called me in and he said, "Well, Frank, it looks like we missed out."[‡] [Chuckles]

I remember saying, "Yeah, that's just too bad." Of course, he'd spent his time pretty much in the Atlantic, and he didn't think this would do his career any good, not to be in the Pacific. But it turned out he made admiral, anyway.

---

[*] Lieutenant Paul B. Smith, USN; Ensign James G. Townsley, USN; Ensign Robert Clarence Thomsen, USN.
[†] In the first combat use of atomic bombs, U.S. B-29 bombers hit Hiroshima, on the island of Honshu, on 6 August 1945 and Nagasaki, on Kyushu, on 9 August.
[‡] Commander Odale D. Waters Jr., USN, became skipper of the *Laffey* on 26 June 1945 and commanded her until the following year. The oral history of Waters, who retired as a rear admiral, is in the Naval Institute collection. He died 7 May 1986.

Paul Stillwell: I interviewed him. He died, I guess, last year. I talked to him not long before he died.

Captain Manson: Yes, very fine man.

Paul Stillwell: A courtly gentleman. The thing that impressed me was that he had very dark brown eyes.

Captain Manson: Yes. He had dark brown eyes and silver-gray hair, even as a young man. But he was always, as you say, courtly, a keen sense of humor. And I liked him too. I mean, he was just a splendid gentleman.

Paul Stillwell: Did you stay on board for the tests at Bikini, the atom bomb tests?*

Captain Manson: No. I left the ship on October 28, the day after we celebrated . . .

Paul Stillwell: Navy Day.

Captain Manson: Navy Day.

Paul Stillwell: Was that still at Pearl Harbor?

Captain Manson: The ship was still out there.

Paul Stillwell: So evidently you had been on your way back out to get into action when the hostilities ended?

Captain Manson: Well, no, actually, we were still in Seattle, but we were all ready. There's no doubt that we would have been in the vanguard. But in all that Pacific action,

---

* In July 1946 Vice Admiral William H. P. Blandy, USN, served as Commander Joint Task Force One for atomic bomb tests at Bikini Atoll in the Marshall Islands

I suppose one of the things out there that probably shook me up as much as anything was the afternoon we were supposed to make a torpedo run on the *Yamato*.* I tell you right now, that did not appeal to me. We were going to be the number-two destroyer going in, *Barton* number one, and we'd be number two. I thought we had not even a Chinaman's chance of surviving it, but it turned out we didn't have to attack.

Another thing that disturbed me about that is when we were preparing for the torpedo attack, we were trying to find the old battleships, our own, that were going to support us. They were so far behind us we couldn't even see their masts. I thought, "My, it looks like they ought to move in a little closer and give us a little closer support." This preparation for attack on *Yamato* really gave us the creeps. Any surface action like that—destroyer against battleship—was lights out for the destroyers, certainly the first three or four destroyers and perhaps all of us. We had to close within eight miles to fire, and they could start pounding us at 20 miles.

Paul Stillwell: You were viewed as expendable, really.

Captain Manson: Oh, yes. And the gun crews were all asking me a lot of questions, because our eight destroyers were sort of like a bunch of young colts dancing on those big waves going up to intercept that huge ship. Our crew members were apprehensive, and the skipper was, too, because he'd done that before.

Paul Stillwell: But you probably had the feeling on that also that he would have kept going as long as he had a gun or torpedo to fire.

Captain Manson: Oh, sure. Oh, no doubt about that. He would have delivered whatever we had just like he was trained to do. One thing I noticed about a lot of those Naval Academy graduates of the same class or era, they almost knew what the other one was

---

* Displacing 72,000 tons and armed with 18.1-inch guns, the *Yamato* and *Musashi* were Japan's two largest battleships. American aircraft sank the *Musashi* in the Philippines on 24 October 1944 and the *Yamato* on 7 April 1945 when she was en route to Okinawa. The sinking of the *Yamato* was a little more than a week before the *Laffey*'s kamikaze ordeal.

thinking.* I mean, they were all practically from the same class, or they all knew each other and they could work together so well. It was like our air group commanders; they, too, seemed like they were cut out of the same cloth. I was impressed, as a reserve, at the way they could work together to coordinate their attacks or their defense.

Paul Stillwell: They were the nucleus around which the reserves were built.

Captain Manson: Yes, they were, and extremely well trained. And now—dropping back to my training at Cornell University—the way they ran that training school and all the other things to bring all these thousands and thousands of civilians in and utilize them in combat. It was a remarkable training program. Admiral Carney once said to me some years later, "Well, the Navy is really an organization to train men to train men to train men," and I think that's about right.†

Paul Stillwell: Herman Wouk had another way of putting it. He said, "The Navy is a master plan designed by geniuses for execution by idiots." [Laughter]

Captain Manson: Well, I think that's pretty good. I knew him too.

Paul Stillwell: Where did you encounter him?

Captain Manson: He had done this book on *The Caine Mutiny*, and he wanted the Navy to cooperate in the subsequent movie.‡ He came to my office, I was working with Captain Walter Karig and wanted our cooperation, and we gave it to him.§

---

* Commander Becton graduated from the Naval Academy in the class of 1931.
† Admiral Robert B. Carney, USN, served as Chief of Naval Operations from 17 August 1953 to 17 August 1955.
‡ Lieutenant Commander Philip F. Queeg, USN, was the fictitious commanding officer of the destroyer-minesweeper USS *Caine* in Herman Wouk's classic naval novel of World War II, *The Caine Mutiny*, published by Doubleday & Company in 1951. The movie version appeared in 1954.
§ Captain Walter Karig, USNR, was a Navy public information officer, historian, journalist, and novelist. He wrote a series of *Battle Report* books on the Navy in World War II and Korea. He was also the author of three Nancy Drew detective novels under the pseudonym Carolyn Keene.

Paul Stillwell: I think Admiral Fechteler had a hand in that. He blessed it from on high.

Captain Manson: Well, I didn't know about that, but I'm sure he did. But we spent an afternoon with Mr. Wouk.*

Paul Stillwell: What are your impressions of him?

Captain Manson: Well, first of all, I thought he was bright. But we were so preoccupied with just getting his book approved for the movie that we really didn't cover anything else but the contents of the book and how it might reflect on the Navy. So I didn't have a chance to know him well. I had a favorable impression, and that's about all I can tell you about that.

Paul Stillwell: He's a marvelous storyteller.

Captain Manson: Yes, he is. He's all right.

Paul Stillwell: Well, you left the *Laffey*. Did you contemplate getting out of the Navy at that point?

Captain Manson: Yes, yes, I was through. Well, I thought, "This is the end. I'm going to go back and get in civilian life and either finish my law degree or get in the Foreign Service." I thought there was no way I could compete aboard ship with the kind of people that the Naval Academy had developed. They were just so superior to my background, and I thought what's the point in my trying to have a career when there are other areas where I can have a very fulfilled life and compete? So I was just not going to have anything to do with it anymore after leaving the *Laffey*.

But I got back to the States, and I couldn't make up my mind. I was fiddling around after two or three weeks trying to figure out what I was going to do, whether I

---

* Admiral William M. Fechteler, USN, served as Chief of Naval Operations from 16 August 1951 to 17 August 1953.

was going to go to law school. So I went down and checked with the legal department of the Navy, and they said they would be happy to send me to finish law school. So I said, "Well, that's something I can think about to stay in the Navy."

Then I dropped down to the PR department, which I'd always been interested in, although I still didn't know quite what they did. I'd been a PR officer in the fleet, but I didn't quite know. I dropped by there and they quizzed me about my writing background, and I told them about that speech I'd written for Captain Menocal and that was about it, although I had done quite a little bit of writing in college; nothing, I don't think, had ever been published, however. Anyway, they said they'd be most interested in bringing me back on active duty.

Paul Stillwell: Did you actually get out and separate?

Captain Manson: Yes, I went through the separation center, sure did. And so I was a civilian. They said, "That doesn't matter a bit. We can fix all those papers up over in no time at all and you'll be back on board." They really wanted me to come down and join this Secretary's Committee on Research on Reorganization, called SCOROR.

I suppose the fact that somebody wanted me appealed to me, simply because I was sort of at loose ends. I was in a transition period, didn't know quite what I wanted to do or what was best for me. So I thought, "Well, this will be a good thing. I can do this for 30 days or 60 days." So I never did get out after that.

But I got into that thing, and I saw a battle the likes of which I had never seen in World War II.

Paul Stillwell: I'd like to hear you describe that battle.

Captain Manson: Well, this was a battle that the armed services were having over, really, the Navy. I couldn't imagine that the Navy I knew could be under attack back in Washington for the job it did in the war. I thought I had seen the very best, the very finest, and I knew I had. Yet in Washington, we were under severe attack, in Congress to some extent, but mainly, I suppose, by the Army Air Forces and the Army.*

Paul Stillwell: The Air Force had a marvelous PR organization.

Captain Manson: Yes, they were absolutely outstanding. Stuart Symington and Steve Leo were the two leaders, and beyond that they had a lot of others that were just topflight.† The Navy didn't have much. So the Navy was really taking a beating, and it was like the Navy was in kindergarten, and we were working against a bunch of guys who had postgraduate degrees.

Paul Stillwell: What was your specific function in this battle?

Captain Manson: I was sent to the writing division of Captain Walter Karig. Our job was to write speeches for the admirals and congressmen, just as fast as we could, on basically why a Navy, what the Navy does, why we need it, why we should keep it. Those were the things that I was writing about. Those speeches would be about 20 or 30 minutes long. We were turning those things out just as fast as we could, and then we'd talk with editors.

I remember one time I was sent on a trip across the country to talk to editors. See, we were trying to stir up a congressional investigation and hearings. We thought if we could get these hearings, then the whole thing would be put out in public view in open debate, and maybe we'd have a chance. But that wasn't easy. The cards were pretty much stacked against the Navy. William Bradford Huie wrote those articles in *The Reader's Digest* just really ripping up the admirals and their alleged mistakes in the war.‡

---

* On 20 June 1941 the U.S. Army Air Corps was officially redesignated the U.S. Army Air Forces and retained that title until the establishment of the U.S. Air Force as a separate service on 17 September 1947.
† Stuart Symington served as Secretary of the Air Force from 18 September 1947 to 24 April 1950. Stephen F. Leo was the first public relations director for the newly formed Air Force.
‡ William Bradford Huie, "Navy, or an Air Force," *Reader's Digest*, December 1948, pages 62-67; "Facts Which Must Prevent War, *Reader's Digest*, January 1949, pages 23-30; "Why We must Have the World's Best Air Force," *Reader's Digest,* March 1949, pages 27-34; "Struggle for American Air Power," *Reader's Digest,* April 1949, pages 1-6. He also wrote articles on the subject for the magazine *American Mercury* in that period.

Paul Stillwell: It was a myth that air power was the solution to everything.

Captain Manson: Yep.

Paul Stillwell: "You don't need a Marine Corps, you don't need naval aviation." That was hard to work against.

Captain Manson: It was.
     I did put some notes down. Let me see if I can find them here.

Paul Stillwell: Sure.

Captain Manson: Yes, the Navy, our SCOROR was led by Admiral Arthur Radford.[*] That later became OP-23.

Paul Stillwell: Arleigh Burke.[†]

Captain Manson: Arleigh Burke took that over in about '49. I remember the day he walked into the Pentagon. He came in in civilian clothes, a blue civilian suit. I had known him. I had helped him on the General Board when he was writing a paper on "If war should come in the next ten years," so I knew him. But I couldn't imagine the Navy would bring such an excellent combat officer into that ugly job, because I knew he was going to get messed up. Captain Burke didn't know anything about that dirty type of ugly Washington politics. He just didn't know about it, and the Navy didn't have anybody really that was any superior to Captain Arleigh Burke as a combat-experienced man. I thought, "What a shame it is that this guy is probably going to get his career ruined right here," and he almost did.

---

[*] Vice Admiral Arthur W. Radford, USN, served as Deputy Chief of Naval Operations (Air), OP-05, in 1946-47. As a four-star admiral he was Vice Chief of Naval Operations from January 1948 to April 1949.
[†] In 1949 Captain Arleigh A. Burke, USN, headed OP-23, a Navy research group that gathered information critical of the Air Force B-36 bomber and its capabilities. Burke's Naval Institute oral history includes his memories of OP-23 service.

Anyway, the two congressmen that were key in those days were Carl Vinson—who had Bryce Harlow and Russ Blandford working for him—and Dewey Short, who was the Republican minority leader in the Armed Services Committee.[*]

The people that were really key in that, you don't ever hear much about them on the Navy side. Hugh Hansen, a civilian naval engineer about 28 years old, a sharp Rensselaer man. He was keen, and he would always be writing two or three letters to *The Washington Post* and to the *Evening Star*. Hansen's letters just sent Stuart Symington up the wall. All Symington wanted to do was get rid of Hugh Hansen. Then we had another one, Tom Davies, who was an aviator and, boy, he was exceptionally bright.[†] William I. Martin was another one that was plenty keen.[‡] He was serving down at tactical tests at Patuxent. There were two or three others that were really very competent people.

In fact, the Air Force was saying that the carrier was obsolete, surface ships were, that the bomber with the A-bomb was all you needed. And that's in essence what it was all about. I thought it was a dreadful shame that our country could lose everything that we had won, really, if we sat around and destroyed each other, and it looked to me like this might happen.

---

[*] Carl Vinson, a Democrat from Georgia, entered the House of Representatives in 1913 and was appointed to the Naval Affairs Committee in 1917. He became the ranking Democrat in 1923 and chairman in 1931. When the Armed Services committee was formed in 1947, Vinson became chairman and held that position, except for two short periods when Republicans held the House, until his retirement from Congress in 1965. Bryce N. Harlow served during World War II on the staff of General of the Army George C. Marshall, USA. After serving on the staff of the House Armed Services Committee, 1947-51, he was later an advisor to President Dwight D. Eisenhower and President Richard M. Nixon.
John Russell Blandford became counsel for the House Armed Services Committee in 1947 and chief counsel in 1963. He retired from the latter post in 1970 and the same year from the Marine Corps Reserve as a major general.
Dewey J. Short, a Republican from Missouri, served in the House of Representatives from 1929 to 1931 and from 1935 to 1957. Short died at age 81 on 19 November 1979.
[†] Between 29 September and 1 October 1946, a Navy crew headed by Commander Thomas D. Davies, USN, flew a P2V Neptune nicknamed "The Truculent Turtle" from Perth, Australia, to Columbus, Ohio. Their flight lasted 55 hours and 17 minutes and covered 11,235.6 miles. They established a world's distance record in an unrefueled flight.
[‡] In the last year of World War II, Commander William I. Martin, USN, commanded Night Air Group 90 on board the USS *Enterprise* (CV-6). It was the Navy's first carrier air group specialized for night operations. The Naval Institute oral history of Martin, who retired as a vice admiral, covers his work with Representative Short in this period.

The Secretary of the Navy first was Forrestal, and after him was Sullivan.* Sullivan didn't fight hard enough, in my judgment. When Denfeld was fired for going up there before the committee and telling like it was, telling the truth, the Chairman of the Joint Chiefs had changed his mind on the need for aircraft carriers.† Sullivan resigned then.

Paul Stillwell: I thought he was already gone. I thought that the cancellation of the USS *United States* was what sent Sullivan off.‡

Captain Manson: You know, you may be right. I was thinking it was Denfeld. Wait. Denfeld. Yes, you're right.

Paul Stillwell: I think it was Secretary Matthews that fired . . .

Captain Manson: Matthews is the one that fired Denfeld, you're right.§ My memory is a little skewed right here.

Paul Stillwell: What was your role in that particular incident?

Captain Manson: At that time I was on Admiral Denfeld's staff, and we were writing the history of World War II at that time—Captain Karig and two or three others.

---

* James V. Forrestal served as Secretary of the Navy from 19 May 1944 to 17 September 1947. John L. Sullivan served as Secretary of the Navy from 18 September 1947 to 24 May 1949. Forrestal was Secretary of Defense, 1947-49.
† Admiral Louis E. Denfeld, USN, served as Chief of Naval Operations from 15 December 1947 to 2 November 1949.
‡ In the late 1940s, the Navy and Air Force were competing for scarce defense dollars. Secretary of Defense Louis Johnson accelerated production of the Air Force's B-36 bomber and canceled the aircraft carrier *United States* (CVA-58). The keel for the carrier was laid 18 April 1949, and construction was ended five days later. The Navy fought back, as detailed in Jeffrey G. Barlow, *Revolt of the Admirals* (Washington, D.C.: Naval Historical Center, 1994).
§ Francis P. Matthews served as Secretary of the Navy from 25 May 1949 to 30 July 1951.

Paul Stillwell: That was the *Battle Report* series.*

Captain Manson: *Battle Report* series.

Paul Stillwell: How did that come about?

Captain Manson: The *Battle Report* was started by Frank Knox, and he wanted a history written that was graphic—the smell of battle—for women, children, everybody, but one that wasn't too bogged down with detail and technical things that would turn the average reader off.†

Paul Stillwell: More of a popular-type history?

Captain Manson: More of popular-type history. Captain Karig was a popular writer, and Knox started him on the project.

Paul Stillwell: What was Karig's background?

Captain Manson: He'd been a newspaperman primarily and a book writer, head of a news bureau, Gridiron Club, a very skillful writer, could write plays, musicals, narratives, fiction, and non-fiction.

Paul Stillwell: So you got drafted into his organization.

Captain Manson: So I really got sort of swooped up, and he and I became sort of like, in a way like Becton and I. We hit it off right away, and he wanted me to help him write these books. I told him I'd like to think about that a little bit, because I realized that

---

* *Battle Report* comprised six volumes of U.S. Navy operations from the beginning of World War II to the early part of the Korean War. The first volume was published in 1944 and the last one in 1952. Karig was involved in all six volumes. Manson was one of the coauthors on volumes IV through VI.
† William Franklin Knox served as Secretary of the Navy from 11 July 1940 until his death on 28 April 1944.

might cause me to stay in the Navy, at least for quite a while. Another fellow standing there said, "I'll do it, Captain. I'll be glad to help you write the books."

Captain Walter Karig just kept looking right straight at me and said, "Well, you've got all the time you want. Take your time and let me know."

So I took my time and decided to do it. The decision was to do that or go to law school. The Navy, as I said, agreed to send me even to Edinburgh, Scotland, if I wanted to. I decided to help him write those books, and that's how I got started. I didn't know how to write books, so I told him I didn't. I said, "How am I going to do this?"

He said, "Just sit down and start."

Paul Stillwell: Did that mean you got transferred away from speechwriting in the OP-23 function to that?

Captain Manson: Well, we carried both burdens. I suppose maybe 50% of the time was spent with speechwriting and that sort of thing and maybe 50% was spent on the books. But at night, too, I worked on the books at night and weekends, to the dismay of my new wife.* But she was pregnant and helped me sometimes, typing and whatnot. So that was the way that worked. I sort of ran on dual tracks.

Paul Stillwell: Those books were published commercially. Did you get some extra income from that?

Captain Manson: No, I never did. Captain Karig may have; I don't know if he did or not. But they were written under the agreement by the Council of Books on Wartime, so I never did get anything out of it. Captain Karig and I did a story for *The Saturday Evening Post* that we were paid $1,500 for, which we split. It was a story about the

---

* Manson married the former Orie Lee Pickren of Brunswick, Georgia, in Annapolis, Maryland, on 26 May 1948.

submarine *Barb*.* Eugene Fluckey was the *Barb*'s skipper, a wonderful man.† He was aide to Nimitz back in those days, and I really admired him.‡ But, anyway, we did get some money, and I guess maybe we did get some money from the Naval Institute, because they always paid for articles that were taken from the books.

Paul Stillwell: Not nearly so much as *The Saturday Evening Post* paid, I dare say.

Captain Manson: No, no. The Naval Institute, probably paid $200.00 or $300.00, I think.

Paul Stillwell: Would Fluckey be a good example of people that you interviewed to get your material for the book?

Captain Manson: Yes. We went to the skippers, air group commanders.

Paul Stillwell: And undoubtedly the action reports.

Captain Manson: All the action reports of units, divisions, squadrons, groups, task force, task group, on up to fleet commanders.

Paul Stillwell: Were these people that were stationed in Washington so it was convenient to talk to them?

Captain Manson: Well, sometimes I had to go out to Jacksonville or San Diego or somewhere. Admiral Nimitz gave us his "gray books," those were his diaries. He asked us, I'll never forget this, he gave us a Turkish cigarette to smoke in his office while we

---

* Walter Karig and Frank Manson, "Hairbreadth Escapes of the Barb," *Saturday Evening Post*, 22 October 1949, pages 28-29 plus continuation later in the magazine.
† During World War II, Commander Eugene B. Fluckey, USN, earned the Medal of Honor for his service as commanding officer of the submarine *Barb* (SS-220). He described his experiences in the book *Thunder Below!: the USS Barb Revolutionizes Submarine Warfare in World War II* (Urbana: University of Illinois Press, 1992).
‡ Fleet Admiral Chester Nimitz, USN, served as Chief of Naval Operations from 15 December 1945 to 15 December 1947.

talked. Russ Harris was helping me on this volume.* Admiral Nimitz said to us, "Now, remember, we had to fight all these battles, fight them out, and we don't want to have to fight them again in our lifetime." So I respected that. That was before we had conflicts, like Leyte Gulf and the Philippine Sea and different places. So I didn't see it serving any great function or purpose anyway.

Paul Stillwell: You mean not getting into the controversies surrounding—

Captain Manson: Well, not making it to the point where they would have to re-fight some things that had been rather embarrassing to them. They had already fought it out during the war, and they didn't want to do it again in their lifetime.

Paul Stillwell: Well, Halsey and Kinkaid had their battle anyway.†

Captain Manson: Yes. I went to interview Kinkaid, and you couldn't write about Kinkaid without writing about what he thought about Halsey. Halsey didn't have the same intensity that Kinkaid did.

Paul Stillwell: Kinkaid viewed himself as having been the victim in that episode.

Captain Manson: Yes, yes, he did. I liked him. At one time, I figured I knew personally about 300 admirals. I don't know if it was the accurate count or not, but it was pretty close.

Paul Stillwell: I would guess that a fair amount of that material had not yet been declassified. How did you get around that problem?

---

* Captain Walter Karig, USNR; Lieutenant Commander Russell L. Harris, USNR; and Lieutenant Commander Frank A. Manson, USNR, *Battle Report: Victory in the Pacific* (New York: Rinehart and Company, 1949).
† After the war Fleet Admiral William F. Halsey, USN, and Admiral Thomas C. Kinkaid, USN, feuded publicly about who was to blame for missed opportunities in the October 1944 Battle of Leyte Gulf.

Captain Manson: We went ahead and wrote it as if it had been and then sent it to naval intelligence for review. That's how we handled that.

Paul Stillwell: Did you have any idea then of the existence of Ultra?[*]

Captain Manson: No, I did not. Didn't know a thing about it. If it wasn't in Admiral Nimitz's books, I didn't know.

Paul Stillwell: I guess it surprised a lot of people when that came out of the 1970s.

Captain Manson: Oh, I tell you, I knew nothing. I did get on to some very highly classified information in communications. A fellow named Horne, captain or rear admiral, told me whatever I did, not to divulge that, in some kind of a way we had broken Japanese communications. I don't know even now exactly everything I was on to on the thing. He told me just to drop it and forget it, which I did.

Paul Stillwell: There was a great deal of controversy about the attack on Pearl Harbor, of course.[†] Did you get involved in that?

Captain Manson: No. I attended those hearings every day, but I didn't write about that because when I joined the *Battle Report* project, that volume had already been written.[‡] I did meet Admiral Stark and Admiral Kimmel.[§] I later got to know Admiral Kimmel's son quite well at the Naval War College.[**] A fine man, submariner.

---

[*] Ultra—short for ultra secret—was a special security classification given by the British to information gained from breaking the code of the German radio-enciphering machine. It has come to be used more broadly to encompass other information obtained from interception and decryption of German and Japanese radio communications.

[†] On Sunday, 7 December 1941, Japanese carrier planes attacked and heavily damaged American warships at the naval base at Pearl Harbor, Hawaii. The U.S. Congress declared war on Japan the following day.

[‡] After World War II ended, a joint congressional committee of House and Senate members held hearings to investigate the Japanese attack of 7 December 1941. The hearings lasted from 15 November 1945 to 31 May 1946 and produced a 37-volume report of testimony and conclusions.

[§] Admiral Harold R. Stark, USN, served as Chief of Naval Operations from 1 August 1939 to 26 March 1942. Admiral Husband E. Kimmel, USN, served as Commander in Chief Pacific Fleet from 1 February 1941 to 17 December 1941.

[**] Commander Thomas K. Kimmel, USN.

Paul Stillwell: Except his wartime career was cut short in submarines because his brother had been lost and there was concern about him, also.*

Captain Manson: Yes.

Paul Stillwell: What are your impressions of Stark and Kimmel from those meetings?

Captain Manson: Well, with Admiral Stark, he was a very nervous and upset individual. He was noticeably upset about that whole thing. The few conversations I had with him, he was not trying to explain what happened, but thought that he was sort of more a less a victim of circumstances, as did Admiral Kimmel. That's sort of the way they felt about it. Like the skipper of the *Indianapolis*, Captain McVay.† I got to be friends with him. He thought that he had been given a bum rap. Of course, he wasn't zigzagging, but none of the ships were zigzagging in those days. We'd been across that Pacific, in the *Laffey*, with our keel practically widening the bow, and we weren't zigzagging prior to that. So we were not expecting submarine attacks. But, again, I guess it comes down to the idea that the Navy has to be a stern taskmaster.

Paul Stillwell: That was more vengeful than most.

Captain Manson: Yes, I thought so. Anyway, the history books, the *Battle Report* series, were mostly made up of diaries, interviews, action reports, press clippings, radio reports, and that's about it, because there wasn't anything else.

Paul Stillwell: You had to do so much condensation because you consider Admiral Morison covered the same amount of territory in three times as many volumes, 15 compared with five.

---

* In July 1944 Lieutenant Commander Manning M. Kimmel, USN, was in command of the submarine *Robalo* (SS-273) when she hit a mine and sank two miles of the coast of Palawan Island in the Philippines.
† The Japanese submarine *I-58* torpedoed the heavy cruiser *Indianapolis* (CA-35) on 30 July 1945 while en route from Guam to the Philippines. Because of delays in discovering the loss, rescue forces were able to save only 316 of the 1,199 men in the ship's crew. The cruiser's commanding officer, Captain Charles B. McVay III, USN, was subsequently court-martialed after his return to the United States.

Captain Manson: That's right. I gave his people two or three of our chapters that I had written so they could use them in beginning their writings. Like the Gilberts, the Marshalls, and those operations, and I forget, I gave him some drafts because I knew that they were going to go into it much more extensively than we had.

Paul Stillwell: Are there any of his people that you remember working with?

Captain Manson: Jim Shaw, who was one of his principal helpers, Henry Reck, Henry Salomon, and Roger Pineau.[*] That's about all I can remember.

Paul Stillwell: Shaw was later the technical advisor on the movie *The Caine Mutiny*.

Captain Manson: Yes, Jim did. He went back to Connecticut, I think.

Paul Stillwell: He's somewhere up in New England.

Captain Manson: I liked him; he was a friend.[†] I served with him. What were we doing? I can't remember, but we served together for a while. Maybe it was in SCOROR. I don't know where it was exactly. But I got to know him quite well.

Paul Stillwell: Did you turn your files over to Morison's people when you were finished?

Captain Manson: No. I seem to recall we gave them to Naval History.

Paul Stillwell: Where they could draw on them, of course.

Captain Manson: Right.

---

[*] Commander James C. Shaw, USN; Lieutenant Commander Henry D. Reck, USNR; Lieutenant Commander Henry Saloman, USNR; Lieutenant Roger Pineau, USNR, who had studied the Japanese language, interviewed a number of Japanese officers after the war.
[†] Captain Shaw died 4 December 1988, subsequent to this interview.

Paul Stillwell: Salomon, I guess, broke off and went with the "Victory at Sea" series.* What do you recall about him?

Captain Manson: I didn't know him well, didn't know him well. He was a good writer. Captain Karig knew him a lot better, because Captain Karig was the technical advisor on that series. But I don't remember Saloman too well, except we were in the common pursuit of research, and that's about all.

Paul Stillwell: I heard that he had a falling-out with Morison, that he wanted greater credit than Morison was willing to give, and that's why he went into this television instead of the book series.

Captain Manson: Well, all of them wanted that. Jim Shaw wanted more recognition, and so did Henry Reck. I don't know that Roger Pineau ever said as much to me, but Jim Shaw used to really get upset about that. Of course, Captain Karig was just the opposite. He gave us more credit than we deserved. He didn't care. He was a big man. He even helped his competitors when it was to his detriment. He taught Rear Admiral Gallery and Bill Lederer and others to write.† He gave them guidance and advice.

Paul Stillwell: How did a collaboration like *Battle Report* work? Who wrote what?

Captain Manson: In our case, I'd write the first draft. If he wanted anything more, he'd send me after it. Normally he didn't. I usually had too much. So then he would edit down and out, and he would soup it up at times to give it a little more pizzazz. When Russ Harris and I were dividing up the chores, that first volume I worked on, from the Gilberts to the Philippines, I generally took amphibious operations across the Central

---

* "Victory at Sea" was a 26-episode television series produced in the early 1950s by NBC. It was famous for its music score, eloquent narration, and combat footage of World War II. The composer was Richard Rodgers, who was involved in a great many Broadway shows.
† Captain Daniel V. Gallery, Jr., USN. While in command of the USS *Guadalcanal* (CVE-60) in June 1944, his forces captured the German submarine *U-505*. Gallery eventually became a rear admiral and wrote a number of popular books about the Navy. His oral history is in the Naval Institute collection.
Captain William J. Lederer Jr., USN, was a public information specialist and prolific writer. He was best known as coauthor, along with Eugene Burdick, of *The Ugly American* (New York: Norton, 1958).

Pacific, and he covered the Southwest Pacific. I wrote a good bit of volume five, because Russ Harris had left us before we finished. But I had participated in all those operations. I really did have a good insight into that part of the war, having been there. Then, after reviewing it all, I knew about it.

Paul Stillwell: That may have been one of the real reasons that Karig wanted you, was for that background.

Captain Manson: I expect. I'm sure that must be. He didn't say.

Paul Stillwell: You had to learn a lot beyond what you'd observed firsthand.

Captain Manson: Oh, you get such a narrow view firsthand. Of course, I had a lot to learn. But one thing I did during the war is that when we'd get into an anchorage with the *Laffey*, the skipper, Becton, would send me around to pick up all the intelligence, so I'd visit people I knew and get all the information I could. Then I'd come back and brief him on where we'd been and where we were going, and he loved that. I suppose for me that was one of my big jobs, but I didn't think that it was anything at all when I was doing it.

Paul Stillwell: In the *Battle Report* series, what did you use as a yardstick for things to include and things to leave out? Did you focus more on the exciting-type things?

Captain Manson: Yes. We looked for the action, where there was a lot of excitement. If there were many conferences and stuff, we didn't go into that too heavily. They were usually dull.

Paul Stillwell: Not so much on strategy.

Captain Manson: Not so much on strategy. Not even a great deal on tactics, but more on how it felt, how it looked, how it smelled.

Paul Stillwell: I think you certainly succeeded in that aspect of it.

Captain Manson: I thought at one time that I would condense those five volumes into about two volumes, but I never got around to it. But it certainly did make it very easy when I got to writing about the Korean War. That was duck soup after having done World War II.

Paul Stillwell: You had your technique refined by then.

Captain Manson: Oh, yes, I knew what I was doing. A lot of World War II, from my point of view, was adventure and exploration. You know, exploratory.[*]

Paul Stillwell: How long did that assignment go on, working on the *Battle Report* series?

Captain Manson: That was finished in 1949.[†] Then we did one on Korea that would be the sixth volume of it, but it covered maybe just the first six months of the Korean War.[‡] Then later, Malcolm Cagle and I did a comprehensive history in the Morison style called *The Sea War in Korea*.[§] But the World War II project ended before the Korean War started; I know that.

Paul Stillwell: What did you do in between?

Captain Manson: I was on CNO's staff, Denfeld.

---

[*] In reviewing the interview transcript, Captain Manson added the following: "Never did I dream that 55 years later Smithsonian Museum would be making an effort to rewrite WWII history as noted in my attached letter to the Wash. Times editor. On 9 September 1994, *The Washington Times* published Manson's letter under the headline "Smithsonian should cancel distorted show on A-bomb." In preparing for the 50th anniversary of the dropping of the first atomic bomb on Japan in 1945, the Smithsonian's Air and Space Museum planned an exhibit of the B-29 bomber *Enola Gay* with a revisionist text that angered war veterans.
[†] The fifth and final volume of the World War II series, *Victory in the Pacific*, was published in 1949.
[‡] Captain Walter Karig, USNR; Commander Malcolm W. Cagle, USN; and Lieutenant Commander Frank A. Manson, USNR, *Battle Report: The War in Korea* (New York: Rinehart and Company, 1952).
[§] Malcolm W. Cagle and Frank A. Manson, *The Sea War in Korea* (Annapolis: U.S. Naval Institute, 1957).

Paul Stillwell: What sort of work?

Captain Manson: We were, I'd guess you'd say, trying to put forth what naval forces were all about and trying to use the mouth of the CNO to get across the idea that navies were very much a part of our strategy, our future. I used to go up and down the E-ring there, trying to get various admirals to have interviews, like Admiral Charles B. Momsen on submarines; Admiral Dan Gallery on missiles, and Admiral Cal Durgin on seaplanes and carriers.*

By the way, I witnessed the death of the seaplane about that time frame, I guess, or a little after that. The seaplane was wiped out.

Paul Stillwell: They were still in the fleet until the mid-'60s, maybe not with their earlier role, but they were still around.

Captain Manson: Well, I don't think we built any more after about the early '50s, because we had a terrible struggle, a terrible struggle, fought out between the carrier people and the few seaplane advocates. Admiral Cal Durgin's son got wiped out in that battle, fighting with Admiral Felt.†

Paul Stillwell: He got wiped out in what way?

Captain Manson: Career-wise. He told me his career was ended—wiped out.

Paul Stillwell: Were you designated a public affairs specialist at some point?

Captain Manson: At some point along in there when they were taking, I think, the last applications for the public affairs specialist, I applied for it, maybe the last day. I remember somebody writing on my application, "Frantic."

---

* The Pentagon has lettered corridors, going from A at the innermost to E at the outermost. E-ring offices, which go around the perimeter of the building, are considered the most prestigious. Rear Admiral Charles B. Momsen, USN; Rear Admiral Daniel V. Gallery, USN; Rear Admiral Calvin T. Durgin, USN.
† Rear Admiral Harry Don Felt, USN. The oral history of Felt, who retired as a four-star admiral, is in the Naval Institute collection. Calvin T. Durgin Jr. retired as a commander in 1960.

Paul Stillwell: Was there a separate designator then?

Captain Manson: Yes, and it was 1650.

Paul Stillwell: That's what it is now.

Captain Manson: That's what it was. I was one of the first 40 or 50, and I think maybe the 40th, to put in my application.* Because I never was really sure; I still held reservations about competing, if I was going to be going to sea and that sort of thing, with the regular line Navy.

Paul Stillwell: Especially after you had been out of it for so long.

Captain Manson: And then I'd been out of it, and I knew then for sure that I had no chance, but I did think that I could compete as a specialist. Well, I knew I could.

Paul Stillwell: At what point did you convert from reserve to regular?

Captain Manson: I'm pretty sure it was about '47.†

Paul Stillwell: The work you'd done on the *Battle Report* series undoubtedly helped your application.

Captain Manson: Oh, yes. And, of course, I knew everybody. I knew the Chief of Naval Personnel, all of the admirals. So I don't think there was any doubt, once the papers went in, that they would go through because I'd been working there in the high command for quite a long time at that point. Actually, I worked closely with 12 four-star admirals, some not for such a long time but some of them for as many as three or four years at a

---

* The first 40 U.S. naval officers to be selected as public information officers (later changed to public affairs officers) received that designation in 1946. In a play on the title *Ali Baba and the Forty Thieves*, they were known informally as the "40 Thieves" because the scarcity of resources forced them, according to the PAO newsletter, "to borrow or outright 'steal' assets to do their job."

† Manson transferred from the Naval Reserve to the regular Navy on 7 May 1947.

time. But I worked for Denfeld, Forrest Sherman, Robert Carney, Arleigh Burke, Robert Dennison, H. P. Smith, H. D. Felt, David McDonald, Thomas H. Moorer, and Claude Ricketts.* I don't know whom I've left out there. I wrote speeches for all those people.

Paul Stillwell: Maybe we could take them one at a time as they fit in context.

Captain Manson: I've had high-command experiences with them too. Starting with Admiral Denfeld and then with Carney, I wasn't what you might call the main person. Captain Karig was the special assistant, and I was the assistant to him. So I did talk with Admiral Denfeld, and I attended meetings with vice chiefs up and down the E-ring there, but I wasn't really a prime contact. Still, though, I was pumping out the information. That's what I was there for. And I was making friends with admirals and all over the city and with newspapermen and magazine people, books.

Paul Stillwell: Newspapers and magazines were still dominant, rather than TV.

Captain Manson: Oh, yes. Oh, yes. TV, in those days, just had no influence at all.

Paul Stillwell: We were talking about Admiral Denfeld. I wondered if you had more contact with Admiral Sherman after he became CNO?

Captain Manson: Well, I made one mistake with Admiral Sherman, but he forgave me for it. But you have to make mistakes if you stay in there long enough. But this one was a serious mistake. Sherman was going to relieve Admiral Conolly as CinCNELM, a

---

* Admiral Louis E. Denfeld, USN, served as Chief of Naval Operations from 15 December 1947 to 2 November 1949. Admiral Forrest P. Sherman, USN, held the billet from 2 November 1949 until his death on 22 July 1951. Admiral Robert B. Carney, USN, was CNO from 17 August 1953 to 17 August 1955. Admiral Arleigh A. Burke, USN, was CNO from 17 August 1955 to 1 August 1961. Admiral Robert L. Dennison, USN, served as Supreme Allied Commander Atlantic, Commander in Chief Atlantic, and Commander in Chief Atlantic Fleet from 28 February 1960 to 30 April 1963. Admiral Harold Page Smith, USN, served in the billet from 30 April 1963 to 30 April 1965. Admiral Harry D. Felt, USN, served as Vice Chief of Naval Operations from 1 September 1956 to 28 July 1958. Admiral David L. McDonald, USN, was Chief of Naval Operations from 1 August 1963 to 1 August 1967. Admiral Thomas H. Moorer, USN, was Chief of Naval Operations from 1 August 1967 to 1 July 1970. Admiral Claude V. Ricketts, USN, was Vice Chief of Naval Operations from 1 November 1961 until his death on 6 July 1964.

four-star job, and send him to the Naval War College and reduce his stars by one.* So Jack Norris, a correspondent for *The Washington Post* and a Naval Reserve commander came by my desk and said, "Frank, it is true that Admiral Conolly is going to be sent to the Naval War College, isn't it?"

I said, "Well, yes, it is."

So then on front page of *The Washington Post*, Admiral Conolly read that he was going to lose one star and he was going to be sent to the Naval War College, and Admiral Sherman hadn't even told Admiral Conolly. Nobody had told him. He read it in the papers first. Well, as you can imagine, they went on a crash alert in the office to find out who was the culprit. I said, "There ain't no use looking. I'm it." And I told him exactly what I had done.

Admiral Sherman said, well, hereafter that he would personally make all releases relative to the change of senior officers in command. Everybody understood that, and that was the last of it.

But for some reason or another, Admiral Forrest Sherman called me in from time to time just to chat with me. I kept his scrapbooks, and he liked that. He very much appreciated the fact that I kept record of everything he did.

One day I heard from Lieutenant Colonel Ted Clifton, the fellow who was working for General Omar Bradley as his speechwriter and later became a general working in the Kennedy White House.† He telephoned me and said, "Frank, how about you and I sharing an article in *Reader's Digest*?" He said, "We can get paid about $2,500, and we'll split it. You write down what the Navy wants as of right now, and I'll write down what the Army strategy is, and we'll just combine them, and this will be it." Sherman was just coming in and hadn't been in very long.‡

So I said, "You mean I'll have to write down Admiral Sherman's thinking?"

---

* Admiral Richard L. Conolly, USN, served as Commander U.S. Naval Forces Europe from September 1946 to November 1946, when the title was changed to Commander U.S. Naval Forces Eastern Atlantic and Mediterranean. In April 1947 the title was changed again, to Commander in Chief U.S. Naval Forces Eastern Atlantic and Mediterranean (CinCNELM). He remained in the billet until December 1950.

† General Omar N. Bradley, USA, served as Chairman of the Joint Chiefs of Staff from 16 August 1949 to 14 August 1953. In 1950 he was promoted to five-star rank, general of the Army. Major General Chester V. Clifton Jr., USA, was senior military aide to President John F. Kennedy and President Lyndon B. Johnson.

‡ Admiral Sherman became Chief of Naval Operations on 2 November 1949.

He said, "Yes, of course. I'll write Bradley, and you write Sherman."

I said, "You know, I can't do that."

He said, "What do you mean, you can't do that? Don't you write stuff?"

I said, "Yes, I do, but I certainly can't write down what Admiral Sherman is going to do with this Navy."

He said, "Well, in that case, I'll write it myself."

I said, "Well, you do that if that's what you want to do."

He said, "But I want you to do it."

I said, "No."

Anyway, I went to Admiral Sherman and told him all about it, and he said, "You tell the colonel to tell the general [Bradley] that if wants to know what I'm going to do with this Navy, all he's got to do is ask me, and I'll be more than happy to tell him. But no other way."

So I went back and told the colonel that this was Admiral Sherman's feeling about the thing. Ted Clifton said, "Frank, I told you not to do that. I told you this would kill the whole thing. Now it's all done."

I said, "Well, so be it." That's the way that was.

But, anyway, I found Forrest Sherman to be a very brilliant man. He kept a lot inside him, but still he didn't kick everybody out in the street when he came in, like everybody thought he would. They thought he would just get rid of everybody. They thought he was some sort of a traitor. This was the discussion going around at high command levels. But Sherman wasn't doing that at all. Actually, he was a most articulate and persuasive advocate of naval air and the Navy in general. He was just a very intelligent man. He understood why we had to have a navy, what its role was, where it was needed, and he just brought things around in a hurry.

Now, Admiral Denfeld wasn't anything like as articulate or as eloquent or as persuasive as Forrest Sherman. Denfeld was a good man of character, a real good man, but he wasn't the strategist. He just didn't have that background. His background was personnel, and he was good at that—tops. But he didn't have anything like the fleet experience or really the strategic understanding of Forrest Sherman.

Paul Stillwell: In what ways was the brilliance of Sherman manifested?

Captain Manson: I thought the brilliance of Sherman came out when everybody still questioned the utilization of aircraft carriers in international affairs, not only in wartime but during the Cold War as well. The manner in which Sherman just de-toothed his opponents was superb. I don't know a better word than de-tooth. The opposition just couldn't refute him, couldn't find weaknesses in his logic. When he presented his case for the aircraft carrier, that was the end of the argument. I can't recall exactly and precisely how he did that, but he did it with such persuasion that it was permanent. There never was another time, as far as I know, that aircraft carriers have ever been seriously threatened. And I have to give Admiral Forrest Sherman credit. He knew best how to say it so that others accepted it.

He was clever, too, when it came to international affairs and working out treaties with Spain. Over in the Sixth Fleet he had developed a very good relationship with the governments surrounding the Med.* So when it came to international affairs, he was out front in getting treaties written and improving the relationships between ourselves and Spain especially but other Mediterranean countries as well.

Paul Stillwell: That was the one that killed him, that taxing negotiation with Spain.†

Captain Manson: Yes, that's right.

Paul Stillwell: Did you work closely with him as a speechwriter?

Captain Manson: No, not anything like as closely as with others. He pretty much did his own. Occasionally he would show me something he had written or read it to me and ask me what I thought about it. But as a general rule, he didn't really ask anybody. He just

---

* As a vice admiral, Sherman commanded the Sixth Task Fleet from 7 February 1948 to 14 November 1949.
† Sherman arrived in Paris on 21 July 1951 after a tiring week of negotiations in Spain and Italy. At 10:40 the following morning he had a mild heart attack, then died in Paris at 1:05 that afternoon after two more heart attacks.

told everyone the policy, issued personals to the admiral on that policy, and that ended any quibbling.

Paul Stillwell: How would you describe his personality?

Captain Manson: I would say that he was quiet, low key, voice was very direct. Thoughtful, and a keen intellect with complete mastery of naval air warfare. I suppose he was a thinking man. I never saw him as devious. Some other people did. Competition gets just very keen near the top. He was not an amphibious expert like Barbey or Struble or Kinkaid or Turner.[*] But he had no superior on carrier strategy. Radford was his equal, however.

Paul Stillwell: Well, he's certainly been portrayed by many people as very ambitious, if not devious.

Captain Manson: Yes, I think that's fair, but I don't see that as detrimental or a criticism. All the admirals I have met were ambitious.

Paul Stillwell: I think some of that might be shown in the fact that he had this appreciation of the scrapbooks you mentioned, that he liked to see himself portrayed in a good light.

Captain Manson: Yes, and that is a human characteristic, I suppose. I never thought of it just this way until right now, but that evidently hit a very responsive chord with him. But I thought we were going to be fired, all of us, when Denfeld was fired, because we were really out in front when Denfeld was surprised. To the contrary, Sherman said he'd like us to continue, and we were surprised.

---

[*] Rear Admiral Daniel E. Barbey, USN, commanded Amphibious Force, South Pacific Force (retitled VII Amphibious Force during his tenure) from September 1943 to July 1945. Rear Admiral Arthur D. Struble, USN, was chief of staff for the Allied landings in Normandy in June 1944 and an amphibious commander in the Philippines later that year. Vice Admiral Thomas C. Kinkaid, USN, served as Commander Seventh Fleet from 26 November 1943 to 19 November 1945. Vice Admiral Richmond Kelly Turner, USN, commanded amphibious forces from Guadalcanal in 1942 to Okinawa in 1945.

Paul Stillwell: What he did so well after all that fracas was to pour some oil on the troubled waters.

Captain Manson: Yes, he did.

Paul Stillwell: And I think that was a pleasant surprise to many people.

Captain Manson: Oh, it was, it was. And there had been such difficulty both inside the armed services and outside. Something was desperately needed, just anything, and Sherman did it. He came along and served a most useful purpose in his life. In the Korean War, he had grave doubts about the Inchon landing and so expressed himself to General MacArthur, but MacArthur overrode all that.* Inchon didn't look like a very probable thing, with the 30-foot tide being what it was.

Paul Stillwell: There was not much time for planning, either.

Captain Manson: There was no time for planning. And that just makes a naval officer want to climb the wall, because it does, as you know, require tremendous detail in putting all these task units and task groups and taking into account all of the possible things that you're going to do and how you're going to intertwine. You know, it's a very complicated thing. Well, anyway, Sherman learned from MacArthur on that one.
    Let's see, following him was Fechteler.†

Paul Stillwell: Yes.

Captain Manson: I didn't work for him. I knew him quite well and liked him. He was down in the E-ring in personnel. I think he was deputy chief of personnel or some such title. I interviewed him about his operation in the Philippines during World War II for

---

* On 15 September 1950, U.S. troops under the command of General of the Army Douglas MacArthur made an amphibious landing at Inchon, the port for Seoul, South Korea. The surprise landing, 150 miles behind enemy lines, temporarily turned the tide of war in favor of United Nations forces.
† Admiral William M. Fechteler, USN, served as Chief of Naval Operations from 16 August 1951 to 17 August 1953.

Battle Report. Yes, he was remindful of Denfeld—both likable and good at personnel. Anyway, I hadn't regarded Admiral Fechteler as a strategist, and I doubt if he thought of himself as such. He was not the kind of thinker that Forrest Sherman was.

Paul Stillwell: I've gathered Fechteler was a much more down-to-earth fellow than most admirals.

Captain Manson: Oh, yes, he was, certainly friendly, amiable. There wasn't any pomp and circumstance about him at all, none. Good guy, smart guy but, again, not a strategist.

Paul Stillwell: More of an operational type.

Captain Manson: Exactly, more an operational type, yes. I didn't work for him, but I knew him. And I've had long talks with him, chances to probe his thinking. He was popular among his peers and a wonderful storyteller.

Paul Stillwell: In the meantime, how did you get on to the Korean project?

Captain Manson: Well, when the Korean War broke out, we were still working there for Forrest Sherman. Captain Karig suggested to this admiral that perhaps we ought to get on top of this quick like and not wait like we did during World War II. Forrest Sherman agreed. So all the directives were sent out that we were going to undertake this project as it was being fought. It was Captain Karig, Commander Malcolm Cagle, and myself. We were designated to do the job.

Paul Stillwell: How had Cagle gotten into the organization?

Captain Manson: I had recruited him, really, through a good friend on Admiral Sherman's staff, an officer named John Smith, a Congressional Medal of Honor Marine.* John told me one day, "Frank, I know a guy down there in Norfolk, a squadron commander who you could really use. His name is Cagle."

I said, "Well, get him up here, John," because I was just being swamped with air and surface and everything. He came in, and Chris and I had a little talk. I asked him how he thought he'd like that kind of work, and he said, well, he didn't know. He had been an operational type, but he had written a few articles for Naval Institute, and I really was impressed by him. He was sharp; I could tell that. I said, "Well, do you think this would help your career?" He said he didn't know but said he was willing to try it.

So that was the basis of his coming in. Captain Karig was all in favor of bringing in an aviator; we needed him. So Chris brought a lot of balance. My not being familiar with the air picture, he filled in a lot for us and for CNO. Then he joined the book project. Captain Karig went out to Korea right away. He'd been out there maybe 30 days or so, and then I went out. He came back, and I went out. Cagle came out then after I'd been out there for about 30 days. Then he and I stayed out there until nearly Christmastime.

Paul Stillwell: So was this a sort of a Morison-type approach you were using?

Captain Manson: Well, no, not yet. In this particular book we were doing, it was still *Battle Report*, and we were still giving them the sounds and smell of battle. It was still not the real Morison-type, because this was going to be published by Rinehart & Company, and they wanted the same style book as they'd had. So that's what we did.

Paul Stillwell: What are some of the highlights you remember from being off the coast of Korea?

---

* Colonel John L. Smith, USMC. He had earned the Medal of Honor as a fighter pilot during the Guadalcanal campaign in 1942. He was then a major and commanding officer of Marine Fighting Squadron 223.

Captain Manson: The first thing I wish to say about Korea is this.* I anticipate the United States will face continuing problems with North Korea, as long as that country is Communist controlled. North Korea's leaders are highly skilled risk takers. They see the U.S. as a big dog that doesn't like to fight, so they don't mind tweaking the dog's nose.

Problems at the Demilitarized Zone (DMZ) have existed from its beginning in 1953.† Admiral Arleigh Burke told me the North Korean truce negotiators were daily claiming territorial conquests they had never made, frequently in areas where they had no troops. Admiral C. Turner Joy was completely frustrated by their dishonesty.‡ North Koreans will respond only to force and power applied to their jugular. They do not fear minor irritations such as limited trade sanctions. They simply turn to other sources, mainly China. No matter how much President Clinton and Carter placed in North Korea's good intentions, that nation cannot be trusted.§

When I was last in Korea in 1970, I was taken to the DMZ for a close-up viewing. A North Korean guard, to show his antipathy for foreign guests, kicked at me when I walked past him at about three feet distance.

It reminded me of December 1950 when I traveled alone with a U.S. Army truck driven to Hamhung, North Korea. It was during that brief historical moment when we thought Hamhung was in friendly territory.

I was taken to the Catholic compound where some 300 Catholics had been killed a few days before. I was shown the huge wall where 22 sisters were drowned. I was taken to the chapel's basement where over 200 Catholics had first been shot and then doused in gasoline and burned. I ran my fingers through human remains and turned debris and came up with torture knives, handcuffs, and .30-caliber shell casings. I still have those moments from North Korea.

---

* Captain Manson added this and the next six paragraphs when he reviewed the manuscript several years after the interview itself.
† The DMZ was established as part of the armistice agreement in July 1953. Rear Admiral Arleigh A. Burke, USN, had been a U.S. negotiator during earlier peace talks.
‡ Vice Admiral C. Turner Joy, USN, was head of the U.S. negotiating team during part of the war. See his book *How Communists Negotiate* (New York, Macmillan, 1955).
§ James E. Carter, Jr., who had graduated from the Naval Academy in the class of 1947, served as President of the United States from 20 January 1977 to 20 January 1981. William J. Clinton was President from 20 January 1993 to 20 January 2001.

If there are those who think North Korean leaders are trustworthy and humane, they will surely be disappointed.

The loss of the U.S. helicopter in December 1994 is typical of North Korea's skating on the edge. Her willingness to risk is the result of knowing the U.S. lacks the will and courage to respond, fearing escalation. It is a sad commentary on U.S. foreign policy. North Korea is a dangerous foe with two or three and maybe more nuclear weapons. The U.S. refuses to engage in the special operations needed to deal with North Korea's nuclear capability. So what we have is "peace in our time."[*]

Paul Stillwell: What do you recall about the naval aspects of your time in Korea?

Captain Manson: I remember those tides at Inchon. I tell you, I had never seen and never will see tides again with such speed, depth, and variables. My gosh, the tide just astounded me. Then going ashore over there and seeing the devastation our planes had wrought. I remember a long string of enemy tanks that our pilots had burned out with napalm near the beaches of Inchon. Our air hit them with napalm. But that Inchon coast, my main memory of it is an awful lot of rugged rocks and just a rough place to make a landing.

Paul Stillwell: Were you there at the time of the invasion?

Captain Manson: No. I was there shortly after the invasion. Didn't get there in time, so I didn't see the men actually going ashore. But I got there in time to talk with everybody while they were still digging the sand out of their shoes. I got there in time to have a battle with Admiral James Doyle, who was the amphibious commander.[†] At that time I was over there aboard the *Mount McKinley*. I had been told before I went out there that if I saw any obvious PR deficiencies, anything that would help PR-wise, to get it back to

---

[*] The quotation is a sarcastic reference. Neville Chamberlain was Britain's Prime Minister from 1937 to 1940. He is best known for signing the Munich agreement with Germany's Adolf Hitler in September 1938. He agreed to the partition of Czechoslovakia in return for a non-aggression pledge from Hitler. Chamberlain hailed the agreement as a guarantee of "peace in our time." Germany violated the pledge, and Britain declared war on Germany in 1939.
[†] Rear Admiral James H. Doyle, USN, Commander Task Force 90.

the department pronto, to the Secretary of the Navy. So I hadn't been there too long, but I had talked frankly with quite a number of officers. I found the Navy had been rather niggardly about recommending awards to its personnel—virtually nothing to that point.

So the more I checked on it, the more I realized that awards were nonexistent. So I prepared a rather comprehensive dispatch to send to the Secretary of the Navy stating that giving out awards would help not only the morale and everything else about an operating fleet, but it would also have other benefits.

Paul Stillwell: Public relations-wise.

Captain Manson: Public relations-wise, it would certainly have benefits, and it just might be that this would be the Navy's last big operation. Of course, that's an opportunity that would not long exist, because I thought Inchon might be the only one in the war.

Paul Stillwell: Did you name individuals that you thought deserved awards, or was it just the concept?

Captain Manson: No, no, no, it was just the concept. But Admiral Doyle called me in there, and he said, "I'm not going to send this dispatch."

I said, "Well, I'm sorry to hear that, Admiral, because I was told that when I came out here that I was to look for things that I thought might be helpful, and this is one area I believe would be helpful."

He said, "You're criticizing my command."

I said, "Well, there's no intention to do that, and it's certainly no criticism of you or anybody else, but it's just a situation which exists."

He said, "Well, I'm not going to send your dispatch anyway."

So I said, "Well, that's your privilege." So I took the dispatch and put it in my pocket and transferred from the *Mount McKinley* as soon as I could to Admiral Struble's flagship, *Missouri*.* I was a friend of Admiral Struble's from way back. I just took this wrinkled dispatch and gave it to him, and I said, "I tried to get this out, but it was refused."

He said, "I'll take care of it." Within two days, he had called a fleet conference, skippers from all around, and had them all in there on his flagship, and he really laid it out to them that he wanted awards recommended, he wanted it done quickly, and he wanted a liberal attitude on this. He asked me to attend the conference.

I remember that the skipper of the *Collett* said, "Well, I don't go along with this, Admiral."†

"Why not?" said Struble.

He said, "Well, suppose you've got gunners on one side, on the starboard side, and they shoot down a plane and you've got just as good of gunners on the port side and they don't even get a chance to shoot at one. So you recommend these guys on the starboard, but these guys on the port, they're just as good and they don't get recommended for an award."

Struble said, "That's because the starboard guys had the opportunity. The people on the starboard side should have been recommended for an award." The skipper of the *Collett* didn't like that, and there were a few other questions from people that had really sincere feelings and doubts about whether people were just doing what they were supposed to do, and for that they didn't deserve medals.

Paul Stillwell: Well, that's a tough call, really, whether you're just doing your job or it's above and beyond the call of duty.

Captain Manson: That's right, it's a real tough call. But quite frankly, after having gone through the B-36 hearings, writing the *Battle Report* series, and all that, I realized what the other services were doing, and I knew the Navy was way behind the times. It was

---

* Vice Admiral Arthur D. Struble, USN, served as Commander Seventh Fleet from 19 May 1950 to 28 March 1951. The oral history of Struble, who retired as a vice admiral, is in the Naval Institute collection. The battleship *Missouri* (BB-63) was the site of the Japanese signing of surrender documents in Tokyo Bay on 2 September 1945.

† Commander Robert H. Close, USN, commanded the destroyer *Collett* (DD-730) from August 1949 to September 1951. The ship participated in the support of the invasion of Inchon.

about time the Navy caught up. In many cases our people were doing tremendous jobs and doing just what the others were doing for medals and the Navy was doing in the line of duty. Well, anyway, Admiral Struble got that straightened out. Then I spent 20 minutes of every day with Admiral Struble for a few weeks.

Paul Stillwell: How would you describe him?

Captain Manson: Again Struble was, in some ways, like Admiral Forrest Sherman in that he was a brilliant-thinking admiral. He was very conscious of his place in history, and he wanted to be there, because he was involved. Again, a very intelligent man—one of the Navy's top amphibious and surface leaders. Not afraid to make a decision, excellent planner of complex operations. He could fit it all together.

Paul Stillwell: Did he have a warm personality?

Captain Manson: Yes, he did.

Paul Stillwell: Certainly sounds more so than Doyle.

Captain Manson: Oh, much more so. Oh, yes. Oh, Doyle was a cold fish, but Struble had a warm personality. Those 20 minutes of each day gave me a chance to quiz him on each and every aspect of his operations. Just 20 minutes, that's all, but that was all I needed.

Paul Stillwell: Were you assigned to the fleet staff?

Captain Manson: Yes, temporarily to Seventh Fleet staff. Then I had 20 minutes with Marine General O. P. Smith, and I had as long as I wanted with Army General Almond, who was commander of the X Corps.*

Paul Stillwell: MacArthur's man.

Captain Manson: Yes, MacArthur's man.

Paul Stillwell: But you had unlimited time for interview with him.

Captain Manson: Yes, I could spend as much time as I wanted. I'll never forget being with General Almond one time, and I said, "General, what are you going to do if we go around the minefields, make our landing, and you find there's nothing left to do, everything's over? What are you going to do?"

Almond said, "Oh well, we'll run out the roads all the way to the Chinese border. That will give us something to do."

I said, "Well, yes, you could do that." I had no idea the Chinese were already there, crossing the Yalu River.† That's what Almond tried to do. I don't know if he knew the Chinese had crossed the Yalu at that time. Anyway, he and General Walker were not getting along well at all.‡ I didn't delve too much into their troubles, but I could tell from talking to Almond they were not getting along.

But, anyway, getting back to Struble, he was a student of naval history. I mean, he had a sense of the important. He'd done a lot of reading. A kind man, but he could be very severe, particularly on admirals.

Paul Stillwell: Did you see examples of that?

---

* General of the Army Douglas MacArthur, USA, Supreme Commander Allied Powers, Commander in Chief U.S. Armed Forces Far East, and Commander in Chief United Nations Command. Major General Oliver P. Smith, USMC, Commander First Marine Division; Major General Edward M. Almond, USA, Commander Tenth Corps.
† The Yalu River separated North Korea from China.
‡ Lieutenant General Walton H. Walker, USA, commanded the Eighth Army until his death in a traffic accident in Korea on 23 September 1950. He was replaced by Lieutenant General Matthew B. Ridgway, USA.

Captain Manson: Yes. One time back in Washington, the admiral was Tex McLean.[*] He was working for Struble, and had been asked to get certain statements from various deputy chiefs on an issue; I don't recall what it was now. McLean was supposed to write the position for OP-03, which Struble was in those days.[†] McLean called me in one Saturday, and he said, "Manson, what do you think of this? I don't think much of it myself, but I'd like to just know what you think."

So I read it over and said, "Admiral, you're right. It's not appropriate. It's not what we want."

McLean blew his stack and started screaming at me, McLean did, and wanted to know who my commanding officer was, he was going to have me detached and all this and that.

Struble, who was in the next room, overheard all this. I'll never forget him yelling "McLean!" but it was as loud as McLean ever heard his name, and he called us both in there. Struble said, "McLean, if you can't perform in the job I've given you in a manner satisfactory to the people representing the Chief of Naval Operations, I'm going to have you detached. Now, I want you to get out of here, and I don't ever want to hear you perform as you did out there just now. I want you to do what you've been told to do and if you can't do it, I'm going to have you detached."

So McLean and I were walking out together, and he said, "Well, I guess we both caught it on that one, didn't we?"

I said, "Yes, I would agree."

Anyway, Struble understood amphibious operations. The *Laffey* had been with him on that Ormoc Bay operation. He was in charge of that. He was a complex man, but he had one of the best amphibious minds in the Navy. Probably Admiral Barbey was one of the others that I'd put up with Struble. Turner was good.

Paul Stillwell: Did you find these admirals welcomed your 20 minutes with them as a chance to unwind?

---

[*] Rear Admiral Heber H. McLean, USN.
[†] Vice Admiral Arthur D. Struble, USN, served as Deputy Chief of Naval Operations (Operations) (OP-03), 1948-50.

Captain Manson: Oh, yes. Oh, yes.

Paul Stillwell: What kind of things did they talk about?

Captain Manson: Well, they would tell me what they were doing during the day and what their most difficult problems were at any given moment. For example, Struble had serious problems with the mines at Wonsan and how to sweep them or avoid them if he could.* He would take me with him into the minefields.

Paul Stillwell: What a thrill that must have been. [Laughter]

Captain Manson: Yes. Yes, it was. Soviet mines were planted all around the place, magnetic, pressure, and contact—all kinds. But, yes, anytime I wanted to go with him, I was welcome, and I did go.

Paul Stillwell: Did you take notes by hand in these conversations?

Captain Manson: Yes, I just had a little notebook.

Paul Stillwell: What became of those notes? Did you turn those over to Naval History?

Captain Manson: I think most of them have gone to Naval History. Only recently, I gave 10 or 15 boxes of notes and history to Naval History.†

Paul Stillwell: Certainly you've collected far more than you could use in the books.

Captain Manson: Oh, many times more. Yes, you know how it is. It's like ten to one, maybe, or maybe more than that back here.

---

* North Koreans mined their port at Wonsan on the east coast of Korea and thus delayed United Nations landing operations there. The minesweeping project took place in October and November 1950.
† This refers to the Naval Historical Center, since renamed the Naval History and Heritage Command.

Paul Stillwell: Another person I know you interviewed was Captain Jimmy Thach of the *Sicily*.* What do you recall of him?

Captain Manson: Well, he was a "go get 'em" person. He was an aviator and a kind of lanky fellow, tall and skinny, but a top-notch person, likable, fun-loving, good-humored, smart. I liked him.

Paul Stillwell: Very engaging personality.

Captain Manson: Engaging personality, yes, that's the word I was looking for. But he would draw you to him and keep your interest. And he was a good man. He invented the Thach weave, and he explained all that to me, how that works so you can get a guy off your tail.†

Paul Stillwell: We have his oral history, and he's a marvelous storyteller.

Captain Manson: Is he? Is he still alive?

Paul Stillwell: No, he died in 1981.

Captain Manson: I wasn't as close to Jimmy Thach as, say, I might have been to Struble or some of them, but at the same time I knew him quite well and I was very fond of him, and I thought he was one of our better admirals.

Paul Stillwell: He was very good at operational matters.

---

* Captain John S. Thach, USN, commanded the escort aircraft carrier *Sicily* (CVE-118) during the Korean War. The oral history of Thach, who retired as a four-star admiral, is in the Naval Institute collection. See also Steve Ewing, *Thach Weave: the Life of Jimmie Thach* (Annapolis: Naval Institute Press, 2004).
† Lieutenant Commander John S. Thach, USN, commanding officer of Fighting Squadron Three developed the Thach Weave shortly before World War II. It was a means of enabling the F4F Wildcat to counter the better-performing Japanese Zero fighter. Thach, who retired as a four-star admiral, described the origin of the maneuver in his Naval Institute oral history.

Captain Manson: Very good, yes. You know, in naval operations, he fully understood them. Running a Navy show is a very complex type of thing, and it takes a good mind just to comprehend the thing and to run it as he did. He was innovative too.

Paul Stillwell: Yes, he was. He said in his oral history that he invented the Thach weave with matchsticks on his kitchen table.

Captain Manson: Well, I never heard that, but it doesn't surprise me, how do you keep the other guy off your tail, or get him off your tail. Well, you know, but the very best ideas are sometimes the most simple.

Paul Stillwell: That's an example.

Captain Manson: That's an example.

Paul Stillwell: What do you remember about living in the flagship *Missouri*?

Captain Manson: Well, I remember my office was in the ladies' head. It was the only space *Missouri* had where I could put a desk. I didn't have a desk, I put a board across the sink. My yeoman, named J. Vettese, and I had the head as our office.[*]

Paul Stillwell: Was it just forward of the wardroom on the main deck?

Captain Manson: Yes.

Paul Stillwell: Starboard side.

Captain Manson: Starboard side.

---

[*] Yeoman First Class Joseph J. Vettese, USN.

Paul Stillwell: I know that place.*

Captain Manson: That was my office. Well, I'd never been on a battleship. It was so big that it took me forever to find anything. I was forever asking somebody where I was trying to go. But I thought the luxury of it was captivating, and you could get used to that, including good food. Well, too, another thing, it's so unlike a small ship. People's jobs were so carefully defined and very specialized. You felt very secure in a battleship. It would take the enemy forever to kill you if you were inside that battleship. It is almost the opposite of being in a destroyer, whose skin is thin.

Paul Stillwell: Yes. You went from one extreme to the other.

Captain Manson: Yes. But I admired the organization of the battleship. I thought the people were on top of their jobs. It was like running a city

Paul Stillwell: You get so much talent in a big ship like that.

Captain Manson: Yes, you do. You've just got people overqualified. They're qualified, so many of them, to command that ship. But at that time I was so interested in decisions that were being made about that Korean War out there that I didn't spend an awful lot of time with the ship itself. I was busy going off to other ships, going off to Canadian ships. The *Athabascan*, for example, I went up and spent some time in her, and generally trying to keep my eye on the whole operation, that I didn't spend a lot of time with this *Missouri*, except to think it was a really nice place to write a history.

Paul Stillwell: What was your working routine? How much time would you spend? Did you go around in helicopters?

---

* The interviewer served in the crew of the *New Jersey* (BB-62), a sister ship of the *Missouri*.

Captain Manson: No, I went around in boats. I'm trying to think if I ever had a chopper ride out there in the Korean War. I think mostly boats. I don't recall ever being in a chopper.

Paul Stillwell: Did you go on a bombing raid?

Captain Manson: I think we were on a reconnaissance mission. I don't recall—no bombs. Dick Fleck, who was skipper of one of the AD squadrons, wanted me to go on the Yalu River strikes.* I was rooming with Dick Fleck and his roommate, Ed Deacon, a Corsair a squadron commander.

Anyway, I told him I didn't want to do that, that I'd been scared enough times, and all I'd do if we got into a real good dogfight was get scared, and that I knew what that was like. In any case, I couldn't see much from looking out a small hole about 12 inches in diameter. I could not get much out of it. So I demurred. I told him I couldn't see what point it would be for me to be up there over the Yalu bridges, except to say I was there. Had it not been for my previous combat experiences, I probably would have gone with him, but I didn't go. Besides, I had a young wife and small son at home during this war. I couldn't see taking absolutely useless risks.

Paul Stillwell: What carrier were you on?

Captain Manson: *Philippine Sea*. Fleck and Deacon, who had what they called the "Corsair crouch," would invite me to their party after their attack on the Yalu bridges.

They would have a cocktail hour. I don't know if this is very well known, and I certainly didn't write about it in the book, but when they'd come in after a hard day, these aviators would gather around, and they'd have a shot of brandy or whatever was around, you know, have a few laughs and talk about the day's flight, relax. Medicinal.

---

* Lieutenant Commander Richard W. Fleck, USN, commanded Attack Squadron 115 (VA-115) from 16 January 1950 to 30 June 1951. The squadron operated the AD Skyraider. Commander Edward T. Deacon, USN, commanded Fighter Squadron 114 (VF-114), which operated the F4U Corsair. He was also the strike leader in Air Group 11, which operated from the aircraft carrier *Philippine Sea* (CV-47). The Yalu River separated North Korea from China.

Paul Stillwell: Was that in one of the ready rooms?

Captain Manson: No, no, in their staterooms. I was rooming with Fleck and Deacon aboard the *Phil Sea*.

Paul Stillwell: I see.

Captain Manson: But I didn't know such things were done until I actually joined the aviators. But I learned it was a common practice. So I would look forward, when they would get back from a raid, to hearing just what happened. Lieutenant Commander Tom Amen was a fighter pilot.* He shot down the first MiG out there. He was in our ship.

Paul Stillwell: Did they let you join in the cocktail party?

Captain Manson: Oh, yes. Sure, I did.

Paul Stillwell: Well, writing about it is pretty rigorous too. [Laughter]

Captain Manson: That's called rough duty. Well, as a matter of fact, we had one operation on the carrier where a young man came on board and sheared his landing gear and ran into a large group of aircraft, and we had a terrible fire.† I think the ship had to scuttle about 12 aircraft as a result of that crash. It burned them up. It was a tremendous fire until they got it under control. The only persons really angry were those who lost their aircraft.

Paul Stillwell: Understandably.

Captain Manson: Yes. That's very understandable.

---

* Lieutenant Commander William Thomas Amen, USN, commanded Fighter Squadron 111 (VF-111), which operated the Grumman F9F-2 Panther jet. He shot down the first Communist MiG fighter on 9 November 1950.
† The incident took place on 12 December 1950 when an AD Skyraider damaged by enemy aircraft fire broke into flames when it crash-landed on the deck of the *Philippine Sea*.

Paul Stillwell: What was your method? Did you just gather raw material, or did you start drafting chapters out there?

Captain Manson: No, I was strictly gathering raw material, because at that point I could not sense what was going to fit into the book, and I could not see whether this or that event was worthwhile. I could be very discerning. But at the same time, I couldn't see exactly how everything was going to fit into the total, because I was missing out on some of the happenings back at CinCPac and the Tokyo headquarters.[*] Also, we needed to balance what we saw with what was happening in other ships at the same time.

At that same time, too, Admiral Burke was asking me, every time I got back to Tokyo, to write up summaries so he could send them back to his friend who was an administrative assistant to the Secretary of the Navy.[†] So I did that. Every time I was back in Tokyo, I would prepare a rather lengthy summary letter, and I'd keep that, too, for my own use. But Admiral Burke, who was then a rear admiral, fresh caught, would send it back to Washington to tell them what deficiencies and mistakes were going on and recommend how they could improve it and how they could tighten up the command. Burke was worried about command relationships. Mainly he wanted to get people on their toes. They were too lax, in his judgment, and in mine.

Paul Stillwell: In what ways?

Captain Manson: They had been in a peacetime situation—absolutely no strain. So their reading of the dispatches, for example, was leisurely. There was no big hurry about getting the dispatches read or answering them. That is, not until Burke reported for duty. Things changed.

Paul Stillwell: You're talking about the Far East headquarters in Tokyo?

---

[*] CinCPac – Commander in Chief Pacific Fleet, based in Hawaii; Commander Naval Forces Far East, based in Japan.
[†] Burke, then a rear admiral, was deputy chief of staff to Vice Admiral C. Turner Joy, USN. Joy served as Commander U.S. Naval Forces Far East from 27 August 1949 to 4 June 1952.

Captain Manson: Joy's headquarters.

Paul Stillwell: Did you deal with Joy at all?

Captain Manson: Oh, yes, many times. I found him to be delightful, amiable, and a good man. His teeth had not been cut in combat, I don't think, or it didn't strike me that he was a combat veteran. I don't know what his combat experiences were.

Paul Stillwell: I think he had some experience. I know he was skipper of a cruiser.

Captain Manson: Was he? In action?

Paul Stillwell: I think so.*

Captain Manson: Well, I could be wrong. He could have seen action. But at that point in his life, he was a relaxed person. And, of course, he'd been out there during a time phase when there really wasn't much to do, and then suddenly there was a war, a full-scale war, and it was hard for people who had more or less adjusted to a social life of two or three hours a day at the office, a lot of time on the golf course. It was the same way before World War II.

Anyway, Burke's mission out there was to tighten things up, get people on their toes. Forrest Sherman sent him out there to do that.

Paul Stillwell: Yes. Joy certainly got his combat experience in those negotiations with the Communists at Panmunjom.

Captain Manson: Oh, he did that. Yes, he did more than he ever bargained for.

Paul Stillwell: That was a war in itself.

---

* As a captain Joy commanded the heavy cruiser *Louisville* (CA-28) from September 1942 to July 1943 during combat action in the Aleutians and South Pacific. He later commanded a cruiser division in World War II combat.

Captain Manson: Yes, that was a war in itself. Now, I never went to any of those meetings in the truce tent. But those North Koreans were so difficult. I was out there one time, I went up to the line, and one of those guards kicked a piece of snow at me just because I walked fairly close to him. Just belligerent.

But, anyway, returning to Admiral Joy, I wasn't with him enough to make a judgment on him while he was running the war. I spent more time with Admiral Burke, Admiral Struble, Admiral Smith, who was out there in charge of fire support and minesweepers.* I spent less time with Admiral Joy than with the others.

Paul Stillwell: Did the people back in Tokyo try to pick your brains about what you'd seen in the operating courses?

Captain Manson: Only Admiral Burke. He wanted to know everything I had to tell him. He always had time to discuss what was going on and in detail.

Paul Stillwell: What kinds of things was he interested in?

Captain Manson: Well, he wanted to know my opinion of how operations were going, whether the ships were performing well, and what results were they getting. He wanted any concrete results from the minesweeping or the fire support groups. He wanted any details I could provide him, and, of course I gave him what he wanted.

Paul Stillwell: You've talked about the air. Any comments you have about the shore bombardment effectiveness?

Captain Manson: I didn't think shore bombardment was too effective. Primarily, there weren't a lot of targets: they were well hidden. They would roll out a gun and shoot and then they'd hide, and you wouldn't see them. I don't think gunfire support was very effective, basically. It probably had a certain heckling benefit, but as far as actually diminishing the other side's will to fight, I don't think it had much effect.

---

* Rear Admiral Allan E. Smith, USN, Commander Task Force 95.

Paul Stillwell: It could be most useful specifically when it was supporting friendly troops ashore, protecting them.

Captain Manson: Yes. Now that you mention troops, in the evacuation there at Hungnam fire support was very useful, because the ships just laid down a rim of fire beyond our perimeter.* And close air support was usually effective. I say usually but not always. Whether it was gunfire or whether it was close air support, I'm sure it caused the North Koreans some loss of sleep and a lot of trouble, and later the Chinese had the same problems.

Paul Stillwell: Do you have any specific recollections of that minefield at Wonsan?

Captain Manson: I can't remember looking in any direction where there weren't mines. The North Koreans, with Soviet help, had planted over 3,000 mines at Wonsan. As we went through it, I was just amazed that we could thread our way through this thing without running into one of them, but we did. The Soviets had given them magnetic, acoustic, pressure, and contact mines.

My only other personal experience with mines had been at Okinawa, where *Laffey* blew up a few contact mines off the coast there. They are the ones with protruding horns. Never in any other operation can I recall finding them. So I knew what mines would do. I have seen them blow up. It's an uneasy feeling to be scooting along in the water when you know perfectly well it is mined. You also know you don't know where they are. The best recollection I have of Wonsan's minefield is that I thought that Admiral Struble knew what he was doing, so I put my confidence in him when we entered the minefields.

Paul Stillwell: What was his purpose, just to detect?

Captain Manson: Yes, he wanted to go in and get some kind of a feel for what the total sweep problems were, what kind of mines our sweepers were encountering, and what

---

* From 10 to 24 December 1950, United Nations forces in eastern North Korea were evacuated through the port of Hungnam. Included in the withdrawal was the First Marine Division.

their forecasts were for a day when they could clear a channel so we could land the amphibious forces. He had a planning conference, planning from his point of view, to determine when he could move the forces into Wonsan. But Struble knew a lot about minesweeping. So he would ask Captain Spofford and Dusty Shouldice and Don DeForest—these were the best minesweeping people in the U.S. Navy—for their opinions of what types of mines we faced and where they were located, as best we could determine, and whether we needed additional sweeping devices and so forth.[*]

Don DeForest had gone behind the lines and found the trigger mechanisms for magnetic mines hidden under a straw stack. North Koreans helped him, of course. Still, he had taken high risk.

In the Wonsan operation, the United States hired some commercial Japanese minesweepers to come over there, about eight or ten, and they were very enthusiastic about helping with the war. So the Japanese minesweepers were doing their job with tremendous industry until they found some mines. Either that day or the next day, someone looked out over the horizon, and all those Japanese minesweepers were headed for Tokyo or Yokosuka or somewhere; they were going home. They left us, and someone wanted to know why they were leaving, they said, "It's dangerous. It's too dangerous," and that was the end of the Japanese effort.

Paul Stillwell: How much longer did you stay out there in Korean waters?

Captain Manson: When our fleet anchored in Wonsan's outer harbor and when we got things under control, I went back to Tokyo. We stayed around Tokyo headquarters a while, and then Chris Cagle wanted us to return to Washington, where we could start putting the book together. We knew at that point it was just going to be a short history. So I wanted to go out and join the British fleet and get an allied flavor in the book. Mainly I just wanted to get some British color. But Chris didn't think it would be worthwhile, because the British were not doing anything of consequence. But my main idea was that we should bring the British operations into it for Allied purposes, but we

---

[*] Captain Richard T. Spofford, USN; Lieutenant Commander D'Arcy Shouldice, USN; Lieutenant Commander Don C. DeForest, USN.

didn't because, again, Chris felt that the Brits weren't doing much. Well, nobody was. A French ship that was out there, but it wasn't doing anything except having dinners aboard and drinking some good wine. As far as I know, the French ship never fired a shot.

Paul Stillwell: So did you come back in late 1950?

Captain Manson: Yes, and then we started writing the book.

Paul Stillwell: How long did that take?

Captain Manson: I would estimate it took about six months.

Paul Stillwell: Was that your principal job then in early '51?

Captain Manson: Yes, on that Korean book. That's what we did; we concentrated on that until we had it out. Just about the time we finished that book, I was sent to record the formation of Southern Command in Naples, Italy, where I joined Admiral Carney.[*] That was quite an experience, an unusual experience, to see a command in the early stages of development, to be there when it was being formed, and to hear firsthand the enmity between the Greeks and the Turks, and the Greeks and the Italians, and to try to get those people to record their feelings toward each other, or even to express feelings, because their feelings were so deeply resentful.

Like Major Hadzianis, whom I assigned from Greece to help me write the book. He said, "It's just too much. I can't write about it. I feel so badly against the Italians."

I said, "But you're going to have to put something down. After all, your country has joined in this alliance. No matter how much you may personally dislike or distrust or whatever, there has been a new relationship." Well, he agreed with that.

But the admiral had all kinds of difficulties, too, with the Greeks and the Turks, trying to get them in the same room to talk about what the command relationships should

---

[*] Admiral Robert B. Carney, USN, served as Commander in Chief Allied Forces Southern Europe from June 1951 to July 1953. The command was established as part of the North Atlantic Treaty Organization (NATO).

be and who would be senior, who would be the chief of staff, for example, in southeast Europe. Sometimes he would have to ask them to enter a room consecutively, one group at a time, and he would work out an area of common purpose or common agreement and then he would bring them both together on that one common point. But Admiral Carney was always getting gratuitous advice from Field Marshal Montgomery, who was up in London.* And General Bertrand came down from France to tell Carney, again gratuitously, how to do it.† Both the general and the admiral wanted Admiral Carney to benefit from their broad experiences. They had much advice.

Paul Stillwell: More than enough advice, probably.

Captain Manson: More than enough advice. I remember Field Marshal Montgomery came down, and he said, first thing, "Well, Mick, where are you going to fight the battle?"

Admiral Carney said, "I don't know where we're going to fight the battle."

Montgomery said, "Well, you understand that's the first thing you've got to know in this command, is where you're going to fight the battle. Remember, Mick, you are now commanding land armies."

Carney said, "Well, I'm a Navy-type thinker, and we don't think that way."

"Well, how do you think?"

Carney said, "Well, we start out by deciding what it is we're trying to do, we try to figure that out, and then after we decide what it is we're trying to do, then we decide whether or not we have the tools and the forces that we need to do those things that we think we might need to do. After that, we find out what our deficiencies are. And then our fourth requirement is how do we make up the deficiencies. That's the way we approach our planning problems in the Navy."

---

* Field Marshal Sir Bernard Law Montgomery (1887-1976) was a controversial British Army officer. In 1942 he commanded the Eighth Army during victorious operations in North Africa. He later commanded Allied armies in Northern Europe and commanded the British-occupied zone in Germany after victory was achieved in World War II. He was Deputy Supreme Commander Europe, 1951-58.
† On 1 November 1951, NATO announced that Admiral Carney had appointed General Rene Bertrand as his special assistant. Bertrand was active in the French Resistance during World War II.

Field Marshal Montgomery just couldn't understand the Navy approach. He said, "Oh, Mick, that's a lot of nonsense. The first thing you decide, where you're going to fight. And then when you decide where you're going to fight, then you decide how many forces you need to win the battle." Inside NATO at that time, no one had any idea where a battle might be joined, if ever. The main thing Admiral Carney was trying to do at that point in time was to get the people who were allies to talk to each other.

Paul Stillwell: What they were saying was not all that dissimilar. It's first what's the job and then what do you need to do the job.

Captain Manson: In a way, yes. It's just an Army fellow and a Navy man expressing it in different ways, except Field Marshal Montgomery did seem to think that we ought to pick out a Normandy the way they did in World War II: "If we're going to fight, we're going to go into Normandy."

Paul Stillwell: Yes.

Captain Manson: "Okay, so now we've decided that." Well, what Montgomery couldn't get the admiral to decide was whether we were going to fight over in Turkey or up in the northern plains up near Yugoslavia, or somewhere else.

General Bertrand came down to Naples from Paris, France, and right off, told Admiral Carney that Carney was lucky that he had been chosen, that he, Bertrand, would be very helpful to him, that Bertrand and his wife would be most helpful to the Admiral and Mrs. Carney in handling the social obligations. Mrs. Bertrand would be helpful in the social activities and he could do much professionally to help the admiral. Bertrand gave Carney quite a rundown, as the French sometimes do, on what his capabilities were. Admiral Carney was not too impressed, so he didn't often call on Bertrand—if ever. Bertrand put out the word in headquarters that his advice was not being sought and that he was unhappy about it. He told General Jim Gavin, who told me. Gavin was his chief of staff.[*]

---

[*] Lieutenant General James M. Gavin, USA.

Paul Stillwell: Did Carney display a lot of patience in dealing with all these different groups?

Captain Manson: Except for Bertrand, yes. Yes, Carney understood that it was a very delicate, sensitive situation in dealing with the Greeks, Turks, and Italians. He knew about all the years of animosities. This was one important characteristic of Admiral Carney. He had knowledge of the sensitivities of people. It went beyond almost anything you can imagine. He understood how they all felt. He respected their feelings, and that's why they respected him.

Paul Stillwell: That's why you need an individual like that in that job.

Captain Manson: Yes. I thought Carney would have been a better Chairman of the Joint Chiefs when he was selected to be CNO. Admiral Carney wanted to be Chairman and hoped to be. He thought that General Eisenhower would make him chairman, because Admiral Carney had given General Eisenhower his first forces, the Sixth Fleet.* That was the first NATO force represented—the only teeth that General Eisenhower had, and Admiral Carney gave it to him.

General Eisenhower thought a lot of Carney, and he had told "Engine Charlie" Wilson, the new SecDef, that he thought, even before they got over to Southern Europe, that he thought Admiral Carney would most likely be his choice for Chairman of the Joint Chiefs.† Wilson had already met with Admiral Radford, and he was tremendously impressed with Radford. Both of these admirals were in the Naval Academy class of 1916, and both of them were outstanding officers. But I personally think Radford would have been better in an advocate role. I think Radford would have been an outstanding

---

* Dwight D. Eisenhower served as President of the United States from 20 January 1953 to 20 January 1961. During World War II he had been Supreme Commander of the Allied Expeditionary Force for the invasion of Europe. In the early 1950s, as a five-star general, he served as Supreme Allied Commander in Europe in 1951-52 when the military portion of the North Atlantic Treaty Organization (NATO) was established. In 1953 Admiral Carney became Chief of Naval Operations, and Admiral Arthur W. Radford, USN, became Chairman of the Joint Chiefs of Staff.

† Charles E. Wilson served as Secretary of Defense from 28 January 1953 to 8 October 1957. He was nicknamed "Engine Charlie" because he had previously been chairman of the board of General Motors.

CNO, and I know Carney would have been an outstanding chairman. Their roles were reversed.

I was told later that Radford used to get President Eisenhower upset by even talking to him about ships. Radford got to the point where he never mentioned ships to Eisenhower. Admiral Pete Aurand told me all this confidentially.* Eisenhower saw the ocean as an obstacle. Anytime it was brought up, it created difficult problems. Eisenhower did not see the oceans as an avenue for commerce or as ocean highways to be used for the national good and national advantage.

Paul Stillwell: Did you see interaction between Carney and Eisenhower when Eisenhower was the NATO Commander?

Captain Manson: Yes. Yes. Well, rather frequently Carney would fly up to Paris to see Eisenhower, and they would discuss the problems encountered with the Turks, the Greeks, and the Italians. He kept Eisenhower personally informed on how things were going there. I used to go with him.

Paul Stillwell: What did you observe about Carney's personality from working with him that closely?

Captain Manson: I think Carney is probably the most brilliant admiral I have known. Now, I'm talking about a lot of bright guys, but I'll tell you that Carney's probably the most brilliant of them all in the sense that he understood the formulation of policy, the implementing of strategy, and the tactics of doing things. (Plus remember during World War II he was the master of "dirty tricks," ideas to confound and confuse the enemy.)† He understood all of this with such clarity. He knew that you first had to have a workable policy, and after that you needed implementing strategies, and then you worked out your military formations, commands, and all that. Carney was also an innovative

---

* Captain Evan P. Aurand, USN, served as naval aide to President Dwight D. Eisenhower from February 1957 to January 1961. He eventually retired as a vice admiral.
† In 1944-45, as a rear admiral, Carney served as chief of staff to Admiral William F. Halsey Jr., USN, Commander Third Fleet.

man, creative thinker. He was not a man who was handicapped by the traditions of the "olden days." He wouldn't hesitate to try something new. Yet he always said that certain principles were immutable. Principles remained the same, but conditions and circumstances changed constantly.

Paul Stillwell: Do you have some examples of that, from your observation?

Captain Manson: Well, the advent of nuclear power was one. After Carney became CNO, he brought me back with him to be his speechwriter.

Paul Stillwell: The decision for nuclear power had really gone on before.

Captain Manson: Yes, but not for a nuclear surface fleet.

Paul Stillwell: I see.

Captain Manson: No, at that point in time it was strictly Rickover's nuclear submarine program.* When Carney got back there in 1953, the situation was that the Vice Chief of Naval Operations, Admiral Wu Duncan, opposed nuclear power for the surface fleet or for any expansion beyond submarines.† I'd been brought in there, and I didn't know anything about all of the involvement of the entrenched forces.

So here it was October 27th coming up, 1953, and I was to write this major speech for Pittsburgh, Pennsylvania.‡ I had a caller, Captain George Miller, from somewhere in the bowels of the Pentagon.§ He came to my office next to the CNO's.

---

* Rear Hyman G. Rickover, USN, was considered the father of the nuclear Navy. He ran the U.S. Navy's nuclear-power program for many years, from 1948 until he eventually left active duty in 1982 with the rank of four-star admiral on the retired list. Rickover Hall at the Naval Academy was named in his honor, as was the nuclear-powered attack submarine *Hyman G. Rickover* (SSN-709), which was commissioned 21 July 1984.
† Admiral Donald B. Duncan, USN, a naval aviator, served as Vice Chief of Naval Operations from 10 August 1951 to 1 September 1956. His oral history is in the Columbia University collection.
‡ At that time 27 October, former President Theodore Roosevelt's birthday, was called Navy Day in the United States.
§ Captain George H. Miller, USN. The oral history of Miller, who retired as a rear admiral, is in the Naval Institute collection.

Miller was white-haired and close cropped, a dignified-looking captain with intelligent-looking eyes. He greeted me and told me he wanted to be helpful to me in strategic plans. He said he had some papers he thought I would like to read before I prepared this October 27 speech. I said, well, yes, I would welcome anything I could get from anybody. I was the new kid on the block and only 33 years old at that time. After two wars, however, I felt like I was 53.

So he brought up these top-secret, highly classified papers on trying to get nuclear propulsion into the surface fleet. He had a number of documents, proposals, and some letters that had been turned down. All this he had brought to me right out of his top-secret file cabinet. I'm sure he'd hit a snag at the Vice Chief level.

So I read over all those things and I thought, "Man, what a speech I can write on this stuff. This is really a new, forward-looking policy if the admiral will buy it." So I just simply used that as a basis for drafting the speech on the U.S. Navy converting to nuclear power. Admiral Carney read this all over, and he liked the idea.

Paul Stillwell: Did he know about Admiral Duncan's opposition?

Captain Manson: I don't know. I really never told him. I don't think he did know, but he might have.

But, anyway, Carney went up and he gave this speech, and, boy, he got praise, a good press, and everything: "The Navy's got new thinking," and all that.

So he said, "Now, Frank, I'm going to be going out to the Far East, and I'd like for you to send me a draft of the next speech. I'm going to commission something up in Bremerton, Washington, a radio transmitter or something. Send me another speech."

Boy, I drafted up another "zinger" one, just as strong as the October 27 speech, calling for a nuclear-powered Navy. I've got a copy of that. I ran across it the other day. I think I've still got one I didn't send to Naval History. Anyway, Admiral Duncan called for me, and he said, "You know you're going to cost the Navy its shipbuilding program, don't you?" That's the first thing he said to me.

I said, "No, I wasn't aware of it."

He said, "Well, you are." He said, "All this talk about nuclear power is going to cost us our whole shipbuilding program. Congress isn't going to appropriate money for steam-driven ships when you're saying they're obsolete. You're putting us in a terrible bind."

I said, "Well, I've read some fairly persuasive documents, Admiral."

He said, "Just the same, I'm not going to send this dispatch to Admiral Carney."

I said, "Well, in that case then, Admiral, I'll send it." I'd learned a little bit, you know. I said, "I can put in this message that I'm personally sending this dispatch."

Admiral Duncan said, "Well, if you do that, I'm going to send him one telling him not to give it."

I said, "Well, I think you should, Admiral. I mean, that's, after all, your job. But my job is to write the speech I think he ought to give. You do your job, and I'll do mine."

So we agreed, and I sent the dispatch, and Admiral Duncan sent a dispatch. We got a message back from Admiral Carney saying that he wasn't going to give the speech that I had prepared, but that he would give parts of it and that he would make the decision on which parts that he would give, but that I had sent him enough material. Lord, I sent him enough for an hour speech, practically.

So I'm not sure yet what the admiral actually said up there in Washington, but Admiral Duncan knew, after reading CNO's dispatch, that he'd lost the battle, that Admiral Carney was going to push for nuclear power. So Admiral Duncan and I never did get along too well after that. There was never any open conflict, but he saw that I wasn't going to knuckle down. Then Captain George Miller became one of my principal sources.

Paul Stillwell: Oh, sure. He found a good channel there. And it turned out that the Navy did not lose its shipbuilding program because of that.

Captain Manson: That's right. That's the way it turned out. But that's the kind of thing you run into at that level. But if that had been the first time that I'd ever encountered something like that, I suppose I would have been pretty upset about it, but I'd been through it a lot and it didn't work. I was only a lieutenant commander, but I'm sure a lot of admirals had a lot of other names for me.

Paul Stillwell: [Laughter] Well, I've gathered that Admiral Carney was a pretty articulate gentleman too.

Captain Manson: Well, that's another thing I wanted to tell you about Admiral Carney. He didn't need a speechwriter. If he had the time, he could draft the best speech you've ever read, but what he would do, the way he would work with me is he would call me in and he'd say, "Frank—" First of all, we'd planned out maybe a year in advance, different subjects that ought to be covered at a specific time. Then we'd figure out angles, how we could work it in through the educational or through some other channel to get the message he was trying to get across. But then, when his thoughts sort of jelled in his mind, he would call me in, and he'd give me everything he was thinking about and I would write just crazy, as fast notes as I could, because he's an extremely able person, in control of his own thinking.

So then I'd take that and then I would embellish it, or I would maybe change it if it didn't fit just right or however, but I didn't have to do an awful lot of really what you might call "starting from the start," because he'd give me a running start every time. Then I'd produce the draft, he'd work on it, refine it, and then I'd maybe work on it a little bit more and that was the end of it. But that was usually the routine way we did it.

But we had a very close relationship. I remember one time when Chris Cagle was speechwriter for SecNav and we were working on *The Sea War in Korea*. He said, "You know, Frank, we'd better hurry and get this book written."

I said, "Why?"

He says, "Because one of our bosses is going to be gone. I don't know whether it's going to Carney or Thomas, but one of them is going to be gone."[*]

I said, "How do you know?"

He says, "Because Thomas said he was going to do it."

"Going to fire the admiral?"

---

[*] Charles S. Thomas served as Secretary of the Navy from 3 May 1954 to 1 April 1957.

"Yeah, Thomas said somebody's got to go around here." Chris told me that.

So I went to Carney, and I said, "You know, things aren't going well with the Secretary."

"How come?" And I repeated what Cagle told me.

He said, "Oh, I can't believe Charlie feels that way about it."

But one thing, Admiral Carney wouldn't let Thomas read the blue-flag messages. That was the talk just between the admirals. And Thomas resented that. He wanted to know every detail, everything the admirals were thinking, what one said to another. Carney thought the admirals should get their thoughts together before they presented them to SecNav. Get a consensus of military or naval thought before presenting them to the political arm of the Navy.

I was going to do a book on Admiral Carney. I thought he was the wittiest admiral I'd ever known up to that point. I went out and talked to his mother out at Pearl Harbor. She was living, about 90-some years old, and she told me what kind of a baby he was and young man and midshipman.

Paul Stillwell: Do you have any examples of his wit?

Captain Manson: Well, I do. One thing I'll never forget is when he was a midshipman and his father was teaching here on the Naval Academy staff, and he was a Catholic. He told his son to get something blessed for him when he saw the Pope. The midshipmen were going to cruise over to Italy that year. And his son said he would.

So when they got back, father Carney went down to meet his son when the ship docked. As they were talking about the trip, the father said, "By the way, son, did you think to have anything blessed for me?"

Young Carney had a package of Bull Durham tobacco in his pocket and he pulled it out and he said, "Dad, I didn't forget. Here's a package of holy smoke." [Laughter] His dad socked him, gave him a whack right there on the deck. But Carney was quick: "Yeah, here's a pack of holy smoke."

If I thought about it a little bit, I could give you some others, but he was always pulling a nifty crack about something. He was head of the Dirty Tricks Department with

Halsey's fleet. I went to interview Halsey about that Pacific war and about Admiral Carney. I believe Halsey spent an hour or more just talking about his admiration for Admiral Carney. Halsey said, "I picked him out when I was over at USNA, when I was teaching here." He said, "If I ever get in a tough situation, there's the man I want," and that's who he got. But Halsey was very fond of Carney. He said Carney was really the brains of so much that went on out there. Halsey told me that.

Paul Stillwell: Right. I know he felt a great loyalty downward.

Captain Manson: Oh, yes, he just loved Mick Carney, and I'll tell you, that love was reciprocated. Admiral Carney told me that Halsey had a—what was the word he used? But it was almost like a magical—the perception or rather the way that he could reach a decision just defied the imagination. But it was intuitive.

Paul Stillwell: I see.

Captain Manson: Intuitive.

Paul Stillwell: A gut feeling rather than rational thought.

Captain Manson: A gut feeling, right. But Carney said, "My, he was tremendous as a intuitive man to decide what was right."

Paul Stillwell: Some of his critics have suggested that he wasn't always right.

Captain Manson: Well, Kinkaid.

Paul Stillwell: Certainly Kinkaid.

Captain Manson: And others.

Paul Stillwell: We're right near the end of the tape, so that will be the point we can resume the next time.

Captain Manson: Okay. I don't know if we've had very much continuity here or not.

Paul Stillwell: Oh, sure.

Interview Number 2 with Captain Frank A. Manson, U.S. Navy (Retired)
Place: U.S. Naval Institute, Annapolis, Maryland
Date: Tuesday, 23 February 1988
Interviewer: Paul Stillwell

Paul Stillwell: Captain, I think you wanted to begin today by going back just a bit to talk about the relief of Admiral Denfeld by Admiral Sherman in the late 1940s.

Captain Manson: Yes. I was on the Denfeld staff at that time, assistant to the special assistant, who was Captain Walter Karig. A conflict had developed between the Secretary of the Navy and the CNO, and it boiled down, of course, to the B-36 hearings and the use of carriers and the need for carriers and the need for naval air. There was a general feeling there on the Denfeld staff that if Denfeld told the Armed Services Committee, if he even said that Omar Bradley had changed his mind on the use of carriers, that he would be replaced.* Captain Howard "Red" Yeager, who was his AA, told him that he would be fired if he did that.† Captain Karig told him that, well, he might be fired, but he said he didn't have any choice, that he simply had to make the strongest Navy case that he could.

So Admiral Denfeld agreed with Captain Karig, and, sure enough, the word around the E-ring was that they were looking for a replacement. The admirals, like Admiral Spike Blandy, who was CinCLant at the time, and Admiral Conolly and other four-star admirals were eligible for taking the CNO job. Most had been mentioned as contenders for it, and they all told Admiral Denfeld that they wouldn't accept the job under these circumstances.‡

---

* General Omar N. Bradley, USA, served as Chairman of the Joint Chiefs of Staff from 16 August 1949 to 14 August 1953. In 1950 he was promoted to five-star rank, general of the Army.
† Rear Admiral Howard A. Yeager, USN, administrative aide.
‡ Admiral William H. P. Blandy, USN, served as Commander in Chief Atlantic Command and Commander in Chief Atlantic Fleet from 3 February 1947 to 1 February 1950. Admiral Richard L. Conolly, USN, served as Commander U.S. Naval Forces Europe from September 1946 to November 1946, when the title was changed to Commander U.S. Naval Forces Eastern Atlantic and Mediterranean. In April 1947 the title was changed again, to Commander in Chief U.S. Naval Forces Eastern Atlantic and Mediterranean (CinCNELM). He remained in the billet until December 1950.

But no word ever came from the three-star level, particularly Admiral Forrest Sherman, who was Commander Sixth Fleet.[*] Sure enough, when Admiral Denfeld was asked to retire—I suppose those are the words, I don't know exactly how Mr. Matthews told him—Admiral Forrest Sherman was in Washington, had come in from the fleet, and he was there to take the job.[†] People in the higher echelons in the Navy thought that Forrest Sherman might have sold the Navy out to take this job and made a deal with the Secretary of the Navy and Secretary of Defense.

But Admiral Sherman told us when he got there that he had just talked faster than the political leaders, that he hadn't made any deal, that he was going to remain a staunch supporter of the carriers, and so forth. He was so eloquent, so articulate, so knowledgeable that he really just had his way.

He had a big article in—I think it was *This Week* magazine, right away and soon he was the on the cover story of all the magazines and everybody was praising him because he was such a brilliant strategist, and he did understand the use of carriers. So it didn't turn out that it was a bad thing for the Navy at all. I must say, to Admiral Denfeld's everlasting credit, that he was a loyal man. His field was personnel, and he was very good with personnel. He also knew surface ships, but he didn't really know carrier warfare anything like Admiral Sherman, who had been skipper of the *Wasp* and had just come from commander of the Sixth Fleet.[‡] He understood the use of naval air power as well, if not better, than anyone in the Navy. So it turned out to be a very good thing. Unfortunately, Admiral Sherman didn't live very long, but what time he was there he was brilliant.

Paul Stillwell: And he had the advantage that he could probably be bolder than Denfeld, because Matthews wouldn't want to fire two CNOs in a row.

Captain Manson: Exactly, exactly, sure. And particularly a man who was coming out with mountains of truth. I mean, he was just filled with it. There was just no one in

---

[*] Vice Admiral Forrest P. Sherman, USN, commanded the Sixth Task Fleet, 7 February 1948 to 14 November 1949.
[†] Francis P. Matthews served as Secretary of the Navy from 25 May 1949 to 30 July 1951.
[‡] As a captain Sherman commanded the aircraft carrier *Wasp* (CV-7) from 31 May 1942 to 15 September 1942, the date she was sunk.

Washington, not the Army, not the Air Force, not anyone that could cope with Sherman. He was the big boy on the block.

Paul Stillwell: Another CNO that I know you had a lot of admiration for was Admiral Carney. We talked some about him the last time, and I think you have some more you want to add today.

Captain Manson: Yes. With Carney, I first met him when I was writing the *Battle Report* series, when he was Deputy Chief of Naval Operations for Logistics.* Of course, the war was over. My impression of him was that he looked like a schoolteacher. He had a professor's appearance, and he had a marvelous mastery of the English language. He could really say what he meant and meant what said and be very precise. He was just a brilliant man; I got that impression. Then I went to interview Admiral Halsey later, about Admiral Carney. I was thinking of doing book on him as the wittiest admiral I'd ever known.

I was at CinCSouth with Carney, and I was command historian over there, to write the first history of the formation of the Southern Command. At first, the admiral and I weren't seeing very much of each other, and then something, I don't know what, broke the ice. He decided he was going to tell me what was going on over there, how he was working to get the Greeks and the Turks to come in the same room and what problems he was having between the Italians and the Greeks. He really did finally just let me have the full story of how difficult it was to bring these three nations on the southern tier there into any kind of harmony, or their thoughts into any kind of a confluence on forming the southern flank of NATO. But Carney would keep some of them in one room and some in another, and then he'd eventually get them together. That was, I would think, one of his great achievements. With the differences that these nations had, to get them under the same tent was a stroke of diplomatic genius, the like of which we haven't often seen in the United States.

---

* Vice Admiral Robert B. Carney, USN, served as Deputy Chief of Naval Operations (Logistics), OP-04, from 25 June 1946 to 8 February 1950.

It was, I suppose, almost comparable to the current situation, to bring Israel and Jordan and some of the others in under a common tent. It was just about that way. But Carney did it, and I had a tremendous admiration for his ability to perform both in the military and diplomatic fields. He was a very accomplished man when he was appointed CNO. I was pleased when he asked me to go back with him and help him with his speeches. That was my point. I'd only been over there a year and had just finished the book, which they promptly classified cosmic top secret.

Paul Stillwell: Which book was that?

Captain Manson: The Formation of the Southern Command. As far as I know, they never did reduce the classification of the book, because I dealt with the conflicts and the differences that existed between the Turks and the Greeks and the Italians, and they were worried that if it were ever published, it might upset the applecart, perhaps destroy NATO. Everybody knew pretty much what the differences were, but when you tell the truth, really the truth about anything, why, then there are always a lot of people around who want to classify it.

Paul Stillwell: Do you know what ever became of it?

Captain Manson: No. I know for a while Admiral Carney and I had kept a copy of it under high classification. It shouldn't have been classified. Admiral Carney left me over there for a few months to try to get it declassified, and he told me that in his opinion it should be declassified, but under no circumstances should it have a higher than confidential classification. I might find it in Naval History or somewhere. I don't know, but I doubt it.

Paul Stillwell: Have you ever had any inquiries or follow-ups on that since then? Have you heard from the Navy Department about it?

Captain Manson: Never have heard a word, never have. They hadn't written anything up in SHAPE about the history of the formation of SHAPE.* The historian up there was busy writing Eisenhower's speeches. He didn't have time to do any history, and the historical staff was working on other things. So I don't know if they ever wrote anything or not on the formation of the total Allied command.

Paul Stillwell: What period did your work cover?

Captain Manson: This would be about 1950, '51, and '52. Those were the formation years. NATO was formed in '49, if I'm not mistaken.

Paul Stillwell: Right.

Captain Manson: So this would be the implementation of the political decision to form NATO. The French were very difficult too. They were in the beginning and never have been anything else.

Paul Stillwell: Did your history deal just with CinCSouth or with NATO as a whole?

Captain Manson: Well, I did some writing about the total NATO formation, but I didn't spend much time with Central or Northern Europe, except only as it related to the Southern Command.

Paul Stillwell: I see.

Captain Manson: The tangencies, that's all.

Paul Stillwell: Was that essentially a full-time job for you?

---

* SHAPE – Supreme Headquarters Allied Powers Europe, the NATO command post.

Captain Manson: Yes, I spent full time. I went around to the different commands if they didn't come to me. I remember going to Northern Italy in Verona and different places to the Italian commands. They tried to laugh me out of the office; I remember that. The rather senior Italian colonels told me what a joke it was to be writing history about something that hadn't done any history. I advised these colonels that this was something of great importance to their commander in chief and that I had been sent by him personally to talk to them. But if they didn't want to cooperate, I was sure that the commander in chief would be most interested in what they had to say. And with that, they stopped laughing and joking and got on with telling me their difficulties.

Paul Stillwell: How candid were the various people that you talked to?

Captain Manson: The Italians?

Paul Stillwell: Well, all nationalities.

Captain Manson: They eventually would get around to being candid, but they'd always start by telling me how bitter the feelings were and how they just didn't feel like they could even talk about them, and they would almost choke up. Then eventually I'd say, "Yes, but, you know, we've got a much larger group to think about here, and we've got your best interests in terms of your total interests that we're trying to do now. The time period has changed, relations have changed, and this is a new world we're living in." So they'd eventually come around.

Paul Stillwell: They were still feeling back to the World War II animosities, then.

Captain Manson: They were, very strongly, very strongly. I remember I appointed a Greek major by the name of Hadzianis—and I don't remember if I can spell that or not—but he had served in the cabinet of the Prime Minister. He was a brilliant man. But he told me at first that it was just useless to try to write anything about relationships between the Italians and the Greeks, because they felt so emotional about it. But eventually they did.

Paul Stillwell: In effect, though, what he said was right if it couldn't be released, that those feelings were so strong that your product couldn't be used for history.

Captain Manson: Yes. True, true.

Paul Stillwell: But maybe it's still in the files and could be resurrected at some point.

Captain Manson: Well, it just very well—I'll tell you one thing. I'll see if I can locate it, and if I could, I'll be happy to let you have it.[*]

Paul Stillwell: That would be a useful thing.

Captain Manson: All right.

Paul Stillwell: What do you remember about life in Italy during that period?

Captain Manson: Well, Italy was still impoverished from the war. A lot of houses were still gutted. Life was tough and hard for the Italians. They were all so poor and pretty much in rags. The main thing that the Italians were doing was trying to rebuild and rehabilitate, because their cities had been pretty well banged up by artillery and by bombing. Life, I guess you'd have to say, had no great meaning.

I'll always remember, we had Italians, of course, serving in the officers' mess at our first headquarters there at Via Orazio. One day one of the waiters who spoke English was talking to me about my job, and he said, "What have you written about Naples?"

I said, well, at this point I hadn't written very much.

---

[*] For whatever reason, Captain Manson did not supply a copy of this history to the Naval Institute.

He said, "Well, you'd do me a great favor if you could just get someone to drop an atomic bomb on this entire area and blow all of us up, including myself." He said life had no meaning for him. He said he was making, I think, $30.00 a month there at the headquarters, maybe, or $60.00, I forget, but anyway, it was very little. He said his brother was in the Italian Army and making $15.00 a month, and he didn't have cigarettes. He was having to take all the money he could get from his job to send to his brother, who was in the Italian Army, and pay the rent and help buy the food. So he said life just had no meaning.

And, of course, when you went down in the ghetto of Naples, it was just absolutely wall-to-wall people. I remember one time I drove into one of these ghettos, and I had our little children in the car. These people got all over the car; they got their heads in the windows. They were all over the place. It was like you had invaded locusts, and I was panic stricken. I couldn't get out, I couldn't go any farther. I finally got on the horn, and I just started inching along and eventually got out of there. But I never dared go back into one of their heavily populated areas like that again.

Paul Stillwell: Where did you live?

Captain Manson: We lived first at Britainique, which was a hotel on the Possillipo, a mountain, and then we lived a short time at Villa Orazia, our headquarters. Then we moved out to Lucrino, an area that was, I think, about seven miles north of Naples, on the seashore. It was next to Arco Felice. Just beyond Arco Felice and just beyond Potsuolli, where I heard Sophia Loren was living at the time in a cave. Potsuolli had to be the dirtiest, filthiest place that I had ever seen. Of course, you know the look of the open market. They hang up these carcasses—animals that look like skinned cats or something about that size. They are hanging up by the tails or feet, just raw meat hanging out there on these little outdoor vending counters. Whatever they had to market was just sort of lying out on the street. Black wet dirt was everywhere. Smells wafted of all kinds and descriptions.

But we lived in a new apartment building. The Bob Hope of Italy was a fellow named Nino Taranto, and he had built this new building. So we had a very nice place to live with three other American families. But the Americans in Italy, quite a number of them, particularly Army types, had come from European commands, where they had grown accustomed to treating the Germans pretty roughly. Harshness, I suppose, is as good a word as any.

The Italians didn't respond as well to people barking and yelling at them, not as well as had the Germans. I never had this experience, but I was told the Germans would jump when yelled at. If spoken to in a normal voice, they might sit there for a few moments without moving, but the minute one yelled, they jumped. But the Italians were not that way.

In our particular building there was an American colonel who had yelled at the porter, and the porter didn't respond too well, so the colonel punched him around quite a bit. The porter's name was Angelo. Of course, we heard the commotion and the pounding and whatnot, and I told Angelo I didn't believe the headquarters would approve this if they knew, and I'd be happy to take him in and let him make a report on the colonel. Angelo said, "Well, fine."

So the next morning I got him in the car and got him about halfway there, and Angelo said, "Turn around and go back."

I said, "What's wrong, Angelo?"

He says, "I can never win this battle with the colonel, not with headquarters."

I said, "Well, Angelo, I'm going to support you. I heard what went on."

Angelo said, "Not enough," so he asked me to take him back.

But, anyway, basically the times were turbulent, and I do think that a few of the Americans were a bit arrogant, perhaps from having had the war experience and hadn't quite figured out that we weren't an occupation force in Italy, not anymore. So the relationships between the Americans and the Italians were not always the best.

Paul Stillwell: How were you treated by your peers on the staff? Did they see value in having a command historian?

Captain Manson: I think that they thought that I was a little superfluous. Not too many people had a lot of respect for history. I think they saw me more as a curiosity than as a contributing member of the staff. They didn't know for sure what I was up to, and they didn't think this was any time to be writing history, while it was being formulated.

There is merit in writing a contemporary history by someone who has had some experience in knowing the significant from the inconsequential. CinCSouth's history is significant, because it brought three nations under the NATO umbrella, all working toward a common goal, when their differences were historic and emotional.

NATO's purpose can be stated in one sentence. NATO's goal was to contain Soviet aggression. Bringing European and allied objective into confluence was a benefit and a spin-off of organizing to contain Communism. In NATO parlance, an attack against one would be regard as an attack against all. Even for the Greeks, Turks, and Italians, this kind of commitment meant something to their own national aspirations. Greece knew from her experiences in 1948 that the Communists could topple a government since Greece had been through such an experience and, thanks to the U.S., Greece had escaped.

The formation of an allied command is important historically because it may become necessary, in the strife and turmoil of human events, to do it again. Although at the moment I can't conceive that we had the international giants needed to form such a partnership and make it work. At the moment, in my judgment, NATO desperately needs a new objective. We need people of the stature of Paul-Henri Spaak, George Marshall, Konrad Adenauer, and the giant leaders of the western world.[*] I know they are working on something now. The contemporary leaders are expanding NATO, putting some sort of structure behind Partnership for Peace, but I have little confidence that we have the type of national and international leaders to envision what we should do or how we should do it. To relax and let nature take its course will wind up in some sort of a nuclear holocaust. Of course, anything nuclear is a holocaust.

Back to the setting up of NATO. As soon as the leaders envisioned what they should do to contain Soviet aggression, they put a command structure together. At the CinCSouth level they set up subordinate commands: AirSouth, LandSouth, and Naval

---

[*] Paul-Henri Spaak was Secretary General of the North Atlantic Treaty Organization from 1957 to 1961. George C. Marshall served as U.S. Secretary of State from 21 January 1947 to 20 January 1949. Konrad H. J. Adenauer was the first post-World War II Chancellor of West Germany. He served in that post from 1949 to 1963.

South. Because the area of Turkey and Greece involved such vast land area, they decided to set up a southeast command in Ankara. Once the structure was decided, they began determination of who would command what. This would be largely done on the basis of which nations were contributing the forces: "Him da givva da gold maka da rules." But that was a sound and acceptable way to put the thing together, except, for example, France. France wanted high-command jobs while contributing virtually nothing in southern Europe. France argued that the French experience in the area counted.

In writing the history I depended on writers like Chester Wilmott to guide me through the Soviet moves that made NATO necessary. Then I picked up with organizing CinCSouth and the command structure known as HAFSE—Headquarters Allied Forces Southern Europe. Carney opened command operations aboard a ship tied up at Naples's number-one pier. His staff soon outgrew that, and the CinCSouth command was moved to a new apartment house on Via Orazio. This Southern Command was a major event in world history, getting the Italians, the Greeks, and the Turks under the same umbrella, senior officers working together out of a common fear, which was real and not imagined.

The NATO staffs were organized along U.S. Army tables of organization: 01, personnel and administration; 02, intelligence; 03, operations; 04, logistics; and 05, communications. Under the chief of staff the Army has what it calls secretary of staff, and in Naples that was Colonel Herbert Sparrow, USA, who later became a major general. He was responsible for bringing all the subordinate command plans and headquarters staff plans together. My history division was set up here, an Air Force sergeant and I under the secretary of staff. Colonel Sparrow, whose father was a Navy captain, told me the Navy blue uniform intimidated him, all that gold and such.

One of Colonel Sparrow's early housekeeping problems was keeping the toilet sanitary. With allied forces using it, he couldn't be sure who was creating the problem, but it was urgent, and it needed correction. He mentioned a few times in staff meetings that careful attention to high sanitary standards was incumbent on all of us. Then he issued a memo or two on the same subject. With his patience exhausted, he stationed a lieutenant colonel, West Point graduate, near the latrine door with instructions to check the latrine after each usage. The culprit was immediately found. It was Colonel

Sparrow's French female secretary. Apparently she had been taught by her mother or nanny never to sit on toilet seats, and the result created one of NATO's early embarrassing situations. The French secretary resigned, and we never had that problem again.

Admiral Carney was the key to getting that command started and by offering the Sixth Fleet to Eisenhower up front played a major role in getting the entire NATO concept off the ground or, in naval parlance, out of dry dock.

One exception on the importance of current history was General Jumping Jim Gavin, as they called him, the paratrooper.[*] He had jumped into France during World War II as CO of the 82nd Airborne Division. He was now our chief of staff and a great leader by the way—a young, dynamic person. He used to have me in rather frequently to talk over books he was reading and what was happening and our philosophy on warfare and what types of war might develop down there in the southern flank. General Gavin later became ambassador to France.[†] He liked to talk about the future need of airheads, perhaps in some situations more important than beachheads.

Paul Stillwell: He was ambassador when Kennedy was President.

Captain Manson: Yes, right, true. And I went to call on him when he was ambassador. I just wanted to see if he was the kind of man that would see me after he became an ambassador, or if he would be the kind of person who would forget that he knew me under much different circumstances. So I called on him in Paris. I went directly to the embassy, and the ambassador sent word that he would be happy to see me.

I'll never forget this. They had a big hall there in the embassy, a ballroom or something. They pulled two chairs right out in the middle of that thing. The ambassador and I went out and sat in those two chairs and talked for an hour or two. He told me how disappointed he was that the United States would not share its nuclear secrets with the French, that Rickover was being obstreperous and that the entire United States Government, he thought, was taking the wrong attitude toward France. He said they

---

[*] Lieutenant General James M. Gavin, USA.
[†] Gavin served as U.S. Ambassador to France in 1961-62.

were going to build the nuclear submarines anyway, and we'd be better off if we shared with them and worked out some kind of an agreement such as the type we had with Britain rather than let them go it alone. He said it made it very difficult for him, because the French regarded themselves as Allies and ones who helped our country in its formation and so forth.

Paul Stillwell: And de Gaulle was difficult in any event.[*]

Captain Manson: And de Gaulle was difficult in any event. Exactly. So Ambassador Gavin was having a fairly rough time over there, and he wanted to know if I could be helpful in trying to convince the United States—well, through the Navy, of course, and Rickover—to change its attitude. I told him that I wasn't too hopeful. I wasn't senior enough in rank. True, I had worked with Rickover, but I knew he wouldn't budge. He didn't want to share with the British, much less the French.

I thought the attitude of the United States had hardened on that subject. What they were worried about was that France, in terms of security in France, would be so unreliable, undependable, that the U.S. couldn't rely on France to keep our nuclear secrets, that somehow or another it would slip out, slip over to the Soviets. Anyway, going back to—

Paul Stillwell: I've got one more question on that. What was the point of having these two chairs in the middle of the ballroom? Was General Gavin concerned about bugging of his office?

Captain Manson: He didn't say. I didn't know at first whether it was just to impress me, that I was meeting with an ambassador, but I later decided Gavin wouldn't do anything like that. He had to be worried about bugging, and he wanted to talk to me about something that was most delicate, very sensitive. So he had to suspect that France was eavesdropping on him. He knew that if there was any way, in the first place, if I shared

---

[*] Charles de Gaulle was a general for the Free French in World War II. In 1958 he was called upon to form a government. He served from 1958 to 1969 as first President of France's Fifth Republic.

his views, and secondly, whether or not I'd be willing to be helpful, because he knew I knew the high command of the Navy. Anyway, I think that that's why he put the chairs there, because he wanted to discuss this nuclear thing.

Paul Stillwell: I know you've got some more notes on Admiral Carney. Maybe we could resume on him, please.

Captain Manson: I came back to be his speechwriter and an idea man if I could think of any ideas.[*] He and I had an excellent rapport on exchange of ideas and things. But he had in his mind, being a very literate type, what he wanted to say, but he wanted to cover a wide spectrum. He told me that he wanted audiences that were everything from Wall Street to high schools and colleges, Navy League. He didn't want to just stick with any particular type of audience, nor did he want his speeches to resemble presidential campaigns where a candidate gets four or five things and just hammers away at those things. But Carney, rather, wanted to talk about many things. Education was high on his list, where the United States was going as a nation, values, and, of course, naval policy, too, but he didn't want to deal strictly with weapons—that is, ships.

Not anything like Admiral Burke.[†] When Burke came in—I have to show what I'm talking about here—he told me he didn't want to talk any more about policy and all these things, that he wanted strictly to talk about the ships and how they were going to be used. Those were his instructions to me. Burke thought Admiral Carney had perhaps gotten into trouble, particularly by talking about foreign policy and domestic policy at times, and that he didn't want to make that mistake. And Burke was correct. He had probably been told as much by Secretary Thomas and Admiral Radford.[‡]

But Carney has a brilliant mind and he had a lot of interests. You know, he had such a rich culture in his background, I don't know, I think maybe his mother's influence as much anything, I guess, his father, too, perhaps. But anyway, Carney wanted his

---

[*] When Admiral Carney became Chief of Naval Operations in 1953, Manson joined him on the OpNav staff in Washington.
[†] Admiral Arleigh A. Burke, USN, served as Chief of Naval Operations from 17 August 1955 to 1 August 1961. His oral history is in the Naval Institute collection.
[‡] Charles S. Thomas served as Secretary of the Navy from 3 May 1954 to 1 April 1957.

speeches to reflect variety and be interesting. He wanted to help lead the military on a broad spectrum of subjects—especially values.

Paul Stillwell: Was it up to you to schedule them as well as write them?

Captain Manson: Well, I would always check everything with him, but a lot of times I would schedule his speeches. He told me he preferred to speak about once each month. Sometimes he would have one every two weeks, but generally he sort of liked maybe one a month. Another thing, he liked to go to different places, because Admiral Carney would always take a little time off and do a little fishing or hunting or relaxing. He'd use this speaking opportunity to do it, and I usually went with him. I like to do that too.

On speech subjects, we would together go over a list of subjects that might be good speech material, and then he would say "Well," and then he would tell me what he thought of the subjects that we had covered, what he thought would be appropriate. Then I would schedule a time with him where he'd call me in there, and he'd tell me generally how he saw this subject. So it was just sort of stream of consciousness from his point of view. I'd write it down as best I could with my left-hand shorthand and then try to read it when I got out of there. But I would have in my head and on my notes, a good idea, when I left the admiral, of what he wanted to put across.

So then I would flesh it out, and sometimes I'd take off in another direction once in a while, but that was up to me. He didn't mind. But generally speaking, I always had good guidance from Admiral Carney. He was in command, never a doubt in my mind whether it was up to me to set the policy because he was setting the policy. That worries you when you're with an admiral, and you don't know for sure if he knows the direction he wants to go. But Admiral Carney always gave me good, clear direction, and we were always talking about policy matters. It's a pretty heavy responsibility for a young officer to be dealing with high command, national policy, foreign policy, naval policy, and to feel comfortable that you and the admiral are in sync.

But the way I would work with the admiral, first we'd have this meeting and I would take the notes and so forth, then I'd come back to him with a draft. Then he would edit the draft, and if I found something in there that I didn't quite understand or agree with, I'd go back to him and we'd hash it out. But generally speaking, when he edited it, it was over and it was ready. Only once or twice I ventured off into something that he didn't quite understand, and his face would get really red, and he'd get busy and mark it out. But he never, never once during the entire time I was with him, was he ever harsh with me or critical, but always just the reverse. He was always kind and sort of uplifting and inspiring, and I just loved to be around him and with him, because it would keep me going then for another few days.

Paul Stillwell: He's a witty man. Did you see examples of that?

Captain Manson: Yes, he was very witty. I remember one. Of course, there was a conflict between Carney and Radford, I suppose, because of the nature of their jobs for one thing. Radford was Chairman and Carney, CNO. Radford's speechwriter was a brigadier general who was always coming by my office and asking me if it would possible for him to see the draft of Admiral Carney's speech before it was finally finished. I told him, no, I didn't think that would be possible; however, I would check it with the admiral.

One of the best times I had to talk with Admiral Carney was when he was getting his hair cut. I could sit up there close to him; he didn't have anything else on his mind. So one day when he was getting his hair cut, I told him Radford was putting a lot of pressure on to see his speeches and, if possible, to approve them in advance of delivery. Admiral Carney said, "Well, I don't see any point. I don't see why he wants to see my speeches. He said, "I can see plenty of reason why I should see his speeches, because he wants to be sure that he's espousing naval policy. But I can't see why he needs to see mine. No, no, I wouldn't approve you showing this to any of Radford's people. And furthermore, I don't see any point in Radford seeing my speeches, nor anyone else." [Laughter] He didn't want me showing them to SecNav either, which I didn't.

Of course, Malcolm Cagle had the same job with the Secretary, and I was the one that got him into the job.* Cagle wasn't too happy with me about that, because he had

---

* Commander Cagle was administrative aide to Secretary of the Navy Thomas. Cagle eventually became a vice admiral.

aspirations for high command and to be one of those top admirals himself. He thought that speechwriting job for SecNav would just about ruin him. So he told me he thought I'd done him a great disservice, and I said, "Chris, I know perfectly well you can do this." He and I had served together on Denfeld's staff, too, and Sherman, too, and we'd written one book at that point together on the war in Korea. But anyway, I said, "Chris, this is made for you. You won't have to study or anything; you can do these speeches."

"Yes," he said, "that's not it." He said he just thought that he'd get enmeshed in all kinds of internal politics, and he thought at this point in his career it wouldn't be a good thing for him.

But I said, "Well, it's already done now anyway." So I guess he thought if he had friends like me, he didn't need many enemies. But he knew I had done it.

Anyway, Chris and I then got busy working on this book, *The Sea War in Korea*. Malcolm, at his suggestion, asked that I draft the outline. We sent it to Naval Institute and they accepted it, and we got going on it. Anyway, we got partially through with the book, and one day Chris said, "Frank, we'd better hurry up and finish this book."

I said, "What's the trouble?"

He said, "Well, either my boss or yours is going to be fired, going to go, going to be leaving."

I said, "How do you know?"

He said, "Because the Secretary told me. This building is just not big enough for the both of them."

I said, "Well, I can't believe that."

He said, "Well, I'm telling you, Frank, it's what he told me. It's true. If you want to tell Carney, it's okay with me."

So I told Carney. Carney reared back in his seat, and he said, "Ah, I don't believe that. I don't know. I don't know why Charlie would be upset."

I said, "Well, Admiral, I'll tell you one thing Chris had told me--that he's upset about the blue flag messages. You won't let the Secretary see them."

He said, "Well, he shouldn't see them. He shouldn't see them until we have decided, until the military Navy has decided the consensus of our policy. No, I don't think I'll let him see the blue flag."

Paul Stillwell: What were the blue flag messages?

Captain Manson: These were messages that the admirals used to send to each other, where only the admirals saw them and perhaps only a select list of admirals. I'm not sure if all the junior admirals were on the blue-flag distribution. But it was really policy-level high-command Navy talking to each other. They put in front of the message "Blue Flag" and that meant "nobody else." This was when they were discussing force structure, strategy, and the things that high-command people try to get their heads together on so they can all be together.

But I also heard, hearsay, that Mrs. Thomas was jealous of Mrs. Carney, because Mrs. Carney was a wonderful entertainer in Washington on a social level. You never know how much these things trickle off into the professional side of things. Mrs. Carney was really one of Washington's best hostesses, a very pretty lady, and she loved to entertain. She'd been over in Europe, in London and in Italy and had entertained large international audiences and groups. She was really very good at it and loved it, so she did a lot of it. I had heard that this was a source of some discontent. I don't know to what extent that ever got into Secretary's thinking that Admiral Carney had to go. But it was a great disappointment to Admiral Carney, a great disappointment. He wanted to stay another two years.

Paul Stillwell: Did he confide in you his reactions and feelings about Secretary Thomas?

Captain Manson: Oh, yes.

Paul Stillwell: Sounds as if he sort of considered that Thomas was beneath him.

Captain Manson: He thought that Charlie Thomas was trying to impose his thinking on naval planning and to trying to alter or perhaps even to control the admirals' thinking on what they thought were the best types of ships, the best—well, everything from organization to weapon systems. Really where the conflict was, the admiral felt that the

Secretary was getting too much into his business. Now, I mean, that's about as well as I can summarize it.

Paul Stillwell: Do you remember any specifics that he especially resented?

Captain Manson: No. No. I do remember one time when I had written a memorandum recommending that the Navy do a program on atomic-powered seaplanes and take perhaps the P6M and put an atomic reactor in that plane.* Admiral Carney sent that memo down to 05, who was Admiral Ofstie at the time, a future Commander Sixth Fleet.† Admiral Ofstie had worked on the strategic bombing survey, and he was a smart man. He didn't like my idea, and he thought of about three or four or five different reasons why it was not feasible, not possible, not much good. So then the admiral took the whole package that he'd gotten on my basic letter and sent it over to Secretary Thomas. Thomas disagreed with all the admirals and thought that my idea had a lot of promise and that it should be further explored. That was getting close to the end of Admiral Carney's tenure, so we weren't able to explore it anymore under Admiral Carney, but we did under Admiral Burke.

As you can imagine, when you're fighting the entire hierarchy of the Navy on something like that, you aren't apt to make it. Not me, anyway. I'll never forget, Commander Dave Walley was the technical nuclear man.‡ The "Rickover of the air," I called him. Dave Walley was redheaded, short crew haircut, big freckle-faced guy, just as brilliant a nuclear physicist as I ever met. He was absolutely convinced that we could put a nuclear reactor, sort of a Model T-type thing, into one of those SeaMasters and get enough shielding, and that we could actually build a patrol plane that would get up there and stay up for two weeks, three weeks, four weeks, and do a masterful job in ASW.

---

* The Martin P6M SeaMaster was a swept-wing seaplane powered by four J-71 engines. It was designed for mine laying and reconnaissance flights. It made its first flight in July 1955. Plagued by technical problems and competing priorities, the plane was limited to prototypes. It never went into production or fleet service.
† Vice Admiral Ralph A. Ofstie, USN, served as OP-05, Deputy Chief of Naval Operations (Air), from 16 March 1953 to 3 March 1955. Vice Admiral Ofstie served as Commander Sixth Fleet from 25 March 1955 to 12 April 1956.
‡ Commander David M. Walley, USN, an aeronautical engineering duty officer.

Well, I believed Dave Walley, and I think he could have built this thing. So I lined up with him, and we put on quite a battle for a few years there. We had opposition, though, amongst the vice admirals and the chief of the Bureau of Aeronautics, who was Admiral Gentleman Jim Russell. Believe you me, Gentleman Jim is a gentlemen, and I like him, but I just happened to disagree with him about the possibilities of an atomic-powered seaplane.*

Anyway, I'll never forget, I was the one who had taken the idea of the ballistic missile, the Polaris system, to Burke, in a memo for the first time, and he'd gotten into all kinds of trouble over that with the Navy power structure.† When I came to Admiral Burke with that atomic-powered seaplane, he threw me out of the office and said, "Frank, don't you ever come in here with one of those ideas again unless you have cleared it all the way up from the bottom to the top."

I said, "I understand that, Admiral."

And he said, "Well, okay, just don't ever do that anymore." He didn't have to tell me what trouble he'd had over the ballistic missiles, because I knew. It had been rough on him, and it had been rough on me, because a lot of people knew that I had been the one who started it off in the first place. I'm sure I never was forgiven by a lot of people.

Paul Stillwell: Who gave him trouble on the ballistic missile idea?

Captain Manson: Basically it was the guided missile people. They called me in right off and told me I'd done a great disservice to the Navy to get the admiral all steamed up about this ballistic missile thing. I said, "How so?" All their experts were there to jump on me. They said that there was no way you could build a re-entry cone, that the Navy had tried that two or three years previous to that, and they found that the re-entry was impossible. I guess it burned out. I don't know why it was impossible, but I said, "Well,

---

* Rear Admiral James S. Russell, USN, served as Chief of the Bureau of Aeronautics from 4 March 1955 to 15 July 1957. The oral history Russell, who retired as a four-star admiral, is in the Naval Institute collection.
† Polaris was the name for the U.S. Navy's first submarine-launched ballistic missile, which became operational in the early 1960s. Its more-capable follow-on was the Poseidon missile, which entered the fleet in 1970.

General Electric thinks you can build a re-entry cone." Because they're the ones that we'd gone up to visit at Heavy Military Electronics at Syracuse, HMEE they called it, and that's where we were briefed on how this could be done.

Admiral Burke, Tom Weschler, and myself were briefed for about three days on it by a young man named Dwight Shetler.* He was crippled, one leg shorter than the other one, but a brilliant young man, 32 years old, and he told us how we could put this ballistic missile into anything the Navy had, basically. Showed us how we could do it and what sizes we were working with and what type of propulsion and guidance and all of it. He was a brilliant man, this guy Shetler.

Well, anyway, our guided missile division, OP-57, was bitterly opposed to the ballistic missile concept, and they said that I had cost the Navy its guided missile program, because it might take a lot of money away from programs that were needed. This was always the battle, taking money away from something that was useful and needed. I said, "Well, you may be right. It may not work."†

Paul Stillwell: In fact, when the Polaris program came to fruition, it killed off the Regulus guided missile.‡

Captain Manson: Killed off the Regulus, sure did. And, of course, the Regulus, I believe, was a cruise missile.

Paul Stillwell: It was.

---

* Commander Thomas R. Weschler, USN, served as personal aide to Chief of Naval Operations Arleigh A. Burke from 1955 to 1958. The oral history of Weschler, who retired as a vice admiral, is in the Naval Institute collection.
† The Polaris ballistic missile program began in 1955 with the establishment of the Special Projects Office. Rear Admiral William F. Raborn, USN, became the first director of SP in December of that year. Initially intended for launch by both submarines and surface ships, it entered fleet service in 1960 in the ballistic missile submarine *George Washington* (SSBN-598). The first version of the Polaris missile, the A-1, was 28 feet long, 4« feet in diameter, and weighed about 30,000 pounds. It had a range of 1,200 nautical miles. The Naval Institute's oral history collection includes a volume of recollections from Polaris pioneers.
‡ Two Regulus missiles were designed to be fired from surface ships or surfaced submarines. Regulus I, which entered the fleet in 1952, was 34 feet long, weighed 12,000 pounds, and had a speed of Mach 0.9 and range of 500 miles; Regulus II, which had its first flight test in 1958, was 57 feet long, weighed 22,000 pounds, and had a speed of Mach 2.0 and range of 1,000 miles. Regulus II did not go into fleet service.

Captain Manson: And maybe not too bad, maybe it was a good one, I don't know. So you never know. I mean, I can't sit here now and say that it was right for us to go into ballistic missiles. It may have been a mistake.

Paul Stillwell: There were advantages and disadvantages. It got the Polaris program going, but, really, cruise missiles were set back 15 years.

Captain Manson: Well, they were. In that sense, I really don't know who in the world has enough wisdom, under circumstances like that, to know whether or not you should pursue new concepts such as the ballistic missile. But I thought we should. I mean, I was young, and I had a lot of fire in my tail, going after it. I tended to be that kind of an officer. I was sometimes called a "firebrand" by my opponents or adversaries. I was always suggesting things like nuclear power, ballistic missiles, things of that nature. I had a lot to do.

Now, going back to the Carney years, I wrote that first major speech on converting the surface Navy from steam to nuclear power, and Carney is the man that gave that speech, but I had the benefit of all the paperwork that had been shoved back down some Navy throats when I wrote that speech. It wasn't my thinking; it was George Miller and a bunch of others. I think we talked about that earlier. But, anyway, so this changed the whole thing. Carney was a man who would go for new ideas, and he'd try them out.

Now, this is another field, but in personnel he wanted to try to improve the morale of the enlisted personnel and the junior officers. He wanted me to get something in *All Hands*, a speech or write an article or something.[*] Quentin Crommelin was the aide to Admiral Holloway.[†] I talked to Malcolm Cagle, who was a classmate of his, about Quentin, and he said, "Yeah, call Quentin, and maybe Quentin can work it out."

So I called him, and he said, "No," that he checked it with Admiral Holloway and it wouldn't be possible for Admiral Carney to put anything in *All Hands*. Of course,

---

[*] *All Hands* is a monthly magazine published by the Bureau of Naval Personnel.
[†] Commander Quentin C. Crommelin, USN. Vice Admiral James L. Holloway, Jr., USN, served as Chief of the Bureau of Naval Personnel from 2 February 1953 to 31 January 1958. His oral history is in the Columbia University collection.

Admiral Holloway was then a candidate for CNO too. So I think this is probably what the problem was, that Admiral Holloway might have thought that anything that he put in *All Hands* might imply criticism of the way he was doing the job. Or I don't know what he thought. But, in any case, he wouldn't let us do it.

So I went and spilled the beans to Admiral Carney and told him Admiral Holloway wouldn't let us do it. I'll never forget Admiral Carney's reply. He said, "Well, my approach to these things is this. I must tell those that report to me my thinking. I have an obligation to do that. But if they have good and sufficient reason why they don't want to do what I have recommended, then I think I have to give consideration to their thoughts too." I thought that was a remarkable attitude.

I was ready to dust Admiral Holloway off over there and tell him, "Put that article in there," but not Admiral Carney.

Later on, finally, after about a year, Commander Merle MacBain was able to get a personnel statement in *All Hands*, and I suppose Admiral Holloway was still there at that time; I don't know.*

Paul Stillwell: Yes. He was there past Carney's regime.

Captain Manson: So he was still there then.

Paul Stillwell: Well, it could be that Holloway had some motives that weren't selfish.

Captain Manson: Oh, yes, absolutely. I don't know what he thought. It's useless to conjecture, because I really don't know. I just know that he didn't want to do it.

Paul Stillwell: You talked about the process of writing a speech for Admiral Carney. Once you got the final draft, did he then read that to an audience, or how did he present it?

---

* Commander Merle MacBain, USNR, a public information specialist.

Captain Manson: Yes, he did. He had a deep voice, a bass voice, and he was articulate, and he knew the subject, but he wanted to say the precise words. A lot of times they were measured words. Sometimes he would veer off and expand on a point. Well, sometimes he'd go deliver a lecture and not even have a note. I've seen him do that at the Air War College.* Just a marvelous lecture. I've seen him do it here at the Naval Academy too. He would read that speech, but it didn't seem like he was reading it.

I remember he'd always want to tuck in a paragraph or two that would be the heart of the message. For example, Carney is a cold warrior. He told me that every speech where we would be dealing with the Soviet Union to put in something new about what the Soviets were up to, and I had CIA, DIA, and ONI helping me, so every time I wrote a speech, I'd tuck in a few things that were new about what the Soviets were up to, whether in ships or personnel or whatever.† After about six months, the Soviets were just absolutely furious, and they were beginning to call Admiral Carney some of the worst names they could possibly think of. So then I'd write that up, too, sometimes. Carney just delighted in pricking the Soviets, so we did right along.

I remember one speech, he was upset because we were always talking about how revolutionaries were bad. He said, "That's wrong. We're the greatest revolutionaries of all time," and he asked me to put some of that stuff in there. So I did, and then *Time* magazine picked that up, I remember, talking about Admiral Carney saying we're the greatest revolutionaries of all time. But Carney would deliver the speech precisely and with force and conviction. That's what he did.

Paul Stillwell: How good was his relationship with Admiral Rickover?

Captain Manson: Well, it wasn't much. It hardly existed. I don't recall Rickover ever coming over even to see Admiral Carney, but he sent me to see Rickover, and I was the liaison. Admiral Carney asked me to establish that liaison and to keep it, and I did. I'd go over and see the admiral and have lunch with Admiral Rickover. I had lunch with

---

* The Air War College, part of the Air Force's Air University, is at Maxwell Air Force Base in Montgomery, Alabama.
† CIA – Central Intelligence Agency; DIA – Defense Intelligence Agency; ONI – Office of Naval Intelligence.

him once when he had a lettuce leaf and a big spoonful of cottage cheese and a tall glass of tea and two crackers.

Paul Stillwell: What are your recollections of working with Rickover?

Captain Manson: Rickover always tried to embarrass me or insult me within the first two or three minutes of our conversation. I think he thought that this would put my thinking at a higher level, get my adrenaline flowing, and he knew that I would fire back at him. I never let him get away with anything. If he had a point, well taken. But if he was firing shotgun or something, I would pick him up on it and go right back at him, and he loved this. So he and I had some lively conversations on everything from Jews to guidance systems.

I remember one time Admiral Rickover called me over there, and he was upset because the Navy was ignoring him on the ballistic missile development. Admiral Red Raborn wasn't asking him for any advice.* He called me in and he said, "Now, Manson, if Raborn doesn't change his attitude, I'm going to call a press conference, and I'm going to tell the whole thing that they're not seeking my advice on these missiles. They should be getting my advice. They're going to make them too noisy. They're going to have all kinds of things wrong with them if they don't get my advice."

I said, "Well, I'd be happy to pass that word along."

He said, "Well, you just tell them. Tell all those—" and I forget what he called them, but I think at that particular time he called a couple of senators, so I could hear him talking to Senator Anderson, I think, of New Mexico, and I don't know who else.† Jackson, perhaps, of Washington because that was a great friend of his.‡ Those two were

---

* Rear Admiral William F. Raborn, Jr., USN, was director of the Special Projects Office, which developed the Polaris submarine-launched ballistic missile system. He held the post from 1955 to 1962, being promoted to vice admiral in 1960. His Polaris oral history is in the Naval Institute collection.
† Clinton P. Anderson, a Democrat from New Mexico, served in the Senate from 3 January 1949 to 3 January 1973.
‡ Henry M. Jackson, a Democrat from the state of Washington, served in the House of Representatives from 1941 to 1953 and then in the Senate from 1953 until his death in 1983. He was chairman of the Senate Armed Services Committee and a strong proponent of nuclear-powered warships. The ballistic missile submarine *Henry M. Jackson* (SSBN-730) is named in his honor.

great friends. He let me hear him really tell them that he was bringing pressure to CNO and so forth.

So I went back, and I explained that the admiral is upset, and I was told it was too bad. I said, "Well, he's going to call a press conference and he's going to blow the lid off." The feeling was, over in CNO'S office, "Let him blow."

Paul Stillwell: This was probably in Admiral Burke's time.

Captain Manson: Yes. "Let him blow." So he did, and he had front pages on *The Washington Post*, that Rickover was being ignored. I don't know what the headline was, but that was the essence of it. But he had told them that he was going to do it and he did it. So that was it.

You asked me about Rickover's contact with Carney, and it wasn't much. Then Burke's was much worse with Rickover, but I stayed on in my liaison capacity with Burke. I got to know a lot of the nuclear officers: Danny Brooks, Dick Laning, and George Steele, who went with Rickover, had worked for me and he became skipper of that ship that went through the North Pole.*

Paul Stillwell: *Seadragon*.

Captain Manson: *Seadragon*, yes. But George used to work for me, and I am very fond of him.†

Paul Stillwell: In what capacity?

Captain Manson: When I was in OP-09Dog as head of plans and policies, I had George working with big labor to bring labor in to support the Navy. I'll tell you about that job later on.

---

* Commander Daniel P. Brooks, USN; Commander Richard B. Laning, USN.
† USS *Seadragon* (SSN-584) was commissioned 5 December 1959 under the command of Lieutenant Commander George P. Steele II, USN. In August 1960 he took the ship on the first submerged transit of the Northwest Passage in northern Canada. The oral history of Steele, who retired as a vice admiral, is in the Naval Institute's collection.

Paul Stillwell: All right.

Captain Manson: But, anyway, I knew a lot of these nuclear officers, and one day Admiral Burke was giving Rickover the business in front of me, because he didn't like Rickover. So I said, "Admiral, I don't know. I think the problem is that you don't know Rickover well enough."

He said, "Well, I don't want to know him any better."

I said, "But would you be willing to meet some of his officers?"

He said, "Yes, I would."

I said, "All right. I'll get about six or seven of them and bring them in here, and you talk to them. They admire Rickover, most all of them do."

He said, "All right, I'll talk to them."

So I rounded up about six or seven of them and brought them in there to the admiral's office, and we had about an hour or two set aside so there could be a free exchange. At that time, the big discussion was over a nuclear-powered frigate, the *Bainbridge*, in the planning and thinking stage.* The discussion got around to weight-per-shaft horsepower, whether the weight of the frigate really made any difference or not. Burke said, "It does make a difference, how heavy that ship is."

There was one, Rickover's most technical man—I can't think of his name right now—but he really did argue with Admiral Burke. Admiral Burke didn't take too kindly to these arguments, and it was getting worse and worse. Finally, Admiral Burke said, "Well, Rickover is just a [expletive, deleted] liar." He called him a something. So this young lieutenant commander fired back at the admiral, and he won.

So at this point I stood up, and I said, "Well, Admiral, I know you've got a lot of work on your schedule today." At this point, Admiral Burke's face was fiery red, and I said, "I know you've got a lot of things to do, and if you'll excuse us, we'll get on out of here and let you get on with your work." Burke was plenty happy to see us go.

As we were walking out, this lieutenant commander came over to me and said, "Well, I'll tell you one thing. Burke doesn't know anything about nuclear power."

---

* USS *Bainbridge* (DLGN-25), a nuclear-powered frigate, was the only ship of her class. She was commissioned 6 October 1962. She had a standard displacement of 7,600 tons, was 565 feet long, 58 feet in the beam, and had a maximum draft of 29 feet. Her top speed was 30-plus knots.

I said, "Well, I'm going to tell you one thing. You don't know anything about admirals."

Paul Stillwell: [Laughter] What was his reaction to that?

Captain Manson: He didn't say anything. But he had set things back a long ways. We were getting along pretty good.

Paul Stillwell: The first skipper of the *Bainbridge*, Ray Peet, worked with Burke.* Did you get to know him?

Captain Manson: Ray Pete, yes, and I knew Ray Peet very well. Ray was a nice guy and a very fine gentleman.

Paul Stillwell: Weschler also, who had that job before him.

Captain Manson: Tom Weschler. Tom's the one that went with me up to Syracuse with the admiral on that ballistic missile thing, and Tom and I stayed awake all night talking about this thing. I don't think we ever slept. If we did, we didn't sleep over an hour.

Paul Stillwell: Then he got involved in the guidance system for Polaris.

Captain Manson: Tom did, yes. I had a great admiration for Tom Weschler. A prince of a man, and Ray Peet, as well. Both of them just fine gentlemen.

Paul Stillwell: What else do you have in your notes about Admiral Carney?

---

* Captain Raymond E. Peet, USN, commanded the guided missile frigate *Bainbridge* (DLGN-25) from her commissioning on 6 October 1962 until 17 July 1964. He was assigned to the ship well before completion. The oral history of Peet, who retired as a vice admiral, is in the Naval Institute collection. Peet had previously been Admiral Burke's personal aide.

Captain Manson: Let's see here. It's funny when you start talking about these people, how they all kind of tie together. Carney got into a difficulty with the Secretary of State. Did I mention that the last time?

Paul Stillwell: I don't believe so.

Captain Manson: He wrote a speech and got on the front page of *The New York Times*. It was called the Crossroads speech. Things were going from bad to worse in the Far East, and Carney went down to the Air War College and, off the cuff, told the students down there that we really were getting ourselves into a bind in the Far East, and we were going to have to be strong, and they couldn't run over us. I'm talking Red China now.

After the speech was over, I told Admiral Carney that I thought that would make an excellent speech for the public. This was classified, I guess, secret, top secret. He said, "Well, all right."

I said, "I've got some notes on it."

He said, "Well, go ahead, write it up."

So I wrote it up, and then I went over to the State Department. J. Burke Wilkinson was Assistant Secretary of State, I guess, at that time, but he was an old Navy type.* He and I had played tennis together and taken figure skating together. We were good friends, had written books together, not as coauthors. Burke strengthened the speech a little bit on this Crossroads—get tough in the Far East. That was the nature of it. And if we did get tough, fine, the Chinese would respect us. If we didn't, our foreign policy was heading into oblivion. That was the essence of the speech.

I've forgotten where Carney delivered that speech. It doesn't make any difference. That speech got on the front page of *The New York Times*, full text, because Dulles at that point was not being tough, or not tough enough, and so that's why Carney made the speech.† J. Foster Dulles leaked a story into—I guess it was *The Washington Post* or the *Star*, I don't know which one now—that Carney had pressured the State Department into approving this speech, and he said a Navy commander had pressured

---

* J. Burke Wilkinson was Deputy Assistant Secretary of State for Public Affairs, 1956-58.
† John Foster Dulles served as Secretary of State from 21 January 1953 to 22 April 1959.

the State Department to clear that speech. That was me, of course, and I hadn't. I had taken it over there, yes, but the speech had actually been strengthened.

So Dulles then went and squealed to the President and told him Carney was getting into his soup, interfered with him. So then Eisenhower had Carney in for breakfast and sort of took him to task, and said that people had to be careful in the administration not to jeopardize what one of the others might be doing, and that they had to keep the policies in confluence and exchange and so forth.

So then Bryce Harlow, who was Eisenhower's speechwriter and a good friend of mine, had me in for lunch that same day. I remember we were sitting next to Milton Eisenhower and Robert Montgomery, and I forget who else was in there.* But Bryce talked quite a while about everything under the shining sun about what was going in presidential politics, and I finally said, "Well, Bryce, why did you want to have lunch with me?"

He said, "Well, I want to know whether this was your thinking or Carney's thinking, this speech, I mean."

I said, "It's Carney's thinking. Carney never makes a speech that's not his thinking."

Bryce said, "Well, I thought it was. But I want you to know I agree with him."

I said, "Well, I appreciate that, Bryce. I appreciate you, and I'm sure the admiral will."

He said, "Well, I approve of it. I know it's caused a lot of trouble, but I think Carney did the right thing."

Paul Stillwell: Did anything ever come of all this?

Captain Manson: Well, I think it was a start of a buildup of Carney's demise, because Dulles then was unhappy with Carney. Then Radford somehow or another picked up the information that there was trouble.

---

* Milton Eisenhower, the President's brother, was president of Pennsylvania State University from 1950 to 1956. Robert Montgomery, who had served as a Naval Reserve officer in World War II, was a noted film and television actor and served as a television coach to the President.

Paul Stillwell: From what you suggested before, it was Thomas more than anybody that led to Carney's demise.

Captain Manson: Well, I think so, but I also think that Eisenhower didn't step in. Eisenhower could very well have stepped in when Thomas was saying, "I want to change my CNOs."

Eisenhower could have said, "Well, not yet," or "Not now," and that's all there would have been to it, but he didn't. Thomas didn't have all that much sway with Eisenhower. There were people, the Secretary of State, for example, that evidently thought that he would be just as happy if Carney weren't around to talk about foreign policy.

Paul Stillwell: Do you have a feel for how the Secretary of Defense, Charles Wilson, viewed Carney?

Captain Manson: Well, I know in one instance shortly after the speech that got on the front page *The New York Times*, that they issued a policy that Carney's speeches would have to be cleared 24 hours, I think, before he made the speech. I believe that there was some kind of a special rule they had for Carney. So I was trying to comply with their requirements, and Carney was furious about this, that he was being given special treatment and not all that complimentary, really.

Paul Stillwell: Who was supposed to do the approval?

Captain Manson: Well, they had a setup down there in DoD called security and review, I think it was called.[*] This would be three or four guys, commanders, captains, colonels. Of course, they'd take Carney's speech, I'm sure they did, and run right up to the front office.

So, anyway, we had this speech Carney was going to make in Kansas City. We didn't have much time on it, and I hadn't had time to give it to them in advance. I'm not

---

[*] DoD – Department of Defense.

even sure; maybe we decided to make it a test case. Anyway, I don't remember the details. But I told the admiral I hadn't had a chance to clear this. He said, "That's all right. Let's go down and clear it with Wilson, Secretary of Defense Wilson."

We got down there. Wilson wasn't there, but Robert Anderson was then the Under Secretary of Defense.[*] He was very sympathetic to Carney's problems and he'd been SecNav before. So Carney and I sat there while Anderson kind of looked over the speech, but he was sort of embarrassed to even be looking at it. He could tell that it was no time to tangle with a man of Carney's intellect at this point, and he didn't. He more or less was apologetic that this was being done, but he really didn't have any alternative. He approved the speech.

But then I don't think that speech was too well thought of later on either. I wish I could recall exactly what the nature of the speech was, but it got to the point where anything Carney said anymore, the press was really watching him. If there was any way that they could—you know how they like to stir up controversial matters.

But, anyway, this was coming close to the end of the Carney era. But I'll guarantee you, if he had stayed there, he would have had a much more powerful influence in military affairs and foreign affairs for the next two years, because he had the knowledge, the mental stature, the conceptual understanding of foreign policy, of national policy. He knew how all these intertwined and worked together. Carney would have been a tremendous influence his next two years in the Eisenhower Administration.

Paul Stillwell: How do you think he would have compared with the actual influence that Admiral Burke had?

Captain Manson: I don't know whether he would have had as much influence on actual weapon systems as Burke, because Burke's concentration was on weapon systems, and Carney's was more on foreign policy and how defense policy worked into foreign policy. So I think Carney's influence would have been more at a policy level, but I think he might have helped us with a lot of our problems that we as a nation didn't do too well

---

[*] Robert B. Anderson served as Deputy Secretary of Defense, 1954-55. He was previously Secretary of the Navy from 4 February 1953 to 3 March 1954.

on. I do wish Admiral Carney could have had those two more years. Admiral Burke could still have succeeded Carney, and he would have been a fleet commander for two years instead of jumping to CNO from a type command.

Paul Stillwell: So it was a difference of emphasis between the two?

Captain Manson: Exactly. Now, Carney on the atomic bomb, I remember one time I was in Carney's office, and it was during Dienbienphu.* Radford was pretty much leaning toward using a nuclear weapon, and Carney told me this. Anyway, I was in Carney's office and the phone rang, and it was Radford. I remember Carney saying, "Raddy, after we burn down the jungle, what next? What do we do after that? We're going to have the animosity of the people, the Asiatics, those that survive, and what do we do after we drop the bomb?" I don't know what Radford said. I didn't hear his answer. But, of course, we didn't drop the bomb. I think Carney had something to do with us not dropping the bomb.

Paul Stillwell: Did you get any feel for Carney's role as a member of the JCS other than what you've mentioned already?

Captain Manson: No, except that Carney had a Marine lieutenant colonel who used to brief him. He'd write just about one page on all these many, many pages and books that the JCS would carry down to the meetings. Carney never read that. He'd just take that one page and see what the subject was, and that was all he ever did. Burke, on the other hand, read it all, and that's one of the things that made him stay up late at night, 10:00 or 11:00 o'clock, was to read that stuff. But anyway, Carney was a powerful force on the JCS, because he knew how naval power fit into the overall scheme of foreign policy and in a joint sense and how it fit, why it was needed. He'd been head of logistics in the Navy. He'd been a tactical officer under Halsey, and he'd been a fleet commander and

---

* The Battle of Dienbienphu took place between 13 March and 7 May 1954 in what was then known as French Indochina. Communist Viet Minh troops defeated the French Army garrison at the time peace negotiations were getting under way in Geneva Switzerland. The French surrender on 7 May paved the way for French disengagement in the region and the later establishment of North and South Vietnam.

all that, and he'd seen it in the context of NATO. So it was very difficult for people to out-debate him. He was familiar with the difficulties in relying on bases, getting the base, keeping the base, and some of the other officers didn't have that kind of experience. So probably Radford, he and Radford were the most experienced.

Paul Stillwell: Anything else about Admiral Carney before we move on?

Captain Manson: One time I mentioned to him that he should start grooming some subordinate admirals for CNO. He said, yes, he should, he'd been thinking about that. I said, "Well, do you have anyone in mind?"

He said, "Two people," he'd thought of already. One of them was Ruthven Libby, and the other was Arleigh Burke.* We talked about what he might do, and he was thinking about, of course, giving them additional rank and a fleet command as the next move. He hadn't decided in his mind, of those two, at the time he talked with me which of the two, but he thought one of the two would be most likely.

Paul Stillwell: It turned out he had settled on his own successor.

Captain Manson: He had. Another thing Admiral Carney told me one time, a lot of people when they came in as head man, that they would just push everybody out in the street and take on a bunch of new faces and people. He said, "I don't believe in that." So he only brought in two officers. He brought in Robert Briscoe as readiness officer, and Carney thought readiness was an important element to get his thinking.† The other one was Slim Beecher as Chief of Public Information.‡ He wrote that song, "Halsey, King, and Me" or "King, Halsey, and Me" or something like that.§

---

* Rear Admiral Ruthven E. Libby, USN. The oral history of Libby, who retired as a vice admiral, is in the Naval Institute collection.
† Vice Admiral Robert P. Briscoe, USN, served as Deputy Chief of Naval Operations (Fleet Operations and Readiness) from 1954 to 1956.
‡ Rear Admiral William G. Beecher, USN, was the Navy's Chief of Information from July 1954 to September 1955.
§ In World War II Beecher composed an amusing song called "Halsey, Nimitz and Me," implying that the war in the Pacific was being fought by three people, the sailor/singer and the two admirals.

Paul Stillwell: "Halsey, Nimitz, and Me," I think it was.

Captain Manson: That's the name of it. By gosh, Paul, your memory is right. That's just what the song was.

Carney, at the National War College, wanted to do a speech on the National Security Council and the OCB, the Operations Coordinating Board. You see, when Eisenhower came in, he wanted to activate the NSC and the OCB. So Carney made a full speech on just how those two organizations were supposed to function vis-à-vis the other branches of the government and the military. Now, the OCB was the implementing part of the NSC. NSC would never get an operational role or never involve itself in an operational role, rather strictly do policy thinking, policy coordinating. More coordinating than anything. And the OCB was then supposed to check and see that everybody did what they were supposed to do. Now, had the OCB been in existence during the Iran-Contra affair, I don't think it would have had the problem.[*] I think it was a mistake to drop the OCB; that's my own thinking. I don't think Poindexter and North would have had to implement presidential policy.[†]

Paul Stillwell: They set themselves up as an OCB. [Laughter]

Captain Manson: That's right, exactly that, because the government didn't have anybody. Carney was frequently in trouble—I've got a note here—with his seniors—SecDef, SecNav, Sensate—because he was imaginative, because he would say what he thought publicly, but he was not intimidated in any way by the enormity of the challenges. Nothing intimidated Carney, and he was used to that, because nothing could ever compare with that war in the Pacific. So Carney was really a battle-scarred, big-time operator. He wasn't worried about little things.

---

[*] Iran-Contra was a political scandal in the mid-1980s, during the Reagan Administration. The United States was selling arms to Iran, an avowed enemy. The proceeds from those sales were then diverted to the Contras, anti-Communist guerrillas in Nicaragua. Both the sale of the arms and the aid to the Contras violated stated administration policy and congressional legislation.

[†] Vice Admiral John M. Poindexter, USN, was Assistant to the President for National Security Affairs during the Reagan Administration. He got caught up in the Iran-Contra problems of the mid-1980s and reverted to rear admiral on 4 March 1987. He testified in the summer of the year, along with Lieutenant Colonel Oliver North, USMC, and others, in the congressional hearings on Iran-Contra.

Paul Stillwell: Admiral Peet told me that Burke was very demanding of those who worked closely with him in a personal sense. How was Admiral Carney in that regard?

Captain Manson: Carney was just the opposite of Burke, maybe too lax. The difference, I think, in those two is this, that Carney had such experience coming into the job, that he knew that if any subordinate didn't write the paper he wanted or didn't perform, he could do it. Carney had this self-confidence, and it was deserved self-confidence, but he just knew that if this subordinate could help him, fine, and if he couldn't, well, he'd get along. He was a policy man, and he dealt at a policy level, always. He says he didn't pick the nits off the nuts of gnats. [Laughter] I don't know whether you can type that up or not.

Paul Stillwell: It won't go as well printed as it sounds when it's spoken orally.

Captain Manson: Anyway, I was telling you the difference between Carney and Burke. Carney felt very secure. The fact is, I think the CNO job was beneath him when he came into it. I think he should have been the Chairman. He could have been Secretary of State. He could have Secretary of Defense. Anything. And he would have been marvelous. But here he was with a job that I thought, my own self and my own measurement of the man and of other people I'd met—I'd spent a lot of time with Cordell Hull and different people, and I thought Carney measured up to any brain I'd ever seen in the United States.*

Paul Stillwell: Was he a workaholic as Burke was?

Captain Manson: No. No, no. No, Carney dropped the bricks when he walked out of there, and he didn't take a bunch of papers with him either. Nor did I when working for him. But it was just that he was so well prepared, and he had a mental reservoir of knowledge of the subjects that he had to deal with, that he didn't need to.

---

* Cordell Hull served as Secretary of State from 4 March 1933 to 30 November 1944.

Now, Burke, on the other hand, came in having been destroyer type commander, had not really dealt as a responsible person with the national agenda.* He was frightened, he felt insecure, and, of course, he reflected this to his subordinates in many ways with anger, with skepticism sometimes, with threats, with all manner of things, because he himself really was doing everything he could do to succeed. Now, I was just there with Burke for the first two years. Admiral Burke and I were close friends. We'd been friends when he was a captain, when we was working on the General Board and when he was OP-23 and when he was OP-30, and when he was out in the Far East. So we'd had a long relationship and a good one. My wife and I been to his house for private dinners, and they'd been to our house. We were just good friends.

But when he walked in there as CNO, and he'd hardly been there any time at all, he said, "Well, Frank, I don't have any friends. I can't have any friends in this job, any personal friends."

I said, "Admiral, I don't agree with that."

He said, "Well, I just can't do it. I've got to be impartial. I don't know who it was that told him that, somebody, and he believed it.

"Well," I said, "yes, you do. You do have to be impartial, but I don't think you have to forget about your friends. You may not be able to do them any favors or let your friendship influence your judgment, but you do not have to give up your friends."

Paul Stillwell: I got the impression that after he'd been there a while, these feelings of insufficiency melted away, and he became very confident.

Captain Manson: Oh, indeed they did. As he gained experience, he gained confidence, after he'd been through these things a few times. I'm told that he was very much in control of the situation. He was there six years, you know.†

Paul Stillwell: Right.

---

* Rear Admiral Arleigh A. Burke, USN, commanded Destroyer Force Atlantic Fleet, 20 January 1955 to 17 June 1955.
† Admiral Burke served as Chief of Naval Operations from 17 August 1955 to 1 August 1961. His oral history is in the Naval Institute collection.

Captain Manson: He has a good mind.* Admiral Burke has a very good mind. He's quick, he's thoughtful, he's analytical, perceptive, but he was very difficult to—I probably got on better with him perhaps than any of the other immediate staff because I'd known him so long. I'd laugh at him. Sometimes it would make him really angry when I laughed at him, but I couldn't help it, because he'd just be having a fit. I could see he was having a tantrum, and I'd just get so amused I couldn't hold back the laughter. It always amused me, because I knew it wasn't the real man here; it was a man under stress. One day all the problems came up just as he was going to the dentist. But on top of a lot of personal things, I mean problems.

But no, Carney didn't take the paperwork home. If it was something new or a new approach to a problem, Carney would carefully read that, but he didn't have to read it again. He had it. I don't know that I ever met an admiral that had any greater intellect or retentive power than Robert Carney, intellectual capacity. I surely never met anyone that had his wit. Absolutely fantastic.

When he was fighting with Bradley and the Joint Chiefs about things, Bradley kept talking about a "division slice this" and a "division slice that," and had to have all that money because he had to have that for the division slice. So Carney said, "Well, Omar, what is a division slice?"

He said, "Mick, I don't have time to discuss this kind of thing with you; it would take years to teach you what a division slice is."

So Carney said, "Fine, good enough."

Next meeting, they came down to the Tank, and Carney was talking about ocean slice.† Every time he said anything, it was, "Well, I have to have this for the ocean slice and the ocean slice and the ocean slice."

He'd gone over it about four or five times, and Bradley said, "All right, Mick, what's with this ocean slice?"

Carney said, "Well, Omar, I'll tell you. When you tell me what a division slice is, I'll tell you what an ocean slice is." So I heard that Bradley stopped talking about a division slice after that.

---

* Admiral Burke died 1 January 1996 at the age of 94.
† "Tank" refers to the room in the Pentagon in which the Joint Chiefs of Staff meet on a regular basis.

All Carney did to prepare for the meeting was write down one sentence: "Tell Bradley about ocean slice."

Paul Stillwell: You wanted to talk about Admiral Carney also with the Navy League?

Captain Manson: Yes. Admiral Carney wanted support from the civilian sector for naval budgets, and after looking at all the civilian organizations, he thought that the Navy League was the best civilian organization to get support, so he decided he'd start trying to pump them up, and asked me to line up some speeches.

This was one of the first that he made to the Navy League, and it was in New Orleans, and it was a tough speech. In essence what it was it said was that too many Navy Leaguers were using the Navy League as a social organization rather than a civilian arm of the Navy. So when he was "waxing hot" on his speech and in the midst of it, I was sitting back in the audience, as I usually did, and I heard this Navy Leaguer say, "He sure is twisting our tails, but we need it."

But he started the idea of getting the Navy League to be more conscious of its role as sort of a vocal part of the Navy. A lot of people took him seriously and tried to do it. But, anyway, so that was the other thing.

I had planned to write a book about Admiral Carney, and I sent most all my notes over to the archives, Naval History. But if he had been appointed for another two years, then I think his imprint on U.S. policy and naval policy would have been much better remembered, and a book would have had much more interest. But the public didn't have much chance in two years to get to know him. I think the people who didn't get to know Admiral Carney are the losers. He's a wonderful man. He plays the guitar, he writes songs, a master storyteller. He's just a marvelous person.*

I remember one time he got caught by the law here in Maryland, I believe it was, for fishing or hunting where he was not supposed to. They hauled him into court, and he was here a four-star admiral, but he was, of course, dressed like a hunter. The judge wanted to know what his profession was, and he said he worked for the U.S.

---

* Admiral Carney died 25 June 1995 at the age of 95.

government. The judge let him off lightly, because he could tell by looking at Carney that he had a much bigger fish in front of him than a pure bureaucrat.

Paul Stillwell: You've described the process by which you and Admiral Carney worked together on getting a speech prepared. How was it between you and Admiral Burke in that regard?

Captain Manson: As with most things on those two admirals, it was a total contrast. Burke would sometimes just have one word. Like he was going to make a speech to get a doctorate at Notre Dame, and he told me he wanted to make a speech on work, on the rewards of working. He said, "So make the thing on work," and that's all that I had to go on. He would sometimes have three or four words that he would say, "Make it on aviation." Sometimes he no had idea at all. He said, "Well, just pick something and do it." But he did tell me, and right off, to stay off of policy. He said, "I don't want to talk about that at all. As long as we talk about the Navy in our speeches, fine." Because he knew my writing, he knew what I could write about. So he said, "You just stick strictly to naval matters."

You know, he'd been jumped over 92 admirals. We actually got off to a rough start, Admiral Burke and I. First thing after he became CNO, *Collier's* magazine came to me and wanted to do a cover story on Admiral Burke. Walter Karig was going to write the piece. He had been retired then, so he could do a marvelous piece. Jim Devereaux, I believe his name was, was the head of the Washington office of *Collier's*, which was a big magazine in those days.

Paul Stillwell: Oh, yes, I remember.

Captain Manson: Anyway, the photographer was going to take the cover picture on Saturday morning.* This was just about the first thing that happened after he was appointed. He was living in a little apartment out there on Wisconsin Avenue, and the photographer was late. Tom Weschler and I were going to be with him and help do

---

* The photographer was Robert H. Phillips, who was in his early 30s.

whatever we needed to do. The young brash *Collier's* photographer had just gotten married, and he was late.

So Tom and I were waiting too. He was supposed to be at Burke's apartment at 8:00 o'clock, and then 9:00 o'clock came and no photographer. Burke was just about to go crazy. This was the first time I had ever seen Burke when he was really getting hot. So probably about 9:30 the young man showed up. It was a Saturday morning, the young man was a civilian, he didn't think anything about it at all. And Burke was furious. Only Tom and I knew that, underneath, if you'd just touch him, his entire lid would have blown off.

So this young man was telling Burke to put this uniform on and sit here and put that uniform on and do this, and all Burke wanted to do was just have the picture and forget it. But no, the photographer wouldn't do that. He was messing around with lights, a lot of lights and all this and that. So pretty soon he blew the fuses in the building, all of them, and he still wasn't satisfied he had the right picture. So he said, well, he wasn't happy with what he'd done so far, wasn't at all sure he had a cover picture.

So the decision was made they'd have to go to the Pentagon, because we couldn't get the building fuses fixed. So we had to saddle up and ride off with all that gear. Mrs. Burke, a lovely woman, just a lovely woman, was frightened even because the admiral's temperature had gone up about ten degrees. So she wished us well as we went out and told me privately, "I hope nothing happens." So we got down there, and Burke brought all of his uniforms down there. The photographer took some more in the blues, and then he decided that he wanted him in khaki. Oh, my, there wasn't anything I could really do about it, and Tom couldn't do anything.

So Burke got all dressed in khaki uniform, and we went out on the Pentagon steps. Now, Burke had appointments all morning, you see, including appointments with people like Admiral Robert Briscoe, a three-star admiral senior to Burke. Burke was going to be seeing them every 30 minutes or so all morning, all the deputy chiefs. He hadn't seen any of them, and it was 11:30.

So we were standing out on the Pentagon steps, and this guy was just shooting Burke with his elbow up on the steps of the entrance and different informal shots.

Briscoe came out, and Briscoe just couldn't stop saying what he said: "Well, Arleigh, getting your picture took?" Something like that, you know. Briscoe, a marvelous person, had kind of a deep voice, and he was kind of joking.

But still, it hurt, and Burke said, "Well, yes." Something just real crisp.

So, boy, about that time I told the photographer, "I'll tell you what. If you haven't got what you want by now, it's too late anyway. The admiral's got to go back to work, and we can't put up with any more shots, so we're going." I said, "Admiral, let's go."

The admiral was mad at me, too, for getting him into it. So he and I were walking along at a brisk pace up the E-ring there. Oh, he was mad. He said, "Well, Frank, I've been getting my picture took."

We walked a while longer, and I said, "Yes Admiral, you've been getting your picture took." And that was the end of it. We didn't say any more, because there wasn't anything I could do, and there wasn't anything he could do. But it had robbed him of his morning.

Paul Stillwell: I'm surprised he didn't blow up earlier, because he's very concerned about promptness.

Captain Manson: He's a very prompt person, always a little bit early for everything. That's the way he is. Well, we all knew, Tom Weschler and Mrs. Burke and I knew that everything was there for a blow. But I'd never seen him blow really big. So that's all there was to that.

Finally the *Collier's* article came out about two months later, and it had this picture of Admiral Burke on the cover, smoking a pipe and blue smoke was kind of coming up toward the overhead.[*] An absolutely handsome picture if you've ever seen one, and a marvelous story by Walter Karig. I'd even helped write the story myself. Burke called me in and he said, "Frank, I just want to tell you, that's the most marvelous

---

[*] The color photo appeared on the cover of the 16 September 1955 issue of *Collier's* with Burke wearing his blue uniform and lighting his pipe. Part of the cover had a blue background.

thing I've ever seen." He remembered what he had done, and he said, "Sometimes we just say things we don't really mean."

I said, "I understand, Admiral," and that was the end of it.

Now, this comes on to the story about Tom Weschler that I wanted to tell you. Tom was the appointments secretary there, and I was the speech man. I went in to talk to the admiral about making a speech or an appointment or something or other that involved his schedule. Burke had looked at it, and the schedule was too tight. Tom had been doing it. Burke let out a few well-chosen words and told me to go get Tom, "Get him in here. Both of you get in here."

So I went out there and said, "Tom, the admiral wants to see us. Tom, it's not good." [Chuckle]

Tom smiled, and he said, "Oh, Frank, that's all right."

I said, "Well, yeah, I know, but he's really hot."

So we got in there, and Burke had that schedule out there in front of him for the whole month or week or whatever. He said, "Tom, I told you not to make this schedule this tight." Now, how tight is too tight?

But Tom was trying to get him all set up the best way he could. The admiral let go with about maybe five minutes of just a stream of well-chosen words about that schedule and how important it was not to get this thing too tight, and this and that and one thing and the other. So I was really pretty shook, and old Tom just braced, and every time the admiral would come to a pause, he'd say, "Well, yes, Admiral. Thank you, Admiral. You're right, Admiral," or whatever. It didn't make any difference, but Tom had some little short, soft words.

Burke finally finished, and he said, "All right. Get out of here."

So we both got out, and I said, "Tom, that was pretty rough."

He said, "No, Frank, that's good for the admiral. He had a chance to get all those suppressed feelings out. That's the best thing in the world for him."

I said, "Man, I never looked at it that way."

He said, "Well, that's the way you've got to look at it."

Paul Stillwell: [Laughter] Was Admiral Burke one to hold a grudge?

Captain Manson: No, no. He would forget. Well, I mean like he remembered about that picture. But I mean, normally if he thought he had done wrong, he would try not to do that again. But he knew he had done wrong from time to time.

One time he'd asked me to do a speech, and it was about 3:00 o'clock in the afternoon, and he wanted the speech before he went home. Well, you can't even think of a speech in three hours, much less get it fully in your mind and then get it typed and all that. It takes quite a long time. It did me, anyway. It took me usually a couple of days to do a good speech. Sometimes I'd even have to work a week on one. But generally speaking, for Burke I had to get where I could get them out really quick. Carney would usually give me a week or so.

But Burke wanted this speech, and he said he wanted to have it before he went home. He planned to go about 7:00, and it was about 3:00 in the afternoon. So by 7:00 o'clock and with that kind of pressure, I couldn't seem to think very well, and I couldn't get much of anything down that I thought worthwhile. So I finally went in at 7:00 o'clock and I said, "Admiral, I just don't have it. I've got to go home, though. The family is expecting to eat dinner and so forth."

So he said, "Well, I'll be here until 10:00 o'clock. Just when you get it ready, I'll be here until 10:00."

So I said, "All right, Admiral." So I took the thing home with me, and by 10:00 o'clock I still didn't have it. So I called him at 1:00 and said, "Admiral, I'm still working on it."

He said, "Okay, Frank, I'll be going home. Just call me when you get it." So he left for home, and I called him at naval quarters at about 2:00 A.M. the following morning, and he was asleep. He hadn't slowly come out of his sleep.

I said, "Admiral, I've got the speech."

He said, "Well, that's fine, Frank. I'll read it."

I said, "No, Admiral, I'll read it to you right now. I want to be sure you've got it. I have put such a tremendous effort on trying to get it ready for you, I think I ought to read it to you."

"Well, go ahead." So I read the whole thing to him right there. And he never asked me for another speech with that short a fuse on it. So he does remember.

Paul Stillwell: When you were writing a speech, what was your technique? Did you dictate drafts, or did you type it on a typewriter, or how did you compose it?

Captain Manson: With Admiral Burke, what I would normally do was propose an outline first. With Carney, a lot of time I didn't even outline it very much, but Admiral Burke did want an outline, because a lot of times it would just be a sentence. So with him I would do an outline and let him sort of check the outline to see if we got the main points in there. He liked that. But then after that, I just went from the outline and would dictate.

With Carney and under Carney, I learned to dictate, because Carney dictated everything and beautifully. But with Burke, too, on his speeches, a lot of times we'd ask some subordinate commander somewhere to send us some ideas, and I would work those into the outline and into the copy. But generally speaking, I would dictate, though. But sometimes, of course, I would do it on a typewriter. But generally speaking, I'd dictate to a yeoman and then refine it.

Paul Stillwell: With Admiral Carney, you described his delivery of the speeches. How good was Admiral Burke at delivering a speech?

Captain Manson: Well, at first Burke was just really kind of worried about the whole picture, coming in as he did 92 numbers junior and all that, that he was having a little delivery difficulty. He was nervous. Sometimes he was a little bit—well, I can't think of the word, but it wouldn't be smooth. But he got very good. As he kept on doing it, Admiral Burke became an excellent speechmaker. I worked on him, though, with it.

There's the thing about Admiral Carney. I never would have thought about suggesting to Carney anything about his delivery. But with Admiral Burke—I'm an old speechmaker, speechwriter, speech teacher—and I would talk to Burke about his delivery. He would listen, and then he would do it.

Paul Stillwell: What were some of the things you suggested to him?

Captain Manson: Well, for one thing, changing his rate of delivery for effect, and I suggested he have certain words he wanted to emphasize, at some points of the speech he should slow down, vary the rate of delivery. Be very deliberate when he was coming to a point that he wanted to emphasize. Change the voice level from time to time, not always full throttle as Admiral McCain did.[*] I tried to get McCain to throttle back at times, but it didn't make a bit of difference. He was full throttle, open throat, all the way all the time. But Admiral Burke could do that, and Admiral Burke did have a good speaking voice. I tried to get Admiral Burke to sometimes, if wanted to expand on a point, just to go ahead and do it, but that didn't work too well. So we decided he shouldn't do that too often. And I told him some gestures to use, too, when appropriate.

But Admiral Burke has a commanding posture, makes a good formidable figure there. He speaks with such conviction. But at times there in the early days as CNO he had sort of a reluctance, a self-doubt as much as anything, and it came through. But as he gained confidence, as he became more secure in the job, why, he really did get to be a good one, as you've probably heard him many times.

Paul Stillwell: Oh, yes.

Captain Manson: But I was there during that transition period, and it was rough, because the admiral was depending on me for so many things. As a matter of fact, he came to see me in my office when he was coming in to see why they'd called him to Washington. My little office was right next door to the CNO, and he wanted to know why they'd called him in. He asked me, and I said, "Admiral, I don't know unless Carney is going to give you a fleet command, because he mentioned you and Libby as possible successors." One day I was asking him about grooming somebody. So I said to Burke, "I think he may be going to give you a fleet command."

Burke said, "No, no, I don't think that's it."

I said, "Why not?"

---

[*] Captain John S. McCain Jr., USN, served 1958-60 as Chief of Legislative Liaison for the Navy. He later became a four-star admiral. A brief oral history with Admiral McCain is in the Naval Institute collection.

He said, "Well," he said, "I've got to see Radford and I've got to see Thomas, too, but I've just come to see Carney first to see what it's about."

I said, "Well, in that case, I don't know." So a little later that afternoon I knew, because Burke came back and told me.

Paul Stillwell: Was Admiral Carney bitter about leaving before he was ready to leave?

Captain Manson: No, I don't think "bitter" is the correct word. I think "disappointment" is a much better word. Carney's not the kind of person to really be bitter, it's just not in him, but he was disappointed.

Paul Stillwell: That's understandable.

Captain Manson: Yes, and I was disappointed. As much as I liked Admiral Burke and wanted Admiral Burke to be the CNO, I knew Burke was young. He was only 53, I think, when he came in, and in another two years he would have only been 55. Carney was 60 and would have been 62. I just knew that Carney had some more work to do, and he wasn't finished, so therefore I wanted him to have a chance at it.

I had such a profound regard for Carney as distinct from the people who were firing him, although I had a high regard for Admiral Radford. I mean, although Radford and Carney didn't get along, I still had a very high regard for Admiral Radford. I didn't like the fact that he didn't like Admiral Carney, but that wasn't enough to cause me not to think highly of Radford.

Paul Stillwell: They were classmates at the Naval Academy, so they'd probably been rivals for a good long time.

Captain Manson: Yes, I'm sure ever since 1916.

Paul Stillwell: Anything else in your notes?

Captain Manson: I wanted to mention their wives too. All the wives, I think, particularly when their husbands get into high command, have an influence on whether the admiral ever gets there, for the first thing. If the admiral's wife is given to excesses of any kind—drinking, talking, or any kind of manner that might not fit in at a high command level—I think this hurts when they're considering the people for high command. I've never been in on these discussions, but I don't see how it could help.

Anyway, Admiral Carney's wife was a great asset to him, because she was a marvelous entertainer, a marvelous conversationalist, and she'd had the European experience and whatnot. So she fit in. She helped. She was a great asset, although on professional subjects, she never ever got into policy matters on anything.

I remember Mrs. Denfeld was a marvelous sort of a homebody type. The only thing I can remember Mrs. Denfeld ever said is, she called Secretary of the Navy Sullivan a "baking-powder-biscuit Secretary." She was mad at him, because she thought he wasn't sounding off when Admiral Denfeld was having to do all of the talking in those very critical times. She thought the Secretary of the Navy should have been more forthcoming, so she called him a "baking-powder biscuit." I never knew for sure what that meant. I was out at their house at the observatory one time, and she said that.* But you know how wives are; they can defend their husbands pretty eloquently.

Mrs. Burke, though, is a very religious lady, so she had a profound effect on Admiral Burke on the moral leadership side of things. The admiral is a rough, tough, slam-bang-type admiral, and Mrs. Burke, on the other hand, is one of the most feminine people you ever wanted to be around and one of the nicest people. She reads the Bible daily and practices what she reads. She'd slip things in Admiral Burke's pocket when she thought that he was about ready to take off in the wrong direction on something that involved what she thought was a question that she could deal with. She'd slip a note in his pocket, and he knew to check there. It was a marvelous method of communication.

Paul Stillwell: She wouldn't tell him directly?

---

* Through the end of Admiral Elmo Zumwalt's tenure as Chief of Naval Operations in 1974, the official residence was a Victorian mansion on the grounds of the Naval Observatory in Washington, D.C. After Zumwalt left, the house became the official residence of the Vice President of the United States.

Captain Manson: No, no. She'd put a note in his pocket.

Paul Stillwell: Why did she choose that rather than direct conversation?

Captain Manson: Well, I think she probably thought that he was so maybe emotional about something or other that it wouldn't do much good. He probably wouldn't listen.

I remember one time I had gotten him into building a log cabin out there near Great Falls, Virginia. He was slamming the earth with a sledgehammer, breaking a rock or something in the nature of building the thing, and I told the admiral I thought he was in danger of breaking something. I said, "You shouldn't be hitting like this, Admiral. You don't have this much physical exercise."

"Aw, it won't hurt anything."

Mrs. Burke said, "Let him go ahead, Frank. He's not hitting somebody's head anyway." It was the roughest thing I ever heard her say about him, I think.

My wife and I had a daughter, Melanie, who had terminal cancer at five years old when we were working there at CNO. It was a very rough time for me. Cagle had a child that had a terminal heart problem, too, at this time I was working for CNO. So we had a lot of health problems. Mrs. Burke, as busy as she was, almost every day visited our daughter in the hospital. I just will never ever forget that kind of thoughtfulness and friendship. But Mrs. Burke was always a powerful influence on the admiral's life. He recognized it and told me from time to time that she was a good influence. Mrs. Burke would sit out there alone at the mall entrance to the Pentagon and wait for him to leave the building until 10:00 o'clock at night.

Anyway, I think the only real leadership that ever amounts to anything is moral leadership, moral authority. I mean, all people have technical qualities and qualifications. It comes down to a question of principles, values, and a question of morality. Mrs. Burke was able to provide that. She helped sustain Admiral Burke during periods of trouble. He was always in a crisis. It seemed like he never got out of one, really, until he was in another—even to the very end, with President Kennedy.*

Burke, another thing on weapon systems and whatnot. Lord Louis Mountbatten came over to visit us one time, and Admiral Burke wanted to show him the P6M.† So he asked me to join them. I guess Tom Weschler went too. I don't recall. We went over to Baltimore where they were keeping the P6Ms.

Paul Stillwell: That was at the Martin plant.‡

Captain Manson: Yes, right, the Martin plant. Burke asked Lord Louis if he'd like to take a ride. Mountbatten was sort of intrigued by the idea, but we were able to talk the two of them out of it. The thing was still being tested. I'm very thankful that they didn't take the plane up, because in a week or so the first one crashed.§ It wasn't any time at all after that. So I'm really thankful that the two admirals weren't up in that airplane. But Burke was going to take him for a ride in it.

Paul Stillwell: It sounds like something that would have appealed to Mountbatten's sense of adventure.

Captain Manson: Oh, yes, it did. Oh, it did. Oh, they were both saying sort of the same thing. So I guess Tom and I prevailed on them; I don't know. Maybe some of the people over there at the plant, I don't know how we talked them out of it, but I know I was really against it because the plane was still in its testing stages, and we simply didn't know whether it would be all right or not.

It was under the leadership of Burke and Carney, and I don't know really, it happened on their watch anyway, that we saw the demise of the seaplane and also of the

---

* In mid-April 1961 a force of 1,400 Cuban exiles, secretly trained by U.S. personnel in Guatemala, landed in the Bay of Pigs, on the southwestern coast of Cuba, in an attempt to overthrow Fidel Castro, that nation's Communist dictator. The invasion attempt was a disaster. President John Kennedy decided that U.S. naval intervention would worsen the situation, so ships and aircraft offshore were prohibited from taking part.
† Admiral of the Fleet The Earl Mountbatten of Burma served as Great Britain's First Sea Lord and Chief of Naval Staff from 1955 to 1959.
‡ The Glenn L. Martin Company built the plane.
§ The first flight of the XP6M prototype was on 14 July 1955. On 7 December of that year the prototype exploded in flight because of a control system problem, and all on board were killed. The crash was near the junction of the St. Mary's and Potomac rivers.

airship. I was opposed to letting those systems go by the board. I thought we should have kept a certain amount of money in those programs, because you never know what type of weapons you might get that would depend on a seaplane or an airship. But Admiral H. D. Felt, who was down there in OP-30, didn't want that money going into seaplanes.[*]

Young Cal Durgin, Commander Cal Durgin, wrote an article for Naval Institute on seaplanes and the future of seaplanes, and he was at the same time working for Admiral Felt.[†] And Admiral Felt called him in and really did a number on him. Then young Cal Durgin—well, he was my age—came in to me and said he thought his career was wiped out because of that, and it turned out it was. I told him I didn't think so because his father, Admiral Cal Durgin, had had a long Navy aviation tradition.[‡] But he said, no, he was pretty sure he was all wiped out. Admiral Felt thought he had gotten out of line on seaplanes.

But this is the way you shut down a program. You stop the guy who's in charge at the lowest level for setting up a requirement, and you put the heat on this fellow, and then if he drops out, there's no requirement. Nothing comes up the line, and that's the way the seaplane and the airship were stopped. But, anyway, I regret that this happened and I still regret it. I think we could have found room somewhere.

Paul Stillwell: Well, there's talk about bringing back the blimps, so it's not dead yet.

Captain Manson: No, it's not dead. I used to talk with the Goodyear people a lot about it. Peter McDonald was Washington rep for Goodyear, about trying to come up with some ideas that would catch the Navy's imagination, but they couldn't do it. Anyway, I guess that's about all for all that.

Burke wanted to bring younger officers into the Navy's policy planning so that they would have an understanding of some of the considerations that went into making

---

[*] Rear Admiral Harry Don Felt, USN, served as Assistant Chief of Naval Operations (Fleet Readiness), 1954-56.
[†] Commander Calvin T. Durgin Jr., USN, "Nuclear Power and the Seaplane," *U.S. Naval Institute Proceedings*, January 1956, page 18.
[‡] Vice Admiral Calvin T. Durgin, USN, served as Deputy Chief of Naval Operations (Air) from 16 May 1949 to 25 January 1950.

up the budget, to have a Navy-implemented national policy and so forth. So I went out and scavenged around and got four or five officers.

One of them was Lieutenant Stansfield Turner.* We put him in OP-35 with Admiral Smedberg, and he was absolutely a brilliant young officer.† I used to go to him and get him to help me. When I was writing speeches or anything at all that dealt with the younger officers, I'd go get Stan Turner to help. He always had some ideas.

Paul Stillwell: Do you remember anything specific?

Captain Manson: Well, we were trying to retain young officers. The retention rate was down, was suffering, and we were trying to say things to the young officers that would cause them to make a career of the Navy. I don't recall specifically what Stan recommended, but he had some positive recommendations that we did use. Also on aviators. Admiral Burke sent me to spend a few days there with the Chief of Naval Air Training, who was a big, heavyset fellow and I can't think of his name.

Paul Stillwell: Artie Doyle?

Captain Manson: Yes, Artie Doyle.‡ He wanted me to convey to Admiral Artie Doyle that he wanted aviation support. He wanted support of the aviators, and he wanted to help young aviators to make a career of it, but mainly he wanted to let the aviators know that he had a profound interest in their future. So Doyle had some ideas. One was to bring Burke down to Pensacola, get a bunch of young officers together, get their ideas, free exchange, and we did that. It did help to get Burke down there, because Burke was not an aviator, and Marc Mitscher had not been too kind to him when he came on as chief of staff there.§ They said, "Get on the MC." I'm told, the 21MC, when Burke landed and say, "Attention all hands. Captain Burke has just landed in an airplane," or

---
* Turner eventually became a four-star admiral. His oral history is in the Naval Institute collection.
† Rear Admiral William R. Smedberg III, USN, served from 1953 to 1956 as director of the Politico-Military Policy Division of OpNav.
‡ Vice Admiral Austin K. Doyle, USN, Chief of Naval Air Training, 1954-57.
§ In late March 1944 Commodore Arleigh A. Burke, USN became chief of staff to Vice Admiral Marc A. Mitscher, USN, Commander Task Force 58, in the Pacific. See Burke's article "Admiral Marc Mitscher: a Naval Aviator," *U.S. Naval Institute Proceedings*, April 1975, page 53.

"Captain Burke has just taken off," or whatever. I don't know what all they did, but hazed him a little bit.

Paul Stillwell: But Mitscher came to have a profound respect for him.

Captain Manson: Yes, Mitscher did. As time wore on and he found out what he had, he had a real jewel of an officer. So he did. But at first, though, he thought that anybody that didn't fly wasn't fitting. But anyway, Mitscher did respect Burke, and it was mutual.

Anyway, those are the thoughts right now, and I guess I'll call it for today.

Paul Stillwell: Well, all right. Thank you very much.

Interview Number 3 with Captain Frank Manson, U.S. Navy (Retired)

Place: U.S. Naval Institute, Annapolis, Maryland

Date: Tuesday, 8 March 1988

Interviewer: Paul Stillwell

Paul Stillwell: Captain, the last time you made some fascinating comparisons between the two Chiefs of Naval Operations for whom you worked as speechwriter, Admiral Robert Carney and Admiral Arleigh Burke. I think you have some more you want to add to that today.

Captain Manson: Yes. I've been thinking a little about that. Admiral Burke, in contrast to Admiral Carney, was quick to praise people and his speechwriter or whomever, and he was quick to punish. On the other hand, Admiral Carney just assumed, I think, that everybody was highly qualified and doing his best. So he didn't spend a lot of time, as Admiral Burke did, with individuals—pumping them up or shaping them up. He didn't do that; Admiral Burke did. This was really a different type of leadership. Admiral Carney spent most of his thinking time on policies—international, national, military, naval policies—and how they all meshed, integrated, how they could be utilized, how one could be supportive of the other and so forth.

Burke, on the other hand, in his early years as CNO, and those are the only ones I know about with detail, was more concerned with getting people to know what he was thinking, getting to know their thoughts, and then trying to work a consensus. This is one of the big differences of the two.

I actually suggested to Admiral Burke that he might want to put out a "CNO Personal" like Admiral Forrest Sherman did to all admirals. Burke decided to call it a "dope sheet," and I drafted those "dope sheets" for perhaps about two years. They were largely based on letters that he had received, information that he had gotten from the Joint Chiefs that he wanted to put out, or things that were emerging to the top that he wanted all admirals to know about.

Paul Stillwell: How frequently were those published?

Captain Manson: My recollection is it was once a month.

Paul Stillwell: What sorts of issues did he cover?

Captain Manson: Well, he would talk about personnel changes, things like the conditions, the habitability of ships, or anything that would affect personnel—pay, uniforms, anything that happened to be on the agenda with regard to personnel. With respect to ships, he dealt with the types of ships, changes that we were making, equipment, weapons, and so forth that were coming on line. He would talk about items that we had in research and development. On operational readiness, he would discuss some of our deficiencies at times—where we were doing well, where we weren't, our shortcomings. Generally, he covered the whole spectrum of what the admirals needed to be thinking about. He more than anything wanted them to know what he was thinking about.

Paul Stillwell: So it was more than just information; he was giving some philosophy along with it?

Captain Manson: Oh, yes, of course. Sometimes he'd get a little robust in his language. I remember one time Admiral Smedberg called me down there. He was head of OP-35, I guess it was, because Admiral Orem had been there once in that job.* But, anyway, Smedberg called me in, and he said, "Say, Frank [he always called me by my first name], "I want you to tell Arleigh that some of his language is offensive to me."

I said, "Well, I certainly will."

So I told Admiral Burke that some of the language had offended Admiral Smedberg, and he said, "All right. We'll try to be more careful," and that was the end of it.

---

*Rear Admiral Howard E. Orem, USN.

Paul Stillwell: What was this language?

Captain Manson: Well, you know how some people, when you're making a point you get sometimes a little exuberant, sometimes to the point of using a bit of slang. Sometimes, oh, I suppose there might have been a few curse words from time to time thrown in that you'd hear in the wardroom. Admiral Burke is an old wardroom type.*

Paul Stillwell: That's the way Navy men talk.

Captain Manson: So if he felt like doing that, he did. But, of course, there's this nicest sense of change that some people—well, some people never use that language anyway. But then some of them, when they become admirals, that's one of the changes that comes about. They clean up their vocabulary a little bit and think that they've just got to set a little better example. So they get used to that, and if they hear somebody who's still using some of that language that some of the World War II admirals were rather fluent with, why, then it does upset them.

But, anyway, one of the subjects that Admiral Burke liked to talk about was leadership. He was dead set on getting individuals to do more leading. He thought that his job would be a lot easier if he could just get more people accepting responsibility and doing things that he wouldn't have to do. He thought the captains, especially in the Pentagon and, I guess, perhaps throughout the Navy, but certainly in the Pentagon, were not doing nearly as much as they should be doing.

They were sitting there too much of the time covering their own person and minding their desks, so to speak, and perhaps a lot of daydreaming, but not doing really the work that had to be done that their jobs called for. So he told me to get all the captains together one day, and he wanted to talk to them. He said if I had any thoughts I could put those out for a few notes. But he said he had a few things that he could think of to say that he didn't need any.

---

* Ensign Burke's first commissioned service was on board the battleship *Arizona* (BB-39) after he graduated from the Naval Academy in 1923.

So we got them all together, and, my goodness, there must have been 700 of them. I don't know, it was a big roomful. It filled up one of the theaters up there in the fifth floor of the Pentagon. It was about 5:00 o'clock, I guess. Most of them would have gone home, but they were up there. The admiral really did give them a stern lecture on accepting responsibility and doing at least all they were supposed to be doing and perhaps a little bit more.

One of the points he made was that about 80% of the work, his observation, was being done by about 20% of the captains. My own experience in the Pentagon, I think maybe the admiral was being charitable, because I'll tell you, when I wanted to do a speech or anything like on the admiral's dope sheet, it was all I could do to find anybody that could even talk to me about it. I'm talking four-stripers, two stars. Most of the people simply didn't have any thoughts about what the Navy ought to be, where it should be going other than just doing precisely maybe what their job called for. Hopefully they'd get one letter advanced up to as high as CNO in a year or something like that. But basically they were just waiting to go to sea again where they could do their thing and show their command ability with a ship that was commensurate with their rank.

Well, anyway, Burke gave them a very strong lecture, that they had to do more and that they weren't doing anything nearly as much as their potential. So this didn't sit well with the captains. I guess a few of them thought it was my fault. So they came down to my office, and some of them were complaining pretty bitterly that they didn't like the idea of Admiral Burke questioning what they were doing, that they thought it was denigrating and that it was, in their case, untrue, and gave me quite a talk about how well they were doing.

I said, "Let me tell you something. If you're doing what you're supposed to be doing and if you're doing a little bit more, you're part of that 20%. He's not talking to you, so don't worry about it anymore. And, of course, if you're not, then you're part of the 80%. So you've got to evaluate that yourself, but I wouldn't be upset about it. Just figure out which percentile you're in, and then act accordingly."

"Oh, well, okay."

Paul Stillwell: You're a real diplomat. [Laughter]

Captain Manson: So they'd go off whistling a tune.

Paul Stillwell: You said that Admiral Burke would punish people who didn't measure up. In what ways?

Captain Manson: Well, generally if it was just not too severe, he'd give them a good lecture, sort of a tongue-lashing, which he is very capable of. But if he thought that their conduct was—or if you want to use punishment as an example, he'd tell them to go pick up their papers and get going, that they were fired, they were through, and he'd do that occasionally.

I remember he did that to one captain on a presentation from general planning. Then he sent me around to see what the reaction was, and quite a few of the officers thought he should have fired the admiral, the captain's boss. But it was the captain, after he made the presentation, that was telling Admiral Burke what a splendid job the presentation was, and Admiral Burke was telling him the presentation was no good.

When the captain then argued with Admiral Burke, Burke said, "Well, your work here is finished. So as soon as you clean out your desk, and I hope it won't be longer than two hours, why, you're through." That was in an extreme case. He didn't do that often, but once in a while.

Paul Stillwell: You don't need to that too often; word gets around.

Captain Manson: Well, yes, like ten minutes. I mean, when something like that happens in the Pentagon, in about ten minutes everybody knows, or 30 minutes, anyway. So then everybody starts shaping up. Of course, Admiral Burke, on his fitness reports, was the same way. I mean, if an officer was doing an outstanding job, it certainly reflected in what the admiral had to say. On the other hand, if he thought that the person was derelict in any way, then it reflected also. So Admiral Burke was just a tough taskmaster. That's about the only way you can sum him up.

Paul Stillwell: And those people who produce the best work got the most work to do, probably.

Captain Manson: Unfortunately, that's the way it worked. The people that were performing, there were only a handful, really. Every speech I would write, I would get called in before the murder board, and there would be five or six of these guys in there.[*] Boy, I'll tell you, sometimes it was pretty rough. But I didn't mind, because they were trying to improve it.

Paul Stillwell: Who were some of the shining lights that you remember?

Captain Manson: Well, the best officers at that time that we could rely on for judgmental calls like this, it would have to be Bill Martin, William I. Martin, George Miller, Draper Kauffman, who was then in the Under Secretary of the Navy's office, and Jack McCain.[†] Let's see, who else. Pete Aurand, do you remember him?

Paul Stillwell: He was President Eisenhower's naval aide.[‡]

Captain Manson: Yes, that's right, that's the guy. Pete wasn't in there as often, though, as these others I'm talking about. And of course, Tom Weschler sometimes would come in when he was there.

Paul Stillwell: Every one of these men you mentioned was a flag officer, eventually.

Captain Manson: Oh, every one of them, that's right. There were perhaps one or two others whose names don't pop up right in my mind right now. But, yes, they all made admiral, and they deserved to, because they were extremely bright.

---

[*] A murder board consists of individuals asking questions of the person who is going to speak publicly, perhaps to testify before Congress, so that he or she can mentally prepare practice answers.
[†] Captain William I. Martin, USN, later vice admiral. Captain George H. Miller, USN, later rear admiral. Captain Draper L. Kauffman, USN, later rear admiral. Captain John S. McCain, USN, later four-star admiral. The oral histories of all four are in the Naval Institute collection.
[‡] Captain Evan P. Aurand, USN, served as naval aide to President Dwight D. Eisenhower from February 1957 to January 1961. He eventually retired as a vice admiral.

Paul Stillwell: And it sounds like also he was looking for people with imagination.

Captain Manson: Always. Burke was always looking for imagination and creativity, new ideas. He wasn't happy with the status quo. If you fit in that category, why, you wouldn't last very long with Burke, because he thought there was room for improvement, and, of course, there is. When you're not really in a war, things tend to get stultified in the Navy, and people get used to the golf course and the cocktail hour and whatever. Social amenities of life in the Navy can be pretty attractive.

So Burke would usher them into reality right away, because Burke was always of a mind that war could come anytime—maybe not a big war, but a small one. Now, Carney was quick to react when something did happen. Carney would call in his senior admirals if something was popping in some part of the world, and they'd make some quick decisions.

I remember when Admiral Stump was having some difficulty out in the Far East, and Stump said that you had to be quick on the trigger.* I believe two of the pilots had shot down some Chinese aircraft, as I recall. Stump said, "Well, you've got to be quick on the trigger." Carney was quick to praise Stump, said he was absolutely right, and then Carney had a different opinion of Stump from that time on. I noticed that Stump came up more frequently in his conversation.

But both Carney and Burke were men of action. If they saw, for example, something going on in Panama or like things that are going on now where it just appears that we just can't do very much about anything—†

Paul Stillwell: The Vietnam situation was a case in point during that time, Dienbienphu

---

* Admiral Felix B. Stump, USN, served as Commander in Chief Pacific and Commander in Chief U.S. Pacific Fleet, 10 July 1953-14 January 1958. After he was relieved as CinCPacFlt on 14 January, he remained in the joint billet as CinCPac until 31 July of that year.

† Manuel Noriega was de facto ruler of Panama in the early 1980s and in August 1983 promoted himself to general. Relations between the United States and Panama deteriorated in the late 1989. Following harassment of U.S. service personnel in Panama in December 1983, the United States invaded Panama. Noriega was captured in December 1984. He was subsequently convicted in U.S. federal court and imprisoned.

and so forth.*

Captain Manson: Yes, exactly, and it just really was a frustrating situation. But they were always figuring out how some ships could be deployed, how something might be able to bring some pressure, political pressure and diplomatic pressure.

The story I had mentioned about Burke and his leadership lectures, one time—and I don't know why he told me this story, but you don't have to be too smart to figure it out—he was telling me that when he was aboard the battleship *Texas*, when he was a two-striper, they had a monkey who would steal the cookies about 3:00 o'clock in the afternoon.† When the baker had finished cooking a batch, he'd slip his paw around where the cookies were kept, and open the cookie jar, take two or three, and scamper up the mast, and he would sit up there and eat those cookies. Not only did he get away with cookies, but he was making a mess down on the deck.

So there was quite a discussion aboard the deck apes and the oil guys about what they could do to stop that. So one of the men dealing with oil said, "Let's grease his tail." So they greased the monkey's tail, and the next time he stole the cookies he rushed up there and wrapped his tail around the mast and fell right down on the steel deck there and it knocked him out. Not serious, though, he was able to get back on the cookie jar within a few days.

But, anyway, from that time forward, the monkey would go in and he'd think before he got those cookies he'd better go check his tail to see if he had friction. So he'd scamper up there and priss around, and then he'd come back down and take his cookies and go back and do his thing. The point, of course, was that it doesn't pay to make the same mistake twice. This monkey even had enough sense to know that. So I thought that was a pretty good way to illustrate a point.

---

* The Battle of Dienbienphu took place between 13 March and 7 May 1954 in what was then known as French Indochina. Communist Viet Minh troops defeated the French Army garrison at the time peace negotiations were getting under way in Geneva Switzerland. The French surrender on 7 May paved the way for French disengagement in the region and the later establishment of North and South Vietnam.
† The only battleship in which Burke served as a junior officer was the *Arizona* (BB-39) from 1923 to 1928.

Paul Stillwell: Admiral Burke had another saying that he passed on to me once. He said, "When you've figured out what you're going to do, you always need a plan for what you're going to do if what you've planned to do doesn't work."

Captain Manson: Well, yes, Admiral Burke was always considering a range of options and always thinking about half a dozen things if he could. Admiral Burke always liked to think in terms of a half a dozen. He'd have a half a dozen officers to check you out, or he'd have half a dozen ideas. One or two wouldn't be enough; he'd have quite a number of ideas, which is good because it gives you a number of options.

Paul Stillwell: Was he the sort of individual who would give the same job to several people to see who would do it the best?

Captain Manson: He frequently did that, and that used to aggravate the people in the Pentagon, because they'd come to me and complain and say, "Well, my God, you've got So-and-so over here and he's asked him to do the same thing." Sometimes in speechwriting, he'd say, "Frank, get five or six of them to give some thoughts on this." Then they would complain and say, "Well, I found three or four doing this same thing."

I'd say, "That's right. Now, you do your best and everybody else will, and maybe we'll have something good come out of this." The admiral wanted as many ideas as he could get.

Yes, frequently he did ask as many as half a dozen people to give him their best thinking on a subject, which I thought was a splendid way to approach it. Carney would never do that. I say never; I never saw him do it. The way Carney would work was he would put his thoughts down and then farm them out for comment. But it was just a different way in approaching things.

On that subject of leadership, there isn't any question but what both of these admirals were absolutely inspirational admirals. But their styles were quite dissimilar. I used to always be looking for the secret to leadership. For example, Vice Admiral Flatley had taken two aircraft carriers and had, almost overnight, converted those two ships from sort of also average, also-runs, to outstanding.* They got the pennant for being the best ships in the fleet.

One day he and I were flying going to New York to try to stimulate the Navy League to do a little bit more for the Navy, and I asked him what his secret was to leadership. He said, "Well, there are really a lot of secrets to it. Of course, moral leadership is a secret. The first thing that you must do is to discredit the bums. If the bums are the champions, then you've lost." I've thought of that so much in our country, our national leadership. If you can't control the bums, and if the bums are the leaders, then what are you going to get but bad? If the crime syndicate is in charge, then your government is going to be pretty sad.

In the Navy, he gave me an example, he said that one time he took a carrier into the Mediterranean, and their first stop, their first port, I think he said more than 30 of the men caught VD during the two or three days that the ship was in port.† Anyway, they were all reporting, and he checked with the doc and the chaplain when they got back and they told him they had these 30-some cases of VD. He said, "I'd like to see all of them in my cabin today."

So on the ship's speaker they put out the word that the captain wished to see all the men that had been to sick bay as a result of the port call. He got them inside and he said, "Now, I told these men that I was really saddened to hear what had happened to them." Being the captain, he knew their competence, after a while, would be diminished in their jobs and that they were ill. He said that he knew that their families back home, their wife or their mother, would certainly be concerned about them if they knew.

But he felt as the captain, that he should tell them how concerned he was. So he said, "Now, I'll tell you, I'm going to hope you're feeling better, but tomorrow I'm going to call and I'm going to have you up here tomorrow to see how you're doing." So the next day at 11:00 o'clock, he put the word out over the loudspeaker for all the men that were afflicted to lay up to the captain's cabin, the ones that he'd seen the day before.

---

* Captain James H. Flatley Jr., USN, commanded the escort aircraft carrier *Block Island* (CVE-106) in 1952-53 and the large carrier *Lake Champlain* (CV-39) in 1955-56. Both ships won Battle Efficiency Pennants under his command.
† VD – venereal disease.

Pretty soon, I mean in a day or so, the word has passed throughout the ship, "Well, who are those people the captain keeps calling up to the cabin all the time?"

The word was passed around, "Oh, those are the guys that got VD."

"Oh, is that who that is?"

"Yeah." But he went on for a few days calling these people up, and the first thing you know, the whole crew, these guys were not exactly the leaders of their gangs anymore. Their flag wasn't flying so high. So the word was passed, "Man, that's one thing you don't want. You want to shape up when you go offshore. You certainly don't want to come back to this ship with anything like that."

Well, anyway, that ship on the whole rest of the cruise, he said there were only two cases of VD for the rest of the cruise, and then the church attendance improved, a lot more people were going to church. He said that's just one way that he was able to grab a situation that existed and put the top man in charge. So I thought that was a fairly interesting testimony to human history, I guess you would say. I suppose if he were living today and he saw some of these evangelists like Bakker and Swaggart and their form of leadership, I expect that he would be terribly upset.[*]

I once had Jimmy Flatley out to my church, St. Paul's Episcopal Church there in Falls Church, to talk on leadership. He spent most of his time talking about the dangers of secularism, a country trying to proceed without any faith in the Almighty. Of course, Jimmy Flatley was a very devout man. But, anyway, I just use that as an example of leadership, how different officers were able to acquire it.

One time Admiral Cat Brown, commander of the Sixth Fleet, was telling me about John Crommelin, what a great leader he was and how the men loved him.[†] He was saying that he was such a good pilot, and to illustrate the point, he said that one time John Crommelin had a bunch of young ensigns aboard and they were afraid to land on the carrier. Word was getting around that these guys were just really shook up.

---

[*] Flatley died of cancer in 1958.
James O. Bakker and Jimmy Lee Swaggart were television evangelists who were brought down by sex scandals in the years shortly before this interview.
[†] Vice Admiral Charles R. Brown, USN, commanded the Sixth Fleet from 4 August 1956 to 30 September 1958. Captain John C. Crommelin, USN, was an outstanding naval aviator who had positions of leadership in World War II.

So Captain Crommelin sent word that he was going to give them a demonstration. So he went out there, and I guess it was probably an F6F.* He took that plane off and came in and did a slow roll and landed it flat on the deck, and it was a perfect landing.

He said never did Crommelin every hear any more about any pilots that didn't want to take off, if the old man could go up there and slow roll that airplane. But Cat Brown, in telling me that story, tears came to his eyes because he was so devoted to Crommelin, and they were great friends.

Paul Stillwell: Are there any more good Cat Brown stories? He was a colorful guy.

Captain Manson: I know one Cat Brown story. Cooper Bright was over there commanding an ammunition ship in the Med when Cat Brown was Sixth Fleet commander.† Cooper Bright, who once relieved me in Washington, knew that Cat Brown loved excitement and anything at all. Well, he said he tried to put him on a show every time he went alongside to give him ammunition.

Cooper Bright had the *Wrangell*, so he was always resupplying the flagship. Brown would always, when he heard they were going to do anything, he'd go out and see what Cooper Bright was up to. This one day, he dressed a couple of sailors, or one of them, anyway, in a stocking suit to resemble a female. He then had a male chasing her all over the ship. He had her appropriately worked up with balloons and whatnot, you know, and a wig. Everywhere Cat Brown looked, here they were going, and every time he looked over the side, the big chase was on. Finally, near the end, they didn't know how it was going to work out, but it worked out that he had them both jump over the side up near the bow somewhere. Then they picked them off the stern. Brown thought that was a marvelous deal. He enjoyed it thoroughly. I don't recall exactly everything that Cooper Bright did to entertain Cat Brown.

Paul Stillwell: What kind of a reputation did Cooper Bright have?

---

* Grumman F6F Hellcat fighters first entered fleet squadrons in early 1943.
† Captain Cooper B. Bright, USN, commanded the ammunition ship *Wrangell* (AE-12), 1956-58.

Captain Manson: Cooper Bright was perhaps as innovative—although his ideas rarely ever did get implemented. When he was with me there in OP-09Dog he wasn't happy with my office, said it was too small for a captain. I was a commander, and he was a captain. He said, "You've got to have much more space here. You don't have enough telephones."

I said, "Well, I've got about 20 telephones."

He said, "That's not enough for a captain." So he called up the administrative office to tell them he needed more telephones, he needed more desks, and he needed more space. They told him they'd try to do that, but it would take a little time, that you can't just call on the phone. He said well, he wanted it pretty soon, and he wanted some walls knocked down and a few things like that. A day or so went by, and nothing happened. Now, this was before I had been relieved. He said, "Have you got a power saw at home?"

I said, "Yeah."

He said, "Do you have anything that could cut these telephone wires?"

I said, "Yeah."

"Well, would you bring them in?"

I said, "Sure." I told him that I'd prefer, though, that if he was going to make any major changes that he'd wait until I had been detached.* [Chuckle]

He said, well, he'd do me that courtesy. Anyway, as soon as I left there, he went and cut all the telephones loose in the whole four- or five-office complex, however many. Piled all of the telephones up in a big pile, and then he sawed some holes and took walls down with the power saw. Then he called for the administrative people to come over, told them he had a problem. [Chuckle]

Paul Stillwell: I guess he did.

Captain Manson: Then he told our secretary, Betty Lilly, to find out from admin what kind of coffee their man liked—LeMay, I believe his name was—whether he liked sugar and cream in it or not, just however he liked it. And then he instructed her that when this

---

* Commander Manson was detached from the OpNav staff in July 1958 to attend the Naval War College.

guy walked in, that she was to run over to him with this coffee just the way he liked it and say to him, "Mr. LeMay, this coffee has got sugar and cream in it, just the way you like it." And about the time he's looking at the pile of telephones, he said, "That's when you give him the coffee." [Laughter] So the guy came in, and he looked, and, my goodness, the office was in a shambles. And Betty, standing there with the coffee, said, "Here, Mr. LeMay, is your coffee. We know you like it with cream and sugar." And the guy started laughing. Eventually, they did get more telephones and got that office straightened out, but it took a while.

Paul Stillwell: Well, I heard about Bright that his imagination exceeded his judgment.

Captain Manson: Well, like he had these rubber aircraft he was pushing.

Paul Stillwell: Inflatable airplanes.

Captain Manson: Inflatable airplanes. I went with him on one, briefing Admiral Combs, and Bright was telling him how good this rubber airplane was.* You could just take it out of a box, zip the motors in, and then take off. He said you could put it in any kind of a ship—everything from a tender to a destroyer to a submarine. Make the box so it will fit in any hatch was Bright's idea. So he got through with his presentation. Bright was a little bit cross-eyed, so I never forget he was looking straight at Combs, and he said, "Well, any questions, Admiral?" [Laughter]

The admiral looked at him a long time and said, "How many holes can you shoot in that thing before it'll fall? How many bullet holes will it take?"

So Bright said, "Well, what kind of bullets?" The admiral said, well, he thought .50 caliber, and Bright said, "Oh, it would take about 130." [Laughter]

Paul Stillwell: Oh, gosh. [Laughter]

---

* Vice Admiral Thomas S. Combs, USN, served as Deputy Chief of Naval Operations (Fleet Operations and Readiness) from August 1956 to November 1958.

Captain Manson: And I'm telling you, he didn't even crack a smile. The admiral couldn't think of anything else to ask him. [Laughter] I think he just wanted Bright to leave before he broke right down and—

Paul Stillwell: Well, that rubber airplane was a personal crusade for Bright.

Captain Manson: Oh, I'll tell you another one. I was at the war college after I was relieved, and Bright told me that he was in trouble with Admiral Burke. He said, "I wish you'd write Admiral Burke a letter and tell him that I'm qualified and that I'm not crazy." So I wrote Admiral Burke—I wish I could see the letter; I don't know what I said in it, but I'm sure I told him that Captain Bright had a lot of unusual ideas, and perhaps some of them ought to be checked into. I never heard from Admiral Burke, so I don't know what happened. Oh, geez.

Paul Stillwell: Do you have any more on that time with Admiral Burke to put on the record?

Captain Manson: I told you about getting the ballistic missile idea started when I went to Heavy Military Electronics near Syracuse. And he went swimming up there in a lake, and that's the only time in as long as I knew Admiral Burke, which was 20 years, I guess—the only time I ever saw him taking time off to swim or do anything. He did that.

Anyway, I know one thing about him that goes back to our leadership subject, and it gives you some insight into Burke. People would come to me with the delicate questions, and this particular thing, the admiral had gone down to New Orleans to make a speech, and I had gone with him. We were on our way back, the people in OP-05, the aviation division, had a fast airplane. I suppose they thought it was the fastest fighter airplane, faster than anything the Air Force had or anything in existence. And they wanted to race the airplane, but the situation between the services was such that if the Navy went out and made a big splash about a big, fast airplane, it would cause quite a brouhaha there in Washington, in the Pentagon, in the Congress. I forget now what admiral it was asked me to find out if Admiral Burke thought it was okay, but one of them asked me if, please, I would check it out with him. So I did, and I described the plane to him. He knew about the plane, and I said, "Admiral, do you have any objections if they race the airplane?"

The admiral's face turned fiery red, and he said, "Haven't any naval aviators got any guts? Do I have to approve everything that goes on in this entire Navy?"

I said, "In my opinion, Admiral, you don't. I appreciate your answer."

So it wasn't very long before the airplane was up there flying.

Paul Stillwell: Which plane was it? Do you know? It must have been a fighter.

Manson: There were two planes that really were fast, and this would have been in 1956. So whatever plane it was at that time that was coming on the line.

Paul Stillwell: An F8U, maybe?

Manson: It might have been an F8U, could have been.[*] I don't recall the airplane, but it was supposed to be the fastest airplane. The Navy thought it was the fastest plane, and they wanted to try it out, so they did. But that was Admiral Burke's reaction to it.

Paul Stillwell: Let's talk about your second Korean war book, which you coauthored with Malcolm Cagle.[†] How did that project come about, and how did you interact with the Naval Institute on that?

Captain Manson: Well, the way it came about was Malcolm Cagle and I had written with Captain Walter Karig a book called *The War in Korea*, but it was actually the naval side of it, the sixth volume of the *Battle Report* series.[‡]

---

[*] The F8U Crusader was a jet fighter built by Chance Vought. It first entered fleet squadrons in 1957. On 16 July 1957 Major John H. Glenn, Jr., USMC, broke the transcontinental speed record when he flew an F8U-1P Crusader from Los Alamitos, California, to Floyd Bennett Field, Brooklyn, in 3 hours, 22 minutes, and 50 seconds.

[†] Malcolm W. Cagle and Frank A. Manson, *The Sea War in Korea* (Annapolis: U.S. Naval Institute, 1957)

[‡] Captain Walter Karig, USNR; Commander Malcolm W. Cagle, USN; and Lieutenant Commander Frank A. Manson, USNR, *Battle Report: The War in Korea* (New York: Rinehart and Company, 1952).

Paul Stillwell: And it was really just the early part of the war.

Captain Manson: Just the early part of the war. So I had been responsible for getting Malcolm Cagle back to the speechwriting job in the Secretary of the Navy's office, for which he was not grateful. He was upset because he didn't want to do that. But, anyway, it didn't cost us our friendship. So one day he said, "Frank, why don't we do a real thorough job on the Korean War. I have a hunch that Naval Institute would want to publish it."

I said, "Well, that's very possible, Chris." I called him Chris.

I wondered whether we had time to do it, and he said, "Oh, well, we could do it easily. It wouldn't take up much of our time," which I questioned. But in any case, he said, "Well, would you do the outline?"

Chris asked me, and I said, "Oh, that's the easiest thing." So I drafted an outline of the war, the whole thing, and Chris looked it over and said there wasn't anything he could add or detract from it; it looked good enough to him. "Let's send it down to Naval Institute." Let's see. Who was the top man down here at that time?

Paul Stillwell: Roy Horn was here.

Captain Manson: I guess it was Roy Horn.[*] I'm pretty sure it was Roy Horn. So he called us down here and said he liked the idea and wanted to know if we had access to—well, he knew we did have, but he just checked with us.

Paul Stillwell: Access to what?

Captain Manson: To the records, if we'd have any trouble with Naval History. We had had a little trouble getting records from Naval History because Admiral Heffernan didn't always grant access to the historical records.[†] But we told him we thought in this case, with Chris being there in the Secretary's office and I being in the CNO's office, that we'd

---

[*] Commander Roy de S. Horn, USN (Ret.).
[†] Rear Admiral John B. Heffernan, USN (Ret.), served as Director of Naval History from July 1946 to October 1956.

be able to get the records. And if not, we'd just take the records out that we'd had access to in both of these offices.

Well, anyway, we decided to go ahead, and they told us the sooner we could get this book out, the better they would like it. So we did it. The way Malcolm and I decided to divide the book up was that he would write mostly about carrier operations, and I would write mostly about amphibious operations and mine warfare and more or less surface operations. He would concentrate with the air group commanders and so forth.

That's sort of the way we'd do it, and I'd write the beginning of the war. I wanted to do that, and he said he'd prefer I did that. So I did all that buildup for the war, and then we started, sort of chapter by chapter. Then he'd let me read his chapters, I'd let him read mine and so forth.[*]

Paul Stillwell: That explains why it's topical rather than chronological.

Captain Manson: That's right.

Paul Stillwell: Did you find there were things that you couldn't say about the war because they were still classified?

Captain Manson: There were two or three sticky points. One of them, the State Department did not want to release the information about Dean Acheson saying in a speech before the National Press Club that we were no longer interested in a line between Japan and Korea.[†] By inference, that made Korea an area that was of no longer a strategic interest to the Unites States. We, of course, put that in the book, and the State Department wanted us to take that out.

Paul Stillwell: Well, it was on the public record.

---

[*] The Manson-Cagle papers related to the research and writing of the book are on file in the Operational Archives Branch of the Naval History and Heritage Command in Washington, D.C.
[†] On 12 January 1950 Secretary of State Dean Acheson made a speech at the National Press Club in Washington and talked of a U.S. "defense perimeter" that defined national interests. He did not identify Korea as being within that perimeter. When North Korea attacked South Korea in June 1950, Acheson urged President Truman that the United States should go to the defense of South Korea, which it did.

Captain Manson: Well, it was a part of public record, exactly. So we refused to take it out.

Paul Stillwell: As a matter of fact, it's been said that that speech encouraged the North Koreans to start the war.

Captain Manson: I think it probably did. After all, our number-one diplomat was saying we were not interested in that part of the world. Why not? Terrible, terrible blunder on the part of the Secretary of State. But, no, there may have been some things that we couldn't write about, mine warfare, perhaps, pressure mines. We probably did get into some classified information, but, of course, we wouldn't go into the details of how some of these mines worked and countermeasures.

Paul Stillwell: You had dealt with a commercial publisher on the *Battle Report* Series. How would compare that with dealing with the Naval Institute as a publisher?

Captain Manson: Well, when it came down to indexing the book and correcting errors, I believe that we did more work with the Naval Institute in checking that sort of thing, because the Naval Institute at that time simply didn't have the staff to do the job that the commercial publishers did. They had a lot of people. So Rinehart and Company did more of the backbreaking editing and all that than the Naval Institute. It was pretty much left up to us to get the book in apple-pie order.

Paul Stillwell: So however you turned in it, that was the way it would be published?

Captain Manson: That's pretty much the way it was, yes. Whereas with the commercial publishers, you'd have an editorial conference, and they would do quite a bit of editing on their own. But not here with Naval Institute. They simply didn't have the staff or didn't have the competence; the talent wasn't here. They published 12,000 copies right off. Their only printing was that number, but it was bought right up. The Navy League sent a copy of it to each congressman, and it had a rather wide distribution, because people were hungry to know at that time what the real situation was.

One of the things about the book that we, Chris and I, wanted to be sure and make plain was that the Korean War may have also been brought on by virtue of the budget cuts on the Navy side, at least, and all of the armed forces, but generally the Navy had been cut down to the point we only had four carriers. There was considerable talk that we really had four more than we needed—that we didn't need any.

I made that point pretty plain in the first chapter, that this was a sad moment in the history of the Navy. And then, of course, the mine warfare had been completely eliminated from the Navy's budget so we didn't have minelaying, we didn't have minesweepers, and yet, of course, the Soviets knew that.

Paul Stillwell: Wonsan was very embarrassing.

Captain Manson: Very embarrassing. Of course, they knew that we didn't have any competence or any capability.

Paul Stillwell: Why was Admiral Heffernan not cooperative?

Captain Manson: I guess perhaps I will never know why. Timmy Mertz was Admiral Heffernan's administrative assistant, and I guess the kindest thing I can say about her is that she was paranoid. Somehow or another, she had in her mind that these historical records were to be preserved but apparently not to be written about or published. It's strange how a woman like that can get such a toehold or a stranglehold on an admiral, but I'm pretty sure she convinced Admiral Heffernan.

I don't see why there would ever been any other reason, because Admiral Heffernan is basically a very fine gentleman, and an old skipper of the *Tennessee* and all that. Just a fine, fine man. Yet as he got older and in that job, he didn't want any of us, he didn't want Jim Shaw, who was working with Morison, nor Cagle, nor me to have access to those historical records.[*]

---

[*] Commander James C. Shaw, USN.

There was always a struggle when we were trying to see them, because we couldn't see any point in not permitting. I never did have any other reason other than the fact that they just didn't want us to do it. Now, earlier Miss MacCrindle was there, and we had absolute total access during much of the *Battle Report*.* Admiral Nimitz even gave us his Gray Books to work with—you know, those were his personal diaries. But it's always been a question. Then I was telling Admiral Carney when he was CNO that Heffernan had this problem with letting other people have access. Carney said, "Well, we're going to have to make a change there."

We were discussing that when Admiral Wu Duncan walked in, Vice Chief of Naval Operations and a classmate of Heffernan.† So Admiral Carney quickly changed the subject and said, "Manson and I were discussing a speech." I don't know what he said, something or other, and Admiral Carney's conscience starting hurting him right quick. He realized that it was really wrong for him to be talking to a lieutenant commander and then tell an admiral, a four-star admiral, his Vice Chief, something that wasn't correct. So in the midst of his sentence, he just blurted it all out to Duncan. He said, "Wu, we were talking about Naval History and Heffernan's problems over there."

Duncan said, "Well, I've been trying to get things straightened out over there, and I think we're going to be able to do it," and he had a very soothing voice. Carney told him in very straight English that he wished and hoped that he would take action and do it quickly, get it promptly, because from what I told him that things were not running well at all, and it was not for the best interest of the Navy to keep those records from writers. Oh, one of the reasons he objected, they didn't want civilian writers to have access to the records. Of course, that's exactly the opposite. Their whole attitude was 180 degrees out of phase. They should have gotten those records out to everybody they could and made them declassified and available to writers, particularly magazine writers, but anybody. But that was not the prevailing attitude. So it was sort of what I guess you'd call the "sea cabin complex," for a better word I don't know.

Paul Stillwell: Why do use that term?

---

* Loretta I. MacCrindle.
† Admiral Donald B. Duncan, USN, served as Vice Chief of Naval Operations from 10 August 1951 to 1 September 1956. He and Heffernan were in the Naval Academy class of 1917.

Captain Manson: Well, you're all alone, you're in that sea cabin, and in a way it's you against the sea and you against the fleet. I never could understand why.

Paul Stillwell: Did Admiral Duncan rectify the situation?

Captain Manson: No. No. The way we rectified it is we finally had what you would call a hearing. They set up a committee of which Admiral Eller was a member, and I guess they had two others. They had three main witnesses, I guess: Cagle, Shaw, and myself, and I don't know who else. They probably had a few others. They told this committee what was wrong. Admiral Eller, who was sitting on that committee, they made recommendations, and then Admiral Eller became the Chief of Naval History after that.*

Paul Stillwell: Did that solve the problem?

Captain Manson: Not entirely, because Timmy Mertz stayed on then as Admiral Eller's administrative assistant, but it helped.

Paul Stillwell: Were there any things that you were frustrated in trying to see that would have useful?

Captain Manson: Well, I suppose we would like to have had access to letter files, but pretty much we were restricted to action reports from the ships at various levels of command. Some studies we had access to and some narratives, but I don't recall that we ever did really have access to letters and dispatches. My mind is hazy on where we got dispatches, but we did get them somewhere.

Then the Office of Public Information had a historical file on news clips, so we got all those from public information. They were very helpful, by the way. Kimball was the man's name that was in charge of that, Dan Kimball, who later worked for me. Well, anyway, that's about all there is to that.

---

* Rear Admiral Ernest M. Eller, USN (Ret.), served as Director of Naval History from October 1956 to January 1970.

But there's one thing about Naval Institute back in those days. It was small, but they were most cooperative and would work with you. I remember that.

Paul Stillwell: Were you satisfied with the way the book turned out?

Captain Manson: I was. I thought that they did first-class job in all respects. I mean, I was very happy with the book. I'm sure Cagle was too. I know he was.

The book got me in trouble. I was out with Captain McCain and Captain Hank Miller at a Navy League meeting in Chicago, and we were all sitting on the stage.[*] The fellow who was in charge of the meeting was Jack Bergen, national president of the Navy League.[†] We were on a barnstorming tour, and we were just starting in Chicago. Jocko Clark was also on this barnstorming tour.[‡] We had a plane, we were going to go set up some new Navy League chapters, and I was going to do the speaking and somebody else was going to do this and that. Then I would write everything that Admiral Bergen wrote, too, for the two weeks. Everything that Admiral Bergen said, I was to do; that was my job.

We got out there, and they spent entirely too much time talking about this *Sea War in Korea*. I remember Hank Miller turned to McCain, and I overheard him say, "Frank and that damn book." That somehow burned me up. I was really fit to be fried. I was so furious about it that when they asked me to say a few words, I could hardly think of anything to say.

Then I got on the plane and exploded to Jocko Clark and told him how much difficulty that Chris Cagle and I had had in writing this book, how hard it was for both of us, both of us under tremendous pressure from both our jobs and our family, because we both had very sick children during that period. I was just absolutely—it had been an effort that was almost above and beyond the call of duty for both of us, and I could not in good grace accept somebody making a remark like that.

---

[*] Captain Henry L. Miller, USN. The oral history of Miller, who retired as a rear admiral, is in the Naval Institute collection.
[†] Rear Admiral John J. Bergen, USNR (Ret.).
[‡] Vice Admiral Joseph J. Clark, USN, served as Commander Seventh Fleet from 10 May 1952 to 1 December 1953, during the Korean War. By the time the Cagle-Manson book was published, he had retired from active duty as a tombstone four-star admiral.

Jocko Clark said, "Well, Frank, I agree with you 100%." He said there was absolutely no point in that, and it was wrong. And I'm sure that if Hank had realized how hard it had been for us, he would never have said that.

Paul Stillwell: What was the cause of his resentment?

Captain Manson: Because they were going to do a lot of talking about sea power. I suppose he thought they should spend more time talking about sea power rather than just how this book came about. They were, in his opinion, spending too much time. Of course, this book is sea power. It's a documented sea power. But they had a sea power presentation to talk about.

Paul Stillwell: Never mind the real sea power, we'll just give them this lecture. [Laughter]

Captain Manson: Yes, right. [Laughter]

Paul Stillwell: Well, I'm sure that was very emotionally draining for you to have your daughter that sick when you were trying to do a hard job at the same time.

Captain Manson: It was virtually impossible, but somehow or another we were able to do it.

Anyway, we went on our barnstorming tour, though, with that old C-47, R4D, and had cots rigged in it so we could lie down.* We went out and set up a Navy League chapter up in Northern California. Came back through Minnesota. Admiral Bergen had to go see the Mayo Clinic to see about something about his health, so we stopped off there. I don't know what other stops we made, I don't recall. But it reminded me of the old barnstorming days, when people used to land in the pastures. Of course, this plane would land almost anywhere.

---

* The Douglas DC-3 cargo-passenger plane had the Navy designation of R4D and the Air Force designation C-47.

Paul Stillwell: Well, we're really getting into your next job now. Maybe you could explain what the overall job was.

Captain Manson: Yes. Well, when I was leaving Burke's staff, Admiral Burke said I could have any job that was commensurate with my rank. What I really wanted to do was to go to school and study mass communications. But I was, I guess, making the mistake of calling it mass persuasion. I really was interested in mass persuasion. So I called all the big Ivy League and all the schools in the East, starting with Harvard and going right down the line: Yale, Princeton, Cornell, all of them.

I finally wound up on the West Coast asking if they had anything in their curriculum that dealt with the kind of thing that I was interested. I said, "I've been trying to persuade people, and I'm just making small drops here in the ocean. I'd really like to become more competent at persuading more people, because the world is so big and my left arm is so small."

So anyway, they were a little bit upset that I would even be interested, when I talked to the people who were in charge of curriculum. They said, "There's no point in having a subject like that. That would be dangerous. That's what Hitler was doing." So they were as fearful almost, it seemed like, in talking to me about what I was interested in. So there wasn't any way to do that. So I couldn't figure, "Well, I guess the only thing I can do is to set up my own brand of it."

Captain McCain was coming by my office every day, every day when he knew I was about to leave. I had to find my relief first. Admiral Burke said, "You've got to find someone I'll accept." I knew he liked Ralph Williams, who had won a number of essay contests down here at the Naval Institute, a Supply Corps officer, good writer.[*] So I talked Ralph into coming up there after a few weeks of persuasion.

Then I said to McCain, "Okay, Captain, I'll join your staff."

So he set up a special division in the Progress Analysis Group, which was OP-09Dog2.[†] We had to think of title, so I became head of plans and policies analysis. The first thing was to try to be vague with that title so no one would know what in the

---

[*] Commander Ralph E. Williams, Supply Corps, USN, won Naval Institute Prize Essay Contests in 1951, 1953, 1954, 1955, and 1958.
[†] "Dog" was the word used for the letter D in the phonetic alphabet of the time.

world plans and policies—nobody knows what that is. But Captain McCain and I had a very good understanding of what we were going to do.* Basically we were going to establish a friendly atmosphere for the Navy, completely within the entire power structure of the United States. We were going to establish contact, and then we were going to get a presentation together that would be persuasive on why we needed to build a stronger fleet and what that fleet would do when we had it, and where it fit into the national policy.

So my job was to set up sort of an external affairs, I guess you would call it in this day and time, and to go around the Navy's entire periphery of all the power structure, the people, everything that we had contact with. This would encompass public relations, congressional relations, labor relations, labor management, civilian organizations, the entire periphery of every tangency that the Navy had, and to establish, first of all, contact, and then tell them that we wanted to get together with them and tell them why we had to start building a stronger Navy and what types of ships we needed and all about it.

By the way, when we started, there were only two of us, Captain McCain and myself, a commander. So we had to find offices, I had to get personnel. This was not an easy thing because space is always at a premium. Captain McCain already had a progress analysis group that was studying warfare—new concepts of warfare, old concepts—to see whether we were up to speed and whether we were making progress or going the other way. That's what that job really called for that he was in. But when we put my part on there, then we were going into the phase of the public, the total public.

Paul Stillwell: Mass persuasion.

Captain Manson: Mass persuasion, exactly that. So almost as fast as we could, I looked up in the telephone book to see if we had anybody in the Navy who had contact with anybody. So one fellow who represented labor was Julius Kuczma, who is dead now, but who looked like he'd been boxer, had a broken nose, big tall fellow.†

---

* Captain John S. McCain Jr., USN, was director of the Progress Analysis Group in OpNav, 1955-57.
† Julius E. Kuczma was labor relations advisor on the staff of the Office of Naval Material.

I told him that Captain McCain and I wanted to call on him, and he was shocked. He couldn't believe that somebody from CNO or OpNav wanted to visit with him. He just had a little office over there, and I don't know what he did. McCain and I went over there, got a sparse little place, and told him we wanted to establish good relations with labor leaders. "You do?" he said.

"That's right. We don't even know who they are or what their names are."

He said, "All right, we'll meet at Harvey's restaurant." That was a swank restaurant up there by the Mayflower Hotel in Washington. And he said, "Those people we'll ask you to watch."

So McCain and I weren't adverse to be going to Harvey's. We went up there, and they had a labor delegation. Bill Schnitzler, was secretary/treasurer of the AFL-CIO and, for all intents and purposes, was the top man. Meany was really the head of it, but Schnitzler did all the work and thinking.*

Schnitzler was really intrigued with us and our idea. He said, sure, labor wanted to get behind the Navy and support all the Navy's programs. It would be in labor's interest to do that. Of course, they'd want to do it. So we started thinking then, what could do we do to get things really moving? So out of that meeting we decided maybe we ought to hold an annual labor meeting aboard an aircraft carrier. Oh, everybody thought that was the best thing. So the next big labor meeting was scheduled for an aircraft carrier off the coast of Florida. So that's what we did, and we had those labor guys right out there, all of them, the head of every major labor union in the United States. We flew them out on helicopters and boats and everything else.

Paul Stillwell: What year was that?

Captain Manson: I'm pretty sure it was 1957, not long after I left Admiral Burke's office.† Even in this new job I was still working for Admiral Burke. It was just in a much broader capacity, and I was implementing then what we were talking about.

---

* William George Meany (1894–1980) became president of the American Federation of Labor in 1952. The AFL merged in 1956 with the Congress of Industrial Organizations to form the AFL-CIO.
† Manson had made the transition from Burke's immediate staff to Captain McCain's in September 1956. Manson's date of rank as a commander was 1 January 1956.

Anyway, we got labor set up, and then I was gradually getting officers assigned to me. George Steele came in, and I put him in charge of labor liaison, or whatever we called the job.* But I know I'll never forget George Steele. He'd never even seen a thing like we had there, and yet in two or three days he had a yellow notepad, and he had about three pages of organizations that he thought he should get in contact with. I told him absolutely. He was off and running without any more instruction with that. He caught on immediately to what we were up to.

Paul Stillwell: He's an extremely capable guy.

Captain Manson: Oh, gee. When Rickover wanted him, he was called over to be interviewed to get a nuclear sub. Rickover asked him where he was working, and, of course, he told him, "I want to see whether you're any good or not. I want you detached today," tonight—Saturday, I think it was. It seemed like it was Saturday, and it might have been Friday then.

George Steele called me and said, "Frank, Rickover wants me. He says he wants to see whether I'm any good or not, and I want to be detached." So I called Captain McCain and, boy, he was detached. Got him loose from there in a few minutes. So Rickover was impressed with the speed with which he could be detached.†

Another officer that I had was Mitchell Parizo, who was a lieutenant commander in the reserve. I brought him in from Minnesota, where he'd been in the cabinet, in the state government in Minnesota. He was a reserve. He'd come to Washington to find out—he was a great friend of Hubert Humphrey and Senator Eugene McCarthy and all the congressmen.‡ He knew his way around politically because he'd already been—I believe he was head of the air department of the Minnesota state government. I don't know really what exactly his title was.

---

* Lieutenant Commander George P. Steele II, USN, served in February and March Mar 1957 as part of the Office of the Chief of Naval Operations, Progress Analysis Group. The oral history of Steele, who retired as a vice admiral, is in the Naval Institute collection.
† Admiral Steele told this same story in his oral history.
‡ Hubert H. Humphrey Jr., a Democrat from Minnesota, served in the Senate from 3 January 1949 until 29 December 1964, when he resigned to become Vice President. Eugene J. McCarthy, a Democrat from Minnesota, served in the Senate from 3 January 1959 to 3 January 1971.

We put Mitch in charge of our congressional liaison. His main job, though, was to go up there and find out, on the Hill, what programs were being discussed that had any influence on the Navy one way or the other, what congressmen and senators and so forth were leaning our way, which ones needed to be persuaded and so forth. In a way, he was sort of an intelligence officer, and every day he'd spend at least a half a day on the Hill, going from committee room to committee room, from office to office, and then he'd come back and prepare a memo of things that were really vital, he thought. He was a perceptive, extremely intelligent officer and switched on politically, more so than anybody else in the Navy. So he took over that area of our work.

Then we went into the educational field and established links with top educators, and we started giving briefings, later, to meetings of senior universities. Worked ourselves into that area. Industrial, we worked through the Navy League as much as possible because the Navy League was made up of industry, pretty much so. So we depended a lot on the Navy League, and we worked through the Navy League. We helped print their magazine and provided about 90% of what went in their magazine for a year or so there.

Let's see. The Congress, the labor, the management, the education, civilian organizations. Well, anyway, when we got all this set up, we were overlapping with PR, with congressional liaison. They had some shop over there called industrial liaison or management, but, anyway, we overlapped all those, but at the same time, we brought it all together, too.

The way our office worked was that we had a brainstorming session every Wednesday. We fanned out and we did establish contact with the power structure. We had a little trouble deciding how many ships we wanted to build, but Captain McCain and I decided we'd build 1,000. We couldn't find anybody else that had any better idea about it. I think we said 600,000 men.

Paul Stillwell: Did these other areas that you were getting involved with object that you were infringing on their turf?

Captain Manson: They did, and yet they didn't. They realized that they weren't doing as much as needed to be done, and in some cases they were doing hardly anything. For example, Admiral Kirkpatrick, who was chief of public information, called me in one day.[*] He said, "Frank, you know, your shop really ought to be under me." I told him that I agreed to at least part of it, that part that dealt with public information ought to be under him.

I said, "Admiral, until you can get your shop under way and fully functioning, it would be a mistake to put out something like ours that's really under way. Because what might happen is that we might be fully stopped."

He said, "Yes. No, it's better to leave it the way it is." And that's what we agreed to do. But he was right.

Ira Nunn was legislative liaison, and he complained to Admiral Burke, and then after that Ed Stephan was OLL.[†] Nunn complained that Captain McCain was going up on the Hill and briefing congressional committees without his approval or authority. So Admiral Burke said, well, he'd have to get McCain in there and get him straightened out.

So here was sitting with all the admirals, and he called for Captain McCain. He had this little paper all written up, and he told McCain, "I understand you've been going up on the Hill without getting approval or the authority of the office of legislative liaison."

"Yes, sir." That's McCain—you know, he clicked, "That's right."

"And that you've been briefing Armed Services Committee and other committees."

"That's right, sir."

He said, "Well, therefore I've got to take appropriate action here. Hand me this paper." He had it all written up. "A reprimand to Captain McCain for exceeding his authority." But in the way it was written it was really commending him, and, in effect, saying "Go to it, Jack."[‡] I don't think Nunn liked it too much.

---

[*] Rear Admiral Charles C. Kirkpatrick, USN, served as the Navy's Chief of Information from December 1957 to August 1960.
[†] Rear Admiral Ira H. Nunn, USN; his oral history is in the Naval Institute collection. Rear Admiral Edward C. Stephan, USN.
[‡] This same anecdote is in the oral history of Vice Admiral Thomas R. Weschler, USN (Ret.). Weschler was Burke's aide at the time.

Paul Stillwell: So he was sort of taking the attitude toward McCain that he'd had toward these fighter pilots.

Captain Manson: Yes.

Paul Stillwell: That they should go ahead and break the rules once in a while.

Captain Manson: That's right, and if you're out there selling the Navy, you can do no wrong. That's the way Burke was.

One time we spread this sea power presentation—well, first, the way I described this structure was you set up your wiring and your pipelines and everything. Then we used this sea power message to put it out in movies and presentations and speeches, through the Naval Reserve and through the education and every way we could get it out.

But sometimes these speakers would change it and modify it. One of them did one day, and I'm pretty sure it was Hank Miller who did this. Anyway, he got a little bit excessive in changing the thing, and in some way Japan took offense after it was reported in the press. I don't recall exactly, but all I can recall is that Japan was offended by what he had said.

I remember that one day Burke and I were walking down the hallway. He looked over with a half-smile on his face, and he said, "Well, Frank, I see you've been getting the sea power presentation into Japan."

I said, "Yeah, that's right." [Laughter] He didn't say another word. He just kept walking. He didn't care.

Paul Stillwell: Did you try to cultivate the press as you'd tried to cultivate labor?

Captain Manson: Yes, yes, and there's something that I have tried to get a lot of people to understand, that the press is made up of people just like everybody else. They're no different than anybody else. Different in a sense that they're explosive if you're dealing with something that can really burn you.

But the way what Captain Walter Karig taught me was, first of all, to be friends, to be honest, and shoot straight. If there's something you can't tell them, tell them you can't tell them. Tell them, if you can, why you can't, but if you can't tell them why, just tell them you can't. But if you can, if there's no real reason why not. But don't be phony, flaky with the press. That will not work.

So I had that attitude then right from the start. I joined the National Press Club because Captain Karig suggested that I do that. I got to know all the top reporters, the top writers right away, and became their friend. They trusted me; they counted on me, and in turn I counted on them. And I never, in all the history of 25 years of dealing with them, I had only one person let me down in all that time. On the other hand, many, many times they covered when I was in trouble, you know, for one reason or another.

Paul Stillwell: Who was the person who let you down?

Captain Manson: There was a fellow named Ennis. I think it was John Ennis from Norfolk, Virginia. It was when I was chief of information for Allied Command Atlantic, and I was setting up a thing called the NATO games. I had decided there were two ways that we could push NATO. One was with sports and one was with, well, some kind of music, but sports especially.

In the Tidewater area, we were going to have the NATO games, and I had gotten the approval of all 15 nations. I had already gotten the cups in there that we were going to give out for winners, and I'd gotten the prizes and everything. One of the fellows who was going to run in the track and field events worked for one of the high schools down there in the Tidewater area, and apparently he had a reputation for having excluded blacks in some of his track meets.

Well, without ever asking me anything about it, I was not even in the city, I was in Houston, Texas, with the NATO briefing team, John Ennis put on radio and television that NATO was reverting to Jim Crow, I guess is the name they used, and that we were going to have nations participating in sports and games that would discriminate against blacks."* It was a terrible story, absolutely wrong, absolutely totally wrong. I didn't even know the man that was going to be working in this track thing, because we had a committee set up there in Norfolk.

I called John and said, "John, this is a terrible thing you've done, and there is no way we can correct it. You didn't check with me. You know perfectly well that's not the way I think or the way I feel, or it's not the way NATO works, and yet you've done this."

I don't recall what he said, but it was too late to save it, and it killed the whole concept. Then that was end of it. Because we were going to have water sports too. It would have been a marvelous thing to have had those games maybe every two years or four years.

Paul Stillwell: What year was that when that flap took place?

Captain Manson: That was in 1966, I believe.

Paul Stillwell: You said there were examples where media people covered for you. What would be those cases?

Captain Manson: Well, for example, in London when I was chief of information for the Navy and also for the Middle East Forces, a command in those days called CinCNELM and CinCUSNavEur areas. But, anyway, it was when McNamara had come in as Secretary of Defense.† His chief of information was Arthur Sylvester.‡ All right. Arthur Sylvester had come over there with McNamara, and we'd had lunch. He told me that I would be well advised to tell the admiral not to make any policy statements or any policy remarks, that nothing like this should come out except out of the Pentagon. This was

---

* Thomas D. Rice, a black minstrel singer, wrote a song and dance titled "Jim Crow" in 1832. Later in the century, the term took on the meaning of segregation of the races, as in "Jim Crow laws."
† Robert S. McNamara served as Secretary of Defense from 21 January 1961 to 29 February 1968.
‡ Arthur Sylvester was Assistant Secretary of Defense (Public Affairs) from 20 January 1961 to 3 February 1967.

Kennedy's wish, this was McNamara's wish, and, in effect, the admiral, H. P. Smith it was in those days, was finished.* He really couldn't say anything.

So we had a whole group of press come in, 50 or 60 of them, sort of a cook's tour of Europe, and Admiral Smith, and we had them up to lunch. Admiral Smith, who had been deputy chief of information, just simply told them that he had been gagged. He had been told that he couldn't—because I told him everything that he couldn't do, and Admiral Smith said, "So they said, 'Admiral, in effect, you've been gagged.'"

He said, "Yes, that's right." So Mark Watson, knowing the impact that this could have had in Washington—did you ever hear of Mark Watson from the *Baltimore Sun*?

Paul Stillwell: No.

Captain Manson: Oh, a marvelous person, good writer. He wrote some of the Army history of World War II. He was sort of a little fellow and one eye was gone, he was about 75 years old. He stood up on a chair and said, "I just want this group to know that we have one of the finest admirals here in H. P. Smith in the Navy, and he's been honest with us. But I just want a gentleman's agreement here amongst all of you that none of you will write one word of what the admiral has told you here about what the real truth is, about the gag that's been placed on the military."

Mark Watson and I had been friends for a number of years, and I think if we hadn't been close friends he wouldn't have done that. But that was the end of the problem.

Paul Stillwell: What would have been the repercussions if that story had come out?

Captain Manson: I suspect that Admiral Smith would have been relieved within no time at all.

Paul Stillwell: Well, he must have known that when he said it.

---

* Admiral Harold P. Smith, USN, served as Commander in Chief U.S. Naval Forces Eastern Atlantic and Mediterranean (CinCNELM), U.S. Commander Eastern Atlantic, and Commander in Chief U.S. Naval Forces Europe (CinCUSNavEur) from February 1960 to April 1963.

Captain Manson: I'm not sure that he cared all that much. [Laughter] Because he was hot. You find this amongst admirals, that when they feel really strongly about something and they think it's absolutely wrong—well, here's the admiral, Admiral Smith, in charge of Europe and the Middle East for all naval activities, you see—Morocco and everything, Holy Loch, Scotland—and yet was being told that he couldn't say anything at all about policy. It was a tragic circumstance. A most knowledgeable man. Spain, Italy, everything, and we were having real problems in Morocco at that time, for example. They were going to force us to leave there and take our Navy somewhere else.

Anyway, that's just an example of how being friends can, instead of—my daughter Joy has been high in politics and still is, and I've tried to put this point across to her, that if you will establish friendships, get to know them and don't be afraid. That's the very worst attitude you can have toward the press or the media.

The very top journalists in those days in the United States were my friends. I took a whole bunch of them out to China and Japan to investigate the disposition of surplus property in 1945. I had Bob Whitney of the *New York Times*, Bill Clark of the *Chicago Tribune*, Frank McNaugton of *Time* magazine, Leo Cullinane of the *New York Herald Tribune*, and Phil Woodyat [phonetic] of CBS. All these people top flight, and I was with them for a little over a month. That's the way I worked with him. Captain Karig had already given me—and besides, that's my attitude anyway. But he reinforced it, Captain Karig did. Anyway, so those are examples.

But going back to this 09-Dog setup, this word passed around the whole [unclear] and through the Navy League in different ways, that if you wanted to get anything done or you wanted to know something, go to 09-Dog. But this little sea power presentation, which we had in little boxes, was available to anybody who had a slide machine. This was really the gimmick, you might say. It wasn't necessarily a gimmick, because it had the full message in there.

Paul Stillwell: Did you write that, or part of it?

Captain Manson: Well, the first draft of it came out of some of the speeches that I had worked up for Admiral Carney. Then we kept changing it all the time. Captain McCain had a fellow up in Connecticut named Tom Watson, and Watson was very good with a few words, like a headline writer. He would keep revising these few words, and Captain McCain could remember those words. I remember when we were first sort of shaping it up, most of the time we went to the top, start with the top, top leaders.

But in this case, with the Veterans of Foreign Wars and the American Legion, we started at the bottom. We thought that if we could get a chapter or two to hear it and like it, maybe they would recommend to the national leaders, and then we'd get it to the top. So we went out to Midland, Michigan, one time at a chapter meeting of the American Legion, and they insulted us. They didn't want us out there, because the head of that group and his father, who was an old Navy submariner, were not getting along right then. So I told Captain McCain, "Captain, let's get in our airplane and go home. I haven't come out here to be insulted."

Captain McCain said, "Hold on, Frank. Something's going to change."

Along about 10:00 o'clock, the head of the thing came out, and he said, "If you guys have anything to say, come on in." Then that's the way we were presented to the group. But we put on such a show, he gave half of it and I gave half of it, that they stood up and applauded after we were through and said they were going to recommend that we go to national convention, which we did that same year. But it was just that one shot, and that's all it was, but it was a good clean shot and we made it.

But we kept working on that presentation all the time. This guy Watson was always—every two or three weeks he was changing the words around and changing the presentation. One of the best slides in it was about 450 Soviet submarines, and then 57 submarines. Have you seen that slide?

Paul Stillwell: No.

Captain Manson: Well, anyway, the story went like this, that Hitler began World War II with 57 submarines, and they had little black submarines up there.[*] At this point in time, the Soviets had 450, and they'd pull that red thing and people would gasp at that slide. But there were a lot of slides like that.

---

[*] Adolf Hitler was Chancellor of Germany from 1933 until his death by suicide on 30 April 1945.

Paul Stillwell: Excuse me. Let me just flip the tape.

Just to go back a little, you've got another story about the Burke era.

Captain Manson: Well, yes, because Felt was Vice Chief of Naval Operations at that time, and he decided that I needed to write some speeches for him.* He wanted four speeches, and he gave me the subjects of all those speeches. They had to do with carriers, I can guarantee, because carriers were fore and aft and alpha and the omega of his life. If there's ever a tailhook admiral, he was one.

Anyway, he told me that he wanted me to write these four speeches, and he didn't want anybody to interfere with me. By this time, I had been detached from CNO's office, and I was in this 09Dog setup. But he told Captain McCain that I had to be used for this for a while, because our line of command actually went through Vice Chief on this 09Dog.

So, anyway, he gave me a flag officer's office just across from his. His instructions to me were, "I want these four speeches, and I want them as quickly as you can get them." These were probably all he'd use for a year. He gave me, in outline, what he wanted in these speeches, but he said, "You're not to leave this office for any reason except to go to the head and to go get a sandwich. If you need to see me, you don't even need to come to my office, I'll come to see you." This was Felt telling me. But he said, "You're not to leave this office until you get these four speeches written."

"Yes, sir."

Now, I'd never had any such instructions in all my life as that, and I couldn't believe it. Yet at the same time, you never know what to expect. So I got working on the speeches, and I guess I'd written one or two and had them approved.

Oh, one thing that Malcolm Cagle had told me about Felt, "He's a tough guy to deal with, but there's one thing about it. If you're wrong with him, admit it quickly, if there's a possibility of being wrong. But if you're right, stand up to him quick," and I always remembered that. So that's the way I dealt with him and got along with him all right.

---

* Admiral Harry D. Felt, USN, served as Vice Chief of Naval Operations from 1 September 1956 to 28 July 1958. His oral history is in the Naval Institute collection.

But in this particular case, I thought these were the most unusual circumstances that I'd ever worked under. I was over there toiling away with my speeches, and in came a first-class yeoman to see me. Of course, he was not supposed to be coming in there. I was not supposed to have any guests, but he was in there anyway. He worked for Felt, and he had to tell me something. I said, "Yes, what happened?"

He said, "Well, you know the chief? Well, the admiral called him in and wanted to give him some dictation, and he told him he didn't want him to miss one [expletive deleted] word." He said, "This really did shake the chief up. He got his pencil up there, and the admiral dictated about three sentences to him and he said, 'Now read it back word for word.'"

Well, the chief couldn't read it back, he was so worried and nervous that he hadn't been able to get it down. So he just opened his mouth and nothing happened, so the admiral said, "What's wrong with you, anyway? You go out in the hallway and you get three sips of water and you get yourself back in here." So the chief went out and took three sips of water, or however many sips. I guess he took as many sips as he wanted.

He came back and got up there in the same position and the admiral said, "Now I don't want you to miss one word." I guess those are the things that really scared the chief, because he couldn't do it. So he dictated and again the chief just did a little marking and the admiral said, "Let me see your notes."

So the chief took them over there, and he'd just marked it all up with a bunch of little circles and didn't have any shorthand at all. He said, "What's wrong with you, anyway, Chief? You get out of here and get yourself together and come back in here when you can take proper dictation." So anyway, that's all there really was to it.

But the first class, though, was so amused about it that he came over to tell me. And under my condition over there where I was sort of in purgatory, I got so tickled that I slammed my head down and cut my head on the desk, laughing. It wasn't serious, so I didn't have to go to the dispensary, but if I had, I suppose I'd to have asked Admiral Felt permission, that I'd been wounded in combat.

Paul Stillwell: Verbal combat.

Captain Manson: Verbal combat, yes.

Paul Stillwell: It sounds like he had the chief just completely intimidated.

Captain Manson: He did. So then the admiral was ordered to go and take over CinCPac, and he sent word around that anybody could go with him that wanted to go.* I don't think there were any takers.

Paul Stillwell: It wasn't a very long list.

Captain Manson: It wasn't a very long list. So he called the chief in and said, "Chief, what's wrong with you? Don't you want to go out to Honolulu?"

The chief said, "No, Admiral, I don't think I want to go."

"What's wrong, Chief?"

He said, "Admiral, I'm scared of you." [Laughter] That was all there was to it. Admiral Felt couldn't imagine that they were afraid of him, but he was a pretty tough guy.

I remember one time Admiral Burke put out the word that we weren't going to go for another aircraft carrier that particular year, and Admiral Felt just plain put out the word that we were going to go for another aircraft carrier. I never could understand how they ever reconciled these two differences, one of them being number one and one number two, but that was the word we received. You can imagine what Captain McCain and I were doing; we were going for it.

[Tape interruption] ...his colleagues, he'd told people not to do it, but they were going anyway, so we did.

Paul Stillwell: What are your recollections of McCain as a guy to work for?

Captain Manson: I'd have to say that he and I had a special relationship in that we found the good humor in each one. We both had a sense of humor in working with each other,

---

* Admiral Harry D. Felt, USN, served as Commander in Chief Pacific from 31 July 1958 to 30 June 1964.

and we both enjoyed each other and working with each other. I never ever felt any compunction against telling him exactly and precisely as I saw a situation or a problem, which he really appreciated, because a lot of people were afraid of Admiral McCain because he had a gruff voice, and he could be rough, he could. But with me it was, I don't know, I can't explain it. Mrs. McCain told me that he had always been very fond of me, and I suppose it was shared. Sometimes he'd ask me to do impossible things, absolutely impossible.

Paul Stillwell: Such as?

Captain Manson: Well, one of the most impossible things that he asked me to do was to work almost seven days a week. I wouldn't have time to do my income tax or whatever personal things I had to do, because there'd be no time to do it. So that's all right, there'd be somebody else that could do that. So one day I told him, I said, "Admiral, I have just got to take care of some personal things."

"Well, what's wrong?"

I said, "For one thing, I haven't done my income tax. For another thing, my wife's got pneumonia, and the children don't have anyone to take care of them, and it's Saturday afternoon, and my grass needs cutting." I don't know, however many things I hadn't done.

He said, "Your grass needs cutting?"

I said, "Yes, it does."

He said, "I can take care of that."

I said, "Well, I don't know, and the shrubs need taken care of." I don't know, I listed him quite a few things.

Anyway, we went on working, and I didn't realize that he'd done it, but he had called his wife Roberta. He told her to get out to my house and get my grass cut. [Laughter] So when I went home along about 3:00 or 4:00 in the afternoon, boy, here were Roberta and Leroy Branch, the guy that was helping her. He worked at their house too. But Roberta and Leroy were out there, and, boy, they were making things fly. They were cutting shrubs and cutting grass. I said, "Roberta, what on earth are you doing out here?"

"Well, Jack said that you need the grass cut, and, Lord, you do, and I'm taking care of it. I got this dumb nigger here, and he's helping me."

And ol' Leroy said, "You tell him, Miss 'Cain." He called her "Miss 'Cain. Leroy was a great guy, and she could say just those words to him, and he loved her. Like one black saying that to another black, but for Mrs. McCain that was perfectly all right. But Leroy was a good worker, and they cleaned up my yard and my shrubs, everything, the two of them, in about three or four hours. That's not exactly an impossible task.

Paul Stillwell: I guess Mrs. McCain had a twin sister named Rowena, and sometimes they lived with him simultaneously.

Captain Manson: Yes, they did, and he was asked, "How do you tell them apart?"
He said, "That's their problem."

Paul Stillwell: "How do you know if you've got the right one?"

Captain Manson: That's right. "It's up to them." She was an identical twin, beautiful girls, both of them. I knew them well. But he never worried about it. I could tell them apart, of course.

Paul Stillwell: And you presumed he could. [Laughter]

Manson: Oh, I think he could, yes. He never did look too carefully, baby. They got married. They ran away, as I recall, to Mexico or somewhere when he was just barely an ensign and got married real quick like and didn't have much approval, I don't think, from anybody's parents. But they had, I thought, a good marriage. Mrs. McCain is a bright, intuitive-type woman, and she was a great asset to him in many ways. She'd question anything. He'd get her told off properly, but that didn't stop her. She'd be right back at him in two minutes.

Paul Stillwell: I take it you had a lot of enthusiasm working in that job.

Captain Manson: Oh, I did. Yes, a full head of steam all the time. We knew we were going for broke, and we knew that if we didn't get it done, it wasn't going to get done, the big picture, because there wasn't anybody else. Both of us seemed to understand that this was our job, our mission, and we simply didn't have very long.

Paul Stillwell: What do you mean by that? Why didn't you have very long?

Captain Manson: Because we knew that he would be detached and go somewhere else and I—two years is usually about all you spend in a job, so it doesn't give you very long.

Paul Stillwell: So you had the feeling it was entirely on you two?

Captain Manson: On getting the start, yes, we had the feeling that the job was not being done. We knew that people didn't know about the Navy. Well, to start with, a lot of Navy personnel assumed that somehow or another—well, like Admiral Nimitz told me one time, "Oh, well, Commander, you never should have worried about the Navy's future. The Navy's roots are too deep." He said he never worried about it when we were under stress and all that. He said he knew the public would never let the Navy sink.

I didn't feel that way at all about it, and neither did McCain. In the first place, we didn't have a constituency except maybe the shipbuilders, and they weren't very vocal. As you know, the fish don't vote, and that's where we are most of the time, out at sea. So the Army, with its bases spread in practically every community throughout the whole country, people understood what the Army was all about, what the Army did. Air Force the same way, once they started building up the Air Force. It was readily available because it was air and people could see.

But the Navy, those ships out there, what are they doing? People have a vague notion, and this was before television. They didn't know what ships do, and it was hard to get the point across. Unless you had someone at the top like FDR, Carl Vinson, or Frank Knox or somebody, then the Navy budget, the tendency was to give service a third and a third and a third or however, but not based on what is really in the national interest or what will really support national policy or foreign policy.[*]

That wasn't the way, and that still is not the way the budget is divided. Of course, now, if we go into space, they're going to have the same problem, I think, in getting space weapons and space power, as the Navy has had all these years, maybe even more so because people won't be up there and they won't know what they're doing. So they'll say, "Well, I'm not so sure I want to spend all that money on space." That's what basically was the problem.

So we knew that was the situation. So we had to devise a plan that would get, as nearly as we could, to Main Street and into the countryside with what the Navy was all about and why it was useful, why it was absolutely essential. And McCain and I understood that.

But our relationship was one in which, I suppose, we were as close as I ever was to another person in terms of communicating and disagreeing if need be. But there was, I guess, a rapport is as good a word as any. But if I was having ever any kind of a problem or if what we were doing troubled me, if I thought we were making a mistake—for example, I'll give you one. We were making movies at the same time we were making this sea power presentation. We had a fellow, Commander Marsden Perry from New York, who was our Cecil M. DeMille and he was out there at the Naval Photographic Center making all these movies.[†] He was technically under me, but for all policy purposes he was working directly for Captain McCain, because I didn't have any confidence in Marsden Perry that he knew what he was doing. I used to tell Captain McCain rather regularly that I thought that "Cecil B." was out there making footage that was of absolutely no use to anybody, most especially to us, as he was spending $250,000 or whatever it might be.

---

[*] Franklin D. Roosevelt served as President of the United States from 4 March 1933 until his death on 12 April 1945. Carl Vinson of Georgia entered the House of Representatives in 1913 and was appointed to the Naval Affairs Committee in 1917. He became the ranking Democrat in 1923 and chairman in 1931. When the Armed Services committee was formed in 1947, Vinson became chairman and held that position, except for two short periods when Republicans held the House, until his retirement from Congress in 1965. William Franklin Knox served as Secretary of the Navy from 11 July 1940 until his death on 28 April 1944.

[†] Commander Marsden J. Perry, USNR; DeMille was a famous Hollywood movie director.

"Oh, no, Frank," he would say, "he's a good moviemaker. He knows what he's doing."

I said, "In the first place, he's putting an atomic bomb in every movie he makes. He starts every war with an atomic bomb. We've had a lot of wars, and every so often we don't have a bomb, and yet he's starting everything with a bomb. So I don't think we'll be able to show these things in the first place, scare everybody out of their wits, and it'll be classified."

"Oh, no."

Well, anyway, I lost. We went ahead making the movies and he made, I think, about 12 of them, Marsden Perry movies. And we couldn't show any of them to anybody. He made some on amphibious warfare and carrier warfare and special mine problem, and all this and that. But Marsden insisted that the war had to begin with these atomic bursts. That was really one of the reasons why the movies couldn't be shown.

But there was a time when Captain McCain and I didn't agree. He didn't know for sure whether they could be used or not. But most of the footage they were using was negative footage from NPC. Still, it took time and effort.

Paul Stillwell: Was he willing to listen to other viewpoints?

Manson: Oh, yes. And sometimes these viewpoints would get almost to the point where you couldn't reconcile. Sometimes people would leave the room in such fury, I've seen that happen. McCain would chew on his necktie and his handkerchief and everything he could find to chew on to keep himself under control, and his cigar, while the verbal blasts were rocketing through the room. I've seen that happen many times. People were in violent disagreement on things, and that was all right. I mean, we'd thresh it out in two or three days.

McCain was the only officer I've ever seen in the Navy do this, but every day he would go to key officers, this was when he was a captain, and he would go like to Draper Kauffman and to Bill Martin and to Pete Aurand and to George Miller. He'd stop by, and he'd tell them what he was thinking and what he was working on. Now, it might only take him two or three minutes, but if they had time, they'd tell him what they were working on and if they didn't, they wouldn't. But yet he'd make those rounds, very important, and he did that every day.

Then maybe once a week, he'd have all of them in for a really big session, and then we'd really chew over all the things that had been discussed amongst each one, and everyone would have his own idea about it. But this was a good consensus-maker. I'd never seen anybody else do that. Nobody would take the time to do it. But McCain, yes, he'd take the time.

Paul Stillwell: How would you assess him in terms of intellectual stature?

Manson: No, I wouldn't call McCain—he used to surprise me in this regard, though. At times I would sort of evaluate him as, well, average maybe in intellectual attainment and depth as amongst other people of his—but then, sometimes he would really fool me, because he would probe the depths of something quickly. It might be nuclear power, it might be missiles, it might be a type of ammunition, it might be some kind of a mathematical equation or something.

But, yes, I have seen him when he would just dart into something and just amaze me with his intellectual depth. But a lot of times you'd think he didn't have really a lot of depth, and I'm sure a lot of people think that. But, particularly in terms of where he was talking public policy or attitudes, he tried to always stick within his frame of reference or stuff that he was very familiar with. He rarely broke new ground.

So he wasn't the kind of a person or the kind of an intellect that you can range off into sort of new horizons. He might not find that very interesting. Unless it was something that you could see, feel, and touch, he might not take too much interest in it. But he sure knew the world of reality.

Paul Stillwell: I've gathered his greatest gift was energy.

Captain Manson: He had a strong, dynamic energy, personality and energy, and he was very engaging. People liked that about him. Senators liked it. Well, his son now is a senator, but he was much more dynamic than his son, many more times.[*] Oh, people like Dirksen and Goldwater who were some of the stallions of those days. Let's see, Dirksen, Goldwater, John Stennis—[†]

Paul Stillwell: Richard Russell.

Captain Manson: Richard Russell.[‡] These were all men that understood McCain well, and he understood them, and they loved him. They'd come to his house for dinner. You've got a lot of people in Washington that invite senators to dinner and they don't go. But when McCain asked them over, they came.

Paul Stillwell: Was he a witty, humorous man?

Captain Manson: Well, yes, he was. He could pull out of you, if you were in sort of a dour mood. For example, I might be looking fairly gloomy, and the first thing he'd say to me is "Frank, what are you so happy about?" That was his first comment. And if he would ask me something and I would be pondering it, then he'd say, "Well, what have you got, the vapors?" [Chuckles] If I wasn't commenting on something quickly enough, he'd tell me or tell others that, "Frank Manson's in his foxhole, he's not talking, he's not doing anything."

George Miller was telling me this the other day, that one time he was speaking to McCain on the phone about something or other and he said, "What's Frank doing?"

"Oh, Frank, he's in his foxhole. He's not saying anything about this," whatever it was.

---

[*] John S. McCain III, a Republican from Arizona, has served in the Senate since 3 January 1987. He ran unsuccessfully for President in 2008.
[†] Everett M. Dirksen, a Republican from Illinois, served in the Senate from 3 January 1951 until his death on 7 September 1969. Barry M. Goldwater, a Republican from Arizona, served in the Senate from 3 January 1953 to 3 January 1965 and from 3 January 1969 to 3 January 1987. John C. Stennis (1901-1995) was a Democrat from Mississippi. He was in the U.S. Senate from 1947 to 1989, including service as chairman of the Armed Services Committee.
[‡] Richard B. Russell Jr., a Democrat from Georgia, served in the Senate from 12 January 1933 until his death on 21 January 1971.

I didn't stay in my foxhole very often, but a lot of times I'd stay in there until I found out for sure what I wanted to do and what I thought was prudent and what I thought was attainable. And, of course, he, too, was that way. He didn't like to get cross-threaded with people like the Chief of Naval Personnel.

I remember one time we had a report in our office, it was very critical of Chief of Naval Personnel Holloway, and McCain didn't know what to do with that report, so he'd just keep putting it down to the bottom of the basket.* I'd see him over there by the window sometimes pulling his tie and chewing on it, and I'd say, "What's wrong, Captain?"

"Aw, it's this damn thing with Holloway."

I'd say, "What?"

"Oh, this report."

"Well, are you going to tell him about it?"

"I don't know whether I will or not." And then he'd probably let it sit for six months or something, and maybe we'd take care of it some other way.

But he didn't like to cross swords with a senior admiral, unless it was on sea power. Then he wouldn't hesitate to cross swords with anybody. But if he was going to have to tell the Chief of Naval Personnel that he wasn't running the personnel thing correctly, he tried to find a way to do that that would not offend the Chief of Naval Personnel, and that's pretty hard to do, but usually he could.

But yes, he's witty.† He had a lot of old salty sayings about his teeth were marlinspikes and stuff like that. He'd go around coming off with some of his little ditties at times, sea ditties, and sing a little tune.

Paul Stillwell: Sounds like a fun person to be around.

Captain Manson: Oh, sure. And here's the type of thing you could do with him. We were on a plane one time going to New York, and we had a special Secretary of the Navy's plane. We were going up to make a special pitch to a Navy League group,

---

* Vice Admiral James L. Holloway, Jr., USN, served as Chief of the Bureau of Naval Personnel from 2 February 1953 to 31 January 1958. His oral history is in the Columbia University collection.
† McCain, by then a four-star admiral, died 22 March 1981.

stockbrokers, and people like that in New York. We got about halfway up there, and I decided it'd be fun to send a message from the Secretary of the Navy telling him that he wanted his plane and to cancel his trip and come on back.

So I went to the radioman and got the message all written up. It said, "SecNav requests you cancel trip and return to Washington immediately," or words to that effect.

So I brought it out of the radio shack and showed it to McCain, "Oh, I don't believe that."

I said, "Well, read it. Man, there it is. He's telling us to turn this thing around right now. He wants us back. Well, you going to turn the plane around?"

"No. I'm not doing it." [Laughter] Of course, I'm sure he suspected that it was a joke anyway, but whatever it was, he was going to go ahead and do what we were set to do.

Paul Stillwell: Did you have a chance to observe Secretary Gates during that period?

Captain Manson: To some extent. I liked Secretary Gates, and he was there at that time.[*] But I remember one time that Captain McCain and I were trying to get him to entertain a group of top bankers and people in industry, and he wasn't inclined to do it. He was giving us a little speech on how everything was going real well and that he thought things were in pretty good shape, and he wasn't inclined to do this.

I said to him, "Yes, Mr. Secretary, everything is going just fine. What ain't we got? We ain't got ships." I'll never forget the look on Mr. Gates's face as he looked at me. He never said a word and neither did McCain. All I said was, "What ain't we got? We ain't got ships." But I forget now whether he went ahead with that luncheon or not. I'm inclined to believe he did. But that could have got me thrown out of the office.

But I knew him and liked him. He was an old Navy type. He'd been an intelligence officer, I believe. He wasn't anything like John Lehman, for example.[†] For Secretaries, though, of that time frame, I would list him pretty high. Certainly his heart was in the right place.

---

[*] Thomas S. Gates Jr., served as Secretary of the Navy from 1 April 1957 to 7 June 1959.
[†] John F. Lehman Jr., served as Secretary of the Navy from 5 February 1981 to 10 April 1987. He was a Naval Reserve officer.

Paul Stillwell: Not only that, but Secretary Gates seemed to have an understanding of the Navy that went beyond that that some just politicians brought to the job.

Captain Manson: He did. He did. He did have an understanding and a belief. He had confidence in the admirals, and that helps, to have a man to have that depth of understanding. I don't remember any specific stories except the one I told you, except that I did see him rather often and found him to be a person that the Navy counted on, depended on, and we weren't afraid to ask him anything. As you could see, we would go right in there and spill the beans. But as far as Navy Secretaries go, I think that's been one of the problems with the Navy is that over the years, starting back in 1940, well, after Forrestal, that we had too few secretaries who would make the political stance that was necessary and talk forcefully enough, like say Symington did for the Air Force or somebody else.* They were not powerful enough, persuasive enough. They didn't carry the political load.

That's my feeling, and it required too frequently the Chief of Naval Operations to bear the burden, and that's where my slot was, and that's why I was always hoping and looking to the Secretary. That's just a general comment. There were exceptional times when sometimes they would. Matthews wasn't very strong as a Secretary of the Navy.† As he got knowledge, he became stronger, and usually they did. Franke was a person that didn't know a lot about the Navy.‡ My recollection is that he was an accountant or something with J. C. Penney or one of those stores.

Paul Stillwell: He was more of a financial type.

Manson: He was a financial type and was good when it came to taking a close look at budget items. But as far as understanding the Navy, no, he didn't have much of an understanding of how sea power is really utilized. I don't recall right offhand all the

---

* James V. Forrestal served as Secretary of the Navy from 19 May 1944 to 17 September 1947.
W. Stuart Symington was first Secretary of the Air Force, holding office from 18 September 1947 to 24 April 1950. A Democrat, he later served as a U.S. Senator from 3 January 1953 until his resignation 27 December 1976.
† Francis P. Matthews served as Secretary of the Navy from 25 May 1949 to 30 July 1951.
‡ William B. Franke served as Secretary of the Navy from 8 June 1959 to 20 January 1961.

different personalities, Navy types, secretaries. But generally, in any case, I didn't have an awful lot to do with—I was always on the CNO side of the aisle. I always thought the politicians weren't doing enough, you know.

Paul Stillwell: Anything else to mention about that job in OP-09Dog?

Captain Manson: Well, that job created such a sort of a tailwind or a wake or whatever that four or five officers made admiral right out of it—McCain, Hank Miller, and those who followed. There were three or four of them that came right in behind. We had such a momentum, "big mo," as you call it, that it was effective for a number of years.

The Navy may still have it. I don't know if they do or not. I checked in maybe ten years ago when they still had it, but much smaller. It was back down to where it was about when we started with it. They were still doing a little bit, not much. You know how things are, it switches around until you can find somebody who'll do a job, and then wherever he is, he does it. That's generally the way things work. It doesn't matter so much where they fit in the organizational chart, but it's whether they have the competence and the knowledge and the will to do it. So that switches around and moves. I often thought that it didn't matter where your desk was in Washington, you'll be doing the same thing anyway, pretty much so.

Paul Stillwell: I wonder if you had a feeling of letdown personally to leave there after two high-powered jobs in the CNO'S office and then working for Captain McCain. Was it anticlimactic to leave from there?

Captain Manson: Well, it was. I went to the Naval War College, and I really looked at it more or less as a year of rest. Sure enough, right in the middle of a lecture, I did pass out up there. They took me to the hospital and found out it was stress that had caused my passing out.

So it was a tremendous change, though, from full-court press to no press at all. All you did was sit back and listen to these lectures and study all these books and charts and diagrams and everything that you go through up there. But I found the war college to be very stimulating because it was wide open. You were absolutely free to explore any concepts or ideas that you might have in your mind.

That's when I went off in this idea of building ships that were to be used for constructive purposes and to use this as an edge of sea power, a cutting edge of it, during a Cold War period or during a period of relative peace that you could still use these platforms, these Navy platforms, and support the foreign policy, implement the foreign policy, and defeat the Soviet Union in a way that in those days they couldn't even compete with us at all.

I was perfectly free up there in the Naval War College atmosphere to explore this. I think that's why Senator Humphrey asked me to do that when I went to the war college, to explore this further. I'd already discussed it with him before going to the war college.

Paul Stillwell: It would be helpful if you could explain that in more detail, just what you had in mind for ships to do.

Captain Manson: Yes. The idea there was that you would take ships that—some of them wouldn't even have to be converted for electric power, for example. I had known of us using a destroyer escort in Pyongyang during the Korean War to light up a good portion of the city. And I've known of other cities where we would move a ship in during an earthquake or something. I'd known of many cases where units of the fleet had been brought in, in urgent situations. Even during World War II, after we'd gone in and wiped out entire little communities like in Guam and different places, we'd send in a Seabee construction battalion, and in a week or two weeks or a month maybe, they'd have a better place there than they had before we tore it all down.*

So I knew that we had a tremendous potential, competence there, for constructive work. So I sort of thought, why wouldn't it be a good idea for us to take ships and load them, with the idea of finding out some of the critical situations, and designing a fleet or at least portions of a ship to cope with those particular conditions—roads, for example, bridges, water. Most everywhere in the world there's a water problem; people just don't

---

* Seabees is the nickname applied to members of the Navy's mobile construction battalions (CBs).

have enough water. So wells, small dams, pumps, generators for electric power, various kinds of plows, fertilizers, seeds, various kinds of health care.

Well, actually, the way the world looked to me like when I was up there at the war college, the way it shaped up, it was sort of like the United States was not all that many years ago when these county agents, they called them, in Oklahoma, anyway, and probably in Missouri, as well, but anyway these county agents had a bag of answers to farmers' problems, everything from trimming fruit trees to getting cut worms to leave the tomatoes alone.

So I thought, well, why would it not be a good idea to systematize the science of constructive effort just as we've systematized the science of destruction? We work the full spectrum of it. So then I set out to find out as many things as I could about what sort of problems existed when I was at the war college and how we might tackle those various problems with the various types of ships and so forth.

Paul Stillwell: So you were sketching a humanitarian role for part of the Navy?

Captain Manson: Exactly, exactly. A humanitarian role that I thought was an area that we could compete favorably with, with the Soviet Union. I thought it would be a way to win the Cold War, for sure.

Paul Stillwell: Were you in any way influenced by the book *The Ugly American*, which came out about then?[*]

Captain Manson: Yes, I was. I knew Bill Lederer very well, had known Bill many years.
Paul Stillwell: He was a Navy public affairs type.

Captain Manson: Yes. I'll never forget one time Bill Lederer came to me when he was starting to write. It was lunch period, and he was eating yogurt. He said, "Frank, c-c-c-c-c-can you help me [he stuttered a lot, you know] on-on th-th-th-this damn story?" He'd

---

[*] William J. Lederer and Eugene Burdick, *The Ugly American* (New York: Norton, 1958). Lederer was a regular Navy line officer until shortly after World War II, when he converted to the public information role. He retired from active duty on 1 November 1958.

taken every sentence and cut it into a little strip, and I'll bet you he had 200 strips. He said, "C-c-c-can you put this thing together for me?"

I laughed, I said, "Bill, there's no way that anybody can ever put this thing together. Why did you cut it up?"

He said, "Well, it wasn't tracking right." So he cut the whole thing, had a whole handful. Well, that's Bill Lederer. Yes, but his book was a good one, *The Ugly American*. Of course, he was all in favor of this fleet too. He came over to see me in London to talk to me about it, after the idea had been in *Life* magazine.[*]

Paul Stillwell: Let's explore the *Life* magazine thing farther. How did that develop?

Captain Manson: Well, I did a thesis on this idea. When you get there at the war college, you do a short one the first semester. Then the second semester you do another one, and it's got to be a real thorough job with all your footnotes and all that. They want to see whether or not you've made any progress since you've been up there.

Well, anyway, so I did both of them on it. My first one was more or less a philosophical approach to this thing, in pretty much the terms that you and I have talked. Then my second term paper, I went into different types of ships and so forth. So when I was finished with it, I brought it down to Washington, and I showed it to Senator Humphrey and Congressman Ed Edmondson.[†] Both of them were Democrats, and they said that they wanted to introduce resolutions in the Congress to get such a fleet into being. I said I thought it would be a mistake if we didn't have Republicans. If we just came into it with one party, I said, "This will never work."

They said, "Well, all right." So Humphrey said that he'd like to select his own Republicans. I said it made no difference to me, so he selected Senator George Aiken of Vermont.[‡]

---

[*] On 27 July 1959 *Life* magazine published a cover story on Manson's proposed "A New Kind of Great White Fleet," which would use Navy ships for humanitarian purposes.
[†] Edmond E. Edmondson, a Democrat from Oklahoma, served in the House of Representatives from 3 January 1953 to 3 January 1973.
[‡] George D. Aiken, a Republican from Vermont, served in the Senate from 10 January 1941 to 3 January 1975.

I kind of wanted Ed Edmondson to select Bob Wilson from California, whom I knew quite well, and he'd wanted me to be Nixon's speechwriter at one point.* So I wanted Bob, and Ed said, no, he liked Bob a lot, but he could work better will Bill Bates of Massachusetts, who was also a Naval Reserve type.†

Paul Stillwell: He had been an active duty officer.

Captain Manson: That's right. And he said, "Bill will understand this 100%, he'll be for it." Ed was really inspired. Ed was a Naval Reserve type, too, and an old friend of mine. He and I had been friends back in college and all that, high school, even. Anyway, they said they'd get a bipartisan resolution up in the House and the Senate. I said, "Well, that ought to do something."

Paul Stillwell: Did they run this through the front office of OpNav before they went to put this in Congress?

Captain Manson: No. I didn't even know exactly when they were going to do their resolution or anything else. I don't think they had a copy of my paper. Maybe they did, I don't remember. Certainly they had some memos from me, and they may have had a copy of it. I don't know for sure. But, anyway, they were going to get those resolutions drawn up.

So then I was going back through New York, and I thought I'd like to call on my old friend Jim Shepley, whom I used to visit frequently when he was head of *Time* magazine in Washington.‡ He and I were old friends, and he used to call me a "battleship admiral." I called him sort of an airhead Air Force type. He and I used to argue good-naturedly about those sorts of things.

---

* Robert C. Wilson, a Republican from California, served in the House of Representatives from 3 January 1953 to 3 January 1981.
† William H. Bates, a Republican from Massachusetts, served in the House of Representatives from 14 February 1950 until his death on 22 June 1969. He served on active duty in the Navy from 1940 until 1950, when he left as a lieutenant commander to run for Congress. He was a Supply Corps officer. The nuclear attack submarine *William H. Bates* (SSN-680) was named in his honor.
‡ James R. Shepley was head of *Time*'s Washington bureau from 1948 to 1957 and later moved to the New York office.

Anyway, I went over. He and I were good friends. I went over to see him, and he wanted to know how I was wasting my time. I told him I was at the war college. He didn't even know that. Then what am I doing up there besides being at the war college, and I told him I'd been working on this idea, as I've described to you. I told him I was working on a fleet like this. He said, "Frank, that's the greatest idea that I've heard in I can't remember when. I don't know if I've ever heard of a better idea. Is there anything written on this?"

I said, "Oh, sure."

He said, "What or where?"

I said, "Well, I just happen to have my thesis over at my hotel room here in New York."

He said, "Would you get a taxi and go over there and get it?"

I said, "Yeah, sure."

So I got a taxi and went over and made a copy of it and gave it to him. He said, "I'll tell you this, Frank. I can tell you that *Life* magazine and *Time* and this whole organization, I can tell you they're interested in this idea. Now, what will be the result, I have no idea." He said he was pretty sure that Luce is going to take an interest in it.[*] He added, "I just know that all of us are going to be real keen on it."

I said, "Well, okay." And that was all there was to it.

I was getting ready to go to London to take up my duties over there as information officer, and on my way back through New York to get my family aboard the ship, I stopped off up there to see what they were doing. They said they were going to run the thing in *Life* magazine. They wanted me to meet with the fellow who was in charge of, I guess, cover stories. They were going to do it in a big way and wanted me to discuss further ideas for art and this and that. They had decided that instead of putting my thesis in there, they wanted me to write another story on how I got the idea for it. I thought, "Well, boy, with this kind of thing brewing, I'd better get down to Washington and tell Admiral Burke and Chief of Information what's going on."

---

[*] Henry R. Luce was a co-founder of *Time* magazine in 1923 and served as publisher until his death in 1967.

I got down there, and I was just going to be there a half a day, I guess, because we were ready to leave. Ray Peet, I believe it was, was in that outer office there, the appointments office. I told him I had an idea that I'd like to talk over with Admiral Burke. I'd already talked to Admiral Burke about it once before anyway. I was wanted to get some hospital ships commissioned to go out in Southeast Asia just strictly for medical purposes, and Burke thought this would be okay if I could get Theda Combs, who was OP-03, to agree with it.[*] He said, "Now, Frank, you'd have to take a couple of cruisers out, you know that."

I said, "Admiral, I'm not going to ever recommend we take two cruisers out."

He said, "Well, you're not going to get the money."

I said, "This is a different job we're going to do. We will get the money."

He said, "No, they'll take it out of our hide." This is Burke talking.

I thought I'd better go in and explain to him that I had written on this up at the war college. Ray couldn't get me in; the admiral's morning was just impossible. So I went down there, and I said, "Well, I'll go down and talk to Kirkpatrick," who was Chief of Information, "and he can tell Admiral Burke and then I'll get on with my journey." So I went down to see Kirkpatrick, and he was sick. I don't know what was wrong with him, but I did talk to him on the phone. He said, "Frank, unless it's just absolutely urgent, I'd prefer that we just talk about it sometime later."

I said, "Well, that's okay with me. It's something, though, that's going to pop." I told him, in essence, that it was something that I had been working on at the war college, and he, in essence, said, "Oh, well, anything you're working on is okay with me," and away we went. But Kirkpatrick had no idea what in the world was going to happen. Nor did I at that point, really. I just knew they were going to do something with it in a pretty big way.

The *Life* people told me to start thinking about how the idea evolved because that's what they wanted to run, was my personal story in the magazine, but I had no idea how they were going to do it.

---

[*] Vice Admiral Thomas S. Combs, USN, acquired the nickname Theda when he was a midshipman, and it stuck. He got coal dust in his eyebrows, leading one of his fellow midshipmen to observe that it made him look a bit like silent movie star Theda Bara.

On the ship going over there to England, I got real good and seasick. It was one of these old converted transports or something that rocked and rolled, and we were in a storm, and I didn't feel like working on the thing on the ship. Got to London and I was trying to figure out where we were going to live and all that. The next thing I knew, the head of the *Life* magazine in London, Dick Pollard, was calling me and saying he had a wire from New York, and I was supposed to have a story on how I got this idea of this fleet. I was supposed to have it to them, and they were ready to run. They were waiting on a cover story, and I was holding the whole thing up, and when was I going to get it to New York?

So I said, "Well, I guess I'd better write it." So I sat down over in London at a typewriter, and in one night I drafted the thing and got it off to them, I guess the next day. Then I got a call in London from Jim Shepley in New York. He told me they were going to feature this thing. They wanted to get my picture, and he hoped I had no objection.

I said, "No, I don't care. Are you clearing it with the Navy?"

"Oh, we're in touch with the Navy."

I said, "Well, that's fine, but you'd better put a disclaimer on that thing that it doesn't reflect the thinking of the Navy Department."

"Oh, we'll take care of that; don't worry about that."

So, anyway, they did feature it.* Meanwhile, they'd been down there in the Congress and they'd been going to Humphrey and Aiken and Edmondson and Bates and all those people, and they had people all lined up and took their pictures. They just really did create a minor firestorm in the United States. The TV people wanted me to come back to be on TV in America and this and that, and the Navy wouldn't let me do it. Admiral Kirkpatrick was just upset, and Admiral Burke was upset in a way, and in a way he wasn't. But I heard that he told some people privately that I was entitled to have a few of my own ideas. So he didn't think it was all that bad. But, meanwhile, he had everybody in the Navy rushing around to prove the Navy had sort of been doing this anyway—any kind of goodwill mission or any kind helping in earthquakes and things of that nature, to get that all, "Pump it out, man, quick, quick, otherwise we're going to be

---

* Manson's idea was a cover story on the 27 July 1959 issue of *Life* magazine, pages 17-25, with the title of "Peace Plan for the U.S.: a New Great White Fleet." In the midst of the article was a sidebar, pages 20-21, titled "Author of the Big Plan Explains," and a photo of Manson in uniform.

overrun with this thing. We're going to have these ships all over the ocean and no Navy." And we were getting the dispatches in from the Middle East saying that was the kind of a fleet they wanted to send to the Middle East. Really, it was creating quite a stir.

Eisenhower was asked what he thought about it at a press conference, and he said that he tended to be suspicious of ideas of this nature that came from U.S. citizens, that he'd prefer to have them come from other nations, ways and means of helping other nations. So he was suspicious of it. So that was really a backhanded way of saying he didn't like it. But Pete Aurand, who was on his staff, came over to see me with Ike and said, "Frank, if you can get Burke to understand that the budget would not be in competition with the Navy budget, and that all the appropriations would be something apart, and if the senator and everybody would get this across to this Navy, you'd have clear sailing." I said, well, I would try to do that.

But these lines got all crossed up back in Washington, and JAG was asked to write a letter saying that such a plan as this would not add appreciably to the emergency capability that already existed in the Navy for earthquakes and floods and things of that nature, and that the Navy was never meant to be in technical aid, not prepared for it, shouldn't be doing it, and that this is the kind of thing that ought to properly be done by the Department of State and AID.[*] That was the kind of letter that went to Congress.

So there had been a special white-fleet committee by this time organized on the Hill under the Armed Service Committee. I don't think it ever should have been under the Armed Services Committee anyway. It should have been under the Foreign Affairs Committee and the Foreign Relations Committee, but they never held hearings. The chairman of that committee was a fellow named Fisher, and he told me personally that he was going to hold hearings, but he never did.[†] I suppose what really happened was that the Navy, I'm sure this is true, was running around with burlap bags and stamping out the fires as fast as they came up.

---

[*] JAG – Judge Advocate General; AID – Agency for International Development.
[†] Ovie C. Fisher, a Democrat from Texas, served in the House of Representatives from 3 January 1943 to 31 December 1974.

Admiral Dennison was my boss over in London when I reported and this thing came out.* He was so proud of it, he sent out and bought at least a dozen, maybe two dozen, magazines and every time anybody came to see him he just handed them a magazine. He said, "That's my new chief of information over here." He was proud of it, Dennison was.

Paul Stillwell: What ultimately came of the whole initiative?

Captain Manson: It never really did take off. We formed up a group in Europe and another group in Britain with industrialists and people like that. It came within an eyelash of taking off.

Paul Stillwell: Was your plan in any way linked up with the Project Hope hospital ship?†

Captain Manson: Yes, it was in a sense. I'd been working on this thing about a year when Walsh and some others got the idea for just a hospital ship.‡ So by the time my second paper was written at the Naval War College, I had mentioned that *Hope*—I think I'd mentioned that there'd been something in *The New York Times* about maybe trying to get a hospital ship named *Hope* to do the medical side, or part of the medical side of this idea. It's about all I knew about it.

Anyway, when the thing appeared in *The New York Times*, I had a call from Dr. George Hyatt, an orthopedic surgeon and an aide to Burke and Radford on the medical side, wanting to know if this was the start of the fleet.§ Also Mitchell Parizo, the one I was telling you about, he called me that day, and I said, "No. As far as I know, this is an entirely new approach, another project, and I don't know anything about it."

---

* Admiral Robert L. Dennison, Jr., USN, served as Commander in Chief U.S. Naval Forces Eastern Atlantic and Mediterranean (CinCNELM) and USComEastLant from March 1959 to February 1960.
† Project HOPE (Health Opportunities for People Everywhere) was founded in the United States in 1958. Included in its operation was SS *HOPE*, a civilian hospital ship that had previously been the USS *Consolation* (AH-15).
‡ Dr. William B. Walsh was a physician who served on board a destroyer in World War II and had seen poor medical conditions in various countries. In 1958 he persuaded President Eisenhower to donate a hospital ship to Project Hope.
§ Captain George W. Hyatt, Medical Corps, USN.

But when *Life* started doing the whole thing, they went to Dr. Walsh and asked him what he was doing, and they put a picture of the hospital ship in the article. This helped him a lot, helped him $2 million worth, because I understand there was about $2 million came in based on that *Life* article.

Paul Stillwell: That's a pretty good success in your mass-persuasion campaign.

Captain Manson: Yes, in a way, it didn't turn out too badly. Just little things, if I hadn't made mistakes along the way, there would have been fleet all over the ocean. But on the Europe side, the meeting was over in Brussels, I had Paul-Henri Spaak supporting it and that whole NATO bunch were in favor of it.[*] I was at a cabinet meeting, and that night we had a meeting of White Fleet Europe, and they got into a big argument, saying that they would have to go to the white fleet committee to get approval for checks over $200.00.

So I sided in with a doctor who said, "Yes, they probably ought to get it approved for that," and that was the wrong thing to do. It killed it. Because they weren't about to. I don't know what those people were going to do with this fleet, by the way. They might have been going to open those copper mines in the Congo, for all I know.

Paul Stillwell: Where were the ships to come from for this white fleet?

Captain Manson: They were supposed to be brought out of surplus.

Paul Stillwell: Mothballs?

Captain Manson: Yes.

Paul Stillwell: What kinds of ships did you envision?

---

[*] Paul-Henri Spaak was Secretary General of the North Atlantic Treaty Organization from 1957 to 1961.

Captain Manson: LSTs, transports, even jeep carriers would be useful—those built on merchant hulls. Just about any kind of a ship where you could have a lot of deck space and move farm machinery, earth-moving gear, clinics, Seabee-type stuff. You can put that on almost any—well, you really can't do it on a destroyer. But it's like Bill Bates said to me one time when he and I were talking, "You know, Frank, we'd probably have to send the fleet in, if we ever get one of these ships going, some of these places. We'll have to send in some destroyers to protect them while they're in there." Entirely possible, just might work out that way. He said, "I think it probably will, but still be a good thing." By the way, Bill Bates was some tremendous intellect. I loved him, a great guy. You know he had an early death.

Paul Stillwell: Died of cancer, yes. He had gotten into Congress because his father died in an airplane crash.

Captain Manson: Yes. But he was sure a strong supporter of this idea, as were a lot of others.

Paul Stillwell: I think you had a lot more impact with your war college thesis than most of your line officer contemporaries.

Captain Manson: Yes. I'm told that they used to hold that magazine up for a few classes after that, spread it around, and say, "We don't expect all of you to be on the cover of *Life* magazine, but if can just do half as well, you will do well."

Paul Stillwell: Was the was college curriculum in any way set up for a restricted line officer to participate?[*]

Captain Manson: Yes, it was. But because of my experience in the Navy's high command as a speechwriter and policy writer, I was not unfamiliar with the things, and

---

[*] A restricted line officer is usually someone in a particular specialty so that the individual is not eligible for command at sea.

writing the history of *Battle Report* and all that, they didn't have anything up there that was strange to me. So they fit me in wherever they wanted to. It didn't matter whether we had a war going on in the Middle East or wherever it was, they just gave me any sort of a job, and that's what I did.

Paul Stillwell: On this war in the Middle East, are you talking about a war game scenario?

Captain Manson: War game scenario. In one war game I remember, I was in charge of land transport in the Middle East. I forget exactly the scenario, but that's what my job was, to handle land transport. It didn't make any difference. They never gave me any special treatment or said, "No, you don't know anything about this. We're not going to let you worry about this." They'd just sock it to me.

Paul Stillwell: Well, of course you'd been a line officer in World War II.

Captain Manson: That's right, so that helped a lot. But my entire exposure had been to fleet operations, so there wasn't anything much different about it. We were talking, thinking different concepts for war situations.

But where the war college helped me a lot was in studying national interest from other viewpoints and other nations, regional conflicts, adversarial situations, and we had the good intelligence to go on where possible conflict could come and our analysis of that.

This was a very useful thing for me. I think it opened avenues and vistas for me that I hadn't seen. I just think the war college was a marvelous opportunity for me to open some horizons for myself which I never had had time for.

Paul Stillwell: Do you think that benefited you in your later career?

Captain Manson: Oh, yes, I sure do. When I went to Europe, I had a much better understanding of how the nations fit into an overall plan, particularly when I got with

Allied Command Atlantic. Dick Colbert and I were able to work hand-in-glove on Standing Naval Force Atlantic and Iberian Command Atlantic.* We organized both of those, the two of us. There's an officer I really admired. He's another fellow I got on with, just like I did with McCain.

Paul Stillwell: What qualities in Colbert did you admire?

Captain Manson: Now, Colbert had a lot of intellectual strength, and very imaginative, creative, constructive, original. By the way on this white fleet, he called me over when he was with Rostow, I guess it was, over in policy planning in the State Department.† He called me over there one day and asked me if I would agree to allow, or permit, this fleet to operate under the aegis of CIA. I told him I thought perhaps it would prove self-defeating. It would certainly be found out sooner or later, and then the whole idea just might go down the chute. Of course, I was very hopeful of the whole thing coming, at that point. In hindsight, I've wished a million times I'd have said, "Go ahead with it."

Paul Stillwell: Whatever it takes.

Manson: Whatever it takes, let CIA run it. But Dick Colbert is the guy who called me over and said, "If you'd agree to it, I think we might try it in certain parts of the world." I told him I thought it would be contradictory to the general idea of the thing. But Dick Colbert, from that point on, really, he and I were always exchanging ideas.

Paul Stillwell: Is there any more to discuss on your war college time? Was it a chance to recharge your batteries after that Washington tour?

Captain Manson: Yes, very much so. That I appreciated more than anything else, that it gave it a chance to be with my family, to reflect on things that were important and things

---

* Standing Naval Force Atlantic, a multi-national group of ships that operated together under the auspices of NATO. Rear Admiral Richard G. Colbert, USN, initiated the concept paper on the subject in November 1966. NATO approved the concept, and the force of ships was activated in January 1968.
† Eugene V. Rostow served from 1966 to 1969 as Under Secretary of State for Political Affairs.

that weren't, and to look back over those years and to see the things that were worth continuing to emphasize and things to drop, but more or less to get your life in a better balance. That the war college did. Plus as I say, it opened up new avenues.

Another thing, too, it had a lot of officers up there that were really outstanding, bright people and from a lot of different—and we used to have a chance to exchange views with each other. If we had professors who were a little bit to the left, we'd get on their case right away. Of course, Commodore Bates was up there, and Admiral Eccles, and I used to get to see them a lot.[*]

Paul Stillwell: Both of them were institutions.

Captain Manson: Yes, they were institutions. They'd come to see me a lot, and I'd go visit them. Eccles was the greatest logistician. Bates was a very bright officer, too, although he at one time told me he thought I was trying to white-feather him back in the *Battle Report* I had written, that he thought that going into Lingayen Gulf was going to be suicide for our ships.[†] I wrote that in the *Battle Report* series, and then Bates was talking with one of his buddies down in OP-06, and said, "What's everybody trying to do, white-feather you?"[‡]

So, boy, he was yelling down the hallway one day and came out there. I walked in the E-ring to see what he was yelling about. He said, "What are you trying to do, white-feather me?"

I said, "Well, Commodore, what did I do, put something in there you didn't say?"

"Well, I mean you're writing in there that it's going to be plain suicide if we take the ships into Lingayen Gulf with all those mines in there. You put that in the book."

I said, "Sure I did. That's what you said."

---

[*] Commodore Richard W. Bates, USN, directed a number of analytical studies of World War II combat actions while on the staff of the Naval War College in the late 1940s. When he retired in 1949, he received a tombstone promotion to rear admiral on the basis of his wartime service. He then continued his studies following retirement. Upon retirement from active duty in 1952, Rear Admiral Henry E. Eccles, USN, began a 25-year second career as head of the logistics department of the Naval War College; he was a prolific author.
[†] Captain Bates served as chief of staff to Vice Admiral Jesse B. Oldendorf, USN, who was Commander Task Group 77.2, the Bombardment and Fire Support Group for the invasion of Lingayen Gulf on the island of Luzon in January 1945.
[‡] A white feather is a symbol of cowardice.

"Well," he said, "I wasn't afraid."

I said, "Well, I didn't say you were. I'll tell you one thing, Commodore, if you're unhappy, on the second printing we'll take all this out."

"Oh, you don't need to do that." That was the end of it.

Paul Stillwell: Just letting off some steam. We're getting right near the end of the tape. I think this would probably be a convenient breaking point unless there's anything else to talk about from that war college period.

Captain Manson: I won an essay contest up there, "Winning Friends for Freedom." It was for all the Navy, I don't know who all, but everybody could participate. They sent to the BuPers when I won this cash award and a big medal this big around, about five inches or six in diameter, and said to present that to me at the War College, and Admiral Ingersoll wouldn't do it.* He said that it was a civilian award, and it would have to be presented to me in private. If it were a Navy award, it would be presented to me before the whole war college, but since it was that civilian award, it couldn't be done that way. So he asked Captain Moorer to present it to me. So he took me down to a room where there was nobody, and said it was his pleasure as a result of award, through the Chief of Naval Personnel, he gave me this award. No pictures, no nothing.

So there were some Marine Corps types up there, including Stud Stallings, who got so angry when I was telling them about this, that they stormed the president's office and told him what a disgrace it was for him to have that kind an award given to one of the students and them not to even be proud enough to show it in front of the entire student body. But Ingersoll didn't care; he'd seen Marines before.

That's enough. If I think of anything else on that, I can pick it up next time.

Paul Stillwell: Sure. Thank you very much.

Captain Manson: Okay.

---

* Vice Admiral Stuart H. Ingersoll, USN, served as president of the Naval War College from 13 August 1957 to 30 June 1960.

Interview Number 4 with Captain Frank Manson, U.S. Navy (Retired)
Place: U.S. Naval Institute, Annapolis, Maryland
Date: Wednesday, 13 April 1988
Interviewer: Paul Stillwell

Captain Manson: After World War II Jim Lucas was interested in writing on naval subjects. He'd been critical, in some of his articles, of Admiral Gallery, severely critical.* So one day I told Jim, who was a friend of mine from Chekota, Oklahoma, "Jim, you know, it's a shame that you're writing these things about Admiral Gallery and his guided missile program."† I said, "He's first class, he's a good man. He's a bright person, one of the brightest we have in the Navy, and here you are, you're writing all these bad things about him."

He said, "Well, I'd be willing to talk to him."

I said, "Well, I don't know whether he'll talk to you or not, but I'll check."

So I went to Admiral Gallery and told him that I thought maybe it would be good for both of them to visit with each other, that I knew both of them, and I had a high regard for both of them.

I remember Admiral Gallery's hands started shaking, and he got very nervous. He said, no, he didn't want to.

I said, "Well, just give it a shot. It can't get any worse than it is," and he agreed with that.

So, anyway, to make a story short, they just met each other and had a high regard from the start. It was the end of their problems, and they became friends. Of course, the moral of the story is the quickest way to defeat an enemy is to make him a friend, and that's exactly what they did.

---

* Rear Admiral Daniel V. Gallery, USN, was Assistant for Guided Missiles on the OpNav staff from 1946 to 1949.
† Jim G. Lucas was a correspondent for Scripps-Howard Newspapers. In 1954 he won a Pulitzer Prize for international reporting. He was also noted for his reporting on the Korean War.

Paul Stillwell: Were there other cases like that where you served as an intermediary to bring people together?

Captain Manson: Yes, frequently that was the case and particularly so when you're dealing with the media and Navy types who have been rather remote from the media. Admiral Momsen was a submariner, and there wasn't a lot of animosity, but he just didn't know what the press was like.* He had a story to tell on submarines at that particular time. That was in the late '40s. He particularly wanted to keep submarines and submarine warfare competitive with carrier warfare and all the rest of it.

The admiral and I became friends quickly. He said that he would like to get to be friends with some of these writers, and I arranged that. As soon as that happened, well, of course, Admiral Momsen began putting his point of view across in the newspapers. Every now and again, the press wouldn't write exactly what was the policy of the department, and there'd be some submarine captain would go to Admiral Momsen and say, "Look what these people are doing to us. They didn't even get it straight."

Admiral Momsen would laugh with me and say, "People that worry about little things like that really don't have much vision." He said he never worried about it. He said if they got the main thrust of the story correct, that was the important thing. But anyway, he became really an advocate at a time when most naval officers were shying away, simply by my working with him.

I've found this has been true all throughout my life. Even my own daughter now, who is assistant administrator at EPA, has been chief of staff to a governor and ran the campaign for John Warner for the Senate and all that, and she's had a lot of exposure to press and all, but she still, even now, tends to be a little standoffish.†

I've told her over and over again that the thing that is important to do with writers and reporters is to get to know them and exchange views, share their life's experiences and share their convictions and whatever. If they have mutual dislikes, share those too.

---

* Rear Admiral Charles B. Momsen, USN, Assistant Chief of Naval Operations for Submarine Warfare.
† Jennifer Joy Manson Wilson (since remarried and last name changed to Pinniger) was assistant administrator of the Environmental Protection Agency (EPA), deputy administrator of the National Oceanic and Atmospheric Administration (NOAA), Assistant Secretary of Commerce for Oceans and Atmosphere, and served as senior executive assistant to Governor John Dalton of Virginia and legislative director for Senator John W. Warner of Virginia. Her final job was as president and chief executive officer of the National Stone, Sand and Gravel Association.

But in all cases, to bring their minds into some kind of harmony and then they can be constructive. So she is trying to do that.

But I used to, particularly in my days on CNO staff, I spent a lot of time with people from Captain John Crommelin starting back in those days, on up to as late as 1948 or '49, working with admirals on this subject, really.* Well, it's not something that just the Navy has problems with; Richard Nixon had a lot of problems with that.† Recently you may have seen that "Meet the Press" the other day.

Paul Stillwell: No, I missed that one.

Captain Manson: Well, anyway, they asked him if there was anything in his life that he might have done differently, and he said, well, he might have been a little bit more friendlier to the press, and he said, "And of course, they might have been a little more friendlier to me, too."

Paul Stillwell: Well, that's a two-way street. If he's more friendly to them, they're more likely to be friendly to him.

Captain Manson: Exactly, precisely. Of course, in college I had been a journalism student, and I'd written things for papers and all that, but then when I got into what you might call the "big time" with Walter Karig, he reemphasized and sort of doubled my conviction that if you would get to know the people you're dealing with, that your chances of making a mistake or having a failure were reduced. So that's what I did.

In those years just after World War II, I became personally acquainted with the top writers in the United States—ones with *The New York Times*, *The Washington Post*, *The Washington Times Herald*, the *Chicago Tribune*, the *San Francisco Chronicle*, you name it, the *Nashville Banner*. I knew either the editor, one editor, *Cincinnati Enquirer*, you could just name any paper, *Kansas City Star*.

---

* For a description of the role of Captain John G. Crommelin Jr., USN, in the "revolt of the admirals," see Edward P. Stafford, "Saving Carrier Aviation—1949 Style," *U.S. Naval Institute Proceedings*, January 1990, pages 44-51.
† Richard M. Nixon was President of the United States from 20 January 1969 until his resignation on 9 August 1974.

I had friends, mostly Washington, that I got to know through membership in the National Press Club. But the thing was if I had something of importance to the Navy that I really needed to get into the public print, there were always two or three people I could talk to. I found this very useful throughout my naval career.

Paul Stillwell: Would you say that for the most part, senior naval officers had a distrust of the media?

Captain Manson: Yes, they did, and I suppose they still do have. I don't know about the '30s, but certainly right after World War II, the press was very critical of the Navy and the role that the Navy played in World War II. The conflict was about air power and the strengths and weaknesses of the carrier versus land-based air. This was a good part of the program, but it was a struggle, really, I guess, for budget back in Washington as much as anything.

Military officers did not understand or appreciate the role of the other services. I thought the Navy had a better appreciation of land forces, for example, than the land forces had of the naval forces. That was one of the problems, and, of course, this trickled out into the press. I don't know whether the problems started there. In any case, the Navy was pretty much a target of bad press, reporters who were very critical of not only what the Navy had achieved during the World War II, but what the future role of the Navy would be.

One time I heard General Leslie Groves, who had a lot to do with creating the atomic bomb; I don't know exactly what his role was, but he almost sounded like he might have built the thing himself at times.[*] I heard him one time talking about the thing and asked him what the future of naval power was, battleships and carriers and so forth, and he said, "Well, I don't want to get into that subject too much, but I know that one bomb will destroy one battleship." That was the end of his answer.

But anyway, William Bradford Huie, writing for *Reader's Digest*, wrote a series of articles and they were just devastating to the Navy, about 1949.

---

[*] Major General Leslie R. Groves, USA, was head of the Manhattan Project that developed the atomic bomb in World War II.

Paul Stillwell: He had a book too, I think, *The Case Against the Admirals*.[*]

Captain Manson: He did, he wrote a book called *The Case Against the Admirals*. He really accused the admirals of everything from bad judgment to just being stupid, to the whole idea of naval warfare, that it was ended. I don't know if you've ever read those.

Paul Stillwell: No.

Captain Manson: Oh, they are so critical, and they burned me to a crisp. So I wrote a rebuttal to them and passed it around for some of my friends to look at some of my first thoughts on the things. The press got hold of it, it was just a rough draft and didn't have any name on it or anything, and I came very close to being crucified myself for being so critical of people who were writing about the Navy and didn't know anything much about the subject.

So, anyway, there was a couple or three hours when it looked like I was going to be transferred to Alaska or the Aleutian Islands or somewhere, for having even drafted a rebuttal to William Bradford Huie and had sent it around, 20 or so copies. Then it had gotten into the hands of the press and they were going to say then that Admiral Denfeld's staff was scuttling unification because I had—well, as my yeoman had said, that I had written the draft. So we had a difficult time with that for a few days.

But, anyway, you asked the reason why the admirals were—well, that's part of it, that they were getting a very bad rap in the press. Second thing was, the Navy has what I call a sea cabin complex, or did then. But so much of the life of a senior officer is spent in a cabin, a small cabin alone, not with a lot of other people. That's another intrinsic difficulty for a man who's been alone a lot of the time and then suddenly he becomes a little suspicious of the environment except that which he knows.

Paul Stillwell: Well, he's used to being in an environment where he says something and that's treated as law.

---

[*] William Bradford Huie, *The Case Against the Admirals: Why We Must Have a Unified Command* (New York: E. P. Dutton, 1946).

Captain Manson: Exactly, precisely. He knows exactly what he has ordered; he has these things under his command. Then when he gets into a world where, even though he's told a reporter or a writer a certain set of facts or whatever, he can't be at all sure that that's what's going to appear. He has little control, so he tends to become suspicious of anything that he can't control. And to be a senior officer, that's one attribute that is, I think, fairly common.

Paul Stillwell: And at the same time, the Air Force was being very successful with putting out its side of the story, and the Marine Corps so successful that Harry Truman accused them of having a propaganda machine to rival Stalin's.[*]

Captain Manson: He did, he said that. But the Air Force were mostly a bunch of people who had graduated from colleges and universities, civilians, who had come into the Air Corps and later the Air Force. They had a civilian outlook. They were people who weren't, as I think their motto was, "unhampered by tradition." Whereas the Navy regarded tradition as a virtue, those young Air Force colonels regarded it as somewhat of a handicap. So they tended to blow off steam in all directions, and they were guided by Stuart Symington and Steve Leo. Steve Leo was a former journalist, very clever man, I knew him. And, of course, Symington was clever, too, in the PR and political world, as he later became a senator and so forth and proved how really clever he was.

But the Navy in those years had a few people who were articulate and could deal with the press, but they were few and far between. There just weren't all that many.

One time I won't forget, during the B-36 hearings, the Navy had brought in all of its top admirals. I mean like 40 of them. Four-stars and three-stars, and I guess a few two-stars were in there, mostly four and three. Halsey and Nimitz and all the big boys were in this room.

My office was just across the hall. So I thought I'd go over there and check. I think I was going to tell them something about the hearing plan or program or something. They were all blowing off steam and being pretty loud and bellicose. And Jack

---

[*] Harry S. Truman served as President of the United States from 12 April 1945 to 20 January 1953. Joseph Stalin ran the Soviet Union essentially as a dictatorship from the late 1920s to his death on 5 March 1953.

Anderson, who was Drew Pearson's assistant, was sitting right in there at the desk writing down everything that he could pick up, and he was hearing plenty.* So when I saw him there I said, "Jack, I can't believe this."

So I went in and to the first admiral I found, Admiral Price or someone, I said, "Do you people know that Jack Anderson is sitting there at that desk and he's Drew Pearson's assistant?"† You've never seen such a flight of admirals in all your life. They scattered, they hit the door and they went up and down the hall everywhere. But in a minute, that whole room was empty.

Paul Stillwell: Was there a great concern about Pearson and his influence?

Captain Manson: Very much so, very much so. There was always a big debate about whether they should ignore him or whether they should answer him. I think that perhaps the strongest, most persuasive force was that where we tried to encourage and particularly if the story was almost all fiction, was to ignore it, because the danger of countering something that is maybe a "puff" piece in the first place, is that it will give that person another story. If nothing more, he can say that Admiral So-and-so denies that so-and-so was true. So we tried to get that point of view through to the admirals, but a few of them, particularly naval aviators, would give him the business.

Then, of course, Drew Pearson would just write another story. Yes, but they were worried, to answer you. The Navy, as a whole, was always worried about Drew Pearson. They never knew for sure which way he was going to jump, but they never expected anything good, nothing favorable.

---

* Jack Anderson was a journalist widely known for his syndicated column "Washington Merry Go Round," which often included muckraking exposés. Andrew Pearson wrote the column before Anderson succeeded him.
† Vice Admiral John Dale Price, USN, served as Deputy Chief of Naval Operations (Air) from 20 January 1948 to 6 May 1949.

Paul Stillwell: At the other end of the spectrum was somebody like Hanson Baldwin, who was a great friend of the Navy.* Were there others whom you would recall as being very supportive?

Captain Manson: The people that were most supportive of the Navy, of course, Hanson Baldwin, class of '24, was a tried and true naval advocate. In the first place, Hanson Baldwin understood the use of naval power. But then more than that, he understood how to explain it. As a matter of fact, I once told Hanson Baldwin that if I continued in the pattern of my career, that when I got to the end of it, I'd like to relieve him because he'd be getting old enough.

He said, "Frank, if I were you, I'd strongly urge you not to do it." I asked why, of course, and he said, well, while what appeared in the press and everything always seemed to be favorable and all, but he said that in his life he'd had so much difficulty with the other people there on *The New York Times* and the staff, and he said it was not a life that he would want a friend of his to undertake, that it was just really too rough.

Paul Stillwell: Did he give any examples?

Captain Manson: No. He didn't specify any details of stories and things where he'd had difficulty in getting them printed. But I can imagine that while he was busy supporting the Navy and the liberal *New York Times* was on an opposite course, that he probably did have all kinds of—I know he did, because he told me he did—difficulty. So he said, "No, if I were you I wouldn't do it."

So I said, "Well, that's good enough for me," and I dropped it.

But, anyway, you asked about other reporters that were friendly to the Navy. Yes, there were some. Robert Sherrod, who covered military affairs for *Time* magazine, was extremely articulate, and he later became managing editor of *Saturday Evening Post*. He wrote, I think, the Marines at war.

---

* Hanson W. Baldwin was a 1924 graduate of the Naval Academy. Following several years of naval service, Baldwin began a distinguished career as a newspaperman, culminating as military editor of *The New York Times*. His oral history is in the Naval Institute collection. See also Robert B. Davies, *Baldwin of the Times: Hanson W. Baldwin, a Military Journalist's Life, 1903-1991* (Annapolis: Naval Institute Press, 2011).

Paul Stillwell: *Marine Aviation in World War II.*[*]

Captain Manson: Yes, he wrote that. And while he was actually writing for *Time* magazine, covering the Pentagon, he was writing that book for the Marines. But Robert Sherrod was a true advocate of naval and Marine power.

Paul Stillwell: I saw him last week. He's still going strong.[†]

Captain Manson: I'm glad you saw him, and I'm glad he's going. The last time I saw Bob, he wanted to dig back into the B-36 days, and he wanted me scratch my head a little bit and see if we couldn't remember some of the details. He was thinking of writing something on that. I don't know if he ever did. Do you know?

Paul Stillwell: I don't either, no.[‡]

Captain Manson: Well, anyway, he wanted me to give it some thought, and I gave it a little thought, but I never did see him again. Anyway, I actually saw one time when he visited in our office with Captain Karig and me. He was trying to get the truth about some story that had just appeared. I wish I could tell you the exact story, but it was regarding, you can be sure, naval power, naval air power, something about that conflict. The Navy had taken a position on it, and Captain Karig was sitting there reading it.

Bob Sherrod said, "Well, I sure would like to see a copy of that."

Captain Karig said, "Well, I sure wish I could let you see it, Bob, but there is no way I can do that. However, I don't have any further use for it, so I think I'll just throw it away." So he wadded it up and threw it in the wastebasket, and Bob Sherrod proceeded to go right over and take it out of the wastebasket and left the office. And that really opened my eyes. I guess they were all thinking about future court-martials and whether

---

[*] Robert L. Sherrod, *History of Marine Corps Aviation in World War II* (Washington, DC: Combat Forces Press, 1952).
[†] Sherrod died 13 February 1994 at age 85.
[‡] The best book on the subject was published a few years after this interview: Jeffrey G. Barlow, *Revolt of the Admirals: The Fight for Naval Aviation, 1945-1950* (Washington, D.C.: U.S. Government Printing Office, 1994).

one could deny he'd ever given anyone a piece of paper or not, or whether he'd ever taken a piece of paper. But that I actually saw. Bob Sherrod just went right over and picked up that wad of paper and left the office.

Paul Stillwell: He even had a witness. You were the witness that he threw it away.

Captain Manson: Exactly. He had a witness. I saw him throw it away.

Paul Stillwell: How about Walter Millis? I think he was with the *Baltimore Sun*.

Captain Manson: Yes. He was favorable and a thorough writer, but I didn't know him personally. Mark Watson, with the *Baltimore Sun*, I would say he was a fair writer on military affairs. In all the many things that he wrote, I don't recall that he ever wrote what I would call a prejudiced article in dealing with the services or the relationship between the services. He was an extremely factual and a strong research person. By that, he tried to get his facts before he wrote. He was meticulous in searching out what was true and not true.

Anyway, Mark Watson was dependable. Mark didn't write so often about the controversy that was going strong between the services at that time, but he did some writing on it.

Another was William Hessler of the *Cincinnati Enquirer*. He used to write articles in the *Cincinnati Enquirer*, and he also wrote for *Collier's* magazine.

Paul Stillwell: He wrote a number for *Proceedings* also.

Captain Manson: And he wrote for the *Proceedings*. Anyway, he understood.

Paul Stillwell: Well, he had been a Naval Reserve officer during the war.

Captain Manson: And he was a Naval Reserve. He was good.

Paul Stillwell: We've mentioned that senior officers were suspicious. Were there some that you treated very warily other than William Bradford Huie, let's say?

Captain Manson: Well, I'll tell you this about all reporters. I never told them anything that I would have been worried about if it appeared in print, because the only way you can prevent anything from appearing is to not tell it. So even like I was talking about Jim Lucas. Now, Jim was a very good friend, but I would never trust Jim to keep something, because he might decide in his own rationalization—I would never have trusted him to keep something that I didn't want known.

Paul Stillwell: You would have trusted Baldwin, wouldn't you?

Captain Manson: Well, Hanson Baldwin was an exception of all the reporters and writers, because he was a Naval Academy graduate, because he put that trust higher. He had what you'd call a higher trust than just journalism. But like Jim Lucas said to me one time, "I don't know." He had found on my desk about 200 or 300 or 400 copies of Robert Montgomery's recent broadcast.* He was slamming the people who were opposing the Navy in this thing, and Montgomery was at a radio program that was very strong. I was going to New York every two or three days and feeding him information that would then appear in the broadcast. Then OP-23, which was Captain Burke's group, would grab this thing when I'd bring the broadcast back from New York, and they'd reproduce 200 or 300 hundred copies of it.

So I came in and Jim was sitting at my desk, and it said right up at the top "Reproduced by OP-23, Robert Montgomery broadcast." So Jim was sitting there reading this thing. I said, "What you got, Jim?"

He said, "Gee, I don't know, Frank. I don't know whether my conscience is going to win on this or my duty as a journalist."

All I could say was "Well, I sure hope your conscience prevails," but it didn't. So the next day was a picture of Captain Burke in a Scripps-Howard newspaper and OP-23

---

* Robert Montgomery was a movie actor who had served in the Naval Reserve in World War II. He and John Wayne starred in the 1945 movie *They Were Expendable* about PT boats in the Philippines at the outset of World War II.

scuttling unification and on and on and on about reproducing copies. It was a pretty factual story, really, but still it added fuel to the fire. But there was a case where a journalist was acting like a journalist.

Paul Stillwell: Well, that was his job, after all.

Captain Manson: Yes, and I didn't get angry with Jim, because I thought he was doing his job. But I could have kicked myself, or I could have kicked—I forget this captain's name that brought all those reproductions down and put them on my desk, and left them out there, but that's just one of the things that happens. When you're in a fight, somebody's liable to put ammunition in the wrong place sometimes.

But there were people that I was wary of. I'm trying to think of the UPI correspondent.[*] I think his name was Dillon. No, that was Don Dillon and he was a friend. It wasn't Don Dillon. But, anyway, it was a UPI reporter in those days. I can picture him in my mind. Then there was a Maureen Gothlin, a woman writer, and I didn't trust her for sour grapes. I wouldn't have told her anything that—I would have been overly cautious with her, and I was when I dealt with her.

But the other UPI writer at that time, likewise, very cautious. Let's see, who was the AP?[†] Well, Lloyd Norman was the *Chicago Tribune* correspondent, and I had to be rather careful with Lloyd Norman. I liked the man, but I also knew that he was a journalist first and if it came to that, well, I knew what was going to win.

Leo Cullinane of the *New York Herald Tribune*, he and I had been on a trip to China at one time, and I knew him quite well. He came to me one day, and he said, "Frank, what's with this nan gear, anyway? Did you ever hear of nan gear?" And you know it's that equipment that was used at night for visual signaling. You know about that?

Paul Stillwell: I think I heard it called "Nancy."[‡]

---

[*] UPI – United Press International
[†] AP – Associated Press.
[‡] An infrared device for visual signaling at night.

Captain Manson: Yes, Nancy. But when it first came out, it was called man gear. I don't even know whether it's ever been declassified. I'm sure it has by this time.

Paul Stillwell: Yes.

Captain Manson: But, anyway, Leo said, "Did you ever hear of it?"

I looked him right straight in the eye and said "No, it doesn't mean anything to me."

He said, "You were in destroyers in World War II?"

I said, "Yes."

"Were you operating?"

"Yes, I was operating with destroyers."

"And you tell me you've never heard of this gear?"

I said, "That's right."

He said, "Well, you are a liar, and, furthermore, you're no friend of mine."

He stormed out of the door, and I followed him out and I said, "Leo, let me just tell you one thing. If you consider this an act of friendship, what I've just done, then you're no friend of mine. Furthermore, I don't think you're a friend of your four sons which I'm trying to protect and you're not." So that was the end of that conversation.

Paul Stillwell: You had heard of it, I take it.

Captain Manson: Oh, sure, used it many, many times, all through the last year or two of the war, certainly. I knew all about it.

But the correspondents in those days, I knew all of the top correspondents. It's like I say, the UPI reporters—

Paul Stillwell: It wasn't UPI yet. It was still UP and INS.[*]

---

[*] UP – United Press; INS – International News Service. The two merged in 1958 to form UPI.

Captain Manson: Right, it was UP. Not UPI, that's right, it was UP. You're absolutely correct. The International News Service, they were generally all right. King Features Syndicate sometimes would write favorably for the Navy. But there was just such a misunderstanding. The people just didn't know about naval power or how it could be used. They didn't understand it. They couldn't see the ships. They weren't out there on the roads and the country roads going around. People didn't see ships, so they really didn't understand what the purpose of them was.

It was about that time that I recommended that the carriers throw a strike on some inland cities—simulated, of course. I didn't want them to use actual bombs. But I thought if the dive bombers and the torpedo bombers and the fighters would go and throw a simulated strike over some inland cities, that there would be such a scramble, at least the chickens and the cows would have a heyday.

But, anyway, it's such a impressive thing to see a coordinated Navy strike. I just thought that if they could do a few of those 200 miles or so up around the coast, all the way around, that we'd have a lot more advocates and a lot fewer critics. There were some naval aviators high up in PR at that time, Captain Leroy Simpler being one.* But they were afraid of it. I suppose the main thing was, they were afraid of some accidents or afraid somebody might run out of gas, or I don't know. But they were just afraid to do it. I thought that the advantages of it would far outweigh the disadvantages. But I still have a file on that effort I made to try to get a few strikes inland.

Paul Stillwell: Did you have some kind of doctrine or policy to follow when there was bad news, an operational accident? For example, the submarine *Cochino* was lost up off Norway.† How did you respond to that kind of emergency?

Captain Manson: Well, first of all, until you could get all the facts, the first approach that you would take was to refrain from giving out any information. Just say that you have no information available at this time, and as soon as you get some, you'll release what you

---

* Captain Leroy C. Simpler, USN.
† USS *Cochino* (SS-345) was lost off Norway on 26 August 1949 as the result of battery explosions and fires. For details see the Naval Institute oral history of Rear Admiral Roy S. Benson, USN (Ret.), and William J. Lederer, *The Last Voyage* (New York: Henry Holt and Company, 1950).

can. But the main formula you had is never to go with a piecemeal bit of information and then fuel a thousand questions. It's much better to withhold information. Of course, now, if you have witnesses, you have to deal with what the witnesses saw, but then limit the information until you can give a full explanation. Then you don't try to hide once you—and admit mistakes. That's just basic common sense, but that's what PR is.

Paul Stillwell: Really, you had a luxury then that the Navy PR people today don't, in that you had more control over the flow of information. Now the TV stations and networks can hire helicopters and go out and stick microphones in people's faces right away.

Captain Manson: That's right, that's right. Yes, we did. Well, yes, we had a favorable situation. Then until we decided that we had the facts within our grasp, we'd just leave it alone.

Paul Stillwell: Of course, the disadvantage of that is that people may have worries that a situation is worse than it really is.

Captain Manson: Well, that's true, so that is a double edge. I mean, we're generalizing here, but if you know that very shortly the information is going to get out anyway, then our attitude and our formula was in those days to put it out and, of course, always put it in as favorable a light as you can, but not to misrepresent.

I had one case, which we'll get into when we get over into the European theater, where I really had to sort of misrepresent the situation. It was shortly after the U-2 and the Gary Powers flight when the summit that Eisenhower was going to have with Khrushchev was obliterated because Ike decided he had to be truthful about the whole thing two or three days there.* This was a similar situation to that. It was one of our

---

* On 5 May 1960 Soviet Premier Nikita Khrushchev announced that Soviet forces had shot down a high-flying American U-2 reconnaissance plane on 1 May near the city of Sverdlovsk in the Ural Mountains. The American pilot, Francis Gary Powers, was tried for espionage and sentenced to ten years' confinement. He was later returned to the United States in exchange for a Soviet spy. On 16 May 1960, because the United States refused to apologize for the overflight of Soviet territory, the Soviets cancelled their planned participation in a multinational summit conference and withdrew a previous invitation for President Eisenhower to visit the Soviet Union. Eisenhower initially denied the flight's intelligence mission but then admitted to it after the Soviets displayed the pilot and wreckage from the plane.

communications intelligence planes, a Super Constellation.* What it would do was make some kind of a big circle, and it would just go along the Iron Curtain and pick up all the frequencies that it could and monitor what was going on. It was sort of a flying electronic monitor, and it was flying out of Rota, Spain.

Well, one day we lost one of them. It wasn't shot down; it just crashed. We really didn't know why it crashed, but we also knew that pieces fell in Iron Curtain territory, a lot of it, even parts of the plane, bodies, everything. Questions started coming from all over Europe, and I called around to all of our subordinate commands and told them to absolutely make no comment and to refer all the calls to me personally.

So that's what they did. Spain, Italy, Germany, wherever, the calls all came to me in London. I said that this plane was on a routine training flight and that it had run into difficulties and it had gone down. "What was it doing?"

"Well, it was training, it was routine training."

"What kind of training?"

"Well, I have no details on what kind of training. But, nevertheless, I do know that it was just a routine flight." I stuck with that story.

Well, they couldn't really get enough to write much than two or three inches on it, except, of course, it was a terrible loss of life. They had 20 or 30 people, maybe more, on that aircraft because they were all communications, electronics experts. It was a big four-engine propeller plane that had been converted to an electronics eavesdropping-type aircraft. But if I had spieled off all I knew about that airplane, we would have been in deep kimchee for maybe a long time, because that was just meat and grist for the Soviet mill in those days, and for the lefties throughout the world, we were over there imposing, encroaching, and so forth and so on. They'd make the most of the propaganda effort. But in this case, we closed it down right at the source, and it never did amount to anything. It could have been as big as a U-2, at least.

So I say, well, tell the truth, yes, but it depends, because there are security missions that absolutely have to be kept secret.

---

* On 22 May 1962 a Lockheed VW-2Q Super Constellation operating out of Furstenfeldbruk, West Germany, crashed with the loss of all 26 crew members on board. The plane was part of Air Reconnaissance Squadron Two (VQ-2), which was based at Rota, Spain.

Paul Stillwell: Arthur Sylvester maintained that the government had the right to lie in some situations.

Captain Manson: Well, I suppose it's a difficult way to put it. I suppose I might say withhold information. I think the government has the right to withhold information. I think I'd word it that way.

Paul Stillwell: There's no question about that, because classified, obviously you're not going to release.

Captain Manson: That's right. And if there's information that is going to be detrimental to the national interest of the United States, then my suggestion is that you consider alternative discussions.

Paul Stillwell: That's an interesting euphemism. [Laughter]

Captain Manson: We sure steered away from what we started on.

Paul Stillwell: Well, we're to that point again. You've brought us back to your time over in Europe. Maybe you could just pick that one up at the beginning—how you got there and the duties that you moved into.

Captain Manson: I was at the Naval War College and had no idea where I might be sent. I never dreamed, never dreamed that they'd throw me in that briar patch over there in London. If I could have written 100 times where I'd rather go, I, of course, would have picked London every time. And so it was, I suppose, an accident of fate, I don't know what. But my orders came, and I was ordered to go take over the PR for naval forces for Europe and then for all the armed forces for the Middle East.

I had three children at that time and they were quite young. Let's see. Our son Frank Karig was ten, Joy would have been six, and Barbara Lynne would have been about two. That's right, they were little folks. We were ordered to get over there in

London and set up shop, our whole household, because in those days, of course, all the families moved, and I suppose they still do. Anyway, this was the second time that I moved the family to an overseas post. I had been to Italy the first time. But the main thing I remember about taking the family on that European tour was that we got in a ship that was top-heavy, and the whole family got seasick, including myself. We had a terrible voyage. We were in the wake of a big storm all the way over there. This ship, I think it was called the SS *Atlantic*, some old converted merchant ship, and she was rolling like 30 or 40 degrees. When you see a little baby seasick, you know it's rolling.

Anyway, we got there, and then I was sort of not feeling all that well because we'd had about five or six days of this. As I told you last time, *Life* magazine was on my case to get the story out about the white fleet. They were urgent about getting the thing back there. So I suppose in about ten days after I arrived, I went over to the *Life* office in London. It was run by a fellow named Richard Pollard, Dick Pollard. I said, "All right, where's your typewriter?"

So he showed me to a typewriter, and I ripped off about three or four pages on how I got the idea and handed it to him and said, "Well, there it is." So then the rest of it is all history, about being on the cover of *Life* and whatnot.

Anyway, the first days there in London were fairly hectic in trying to find a place for my family. We lived in a hotel. London is a sophisticated city, but for Americans to come in cold, it's a foreign country and things are not the same. The food's not the same and all the rest of it. So it represented quite an adjustment for us to figure out the money, how to get dollars and pounds straightened out, what to eat, what the children would eat and they wouldn't eat.

Paul Stillwell: What adjustments did you have to make on the food?

Captain Manson: Well, the breakfast, for example. They serve a lot of fish for breakfast over there, kippered herring and other kinds of fish. Eggs some, too, in addition, but there's only one person in our family who would have anything to do with fish for breakfast, and that was my wife Lee. She's from Brunswick, Georgia, so I suppose she is a little bit more of a fish-eater. But the children wouldn't touch it. They weren't all that keen on eggs either. They liked various types of cereal, and it wasn't all that available when we got there. Breakfast is the starting meal, so that took a little bit of adjusting.

Of course, the British eat differently, too, than we do. They use their fork and knife, they turn the fork upside down and put the peas on it and eat it fast before they roll off or something, I don't know how they do it. But we couldn't make those adjustments, really. Although we were eating in British places and all that, we had to eat like Americans.

Paul Stillwell: Well, also they would cut the meat with the right hand and eat it with the left.

Captain Manson: That's right, that's right, that's one of the things that you just must do. For the rest of the family that was very difficult. I'm left-handed, so it wasn't so bad for me, but still I wasn't used to doing it.

Anyway, generally speaking, the British food was boiled—boiled potatoes, boiled meat, an awful lot of boiled food, and the family wasn't too keen on boiled food, although it's good for you. But they preferred to have French fries and all that.

One of the things that we discovered early over there was the fish and chips. For some reason or another, the children went for that. There were quite a lot of fish and chips stores around. But when they wouldn't eat anything else, we could usually get them to go for that. Personally, though, as far as British food is concerned, I liked most British food, and the family got to where it did. For example, they serve those beets in a green grocer that they've just freshly cooked, and the British just eat them like apples. Well, we wouldn't have anything to do with that.

Paul Stillwell: [Chuckles] I think not.

Captain Manson: But after about two years over there, we were eating them just like apples. Oh, another thing was that our family was very strong on fruits, all kinds of fruits, and there were not all that many fruits at that time in Britain.

If they were, they were either at Selfridges, the big department store there on Oxford Street, or Harrod's, because they had specialty places for all kinds of exotic fruits and things imported from all over the world. But they were terribly expensive. Out on the market you didn't get a lot of fruit, particularly citrus fruits. Orange juice was at a premium. So this was a thing that we sort of had to forgo for a while until we could find out where we could find fruits and how to get them. But we really did, over a period of not too much time, have a yearning for citrus, particularly orange juice. It was in short supply.

Now, milk was available, but you had to sure about milk, how it was taken care of and all. I remember in Italy we had a problem with milk, and the herds had to be examined and certified before our children were permitted to drink the milk. I think, though, as I recall in Britain, the milk was fine at that particular time.

But, anyway, getting in England and getting situated, for every American family, was really quite a chore and undertaking, because we were moving right into the British communities, and we had to deal with their landlords. Writing a contract with a British landlord can get to be a rather meticulous and painstaking task, because they really do look at the fine print, and they have a lot of requirements that are not part of our landlord/tenant relationships.

Paul Stillwell: Such as?

Captain Manson: Well, for one thing, the landlords in many cases have leased the property that they're renting, and they'll have a certain number of years that they have leased that property. So that you're not dealing with the real owner; you're dealing with a landlord who is not really an owner, but a leaser, I guess it would be.

I'll give you an example. The landlord leased us a place. He said, "Now, you'll have this property all on your own, and we, my wife and I, we'll reserve a room in this place. We live out in the country, but now and again we may use it, but it will only be periodic. But you'll pay for the heat and the coal and all that, gas and whatever, fuel, energy." But it turned out that when we were living there, these people were living down there all the time, and they were using almost as much energy as we were using, and yet we were paying for all of it. There wasn't any way to reconcile the agreement, because we had already agreed to pay for all of it, and we'd been told that they were only going to be there part time. Well, to them that was just a very legitimate way to conduct affairs, so there wasn't anything unusual about that. But over here, that would be very unusual.

Paul Stillwell: Sure would.

Captain Manson: The British have what they call council housing. It's property that's rented very inexpensively to the British citizens who are at a lower income level. In some cases, this council housing was rented to Americans, and this created quite a problem. I don't know exactly the details of it, and I never lived in any of the council housing, but I do recall that sometimes this did create a problem.

But the main, I suppose, point in dealing with British housing was that you just had to be much more mindful of what was in the contract, what the contract specified and called for. I thought right off I might just buy a house over there. I didn't know what the problems might be in purchasing British property, but I thought for three or four years it might be very worthwhile.

So I was discussing it on a bus one time with a British realtor, and I didn't know that one of our naval intelligence officers was sitting right behind me listening to the conversation. So we traveled for 30 or 40 minutes, and I'd explored everything I could with this realtor about where we might find some property to buy. This intelligence officer knew that I was a good friend of Malcolm Cagle, who was at that time stationed in Europe. So he called Malcolm Cagle and wanted to know if there was anything wrong with me, if I'd gone crazy or anything. Malcolm said, no, that he'd been talking to me rather frequently. The intelligence officer said, "Well, that nut's about to buy a house up here." He said, "He's got to be crazy." I believe Malcolm was in Paris at that time. He was over there in something to do with a U.S. nuclear weapons officer or something. He had sort of a special assignment over there in the European Command at that time.

Anyway, he couldn't wait to get over to London to tell me that this talk was all over the command that I was nuts for trying to buy a British house. So I gave up on it. I thought, "Well, if everybody thinks I'm nuts, I might be" and I didn't do it.

Paul Stillwell: What would have been nutty about it?

Captain Manson: Well, I still don't know. I still don't know. I think it would have been a good move now. I mean, I might still own the property. There's certainly no rule in Britain that an American can't own a house over there. But I would have been the only one. But it was the first thought that occurred to me because I'd been buying houses over here in America, so I thought, "Well, pretty country, why not?" But, anyway, word was passed through the command that I was a little bit barmy, so I didn't do any more real estate looking.

Paul Stillwell: Did your family enjoy living in England?

Captain Manson: They did. The schools were, I suppose, the main problem. My wife and I enjoyed in immensely, but the children didn't find it all that pleasing. First of all, they went into a British elementary school. The children had to switch from 5s and 10s to 6s and 12s in their mathematics and all the spelling. The Os usually had OUs for spelling and just a lot of different pronunciations and things. They'd never heard British spoken, so it was really an adjustment for our son Frank, who was ten years old when we got there.

On the way over on the ship, he had read a book on Greek mythology that was about 400 or 500 pages long. He was quite a scholar on mythology. He liked that. But, anyway, the children objected to all these differences and changes. Beyond that, the British children sort of turned against our son, because he was different, and they beat him up on his way home rather frequently. He used to complain to me he didn't have a friend in the class, and I used to tell him the thing he should do is work toward getting one friend, just one, and he worked on it. He finally did make one friend, and then I said, "When you get one, then you ask him to help you get two more and eventually you'll have a few friends." So he worked on that and eventually he did.

But the main point of that first year over there was that the 11-plus examination was coming up. That is where they send these kids into an examination that takes two or three days. If they pass it, then they're eligible to go to grammar school, but if they flunk it, then they go into sort of a technical training, industrial. We were worried, because we didn't particularly want our son to get into one of those technical schools, but yet we couldn't very well avoid it.

So, anyway, he took the 11-plus. Two passed it out of about 30-some children, and he was one of the two that passed it. So then the British teachers were so astonished that they all wanted to visit us. So we had a visitation from the entire faculty of this little school. We served tea and crumpets and sat around. They told us because our son had done so well, that they wanted to recommend him for Queen Elizabeth Grammar School. That was way out in the country out there, and he was so young, we didn't want him going way out there. We didn't know what might happen, so we took him with us.

We moved more into toward the center of the city after that and got him into Quinton Grammar School. But it was kind of a rough-and-tumble place. It was a boys' school, but the younger ones weren't watched as carefully as the older ones, and they had all kinds of fighting and kicking in the classroom. The deportment of the students was under severe question, so I called the headmaster and told him that, amongst other things, our son was being beaten up every now and again.

He had a blue spot on his shin that was about two or three inches in diameter where he'd been kicked because he was not a member of the "pen club." That was that every student, when asked if he had a pen, he was supposed to produce a pen, but if he didn't produce a pen, he got kicked. I saw that one day on my son's leg and I said, "What is that?" He said, well, he wasn't a member of the pen club. I said, "Did the faculty know this?"

He said, "Yeah, one of them was standing right near me when I got kicked."

I said, "What he'd say?"

He said, "He didn't say anything."

I said, "Well, then I think I'm going to have do something about your schooling."

He said, "Well, I don't know what you can do."

I said, "Well, I'm going to call the headmaster." So I called the headmaster and told him this had happened.

He said, "Well, I don't know what I can do about it. I have to spend most of my time with the more senior boys that are getting ready to go to university. I just can't spend much time with those youngsters. The particular faculty member you had there, he's from Australia so he probably doesn't think to much about that sort of thing."

Another example of how they treated Yanks over there, they had a debate one time whether it was better to be red or dead in the English class. So they couldn't decide who would take the dead side. So finally, the whole class stood up and pointed to my son, said, "Well, you're a Yank, you'll take the dead side."

So my son came home practically in tears that night, said he was going to have a debate in his English class. They were going to debate whether it was better to red than dead, and he had to be the dead one.

I said, "Well, son, that's not too bad. Let's analyze this a little bit. Now, what you're really talking about here is Communism. Do you know much about that?" Well, he didn't know much about it, so I said, "Well, all right. When you're a Communist, you're dead in your spirit. It's an atheistic world, so you have no spiritual life at all. So you can just start right off that you've got a dead spirit, when you're a Communist. Then when you're a Communist, your material life is void. You have very little in material things." And I went on down the list of what a Communist deprives you of, being a real thoroughgoing Communist. And I said, "So really what it comes down to is that you're dead if you're a Communist. So what you're really going to debate is whether you'd rather be dead or just be dead and think you're alive." So, anyway, he sort of played on that a little bit.

They had the debate, and then they voted on it in class, and he had won the debate. So both my son and I had a real chuckle about that afterwards. But, anyway, that's the kind of thing. I finally had to get him out of that and into a private school.*

Paul Stillwell: What the English call public schools.

Captain Manson: Yes, that's right. He got in a good one, and he just did very well indeed. He stayed in it from 10 to 14 years of age. By the time when we came back to

---

* Frank Manson Karig attended three schools in London from 1959 through 1963: Osidge Primary School, Quintin Grammar School, and Eaton House School. Back in the United States he graduated from Granby High School in Norfolk, Virginia, and later received a bachelor's degree in political science from North Carolina State University. He spent 30 years in broadcasting and public relations. In 2011 he was awarded the American Advertising Federation Silver Medal. He has been a financial advisor since 2009.

the United States, he was so far advanced in math and French and language and all, he coasted over here in high school for two or three years. As a matter of fact, I'm not even sure he ever did really crack a book until he was ready to enter the university here, because he'd already had it all. So they really do pour it on you in the British schools in terms of academic teaching, marvelous teaching.

I was very pleased, and still am, that he had those four years over there. Now, our other children were younger, and they didn't get so much of the British indoctrination. But I must say that I am all in favor of the British, or at least in those years, of the British training, the British teaching. It was absolutely superior to anything we'd known in the States. Our children had been in a few schools in the States, too, before we got over there. But by comparison, I'd have to give the British higher marks for actual academic input, and I suppose even technique, maybe. I don't really know too much about their techniques for getting the kids to learn. But I do know this, that when those children came home to do their homework, they got busy and did it. So there must have been some kind of penalty if they showed up in class without doing their homework. So the study habits were ingrained in them throughout that.

Paul Stillwell: Let's talk about the Navy part of your life in England. What were your duties?

Captain Manson: My duty was chief of public information for Europe and the Middle East. Basically, we had the Sixth Fleet in the Mediterranean, we had the base in Morocco, we had the bases in Italy, and we had Spain.[*] Not too much in Spain when I first got there, but we did have a base there. In the Middle East our command responsibilities were somewhat vague, although it extended all the way over to the Persian Gulf.

Paul Stillwell: In the Persian Gulf it was more a presence than anything.

---

[*] U.S. Naval Air Station, Port Lyautey, French Morocco, was in operation from 1942 to 1978.

Captain Manson: Yes. We had a Middle East Force over there, a seaplane tender and two or three destroyers, and it was a presence more than anything else. So I never paid a lot of attention, quite frankly, to the Middle East. I figured that I could handle that with one little finger, so I paid a lot more attention to what was going on in Europe and our relationship to all the other countries, their navies, and their other military forces.

But getting right down to the nitty-gritty of the first problem I had over there, I'll never forget, some sailor had gone back to Tennessee and married some little girl that was about 14 years old. The British press was just going crazy with the idea that American sailors were robbing the cradle—headline after headline. The person that I was relieving over there was Commander John Pillsbury, and I said, "Jack, what are we going to do about this?"*

He said, "Well, I don't know. What can you do? The girl is here, and they're married." The British were just riding it day after day. The tabloids love that sort of thing.

So we were sort of hunkering down catching the shells as they came in, and we couldn't really figure out a solution. I was so new there, I didn't know what to do. So, anyway, one of the British newspapers, as frequently happens, decided to go down and check all the prostitutes and see their ages. The reporter found one that was 12 years old, and then he put out in one of the British tabloids that the British now had prostitutes that were 12 years old and tied that in with the story about the American bride of 14, and that was the end of it. It died just as fast as it came up. So that was the way I saw right off that the British press was tempestuous, that it would explode on you, but the tendency was that it would away very quickly.

But outside of the routine—first of all, they didn't have really a PR program in Europe, and Admiral Robert Dennison was the commander.† So I said to Pillsbury, "Well, you don't seem to have much of a program here."

He said, "No, I don't."

"Do you have any?"

"No, no, I don't."

---

* Commander John D. Pillsbury, USNR, a public information specialist.
† Admiral Robert L. Dennison, Jr., USN, served as Commander in Chief U.S. Naval Forces Eastern Atlantic and Mediterranean (CinCNELM) and USComEastLant from March 1959 to February 1960.

I said, "Well, what's your policy?"

"I don't have anything."

Paul Stillwell: Did he just mostly respond to things that came up?

Captain Manson: Just responded to things that came up, nothing more than that. And on that child-bride thing, he wasn't even responding, just lying low. I said, "Well, if there's nothing to tell me, I guess I relieve you." He smiled and said the job was mine.

So I went to Admiral Dennison, after I relieved Pillsbury, and I said, "Admiral, what sort of a PR program do you have over here in Europe?"

He said, "Well, I don't know."

I said, "Well, what do you think you have?"

He said, "Well, I don't think I have much."

I said, "Well, the truth is, you don't have anything. But there's another question here, Admiral. Do you want anything?" He and I had been friends back in Washington. I knew him as a two-star admiral, so we were good friends.

So he smiled, and he said, "Well, of course I want one."

I said, "Well, in that case, I'm going to have to staff up and establish what our program is and how we're going to put across the idea of what the Navy is doing over here in Europe, because that, after all, has got to be the mission."

He said, "Yeah, that's a good idea, Frank. You just get going."

So I decided how many people I had to have and what ratings and ranks and so forth and prepared the list. So the first time the CNO, Admiral Burke, came over there, which was just a short time after I got there, I put the thing to him that I needed to beef up that staff and had 10 or 12 pages of justification.

So CNO said, "Do it." That's the way Admiral Burke issued instructions.

So, boy, I started getting people in there and getting the place organized, organizing a group to deal with the media and a group to deal with special events in Europe, and people to deal with all phases of the subordinate commands and all the things we were doing over there. But I divided the office up in the specialized things that you do in public relations.

Admiral Dennison got pretty excited when he saw these people come in, and he said, "Frank, what are you doing down here?"

I said, "Well, I'm getting you a PR program. Isn't that what you want?"

He said, "Well, yeah, but I didn't know you were going to do it with such enthusiasm." [Laughter]

Paul Stillwell: Were you still a commander at that time?

Captain Manson: Yes, I was a commander. I made captain while I was over there.[*] I said, "Well, Admiral, I say if you're going to get it done, we might as well start."

So he said, "Well, go ahead," so we did.

But, anyway, outside of the routine of putting the idea across to the British and to the French and everybody else over there what the U.S. naval forces were all about in Europe, which was one of our main missions, we were bringing these Polaris submarines into Holy Loch.[†] This was a big problem, and I was there for the birth of that. From start to finish, I really had to handle the PR side of it and, to a large degree, the political side of it, as well, because it was a hot political subject in Britain. An awful lot of people were afraid of those nuclear-powered Polaris-launching submarines. The press was not very friendly toward the idea.

We had some meetings with Mr. MacMillan, who was the Prime Minister, with his top people over how we should handle this politically.[‡] My thought was that we should concentrate the publicity and the focus on the *Proteus*, which was the mother ship, the tender, as long as we could. That ship could do no harm, nothing wrong with "old mother ships," tenders. They give out food supply, they take care of the downtrodden and whatever, but they're just an old mother ship, and there's not any harm in those.

Paul Stillwell: Never mind they've got these spare missiles and warheads.

---

[*] Manson's date of rank as captain was 1 September 1962.
[†] USS *Patrick Henry* (SSBN-599) arrived at Holy Loch, Scotland, on 8 March 1961 at the conclusion of her first deterrent patrol. Her first patrol set a new record for submerged cruising, 66 days and 22 hours, breaking by 12 hours the previous record set by the *George Washington* (SSBN-598).
[‡] Harold MacMillan was Prime Minister of the United Kingdom from 10 January 1957 to 18 October 1963.

Captain Manson: Never mind they've got those spare missiles and warheads down in the bowels of the thing. "Don't mess with that, man; that doesn't have anything to do with anything." But, anyway, it was just another really large ship, and the British were used to having large ships.

Admiral Page Smith by this time was the commander in chief, and I had discussed the strategy with him.* He and I were friends from way back too. I'd known him when he was deputy chief of information, so he and I were very good friends. So I told him I thought this would work.

He said, "I do too. Go ahead with it. So I projected the image of the old mother ship.

We had a big meeting with the political leaders of Britain, and the question came up, how are we going to release information about when that ship, the *Proteus*, is going to depart Norfolk and head for Holy Loch? The British said, "Oh, don't release it, don't release the information. Keep it a secret."

I said, "Well, in the Unites States, you cannot keep a secret of a ship that size with all the men that are aboard it leaving Norfolk, and the families and all. The minute that ship leaves, the stories are going to be out. So we should put out a release."

The British said, "No, keep it a secret as long as you can." They were somehow hoping the ship would get in, and then by and by we'd say, "Yes, the ship is in." Well, I just told them that that simply would not work. And they said, well, they wanted to try it that way. It was their country, and they were going to do it that way. I said, "Well, then sure."

So, anyway, the ship sailed, and I guess maybe it'd been gone about 12 hours, and the stories were flying all over the United States. It got to Britain, of course, as fast as you can make a phone call or an electronic transmission. "What's this ship doing?"

I said, "Well, I don't know what it's doing. I have no way of knowing."

"It's not coming over to Britain?"

I said, "I don't know. I have no information available." So the stories went out that the—

---

* Admiral Harold P. Smith, USN, served as Commander in Chief U.S. Naval Forces Eastern Atlantic and Mediterranean (CinCNELM), U.S. Commander Eastern Atlantic, and Commander in Chief U.S. Naval Forces Europe (CinCUSNavEur) from February 1960 to April 1963.

Paul Stillwell: That the Navy didn't know what its ship is doing.

Captain Manson: Yes, that's right and the agreement had been canceled. They concluded that if I didn't know what was going on, that the agreement between the United States and Britain had been canceled. So then the first thrust of that went right to the Prime Minister's office: "Has the agreement between the United States and Britain been canceled, on bringing the submarines in?"

So I had a call directly from the Prime Minister's office. It wasn't the Prime Minister, but it was his deputy. He said, "Commander, I want you to release the information about the *Proteus* immediately." They don't say immediate, it's "immejiate."

I said, "What's that, sir?"

He said, "Yes, yes. Did you understand me? I want the information released 'immejiate' that the *Proteus* has sailed from Norfolk."

I said, "Well, of course, sir, I'd be glad to do that." So I got the information on the streets in about ten minutes, and, of course, that was the end of that problem.

Paul Stillwell: Why didn't you just fall back on "no comment" instead of saying you didn't know?

Captain Manson: Now, in hindsight that we bring it up these many years later, I suppose I should have said, "No comment." I should have. But I suppose I helped to create the crisis by telling them I didn't know.

Paul Stillwell: Well, you also brought about the solution to the crisis too. [Laughter]

Captain Manson: That's right. I solved it really quick. But I'd already told them that this was for sure going to be the result.

So, anyway, I got along better with the Prime Minister's office after that. At least they knew that these people that lived over in the States weren't all completely illiterate on this subject. Anyway, still, though, the concept of putting the mother ship up there and keeping that attention focused on that was not easy—not even in the U.S. Navy.

Now, Dick Laning was the skipper of the *Proteus*.[*] I knew Dick from way back, because he and I used to do a lot of discussing of ideas when I was getting ready to write a speech for CNO. I had a lot of confidence in him, and I knew he had the intellectual imagination and competence to project this rather innocuous ship that would be coming in up there that was just going to anchor up there, and from time to time there would be submarines that would come in, but by and large, that she'd be there alone.

So when we had the planning session in our naval headquarters there in London, I was up before about 40 or 50 officers explaining that the way we were handling the PR, that it was the *Proteus* that was the big ship. She was the focus and would be for a while. Captain Ward was commander of the submarines that were coming in.[†] After he heard me tell them how we were going to handle this, he said, "Well, I don't think you've got the picture. We're bringing in a bunch of ships to throttle down the Soviet Union. These submarines are going to have the capability of dealing with the strategic threat that exists against the United States, and this is a strategic force. The first submarine is going to have all kinds of firepower. We've got to get this story out, and I'm over here to put this out."

I said, "Well, Commodore, I'll tell you what. All of us in this room know everything that you've said is true, but we're not going to put the information out, not yet, because these people are frightened over here, and they might even threaten whether we can bring the force in here or not."

He said, "Well, I'm not going to put up with this. This is my mission, and I'm the squadron commander."

I said, "Well, Commodore, I appreciate your role in this, and if you'll pardon me for a few minutes, I need to leave the conference and I'll be back. So carry on."

I just left and went in to Admiral Smith and told him that we were in conflict in there over we were going to handle this. "Commodore Ward says that he's going to put

---

[*] Captain Richard B. Laning, USN, commanded the *Proteus* (AS-19) from 8 July 1960 to 25 August 1962.
[†] Submarine Squadron 14 was established in 1958; the initial members worked in the Pentagon to do planning for the Polaris-armed submarines. Later the squadron received and operated the SSBNs as they went into commission. The first squadron commander was Captain Norvell G. Ward, USN; the oral history of Ward, who retired as a rear admiral, is in the Naval Institute collection.

the information out, and he's going to handle it his way. I've told him that up to now that we've been doing it our way."

He said, "Frank, I'll handle this. I'll send him on leave for a while. How long do you think he ought to be gone?"

I said, "Well, I think at least six weeks, or at least until we get this thing in hand, until we get everything settled down and then we can gradually, by and by, bring him into it and tell the whole story."

He said, "Okay, tell him I want to see him."

So I went back and told Commodore Ward that the Admiral wanted to see him. So he went on leave then for a few weeks. I don't know how long now, I forget.

Paul Stillwell: Did Ward hold any animosity toward you?

Captain Manson: Yes, he did.

Well, it went off. We had 180 correspondents up there when we brought the *Proteus* in.* Dick Laning was standing up there like somebody at a school for training something. I don't know what he was acting like, but anyway—

Paul Stillwell: A very articulate gentleman.

Captain Manson: Oh, he's articulate, and he just went right down the party line on what the *Proteus* was up there for, and he never veered off. They tried to get him off on these nukes and all that. "No, no, no, this is just a tender here, this ship." He just did a perfect job for the whole world. As I say, we had about 180 TV, everything out there, and Dick was just a marvelous—put on one of the best performances in a PR way that I've ever seen in my life. I was so pleased with him.

Paul Stillwell: Well, he'd had experience. He was the first CO of the *Seawolf*, so he'd

---

* The submarine tender *Proteus* (AS-19) arrived at Holy Loch on 3 March 1961. The *Patrick Henry*, the first Polaris submarine to deploy there, arrived five days later.

gotten a lot of publicity out of that, too, and he knew how to deal with it.*

Captain Manson: Yes, he must have. Well, the only way I can say is, he was just super good. I never was more pleased with a performance than I was with the way Dick Laning handled that crowd of people that we brought in up there.

Paul Stillwell: How did the British newsmen respond?

Captain Manson: They loved it! They ate it up. They thought Laning was marvelous and gave him a lot of publicity. Spreads were going all over the paper about the *Proteus* and Dick Laning and what a nice group they were to bring in. It was very favorable. That was the initial thing. Anyway, the troubles would set in now, mind you, but not immediately.

I went up very shortly after that to see how things were going. I won't forget, this time Commodore Ward had come off leave, and I went to see him first thing. He had a Bible on his bed there. He's a religious man and a good man.†

Paul Stillwell: He is a good man.

Captain Manson: Just a great fellow. I went in to him and held out my hand, and his hand was a little nervous. He looked at me over his glasses, and he said, "Well." I don't know what he called me, but I suppose "Commander." He said, "You've succeeded in ruining my career."

I said, "Oh, Commodore, I'm sure that isn't the case."

Captain Manson: He said, "Yes. You've denied me the opportunity to tell my story. You've denied the world the opportunity to know what our submarines our capable of.

---

* USS *Seawolf* (SSN-575), commissioned 30 March 1957, was the Navy's second nuclear-powered submarine. The first, USS *Nautilus* (SSN-571) had a pressurized water reactor. The *Seawolf* served as a test bed for a reactor cooled by liquid sodium. The latter was not deemed a success, so the *Seawolf* was later equipped with the pressurized water type. For the first skipper's view, see Richard B. Laning, "The *Seawolf*'s Sodium-Cooled Power Plant," *Naval History*, Spring 1992, pages 45-48.
† Rear Admiral Ward died 19 July 2005, subsequent to this interview.

You fiddled around, and you made Dick Laning the king of Holy Loch up here" or whatever, mayor. I called him "mayor," actually. He said, "As far as I'm concerned, I don't even exist or what I'm here for doesn't even exist. You've done me a great disservice."

I said, "Commodore, the only thing I can say to you is this: have confidence and trust in me for a little while. Before you're through up here, everybody will know why you're here, and everybody will know what these submarines are up here for. But for the time being, we're still going to have to soft-pedal."

"Well," he said, "I'll tell you one thing. I'm convinced that you've ruined me." And that's the way we left it, that visit. I felt badly that he felt that way, because I knew that we were going to, by increments, establish our authority and our purpose and all the rest of it, and that he was going to be the new king of the island. But he didn't see how this could happen after Laning had been given such prominence and actually preeminence too. It didn't appear that the squadron commander had anything to do up there.

Well, of course, by and by the first submarine came in. It was the *Patrick Henry*, and I went out on her myself. It had two skippers. Hal Shear and Bob Long were the blue and gold skippers.[*] But there's another submarine, too, and right now I don't recall which one it was.[†]

But, anyway, the submarine got in, and we began to put out stories about the submarines and what they were doing there. By this time the British had accepted the *Proteus*. Then, though, when the submarines started arriving, the opposition, the left-wing press starting really going after us. So then we had a real fire-hose situation on us, because we had to really turn it on, and we did. So then we started putting out information about what the submarines were all about, why they were useful, why they were needed, and how they would be the one surviving strategic system, and how by being over there in the Holy Loch, they were much closer to their targets and they didn't

---

[*] When the ballistic missile submarine *Patrick Henry* (SSBN-599) was commissioned on 9 April 1960, Commander Harold E. Shear, USN, was commanding officer of the blue crew, and Commander Robert L. J. Long, USN, was commanding officer of the gold crew. Both officers eventually became four-star admirals, and the oral histories of both are in the Naval Institute collection.

[†] The missile submarine *George Washington* (SSBN-598) first arrived at Holy Loch on 25 April 1961.

have all that time wasted because we only had a few. At that time, we only had two deployed.

Of course, Commodore Ward began becoming then a very important person. People were interviewing him, and he was getting his story across and, of course, he was happy as a clam. But there was a period there when he thought for sure his career was ruined, and I just had to keep reassuring him that it wasn't and that he would not only survive, but that he would make admiral. I didn't know how far he'd go, but this was just the way we had to handle this from a political viewpoint.

Paul Stillwell: Ironically, Laning retired as a captain and Ward as an admiral.[*]

Captain Manson: Isn't that ironic? That sure is the way it happened. The very reverse of what Admiral Ward thought would happen.

Paul Stillwell: You had the civilian demonstrators to deal with, also, didn't you?

Captain Manson: That was really the problem that Dick Laning and I had. We were on the phone constantly, trying to figure out how we would deal with these demonstrators. They were camping out up there, and they were reporters and just plain opponents from one kind to another and one political belief and another. But they were trying to provoke things that would cause us trouble. They were even trying to get aboard ship. They would go out there in their little various kinds of rubber rafts, anything they could, even swim out there. They even had underwater swimmers.

One time I remember I was up there, and there was talk that there were some unfriendly divers that were trying to attach something to the keel of the *Proteus*. So, anyway, we sent our divers out. By this time, well, I guess maybe we had them to start with, I don't know, but our divers went out and they didn't find anything.

I remember Dick Laning, on one instance, the boom out from the *Proteus* that was holding small boats, and these demonstrators had come, and they were climbing up the

---

[*] Ward was promoted to rear admiral and later turned down a promotion to vice admiral because he wanted a tour of duty that would be pleasant for his wife. See Ward's oral history.

ladder there onto the boom. Dick got some paint and went out there and got the painters to work where they were going to have come along. By the time these demonstrators got on board, they were just loaded with paint. [Laughter] So paint was dripping off of them, and they had a hard time making their case because they were loaded down with paint. It was such a comical thing in a way, yet this was the cunning of Dick Laning, to think of painting the place up for them. Then sometimes he'd grease it, make something really slick, and then they couldn't do anything they were trying to do.

Paul Stillwell: Imagination is his strong suit.[*]

Captain Manson: Oh, it's marvelous. One time I went out on the *Patrick Henry* with Bob Long for four or five days. We were coming back in, and there were demonstrators that had gotten themselves positioned in between the submarine and the tender. So somebody, I think Dick Laning, said, "Get the divers out there." So they brought out two or three big, big divers. I mean, they must have been 6 feet, 6 inches tall. They looked big, anyway, beside these British people they pulled.

So what they did was they got each one of these protesters by the nape of the neck, and they pulled them up on the submarine and then dived off with them. Cold water, and took them up for a good swim under the water and then brought them up. Whatever they were protesting, it certainly did simmer down after that.

But, anyway, we heard—Dick, I think, heard this, and so did I—that some of these people were being paid, even by the newspapers. We heard that the *Daily Express* was paying people to protest, to figure out various little things they could do. We also heard that one American paper was involved in it, and I can't remember which one it was at this point now. But, anyway, the demonstrators certainly were doing all they could to make life miserable for us up there.

Then on top of that, they put out the word that our young crews up there, sailors were impregnating the young Scottish girls and that this was becoming a very serious problem. So Dick was really worried about this and said, "I'd better get up there right

---

[*] Captain Laning died on 5 May 2000, subsequent to this interview.

away," to see if we couldn't figure out a solution. We'd always meet with the mayoress of Dunoon.* She was a lovely lady. Dick and I were both very fond of her.

I said, "Look, you say that our sailors caused an increase in birthrate of illegitimate children, but we don't have any records on this. I think we should have the records from the registry, the birthing office, or whatever you call it up here, and let's just see how the illegitimate population compares this year within previous years."

Because there had already been all kinds of stories in Scottish papers about what these Americans were doing over here to these innocent girls. Well, anyway, when the records were explored, actually there'd been a decrease in illegitimate births rather than the reverse, which had been printed. Fortunately, the records were on our side in that case, and that was the end of the problem.

But the other thing was, with the mayoress of Dunoon, that some of the Americans up there had criticized the shopkeepers and said that they were hiking their prices. Well, I'm sure they did. But, anyway, the mayoress was very upset that this would happen, and I said, well, what I thought that we should do is to get a few of the Scottish press together and let Dick Laning make a statement. So she said, yes, she thought that would be very helpful, so we called a group of the Scottish press.

Dick, in is inimitable way, made a statement of how absolutely hospitable and generous the shopkeepers were in Dunoon, and he made the most remarkable little speech there about the hospitality of the Scots and the shopkeepers, and it just turned the whole thing around. The mayoress, Dick, and I were there and we were all saying what really great people they were to welcome us with open arms and so forth.

Paul Stillwell: He sort of shamed them into being good.

Captain Manson: He shamed them into being good. He sure did. So, anyway, that was, well, just another chapter.

I'd say every week or two we would have something. They were even camping out up there and just doing anything they could do to stir up trouble—trying to get aboard

---

* The town was Dunoon, Argyll, Scotland. It is on the Firth of Clyde, to the south of Holy Loch and west of Gourock.

ship secretly and trying to do anything they could to disrupt operations. However, by and large, I'd have to say that thanks to Dick Laning and to Commodore Ward, because as it turned out, they made a remarkable team up there.

Now, we had one fellow that came up there, the skipper of the *George Washington*, we had a little trouble with him for a while. He was head of strategic plans for the Navy, I guess after George Miller, and he made admiral too. It had gotten to the point now where I thought I could take the British press into one of the big submarines, which I did. This skipper was talking about one thing or another, and he pulled out a .45, one he had on his belt or something, and made some kind of remark about what he'd like to do to the press at about the same time he pulled that gun out. And, boy, I mean to tell you, some of my closest friends in the British press were very upset and came to me privately and said that they didn't know what kind of a joke that was. They assumed it was a joke, but to them it wasn't a joke. They thought that I should know about it, that that's what he had done.

So I said, "Well, I'll take care of it."

So I called Dick, and he said, "Don't worry about it, Frank, it'll never happen again" and it didn't. So that was the end of the problem. But he had flashed that gun around up there. To the skipper it was a joke, but it sure didn't go down that way with the British, because their policemen don't wear guns. Man, they see a .45 lying out there on the table, that just about shakes them out of their boots. So they were really uptight.

But, anyway, we had subsequent visits putting not only press but members of Parliament and leaders of all walks of life aboard the *Proteus* and aboard the submarines, and it wasn't very long before the British wanted some too.

So we went all the way from what you might call a total negative to a total positive. But let me tell you, this was not done by accident. There was much planning and much head-scratching that went over there with Admiral Smith and Dick Laning and myself.

Paul Stillwell: Those two skippers that you've mentioned, Hal Shear and Bob Long, both wound up as four-star admirals. What are your recollections of them as commanders?

Captain Manson: Well, in order to command a Polaris submarine, first of all, you've got to be a master of detail. But I would say of the two, Hal Shear and Bob Long, that Shear was even more a master of detail. Every aspect of the ship, of the submarine, every bolt, every dial he knew. Well, of course, Long did too. But Long was more, I think, of a generalist in a way when it came to that phase of his career.

Now, of course, Hal Shear had been in strategic plans under George Miller, and I knew him as a three-striper. A very fine gentlemen, he was the son of a merchant mariner, an old seagoing family. I think his father had taken him out to sea when he was quite young. I know it's true, that this is the way he was brought up. So he was a real seagoing type and sort of had that New England look about him. But by being a master of detail, there was very little likelihood of an error or a mistake because they were so careful in the dealings with their officers. This is what I observed by the way they handled themselves aboard. If I had to rate one of them above the other, I'd have a hard time because they were different.

Now, I had Hal Shear go around and make a few speeches over in England and different places. I don't think I did Bob. I don't think Bob was so much into speeches at that time, or if he ever was.

But, anyway, I went out to sea with Bob Long on the *Patrick Henry*, and I was able to observe the way he handled command at sea. I must say, though, I got the fright of my life out there on the *Patrick Henry*. First of all, I'd never been in a submarine at sea before, and I didn't know they leaked when you took them down, say, 200 or 300 feet. So when we got down maybe first dive, I guess, we were headed for the North Sea, but water started streaming down different places, just streaming down. "Hey, Bob," I said. "Hey, look."

He said, "Yeah, somebody get a bucket." So somebody would fetch a bucket. At one point there we had five or six leaks and everybody with buckets all over the place.

I said, "Man, what in the world is wrong with this thing?"

He said, "Oh, well, a few valves need to be tightened up. We'll take her down some more." We took her down another 100, still leaking.

I thought, "Man, by the time we get down to where he's going, we're going to have this thing collapsed" or something, I don't know. Man, I couldn't believe this.

Well, eventually we got down to, I think, a depth of 600 feet, and the thing began to tighten up, and the leaks started to close, and I guess the hull got tighter. I don't know what happened, but it quit leaking eventually.

I won't forget, it was Easter Sunday that particular year, and that was the year I guess that they arrived over there, and that submarine was leaking in half a dozen places, and I was really yakking around to anybody I could get to listen to me about all those leaks. No one was paying any attention to me much and I said, "Bob, you know, we've got to get these leaks stopped."

He said, "Frank, let's go to church, what do you say?"

I said, "Man, all this leaking?"

He said, "Sure, it's routine. Don't worry about it. We're going to have Easter service. Let's go."

I said, "Yeah, well, maybe this will help."

So we went into Easter service and had a chaplain aboard. I guess the squadron chaplain. But we had a marvelous service, and I got my mind off of those leaks for a little while there and onto the resurrection and different things. I don't know if prayers had had anything to do with it or not, but the leaks had sort of subsided by the time the church service was over. But I thought to myself, "What a paradox or a contradiction or something, here this submarine is leaking all over the place and the skipper wants to go to church. Man, if that's the way they handle things on a submarine, I don't know whether I would have ever been a very good submariner or not."

But, anyway, it did work out fine, although we subsequently had a thing happen on that particular cruise that I never did get to the bottom of. That is that they decided to scram the reactor? Is that the word they used?

Paul Stillwell: I've heard that term, yes.

Captain Manson: Well, I think it's called scram, but the idea is that you shut it down. They said they had done this for Dr. Teller, and they thought they'd do it for me, just so I'd be a believer, and that the best way I'd ever be a believer of these things was to scram that reactor.* I told them I didn't need that, that I was perfectly happy just to sit and keep everything going the way it was. The food was nice. I didn't need that.

Pretty soon all the things started clanging around there and had damage here and damage there. First thing you know, the submarine took an up angle. I don't know what degree the up angle was, but I think it was at least 15 degrees.

The next thing I knew, the lights went out, the power went off, the ventilation went off, everything went off, and the submarine was dead. The only thing I could see in that entire submarine was a bunch of people running around with these head lanterns on. By this time, I'd gotten back in the control room where they had a lot of these tall computers, and the thing had gotten in such an angle, I was leaning against one of them. I could tell we were sinking. I didn't know any more than that, but I could tell that submarine was sliding the wrong way.

I kept asking if it was a drill or if we were really in trouble, and the only thing I could get back, "I don't know, sir. I'm sorry, I can't comment, sir. We're busy, sir." They were busy. Well, I think it took about 15 minutes to get that reactor activated again. I'm pretty sure that was the time, because if you did it too quickly, you could have a meltdown, but whatever the minimum time was.

Oh, I know what happened. The auxiliary that they were supposed to rely on when they shut down the reactor wouldn't function, so we lost all power.

Anyway, there was a quite a time elapsed there before we got the thing going, lights started coming on and vents and whatnot. I'd been looking for Bob Long. I finally found him, and I told him, "Bob, let me tell you something. This may be good for submariners, but listen, I've been scared before, and I don't need it anymore."

"Oh, Frank," he said, "that's just nothing. Don't worry about it."

I said, "Well, okay, but I'll tell you right now, I don't need that kind of—"

He said, "We want to make a believer out of you."

I said, "Well, you did, no doubt about that."

A few years later, I was a guest at the Naval War College, as was the former diving officer from the *Patrick Henry*. We were guests at lunch at the president's table.

---

* Dr. Edward Teller was a renowned nuclear scientist.

We got talking. I said, "Say, it's been a few years, I guess maybe you can tell me now. What happened aboard the *Patrick Henry* when we had that simulated drill?"

He said, "Well, I'd rather not talk about that, sir, if you don't mind."

I said, "Even yet?"

He said, "Even yet." So he wouldn't tell me, and that's all I know about it. I'm sure Bob Long didn't have any more to say about it either, but I never did get any more information, so I don't know.

I heard from various ones after that that what happened was that the skipper had told them always to keep the submarine properly ballasted so in case they did lose power that it would remain level. But they had failed to do that, and it was heavily weighted on the stern, so that was the reason why it took an up angle. But for whatever reason or whatever happened, I'll never know, but I'll just tell you one thing, that was one frightening moment for me. Anyway, that's when we came in that time and found those demonstrators.

I was most impressed with the operations of the ballistic missile submarines and the way they were targeted and the speed with which they could respond, and the way in which they could communicate.

Although there was one other thing that happened during the trip I might as well mention, too, that I got a little excited about. That is that every day at 4:00 o'clock they tested the liquid or fluid or whatever in the reactor to see how much radioactivity it had.

Paul Stillwell: Just the coolant?

Captain Manson: Yes, they checked the coolant every day at 4:00. So I went down. The man who did that wasn't too keen on me going in with him, but I said, "Oh, no, I don't mind. Let me watch you do it." So we get in there and then he proceeded to get it out and spill it, and spilled it all over the desk in there. I said, "Man, is that stuff radioactive?"

"Well, a little bit, not much." So he was busy with rubber gloves and mopping it up, and I was busy getting out of there. [Laughter]

Anyway, even though it was supposed to be a routine sort of thing, I found life on board to be pretty interesting.

Paul Stillwell: How would you compare the commanders in chief whom you've mentioned, Admiral Dennison and Admiral Smith, as far as their operating styles?

Captain Manson: Both these men could see the big picture. There was never any myopic vision on the part of either Dennison or Smith. But Dennison tended to concentrate more on political goals and political objectives and the nuances of political relationships, more so than Admiral Smith.

For example, I remember when it looked like the United States was going to cancel Skybolt.* This might very well disrupt the political process in Britain, because Britain was buying into Skybolt. In one of the early conversations we had about that, Admiral Smith said, "You know, this may very well cost the government. The government may lose out." And it did, as a matter of fact. Skybolt was just one part of it. Admiral Smith thought politically, but more so Dennison.

Dennison had been in the White House as aide to Truman.† He was truly a strategic thinker, and he didn't get down into the organizational details of how things were going. He was more concerned with the political process and the relationships of forces to power and changes and political attitudes, whereas Smith, having been Chief of Naval Personnel, was very interested in people. His concept of command was working through the people, and he'd get the people indoctrinated, and then he'd figure that they were going to do it. He delegated liberally with his subordinate commanders.

Of course, Dennison, too, but Dennison was not the detail commander that Smith was. I'll give you an example. First of all, I was trying to get anybody, one of the four-stars, Dennison, Smith, anybody, to go down to Morocco and check. We were about to lose that air base down there, and I thought it would be helpful if one of them would go

---

* Robert S. McNamara became U.S. Secretary of Defense in January 1961. The Skybolt program was canceled in December 1962. It involved a ballistic missile, armed with a nuclear warhead and designed for a range of approximately 1,000 miles, to be fired from planes such as the B-52 bomber.
† As a captain and rear admiral, Robert L. Dennison, served as President Harry S. Truman's naval aide from February 1948 to January 1953.

down there and just meet with the King and Crown Prince and, generally, just sort of case the total area and see if their presence wouldn't help a lot in our dealings.

Well, I got Admiral Smith worked up enough to go down there. So the very time we went down there, the commander down there was Captain Jack Counihan, and he had gone to Washington, because he'd been called back there by CNO.[*] He hadn't told Admiral Smith that he was going, so when we got down there, why, the commander was gone. To be absent wasn't exactly the best way to welcome Admiral Smith or anybody else to a command.

So the deputy was there, I've forgotten his name, but he was doing the very best he could, and so we went around. But I was terribly disappointed, because I had been the one that had been encouraging the admiral to make this trip. I never dreamed that—and I'd sort of been an advocate of Captain Counihan. I'd known him back to the B-36 and OP-23 days and he was a pretty good fighter. But I think Admiral Smith was always a little skeptical of how Counihan might perform under certain conditions. Well, he sure hadn't done well on this occasion.

Well, anyway, we were getting ready to leave, just about an hour before departure, and Captain Counihan returned from Washington. We were at a luncheon at his deputy's home, and Captain Counihan came in. "Well, everything's going fine in Washington," he said.

"Well, that's good."

"Well," Admiral Smith said to Counihan, "does Arleigh have anything for me, any special words of wisdom or anything of that nature?"

Counihan kind of puffed his face out there a little bit and said, "No. Well, I wouldn't be at liberty, Admiral, to mention anything that went on in this meeting, that it was just confidential. I'm really not at liberty to discuss what we discussed."

Admiral Smith—I won't forget this—said, "Why, Jack, that's fine. I have good communications with the Chief of Naval Operations. I have ways of finding out, and I appreciate your position." Admiral Smith was quite a gentleman, but yet the atmosphere

---

[*] Captain John L. Counihan Jr., USN, a naval aviator, was Commander Naval Activities, Port Luaytey, Morocco, from December 1957 to August 1961.

was freezing. Counihan didn't realize that he had just destroyed himself with Admiral Smith.

Paul Stillwell: First by being gone and then not talking to him.

Captain Manson: And then not talking to him. Admiral Smith later asked me what I'd been telling him about Counihan, and I said, "Well, I must say, Admiral, I don't understand this. I don't understand his refusal to talk to you. I'll never understand that."

He said, "Well, I won't, either." That's the last time I guess we ever discussed the subject.

But, again, here was Smith, depending on his subordinate commanders to keep him informed back and forth. He was free to discuss things with them, and he expected that likewise. He wanted that flow to go up and down, and that's the way Smith was. I think it had to do with his personnel background, more so than Dennison.

Dennison, on the other hand, didn't seem to worry much about that sort of thing. I mean, he just kept sort of his strategic goals in mind in the conduct of his command relationships, I guess, is the best way to put it.

Paul Stillwell: Well, each person is a product of his own experience.

Captain Manson: That's what it comes down to. Dennison, for example, would come in and from time to time, he'd ask me about some particular subject, and I'd tell him, "Well, I think we have all the information available on this subject, Admiral."

He'd say, "Well, put it on the streets." That was his way of saying give it the full treatment, publicity-wise or whatever. But Admiral Smith would be much more—well, he was not as sort of flamboyant as Dennison in that sense. I don't know if "flamboyant" is quite the word.

Paul Stillwell: Was he more interested in the details?

Captain Manson: Yes, he wanted to know because he had a background in public information. But he was much more interested in this reporter and that one and so forth. He just took more interest. But still, he told me to use his stars liberally, when I was doing my job, to remember that he was backing me with four stars and to not be embarrassed about using them when I had to.

Paul Stillwell: You have to have good judgment on when to do that, because you can really alienate people if you do it too much.

Captain Manson: Well, you certainly can and particularly in your own command setup. Because your deputy commander in chief is a fellow who guards his prerogatives pretty carefully, and when you have a personal relationship with the admiral, many things you don't ever discuss with the number two. You do if it involves command or anything, but there are times when you really don't. A lot of times there are just tentative discussions or exploratory discussions, and you're trying to feel out subjects before you really come down on something that's final and there's no point in bringing somebody into the discussion if that person may not even understand too well what you're talking about.

Roger Mehle, when he came over there—did you ever meet him?*

Paul Stillwell: No, but I've heard he's a fiery guy.†

Captain Manson: Well, he's a bull-in-a-china-shop-type of fellow. They say in the Pacific, he was a fighter pilot and he used to chew the tails of the Japanese planes off with his prop, actually flying into them and chewing them up. Whether he ever did or not, I'm not sure, but I wouldn't doubt it. For example, when he came over there, he was trying to interpose himself in between me and Admiral Smith. I forget exactly the subject of this particular episode that I'm about to relate, but it makes no difference what the subject was.

---

* Captain Roger W. Mehle, USN, a naval aviator.
† Rear Admiral Mehle died 30 August 1997, subsequent to this interview.

Mehle called me in there, and he said, "Hereafter, you will do this such and such, and you will do it this way." It was great detail, and it was a subject that he knew not too much about. I knew perfectly well that this is not the way we were going to handle this.

So I went down and got the command organization chart, and I brought it back to him.

Paul Stillwell: I bet he was thrilled by that.

Captain Manson: He turned purple, his lips turned purple, and I've never seen a man so angry and with expletives deleted, I'd never heard such a profane man as he let me know that that organizational chart had no part of this conversation. I told him, "Well, I can't." I really didn't get upset, because I could tell that he absolutely had lost control totally. Except I kind of smiled, and I said, "Well, I think we'll have to work with the organizational chart. Now, it may be that we'll have to change it, but as long as it's the way it is, well, we'll do it the way we've been doing it," and I walked out.

So I told Admiral Smith that this had occurred, and the admiral laughed about it. He said, "Well, I suppose I'll be hearing from him."

I said, "I suppose so."

He said, "Well, I'll take care of it," so I never heard any more about it.

But, anyway, we had this case, a similar case, over there when we were told to set up the CinCNELM specified command. In the unification process, the first phase of it was to get the Secretary of Defense and all that set up. Then the next phase was to set up the unified and specified commands all over the world.

I never was really too keen on the defense setup anyway, because I just figured they were establishing a fourth department, military department, that was going to be every bit as large as any of the services and maybe larger. I just couldn't see the necessity, still don't see the necessity, of such a tremendous number of people stirring around and stewing around, in many cases not knowing what they're doing, many times political jobs. Generally speaking, I think it's a lot of wasted effort in that Defense Department. I think it's much, much larger than it ever should be, and cumbersome, bureaucratic, and I don't think it's up to our defense all that much. This is just a sort of a quick, dirty conclusion I'm giving you here.

Paul Stillwell: The Frank Manson view of DoD. [Laughter]

Captain Manson: That's what I'm telling you. But I was over on the end of it where they had sent instructions to us to set up a new specified command in the Middle East. I was given instructions to organize the public relations setup for that command. As I told you, I'd been doing it in my hip pocket up to this point. But then I was told that I must have—in Washington and the Joint Chiefs, I think they had decided that we should have about three officers, three or five, I don't recall, but anyway, a sizeable little setup and quite a number of enlisted personnel.

So when I received these instructions from the nucleus of the staff that had been sent over there, a Marine general named Vanryzin, and Ben Pickett was one of the implementing officers.[*] I forget the rest, but I have to remember Pickett's name. He later made admiral, but he's the one I had the trouble with. I told Admiral Smith, "Look, Admiral, I'm not going to try to impose my thinking on these other elements of the staff—operations, logistics, and all that. I'll just summarize by telling you I think it's much, much too large. We've been doing it with 12 officers, and now it looks like we're going to have about 200 or some such thing. I do think I have a responsibility in the public relations, public information, whatever you want to call it, and I am going to recommend against this big staff."

He said, "Frank, you do exactly what you think is right and correct."

I said, "Well, I'll do that."

So they came around to me when the time came to build up the staff and said, "Where's your plan?"

I said, "Well, I think we'll just use the same plan we have now, which is we'll double in brass if the CinCUSNavEur staff will handle the CinCNELM staff."

Then Pickett said to me, "You will establish the command, the billets, and the setup that we told you to."

---

[*] Brigadier General William J. Vanryzin, USMC; Captain Ben B. Pickett, USN.

I said, "Well, I'm going to tell you something, Captain, I'm not going to do it. Who do you think prepared all this mess in the first place?"

He said, "This comes directly from the Joint Chiefs of Staff."

I said, "Who in the Joint Chiefs of Staff do you think did this?"

He said, "I don't care who did it. We're ordered to do it, and we're going to do it."

I said, "Well, I'll tell you one thing, Captain, you're going to be running over one captain's body when you do it with me, because I am not going to do it. I'm not going to move and set up a staff over here that's much larger than the one I have to deal with in Europe and all the other things I have to do, for this mythical staff that's never probably going to do anything except maybe one or two exercises a year when we call in reserves and do that. I'm not going to do it."

He said, "Well, you're going to do it."

I said, "Well, we'll see about that."

So, boy, I made the fastest run I could to Admiral Smith's office and told him that I had just gotten cross-threaded with Captain Pickett, and I told him I wasn't going to implement that PR part of his new command. Admiral Smith told me to stick with my guns, and he'd protect me. So Pickett then was so angry with me, for months after that he wouldn't speak to me. Then we had an exercise, by and by, down the eastern Med with his staff, and occasionally we'd have to sit across from each other at a table, and he never would speak to me again. That was the end of our conversation, but we didn't set that big staff up either.

Paul Stillwell: It sounds as if you had difficult relationships with a number of people in that job.

Captain Manson: Yes, I did.

Paul Stillwell: What was the name of this staff that was being set up?

Captain Manson: The new specified command was CinCNELM.[*]

Paul Stillwell: Well, CinCNELM was a thing that had been in existence.

Captain Manson: We just kept the same name, but it was a specified command. And they brought in a lot of officers and those people didn't have a thing in the world to do except sit around and write papers. All they did. There was nothing to command. No operating forces except that seaplane tender down there and those two destroyers in the Persian Gulf. It was the biggest joke, really, that I had seen.

But I was already disgusted with that whole Defense Department thing, so my background was pretty much tainted by having seen this monstrosity placed on the taxpayers of the American people, and it's still there. I'll never get that out of my craw because I think it's a terrible waste—was and is. That's the way I feel about it.

Paul Stillwell: What came of this plan that you had for upgraded public relations emphasis, for the command?

Captain Manson: I had to use enlisted personnel to put these things together. But we set up something I think we called special events. The idea was that when there was something going on like the Paris Air Show or something anywhere in Europe, that we would have exhibits and things like art shows, displays of all kinds. Maybe we could fill a gymnasium or a big hall with all kinds of exhibits that would display what naval power was all about.

Then I made a television studio and brought that into the command, just a one-camera job, where when we had individuals come in—and that's about all we ever had in London—we could interview them on camera and then send that back and get it into the news at times when other services couldn't—when the regular AP or somebody couldn't get down there.

---

[*] In September 1958, Commander in Chief U.S. Naval Forces Eastern Atlantic and Mediterranean (CinCNELM) was assigned additional duty as U.S. Commander Eastern Atlantic, under Commander in Chief, U.S. Atlantic Fleet. In February 1960 the further title of Commander in Chief U.S. Naval Forces Europe (CinCUSNavEur) was assigned to CinCNELM/ComEastLant. In December 1963 the title CinCNELM was disestablished and that of CinCUSNavEur remained.

Anyway, it was sort of a historical-type setup. It took me forever to get that accomplished, and I barely got it set up when I was leaving there, but, nevertheless, I did set it up. Anyway, we dealt with magazines and books, we had it set up for that, and for dealing with the newspapers and for dealing with community organizations all over Europe, so that we had our hands in external affairs, in a complete periphery of command relations. We had to deal with so many elements over there in Europe. I had some very, very highly qualified enlisted personnel, and many times I had to send them. I had to send them a lot of times to Holy Loch and different places. But I would discuss these things with them. I had a junior lieutenant that I would send.

I had a chief named Bill Prosser, who was one of the most sensitive and highly qualified chiefs I've ever seen before or since. I could use him, and I could send him in a conference with colonels, and he'd do just as well. Everybody in Europe was highly impressed with this man.

In any event, I would send these exhibits out. I'd send out radio programs. We would generate our own and then send them out. Then we had radio stations that we could reach throughout Europe. With the Sixth Fleet, as often as possible, I would get large groups of press and take them to the Sixth Fleet and let them be down there for two or three days. They'd have all kinds of displays and things that they could show them while we were there.

The British loved this, as did other nations too. They liked the idea of getting out in the fleet. I thought that it was particularly good in Britain at that time, because there were, at that time, probably as many as 20 naval correspondents that wrote mostly about naval subjects. They were sort of, still in that time frame, the mouthpiece of naval power and the vocal cords for the world, really. But I could see it was declining. The last thing I ever said to those people, they had a dinner for me when I left Europe and was coming back to the States. They were all there, including Stephen Roskill and that group.* They gave me copies of his books, and they had signed these books and everything. I told them what a shame it was that, first of all, that the Royal Navy was on the decline because it had been such a stalwart force in the history of nations and particularly the

---

* Captain Stephen W. Roskill served on active duty in the Royal Navy from 1921 to 1949, when he was retired for medical reasons. He then served as the Royal Navy's official historian from 1949 to 1960. He was a prolific author. Among his works was the three-volume *The War at Sea* about World War II.

British Empire. Not only was the fleet going steadily down, but that the number of naval writers was on the slide, and that I thought it was a tragedy because they'd been so articulate for so many years, and that I hoped they would reverse this.

They allowed as how maybe if I'd stay over there and keep up, that maybe I could have some influence. But I said I couldn't stay any longer. But, anyway, I used to try to encourage the British chief of information, who was a Captain Wallace—I can't think of his first name—that they should try to strive for more of the budget over there, and he just told me it was a hopeless cause. The money wasn't there, and there wasn't any way he could do it.

The result was that what the U.S. Navy did was take up the slack, and we sent our people out to give presentations at schools and universities. I spoke at universities. We continued, for at least the period of time that I was there, to infuse the Europeans and the British with the idea that naval power had a very strong role to play. That's what we used that office for.

Paul Stillwell: It sounds like a direct outgrowth of your work with McCain in OP-09Dog.

Captain Manson: It was a direct outgrowth. All I did was translate what we had done in the United States to Europe. But I had to, of course, refine it in many ways because the same things didn't work.

Paul Stillwell: You were not talking directly to American taxpayers, for example.

Captain Manson: No, no. And the unions over there were set up quite different. I did get into quite a lot of trouble with one British labor union over there. I suppose the things you can remember are the things where you get in trouble. What was the name of it? "Masterpiece Theater," I believe, was the television show they had over there on TV. They asked me one time if I would be willing to let them use about 15 Marines in one of their TV specials that they were going to do on Korea or Inchon. I believe it was on Korea. I said, well, I'd check it out with the ones who had the Marines, and if they had no objection, I certainly didn't. So, anyway, we agreed to let these 15 Marines appear in this TV production.

I went to a luncheon. They used to have about a monthly luncheon over there between the TV people, the movie people and so forth, and they would invite me to attend these luncheons with them. On this one occasion, I was getting quite a lot of queries about these Marines from the *Daily Telegraph*, of all people. They had a TV correspondent there, and I thought, "Oh, it's safe to talk fully with the *Daily Telegraph*," a very conservative newspaper and always been very friendly to me. I thought, "I might as well tell them exactly." Well, it wasn't any secret about it, anyway. I'd cleared it with the embassy; I'd cleared it everywhere.

They said, "You mean that you're going to allow these Marines to go on the air and take the place of other actors?"

I said, "Well, I don't know about that. I've been asked by this TV production 'Masterpiece Theater,' [It was either 'Masterpiece' or 'Armchair Theater,' and I don't remember which]." But anyway, I said, "Yeah, they've asked, and I'm going to do it."

So the next day, I guess it was, in the paper after this luncheon, there was quite a little story about the fact that these American Marines had been authorized by me to participate in a television production that was going to take jobs away from union members. So I thought, "Boy, I never dreamed that this kind of a thing could happen."

So then I started getting calls from the head of the union. They said, "Are you going to continue with this, or are you going to drop it?"

I said, "No, no, I'm going to continue with it."

They said, "Well, we're going to have to become more severely critical of your activity, and we're going to use the press."

I checked it out with my colleague over in the embassy, and, of course, they had been getting calls, too, in the embassy. I wish I could remember the fellow's name in the embassy.

Meanwhile, the television production people told us that these bit players, that's what they call them over there, were not actually TV bit players, but movie. It was a movie union that was sort of out of work and wanted more jobs, and they were the ones that were really putting the pressure, and it wasn't the TV at all. So I said, "Well, we got into this thing because of you folks. Now, we're visitors over here. What's going to happen here?"

They said, "Well, as far as we're concerned, it's just an outlaw outfit, and we're planning on your Marines doing it."

So I guess that afternoon I received a call from the head of the union, and he said, "I want you to know, Captain, that you're taking bread from the mouths of our union members, and I am going to see to it that this doesn't happen."

I said, "Well, sir, I'm very sorry. I understand you're representing the movie." I told him what I knew about it.

He said, "Well, in any case, you're taking bread from the mouths of our people, and we're going to see to it that you don't do it."

I suppose along about 4:00 or 5:00 o'clock that day I received a call from the *Daily Telegraph* and said, "Well, what are you going to do? Are you going to allow the Marines to participate, or are you going to withdraw?"

I said, "We're going through with it."

So the next day, a great big story there in the *Daily Telegraph*: "Marines Refuse to Retreat Under Fire," and a very favorable story about the whole thing, what heroism we had shown in face of all this pressure to continue with the project. So we did, and it turned out to be a pretty good TV production.

Paul Stillwell: Are there any other events you remember? Certainly the Polaris discussion was very interesting. What other things happened during that period?

Captain Manson: Well, the Agadir earthquake was a great tragedy.[*] We sent ships in from the Sixth Fleet. We sent a cruiser, and I don't recall whether we sent others, but with emergency help in to them, as did other navies in sending fleet units in there. I flew down there, and Agadir had been totally destroyed, just absolutely leveled to the ground. It was certainly the worst catastrophe I'd ever seen. The PR from it was very little,

---

[*] On 29 February 1960, a severe earthquake hit Agadir, Morocco. It killed about 12,000 people and injured another 12,000.

really, from up in London, but the main thing we wanted to get across to the Moroccans was that we would do all we could by way of emergency relief, and we did.

We were pretty familiar with the royal family down there because of a fellow named Leon Blair.[*] Lieutenant Commander Blair was close to the royal family. He was always sending up to London for me to pick up something in the PX for him.[†] On one occasion, Admiral Smith I think loaded on a small sports car for the Crown Prince. I'm not too sure about that, but I believe that's the case.

Anyway, the royal family was friendly toward us, but there were elements down there that were very anti-American in Morocco. I went down there periodically to see how things were going. During that Agadir earthquake I met King Mohammed V.[‡] I think it was Mohammed V. The interesting thing about that was that he was standing out there all by himself in a big circle of people all around, and I asked somebody, I said, "What's the king doing out there in the middle?"

He said, "Well, he's standing out there to shake hands with anybody who wants to meet him or have anything to say to him."

I said, "But nobody's doing anything."

He said, "No, they're all afraid of him."

So I said, "Well, I think I'll go visit with him."

So I went up to him, the only one to go, and told him that I was from our naval headquarters in London, representing Admiral Smith, and that we had come to help at Agadir, do what we could, and that I had come down personally as his representative. He was so appreciative of it and invited me to go on down to Agadir and join him for lunch, which, of course, I did.

But then I was amused, that night Captain Counihan sent out a dispatch from Morocco saying that they'd presented me to the King. I thought, well, that's one of the most unusual presentations that I've ever received. I think maybe I presented myself.

---

[*] Lieutenant Commander Leon B. Blair, USN. He was on the staff of Counihan, who was Commander U.S. Naval Activities, Port Lyautay, Kenitra, Morocco.
[†] PX – post exchange.
[‡] King Mohammed V was monarch of Morocco from 14 August 1957 until his death on 26 February 1961. He died three days before the earthquake, so perhaps Manson met him on another occasion. Mohammned's son, King Hassan II, ruled from 26 February 1961 to 23 July 1999.

But, anyway, I met the Crown Prince, Hassan, who's now the King, and discussed the situation with him. The Moroccan problem was with us the whole time we were there, as to how much we really wanted to put in there and whether we could keep an air station there. We finally, I think, wound up with a communication station, is the way I remember Morocco.

In Spain this didn't have a lot to do with public relations, but Admiral Smith and the general down there, the JUSMAAG, did not get along well.[*] The way this Air Force general wanted to handle things was that he just wanted to strictly deal with the Spanish on a one-on-one, more or less Air Force-to-Spain relationship. This was the conflict, whereas the Commander in Chief of Naval Forces Europe and the Commander in Chief Europe wanted Spain to be integrated on a total basis—I mean, work into the total defense and command security structure rather than just a one-service relationship with Spain.

This was the source of the conflict. As far as I know, it never was resolved during the years I was there, and there wasn't a lot that any of us could do about it. It's one of those things, when you get up in the morning it's still there.

The other thing that this white fleet that had come out in *Life* magazine was something that I really had to deal with. The fact that I had authored the article in *Life* and come up with the concept of it and all, I couldn't hide or get away from it. So this was, in a way, a blessing because it brought me to meet the top-level people in the British government—the members of the Cabinet, the House of Lords, the members of the House of Commons, and the top members of the press. I had access, because of this, to a level of people that I never would have known otherwise. But at the same time, at times it got in the way of things I was trying to do with the Navy and for the Navy. I was just one person, and I could do just so many things. At times it made it very difficult for me.

But fortunately, I had admirals like Admiral Dennison and Admiral Smith. Admiral Dennison never did tell me what to do or what not to do. But Admiral Smith told me when he arrived over there to relieve Admiral Dennison, that anything I had to do in connection with this idea, he wanted me to do it. He said he basically thought it was a

---

[*] JUSMAAG – Joint U.S. Military Assistance Advisory Group.

good idea and that he knew I would be discreet, but he said at the same time, "You do what you have to do."

So I had that, at the very highest level, although back in Washington I was under a cloud on that idea with Admiral Kirkpatrick, the Chief of Information who was very angry with me, who had been a friend up until this thing came out. Admiral Burke was happy about it, and yet he was perturbed too. So this was the thing, as I say, with mixed blessings.

But I should tell you, I think, in this history, that we came within a hair of doing the whole thing worldwide. It had a lot of sympathy in Britain, a lot of interest, as it did throughout Europe. Paul-Henri Spaak of NATO was all in favor of it and sent me a message to that effect. They organized the White Fleet U.K., they called it, and then they called it White Fleet Europe. Then they organized the White Army in Morocco. The thing just really did mushroom for a year or two there. Then because the United States didn't really get behind it, it fizzled out in all these countries. Meanwhile, Willy Brandt was behind it.[*] It had picked up in West Germany. I went over and appeared on nationwide television in West Germany. I appeared on television in Britain. Never in the United States. But I attended Cabinet meetings in Brussels on the idea. I briefed the House of Lords with Lord Attlee present.[†]

While I'm on this, I might as well tell you my favorite anecdote of the whole thing. After I got through with Lord Clement Attlee, he said, "Oh, this is a jolly good idea. It's jolly good." He says, "Have you briefed Churchill on this?" Now Churchill was then in his 80s.[‡]

I said, "No." I guess I called him "Your Lordship;" I don't know what I called him. "Mr. Prime Minister," whatever was appropriate, I know I had the right thing, but I said, "No, no, I haven't." Sir Winston was what I called him. "No, I haven't briefed Sir Winston."

He said, "Well, you should brief him, but you know he's going to oppose this."

---

[*] Willy Brandt was Vice Chancellor of West Germany from 1 December 1966 to 20 October 1969 and Chancellor of West Germany from 21 October 1969 to 7 May 1974.
[†] The Right Honourable Clement R. Attlee, Earl of Attlee, had served as Britain's Prime Minister from 26 July 1945 to 26 October 1951.
[‡] Sir Winston Churchill had served as Britain's Prime Minister from 1940 to 1945 and from 1951 to 1955. He was born on 30 November 1874.

I said, "Oh, no, I wouldn't think that he would. I would think because of his knowledge of geography and the trend of the current world, that he would support it."

"Oh, no," he said, "he will oppose this." I saw a definite twinkle in Atlee's eye when he said of Churchill, "He'll want to save all these ships for the next war."

Then he turned to his Foreign Secretary and told him he thought that Britain ought to look into it in terms of putting something like this in Africa. I think he mentioned West Africa, but I'm not sure which part of Africa.

But, anyway, this idea did at times cause me a certain degree of pressure, really. That's about the only way you can describe it, because every now and again it would break out in the British press, and there would be stories about it. I had to deal with it.

I had visitors from the United States when the Peace Corps came into being. I had been serving on a board of trustees in Britain called the Voluntary Service Overseas, which was the British Peace Corps concept. It had been going on two or three years before. But they put me on that board almost the minute I arrived over in Britain because of this white fleet thing. We'd send young people on sort of Peace Corps missions. We'd interview them and decide who should go and who shouldn't go. But then when they were working on getting the Peace Corps idea in the United States, they'd send people over to talk to me from Kennedy's administration about it, and I'd give them—I remember one piece of advice I told was that whatever they did, they shouldn't start big; they should start rather small and then learn by their mistakes. They started out, I think, with 5,000, so I could see they were taking my advice to heart.

Paul Stillwell: [Laughter] How much dealing did you have with the NATO command?

Captain Manson: Every year I had quite an experience with NATO, because they would send the team to London to run the big NATO exercise, and I would be the U.S. liaison with that team that they set up. They'd usually send a rear admiral over there to run that thing that would be about three weeks to a month. I think my first year they sent Howard "Red" Yeager, over in charge of that command information bureau.* Then I guess two years they sent Admiral Jack McCain, rear admiral. Of course, with Admiral Yeager I

---

* Rear Admiral Howard A. Yeager, USN.

had served on the staff with him and Admiral Denfeld, so he and I were able to coordinate things well. I'd also served with NATO down in Naples, so I had a pretty good idea of how NATO was put together. It didn't cause me any difficulty in dealing with NATO.

Those command exercises were the main thrust of the experience each year, so I did have to get deep into NATO for that period of time. With Admiral McCain, it was a marvelous experience each year.

I think this will be my final anecdote for today, but Admiral McCain was a tennis player. So was I. He'd bring his tennis racket and want to play tennis. I wasn't a member of the Queen's Club there, but Admiral Noel Gayler was.[*] He was the naval attaché. So I asked Noel if he'd let me use his membership with Admiral McCain. "Oh, sure, Frank. Anytime you want to go down there and play, just come get my card and do it."

So one day Admiral McCain and I set up to go down and have a match, and we decided to take our sons with us. His son Joe was over there, and my son, Frank Karig, was also old enough to play. So I went down to the Queen's Club, and Admiral McCain had on his white tennis shorts. He was dressed for tennis, except he was wearing a snap-brimmed hat and smoking a stogie, a cigar that was at least eight inches long, and he'd just barely lit it up. Admiral McCain had long arms, and when he came down, his racket would hit the ground as we walked. He used it like a cane.

Well, we walked out on the court, and we were all dressed appropriately. Well, we all were, but he had this hat on and this cigar. The courts were filled, and everybody stopped playing. You know how the British are, when they see something that's this strange, man, they quit and they all turned to us like we were some visitors from outer space. Admiral McCain turned to me, and he said, "What the G.D. hell do you think these people are looking at?"

I said, "Well, Admiral, it could be that they're looking at your cigar, or it could be they're looking at your hat."

---

[*] Rear Admiral Noel A. M. Gayler, USN, was U.S. naval attaché in London from August 1960 to August 1962. The oral history of Gayler, who retired as a four-star admiral, is in the Naval Institute collection.

"Well, they've got very little to do if that's all they're doing." And he just puffed away, and we kept on walking. They didn't stop watching us until he got over there and took his hat off and put his cigar aside, and we started playing, and then they quit. But I'll tell you, I thought I would pop. But that's McCain for you.

Paul Stillwell: Thank you, Captain, another good session today.

Captain Manson: Thank you.

Interview Number 5 with Captain Frank Manson, U.S. Navy (Retired)
Place: Annapolis, Maryland
Date: Thursday, 21 April 1988
Interviewer: Paul Stillwell

Paul Stillwell: Captain, before we resume the chronological account of your career, I believe you have a couple of stories to tell about previous tours of duty, and you hinted that one has a whiff of scandal associated with it.

Captain Manson: Well, yes, it has to do with the Denfeld administration, when he was CNO.[*] The Navy was under tremendous pressure then to retain its carriers and retain naval air and Marine air. We were just under a lot of pressure for ships in general. So Admiral Denfeld thought it would probably be a wise thing to bring in a person skilled in legislative matters for his personal staff. He had Walter Karig there as his press officer and PR man, and I worked for Captain Karig at that time.

But Denfeld evidently felt that he needed someone who was really close to somebody on the Hill, because the legislative setup in those days was sort of like a group of fiefdoms. I mean, BuShips had its congressmen, like Harry Sheppard and a few others on the Armed Forces Committee.[†] Naval air had its Congress people it could talk to, people mainly who had shipyards or air stations or contracts to build ships or airplanes. So there were those connections all around the Navy.

But Admiral Denfeld himself really didn't have any close connection, so that's how they brought this fellow on the staff. I myself thought it was rather unusual to see a four-striper who was strictly a political officer. It didn't seem to me that he'd had any kind of experience much except maybe on the Hill, and I suppose that's why he was what he was.

---

[*] Admiral Louis E. Denfeld, USN, served as Chief of Naval Operations from 15 December 1947 to 2 November 1949.
[†] BuShips – Bureau of Ships. Harry R. Sheppard, a Democrat from California, served in the House of Representatives from 3 January 1937 to 3 January 1965.

Paul Stillwell: What was his name?

Captain Manson: His name was Captain Harold Latta-Lawrence, and that Latta-Lawrence sounded like a little bit of royalty there or something.* He came from Massachusetts, Boston, and he'd served with Edith Norse Rogers for a number of years.†

Well, in any case, Denfeld was under a lot of pressure really just to stay on in the job. I mean, it was a very critical time there for the Navy, so Latta-Lawrence was going to add a new dimension to us. Red Yeager, I think, had something to do with bringing in Latta-Lawrence. Where he came from, I don't know; I don't even know where he'd been previously. But he was a nice man. I used to enjoy visiting with him and his giving me a little insight on what happened on the Hill.

Well, anyway, he and I were going to get married about the same time there, and his romance had even moved along faster than mine. I was married over here in St. Andrew's Chapel in May of '48.‡ He'd met this woman out in Tennessee when he was on some sort of a trip out there, I think. I'm not sure where he just did meet her, but apparently there was a chemical reaction there, and torrid letter writing went on for about three weeks, so they decided to marry after about three weeks. So nothing would do Diane but to have the big society wedding in New York, and this took everybody by surprise, because I guess none of us around here had ever been in high society before.§

All of Denfeld's staff was going to be involved in it. Admiral Radford, Vice Chief, was going to be the senior admiral representing Admiral Denfeld.** Admiral Jocko Clark was the senior swordsman.†† Captain Thackrey, and Captain Yeager, Captain Karig, and Lieutenant Commander Russell Harris, author of some of the *Battle Report* books along with Captain Karig and myself.‡‡ Harris and I were the two

---

* Captain Harold A. L. Latta-Lawrence, USNR, special advisor to the Chief of Naval Operations. By profession he was a lawyer and economist.
† Edith Nourse Rogers, a Republican from Massachusetts, served in the House of Representatives from 30 June 1925 to 10 September 1960.
‡ Manson's bride was Orie Lee Pickren of Brunswick, Georgia. The wedding was on 26 May 1948 in the St. Andrew's Chapel on the lower level of the Naval Academy chapel building in Annapolis.
§ The wedding was on 22 April 1948. The bride was Eilene Diana Gibson.
** Admiral Arthur W. Radford, USN, served as Vice Chief of Naval Operations from 3 January 1948 to 16 April 1949.
†† Rear Admiral Joseph J. Clark, USN, Assistant Chief of Naval Operations (Air).
‡‡ Captain Lyman A. Thackrey, USN.

lieutenant commanders on this deal, to be the swordsmen. But the thing was that they took two naval aircraft to fly up there with all this Navy brass. If that thing would happen now, why, of course, we'd be investigated by Congress for at least six months or a year. But things were a little looser in those days.

So, anyway, none of us knew very much about it except what we read in *The New York Times*, and it was, of course, covering this wedding and it was going to be at St. Bartholomew's Church.* Oh, it was really one of the most stylish weddings of that era. So we went up there, and, of course, the first thing that happened to me was that Jocko Clark wanted to hold a training session for the swordsmen. So he got us out in a corridor somewhere and we got all of our sword belts and swords and everything on and got all lined up there. Jocko's lower lip was hanging out about an inch—I'd never been around him before—but he wanted to get it straight that when it came our time to perform, we were going to do it properly. So he said, "When I say 'sheath,' I mean sheath. When I say 'sword,' I mean sword. Now," he said, "let's practice." So he'd say "sheath" and we'd put the tip of the sword into the scabbard and get it ready to shove it in.

We did that a few times, and Jocko didn't say he was pleased, but he said he thought we'd do. Then we all went into the wedding, and here came Diane in a lavender dress that, well, I would say, to say the least, she was underdressed for the way she was endowed. I mean, this woman really did have something to say for herself in the upper chest area. And here came Captain Latta-Lawrence with his wife Di and all.

Anyway, they got up there and, gee, you couldn't see anything but that Diana, with the way she was looking, and paid very little attention to the ceremony, to say the least. The wedding got through in very short order, and we were outside with our swords, Jocko came out with his command. The minute he said "sheath," ol' Russ Harris clicked his; boy, he slammed her down. Jocko heard that click and never did the other command. He was trying to find out who'd messed it up.

Well, then there was this "click, click, click, click" all around the—it was the worst show you've ever seen. So Jocko was some—you know, he'd never seen planes launched in that disorder, I'm sure, in his career. Russ Harris, as soon as the bride and

---

* The wedding was at St. Bartholomew's Protestant Episcopal Church. A photo of the newlyweds and accompanying article on the wedding were in *The New York Times*, 23 April 1948, pages 27.

groom passed under the swords, or passed through us, anyway, he took off. He started running because he was afraid of Jocko. And Jocko kept looking for Russ. Anyway, he found him at the reception and started asking him, and Russ ran again. Jocko never did get hold of him, I don't know what he would have done to him. But it was sure a situation there, because we really had messed up Jocko's part of the show.

But Edith Norse Rogers was there, and a lot of New York society was there and all these people in the Episcopal Church, I suppose. Well, anyway, we went back to Washington, all of us, and a few weeks later I told Captain Latta-Lawrence that I thought since my wife and I had just been married recently, it might be appropriate for the four of us to get together and celebrate our weddings.

Well, Captain Latta-Lawrence said he didn't know, said maybe so, but they hadn't quite settled down yet and things were—maybe a little later. He was playing for time. So I said, "Well, sure, we're available anytime."

Well, it wasn't very long after that that the story broke that Captain Latta-Lawrence was having trouble with Diana, and she was suing him for breach of promise and suing Edith Norse Rogers for alienation of affection.[*] This was really big news in the *Washington Times-Herald*.

Paul Stillwell: How could it be breach of promise? He married her.

Captain Manson: Well, apparently he promised to love her, and she claimed that he really didn't love her. Well, on breach of promise, I'm not real sure. But alienation of affection, I'm real sure of that charge. But it was all over the paper there, and those of us on Denfeld's staff were worried that Admiral Denfeld was going to be brought into it, in the least, and then perhaps the Navy, and then it was going to be a disgrace for everybody. Then they'd find out about those airplanes going up there, and we didn't know what was going to happen.

---

[*] On 24 March 1949 Captain Latta-Lawrence was served with papers in a civil suit for maintenance. His wife complained of his "close and intimate" association with Representative Rogers. Both Latta-Lawrence and Rogers denied the accusation. In June 1949 Latta-Lawrence charged that his wife was already married to someone else at the time of his marriage to her. In November 1950, Mrs. Latta-Lawrence, having lost her suit for maintenance, sued for divorce, which was granted.

Captain Latta-Lawrence became a recluse, and he went into seclusion over at the old Main Navy building.* He had a little room he could hide in over there, and the press was just trying to eat him up. Lloyd Norman was a reporter then for the *Times-Herald*; he later went with *Chicago Tribune* and later with *Newsweek*. Well, Diana decided she'd have a press conference. So she called all the newspapermen in Washington to her apartment, had a fifth of whiskey—as I was told, I wasn't there—for each one of them, and then, in addition, she went in and changed her clothes at least five or six times during the time the press was there.

Lloyd Norman came to me and said, "Frank, I'm absolutely convinced that this woman is on the up and up. This guy has really done her dirty, and we're going to support her." So they started writing stories supporting Diane.

Paul Stillwell: Were the two of them living together?

Captain Manson: No, not then, oh, no. They didn't live but maybe two or three weeks. So then I went to Captain Latta-Lawrence and said, "Man, we're in trouble, everybody's in trouble." Well, he knew that, and I said, "Tell me about it."

Paul Stillwell: You'd get that clue reading in the paper about your wife.

Captain Manson: So I asked if there was anything he wanted to tell about it, because maybe I could help him. Well, for a time he didn't want to tell me, and it went on. Finally, he broke down one day over there. No one from the staff would ever go see him but me; they were afraid to. But it was a very touchy thing, and I was trying to get ammunition to give Lloyd Norman to get him to get off Captain Latta-Lawrence's back.

So he said, well, the real story was that when we went to New York, and we all arrived up there, that he had a room that was across from hers. He looked up at her window and saw her doing sort of a Lady Godiva-type thing, as near as you can do in a hotel. She was up in this window without any clothes on. So he said he knew. He said

---

* Main Navy was the popular name for the old Navy Department building at 17th Street and Constitution Avenue in Washington, D.C.

that apparently wasn't just a performance for him, but for the whole hotel or whatever. So he said he knew right then he'd made a terrible mistake. So he went to the rector and the minister and everybody there at St. Bartholomew's and told them he thought he made a mistake, and would they please cancel the wedding. They told him he'd gone too far, that this would embarrass the church, it would embarrass the Navy, he should have checked these things out beforehand, and he was going through with it.

So he said he had to go through with it. He said he knew things were not too good at that point. On top of that, then she was releasing all these letters that he'd written to her. I said, "Did you write—?"

"Yes," he said, "I wrote some very—" He said he was not very discreet in some of the things he'd said in these letters.

I said, "Well, my recommendation to you is that you come out of hiding and make some sort of a statement." He wouldn't do it.

Well, anyway, this thing rode on, and he stayed over there in that little room for, seemed like two or three months. He was just suffering terribly, and I think they did finally get a divorce. It turned out that she'd been living with a dentist for some years out there in Tennessee or somewhere. She was really quite a phony. She really wasn't the true debutante that he thought he was getting, in any case. But Captain Latta-Lawrence decided to resign from the Navy, and he never did any legislative work at all, as far as I know. Finally, some way or another, they got Edith Norse Rogers out of this thing. I don't recall exactly, but I think most of us convinced the press around there that there certainly was not anything going on between them. She was 20 years older than Latta-Lawrence, anyway, so there wasn't any way this could happen. So they finally got off his case.

I didn't see him then for maybe a year or two, but when I did see him the next time, he came over just to say hello, and he'd lost all of his hair. Every hair on his body—eyelashes, eyebrows, on his head, whiskers, the whole thing was gone from nervous shock, and I didn't even recognize him until he told me who he was.

But, anyway, the point of this whole story is that the reason we were so worried about it was that we were afraid that something like this would be such a diversion, and the Navy was already under tremendous stress. We were afraid that this could really do harm to Admiral Denfeld, because they didn't have anything much to go after him on, but this was something. In those days, it wasn't like it is now, because there wasn't all that much of social scandal around. Well, it did get in the papers, of course.

Paul Stillwell: Did the Air Force use that as a weapon?

Captain Manson: No, no, they didn't. They had enough to go on, and they never did, and they never used it against Admiral Denfeld either. Apparently it didn't hurt Mrs. Rogers the next time she was up for election. So the only person that really suffered was the captain.

Paul Stillwell: Well, though, on the other hand, if he was brought in to do legislative work and he didn't do any of that because of this, that was a shortcoming.

Captain Manson: That was a shortcoming, tremendous, exactly. There were, as it turned out, just a lot of mistakes. I didn't think at the time that Admiral Denfeld really needed a political officer like that, but he felt that he did, so that's what happened. Anyway, that's just a little footnote to history. If anybody wants to check on it, they can get the *Washington Times-Herald* for that time frame, and it's all written up.

Anyway, we were in London when we were in the last interview. I remembered, after I left your office, that when the missile crisis came and when it came down to the crunch, those minutes or hours after President Kennedy had challenged Khrushchev, this was the period when the world was waiting for Khrushchev's reply.* We were wondering whether he would blink, or whether he would blast off with a first strike, and we didn't know. In London, we certainly didn't know.

Admiral Page Smith and I just stayed at the office that day, and we went into the little communications control room, the two of us, very small room. Admiral Smith was sitting in there in one chair, and I was in the other one. We both had telephones; he was

---

* The Cuban Missile Crisis was triggered in mid-October 1962, when a U.S. reconnaissance plane photographed a Soviet nuclear missile site in Cuba and the presence of Soviet bombers. On 22 October President John F. Kennedy went on national television to announce a naval quarantine of Cuba, to be implemented on 24 October. On 28 October Premier Nikita Khrushchev of the Soviet Union notified President Kennedy that he was ordering the withdrawal of Soviet bombers and missiles from Cuba.

hooked up to Washington, and I was hooked up to the media outside. Admiral Smith's phone was silent, and mine was just ringing off the hook from the news media. They were all asking the same questions, of course, "What are you going to do with the Sixth Fleet?" and "What are you going to do with those submarines in Holy Loch?"

I was telling the press all over the world that the Sixth Fleet was getting its orders elsewhere and that we hadn't any information, and so was Holy Loch, as far as that goes. I said that we didn't have any information on our submarine operations in the North Sea as of that time, but as far as those alongside the *Proteus*, they are still alongside and as far as we knew in London, they were going to remain alongside. In other words, we were trying to keep any hysteria down and to play it very softly until we heard from Moscow or from President Kennedy or from somebody.

Anyway, I had made this reply, and Admiral Smith was nodding that this was the correct way to handle this. Suddenly one of the calls came in and said, "We have an eyewitness up in Holy Loch, and we see the submarines moving out."

Then I said, "Well, you have better information than I have and that we have, and if you have an eyewitness account, then that's I suppose the best information available." Then the inquiries trailed off at that point. That was one of the most delicate time periods over there, though. The British press was very excited. Well, the international press was too.

Paul Stillwell: You say that the Sixth Fleet was not under Smith's command.

Captain Manson: It was under his command, but operationally—well, now I don't know. If the signal had come to launch, I believe the command would have come straight out of the command center in Washington.* I don't believe that would have been coming through our headquarters in London. We didn't have, at that time, a really, really topnotch command information center. What did they call those things?

Paul Stillwell: Well, that's one term, or war room.

---

* The Polaris submarines were under the operational control of Commander in Chief Atlantic Fleet.

Captain Manson: Well, yes, war room. They later built one over there in London, but at that time we really didn't have the facilities. I'm not sure just how that command—but there's a special command set-up for launching a nuclear strike.

Paul Stillwell: The Polaris submarines were not under CinCNELM's chain of command, but the Sixth Fleet was.

Captain Manson: Yes, the Sixth Fleet was under his chain of command, that's for sure. But I'm now trying to reflect on the operational set-up. There perhaps might have been, somewhere else there in the headquarters, some officers that were dealing directly with the Sixth Fleet. But I recall that the admiral and I were the only two in this room. But there may have been operation officers somewhere; I don't know. But, anyway, we were there until 10:00 or 11:00 P.M. that night, just waiting, and that I do recall.

Paul Stillwell: What do you recall about the general mood around headquarters during that period? That went on for a number of days.

Captain Manson: The atmosphere was tense. We simply didn't know, we didn't know. When there's something like that, and we knew what was involved, but we weren't talking, it was pretty quiet. But the atmosphere amongst the officers was somewhat tense.

Paul Stillwell: That was more of an Atlantic Fleet show than it was a CinCUSNavEur.

Captain Manson: Yes, it was an Atlantic Fleet show; of course, it was. But still, we were over there, and had there been any sort of a launch or first strike from Moscow, I think it's a reasonable assumption that the Sixth Fleet would have been a target, and Holy Loch would have been a target. Admiral Smith was, of course, cool through the whole thing, but he didn't know either. No one knew, not even President Kennedy. I saw a movie recently that showed Robert Kennedy and Jack Kennedy during that time frame. Did you see that?

Paul Stillwell: I saw it some years ago.

Captain Manson: Oh, did you? Well, they were a little tight, too, about it because there wasn't anyone who knew what the Soviets were going to do.

Paul Stillwell: How well informed were you in London kept on U.S. positions and communications?

Captain Manson: We were kept well informed. Not as well, I'm sure, as perhaps they were in constant communication, I would imagine, with Holy Loch, telephone communication, and probably with Sixth Fleet as well. We weren't in continuous, but we were getting ours through dispatches and sometimes telephone.

After that was all over and I was back in Washington, Admiral Dennison had gone with Copley News Service, and he wanted me to write that history of that whole experience.* He said he'd give me all of his dispatches, papers, books, the whole thing. I told him I simply didn't have the time at that point in my life to do it, so I guess it was never done. But he said it would be a marvelous book and I said, yes, I'm sure.

Admiral Ricketts gave me a dispatch that was at least top secret. This was later, of course, but it might have been even a higher classification than top secret. Oh, no, I'm sorry, this was on the Bay of Pigs, and it has nothing to do with the missile crisis.†

Paul Stillwell: Well, that doesn't mean we can't talk about it.

Captain Manson: Well, I was just going to say that he sent a dispatch, which I have since lost, but I had a copy for a number of years, and he told me I could release it at some point if I ever chose to. But, in essence, what Admiral Ricketts's dispatch said to CNO and, I guess, to SecNav, I forget who all the addressees were, but he said that he viewed

---

* Admiral Robert L. Dennison, USN, served as Supreme Allied Commander Atlantic, Commander in Chief Atlantic, and Commander in Chief Atlantic Fleet from 28 February 1960 to 30 April 1963. His oral history is in the Naval Institute collection.
† In mid-April 1961 a force of 1,400 Cuban exiles, secretly trained by U.S. personnel in Guatemala, landed in the Bay of Pigs, on the southwestern coast of Cuba, in an attempt to overthrow Fidel Castro, that nation's Communist dictator. The invasion attempt was a disaster. President John Kennedy decided that U.S. naval intervention would worsen the situation, so ships and aircraft offshore were prohibited from taking part.

his situation with the greatest anguish, that he was there 50 miles off the coast of Cuba with the military power to control the situation, and yet he was not being permitted to do it.* He said he viewed this situation with the greatest anguish. I remember he quoted Churchill in the dispatch as well.

But he just handed it to me one day and said, "Frank, you may want to release that some day," and now I've lost the dispatch. Anyway, that doesn't deal directly with the missile crisis.

Paul Stillwell: Do you have any other recollections to wrap up that tour in London?

Captain Manson: Oh, yes. I wanted to mention, well, for one thing, the Queen's garden party.† I only went to one, and I wouldn't have gone to that except that I went over to the ambassador's office one day and told him that I'd been there going on four years, and everybody had gone to the queen's garden party, I thought, but me and my wife. I understood the ambassador controlled the invitations, so we got one right away to the party.

It was, I'd say, a pretty routine deal as far as the Queen and Prince Philip. They came out to visit with the people who were there, and there must have been at least a thousand—a few hundred, anyway, I don't know how many. Her backyard is rather sizeable, all sorts of growth and a little brook running through. But the reason I wanted to bring it up is, going around meeting people, of course, we were pleased to be in the audience there with Prince Philip and the Queen, but I met a Royal Navy captain who was responsible for the angle deck and the mirror landing system, and, I believe, the steam catapult were the three major contributions that this captain had made to the advancement of naval air warfare.‡ Just to be in his presence was, to me, a great honor. He found out that I'd been involved in writing naval history, so he sort of took a shine to me and our wives hit it off well.

---

* Vice Admiral Claude V. Ricketts, USN, commanded the Second Fleet February 1961 to September 1961.
† Princess Elizabeth of Great Britain became Queen Elizabeth II on 6 February 1952 upon the death of her father, King George VI. Her coronation was on 2 June 1953. She has been Britain's monarch ever since. Her husband, Prince Philip, is the Duke of Edinburgh.
‡ These three innovations greatly improved aircraft carrier operations and were quickly adopted by the U.S. Navy.

So that's the way we spent our afternoon there, visiting with this captain, whose name I don't recall. But, anyway, we invited them then to come to our home for a little visit after, and they did. They came over to our place at Hamilton Terrace and we visited then for another couple of hours. I never saw them again.

Paul Stillwell: Did you get to meet the Queen?

Captain Manson: Not in a personal sense, no. The way they handled that was that you'd have little circles, and the Queen and the Prince would come into this little circle. There would probably be someone in that circle that they would know, and they would discuss rather bland subjects, but just enough so that everybody could sort of get a chance to be near them and see what they were like. That's about all you could get out of it.

I remember Admiral Smith was telling me that he and Dee went to one of these Queen's receptions one time, and they actually did meet Prince Philip and the Queen. He said that Dee tried to curtsy and almost fell down. So I was wondering what my wife would do when she—well, we did meet royalty. We met Tony, Lord Snowdon, and Princess Margaret over at Douglas Fairbanks's house one day.* One of his daughters was getting married, and I was pretty close to Douglas Fairbanks. So Lee and I were invited, and Lee was disgusted and said that she'd thought we'd wasted our time there going to the reception. We didn't seem to know any of those people and they were mostly all royalty, because Douglas Fairbanks was really close. So, anyway, he'd told me that Princess Margaret and Tony were going to be there. My wife was fussing at me about the thing, and I just happened to look around and right next to her, I mean touching her, was Princess Margaret. I said, "Just don't move. Princess Margaret is on your right elbow touching you, and Tony is next to her. I'll go get Douglas Fairbanks, and we'll get a proper introduction." My wife's face froze.

I went and got Douglas, and he gave us a proper introduction, and we had a real nice visit with those two. She was pregnant at the time with her first child, so we were able to give them some pretty good advice on what might happen in a few months and a

---

* Antony Armstrong-Jones, Lord Snowdon and Viscount Linley, is an English photographer. He was married to Queen Elizabeth's younger sister, Princess Margaret Rose, from 1960 to 1978. Douglas Fairbanks Jr. was a noted actor who had served on active duty as a Naval Reserve officer in World War II.

few years, and they were both really friendly and just thoroughly enjoyed our—but it was a light discussion, mostly about being pregnant.

Paul Stillwell: I take it you weren't able to contribute too much to that aspect of it. [Laughter]

Captain Manson: No, that was Lee; she could do much of that. I told Tony, though, what the father's responsibilities were like when the baby was young, which were almost nil.

Another experience I had over there at the Dorchester Hotel, the American Women's Club at one time had contributed quite a sizeable amount of money to the launching of some kind of a peace ship back in World War I or thereabouts. So when they found out about his idea that I had in *Life* magazine for a fleet which would be used for constructive purposes, American Women's Club got interested in having a big dinner over there.

Of course, this got Ambassador Bruce immediately involved, because Mrs. Bruce was sort of the titular head of the American Women's Club over there.* So this brought them right into it. I was not too much involved in it except, of course, naturally, they were calling me every now and again for suggestions and things they were going to do and if I approved it and this and that.

Well, it was getting bigger and bigger, and then they decided to have what they called a stromboli over there. I believe that's the name of it. It's where they go around all over London and pick up gifts. I think it's called a stromboli; I'm not sure if that's the name, but something like that. I'd never heard the name before, and now I can't even— but it's an idea where you go to merchants and you bring all those things there the merchants have contributed and then you sort of raffle them off. They had artwork there, and they had gifts and they had cans of beans, and I don't know what all they had there. But it was sort of a clambake in a way. But they had, of course, the Ambassador and Mrs. Bruce, then they had two cabinet ministers from Britain, I think the Minister of Shipping. Well, I don't recall what two ministers, but there were two.

---

* David K. E. Bruce served as U.S. ambassador to France from 1949 to 1952, ambassador to West Germany from 1957 to 1959, and ambassador the United Kingdom from 1961 to 1969.

The head table was rather large, and I was in the catbird seat. Ambassador Bruce, when he walked in, said to me, "All right, Captain, this is your show, and you're going to have to run it."

I said, "Well, of course I'll do my best, Mr. Ambassador." So right off they asked me to lead the audience in prayer. I'd anticipated they might do that, so I'd written one out, and I had it in my pants pocket. All I had to do was pull it out and sort of read it. But anything that required any sort of talking to the audience, I mostly had to do it. But the British had gone in there, and they'd taken a wall of the Dorchester Hotel, I mean a wall that was 50 or 60 feet long and 20 or 30 feet high, and they had painted on there the type of ship that they wanted for their own type ship and they'd called it the *Morning Star*, had that all painted out on there. It was actually a beautiful thing.

Anyway, they did raise quite a sum of money there. It seemed like it was about $5,000; I gave that money to the British to see if they could get a ship started. The British then wrote a letter to the United States saying that they'd already scrapped all their ships that were suitable and would the United States give them a ship for free. Senator Hubert Humphrey tried to do that, but the U.S. Maritime Commission, I guess it was, said that laws precluded giving ship like this to the British. There are just more reasons than I can think of why the United States refused to give the British a ship.

Later I was in a meeting in Washington with Senator Humphrey and 20 or 30 people from the government at that time, various bureaus and offices. The Maritime Commission said this was really an impossible thing. Although we had hundreds of ships, they said they just couldn't do it. I remember Senator Humphrey at one point got so angry during the meeting that he said it would be better to sink these ships than to just let them sit there and rust away. I think one of the arguments he used was that they couldn't be sure the ship would be used for that purpose in perpetuity, that it might be brought back and used commercially. I think this was the concern. I'm sure it was.

But, anyway, there was an effort made there, and we had clearance with the State Department to go ahead with the transaction. The Assistant Secretary of State for European Affairs was a fellow named William R. Tyler. He and I were on very good terms for a number of years there, and he was very much in favor of Europe getting started with a ship or two ships of this type. He thought it would very useful to help bring the European Community together.

But, anyway, I remember one time, on this same subject, that Edward R. Murrow was visiting over there, and he had a responsible job in the Kennedy administration.[*] I believe he was director of the U.S. Information Agency. Well, he and I had the opportunity to meet, and he wanted to know about this idea. I gave him about a 20-minute dissertation on the whole subject. He liked it a lot, and he said he was going to do what he could when he got back to Washington to get behind this. But there were a lot of political reasons back in Washington why—actually, Dr. Walsh was proceeding with the hospital ship *Hope* at that time and he was creating quite a few storm clouds as he moved along.

Most people just wanted to wait and see how that worked out. They thought probably in any type of program of that nature, it would be pretty much of a prototype, and they'd all be the same. Of course, that wasn't true, but that's the way people looked at it, because there'd been so many storms and fury over getting that project out of dry dock.

Drew Pearson was one who kept after me. He said, "I can get this thing going for you." He sent his brother, Leon Pearson, who was with NBC, to see me a couple of times to see if I wouldn't permit him to take charge of it and go ahead and get the thing going. I told him, no, that I thought that it would have to be done through controversy if he did it, and I didn't think it would serve a worthwhile purpose, so I wouldn't do it and never did.

Anyway, that dinner, though, was quite an occasion, with the ambassador. But anyway, at some point in the evening, he won one of the big prizes, a big painting, and he had to go down and get it from the people who were giving out the prizes. I never did know for sure whether Ambassador Bruce was pleased that he had received this prize or not, but I rather gather that I think he would just as soon not have.

In those kinds of things, when you're the ambassador and when something big like that is going on in country, no matter what else, you have to go ahead with it. So

---

[*] Edward R. Murrow was a noted correspondent for many years for CBS radio and television. He became famous for his radio reports from London in World War II. He was director of the U.S. Information Agency from 1961 to 1964.

that's where he found himself, and I would have excused him. If there'd been any way possible that I could have told him to please forget it, I would have, but there was no way I could.

Stephen W. Roskill was the author of the British official history of World War II, and it's called *The War at Sea*. Well, I've got the books at home that they gave to me at my final farewell dinner there. But during my time over there, of course, I got to know him, and he was interested in this sort of constructive fleet idea. So he wanted me to come out to Cambridge University and meet with some of the dons out there. He said he'd get a whole group of them together if I'd just come up and spend a couple of days. This was quite an experience for me, actually.

I went up there, and they had an apartment all fixed for me up there. Steve Roskill had arranged for all these people to meet at sort of an informal dinner of maybe 40 or 50. We sat in a group and just—I suppose in an Oklahoma phrase, we "chewed the fat" over whether this kind of an idea, the theory of it, whether it would actually work or not, whether it would be too expensive. It was an intellectually stimulating exercise, to say the least. We didn't come up with any conclusions, and we didn't expect to. But they wanted to ask me a lot of questions about it, which they did.

We got off into discussing, I remember, some kind of a birth control or population control idea on the Seychelles Islands. Some of the dons there knew about this program that the British were paying for. But they seemed to think that one of the problems facing the world was one of, in some way or another, population control. It just didn't seem to them like it would be possible, unless we could get some kind of control or handle on the populations that were bursting out all over the world, that it would be possible for the Western nations to come in with various programs without population control.

So anyway, that was sort of the gist of the way the conversation went. But still, I appreciated Stephen Roskill because of his interest in sea power. Now, this is not exactly what I would say is the epitome of sea power, but it's one side of the spectrum of sea power. It is a type of sea power which I believe if not in the near future except in years to come, this kind of effort is going to be placed aboard ships and we will be involved in this kind of thing. This is my own opinion.

Paul Stillwell: What are your impressions of Roskill as an individual?

Captain Manson: Well, now, first of all, he's an extremely intelligent man and a really topnotch historian. His knowledge, even of American naval history, was excellent, but the details he didn't forget. I mean, an operation of a British destroyer in the Mediterranean or the operation of a British fleet in the Western Pacific, whatever subject that you would choose to discuss with Steven Roskill, his memory was so strong. The only problem you had really in really discussing things with him is he'd been a gunnery officer and his hearing was somewhat affected, so you had to talk loud, and sometimes you can't think as well when you're talking loud.* I suppose that he was as impressive a person as I met during the time I was in Britain, and that would have to include Prime Ministers and everyone else. He was a man of substance.

Well, you see a lot of British people over there, particularly in the Navy. I remember I joined the Military Commentators Circle over there. Admiral Sir Michael Denny was one of the sort of leaders of that Commentators Circle.† Here was an impressive man, and I met a lot of retired British military types. For the most part, I was impressed with their grasp of the world as it was then and also their historical knowledge of what had happened. They all knew that Britain was in its decline. This, I think, tended to cause them to be a little sad, for the most part. I mean, none of them liked to see Great Britain, as a nation, in a descent. You could tell it hurt.

Paul Stillwell: Well, that's understandable.

Captain Manson: Yes, it is understandable. It hurt me, because I thought the more the British leave the scene, the more the United States is going to have to come on the scene.

Paul Stillwell: That's proven to be exactly true.

---

* Roskill's medical retirement from the Royal Navy was because of hearing loss.
† Among the billets for Admiral Sir Michael M. Denny, RN, were Third Sea Lord, Commander in Chief Home Fleet, and United Kingdom Representative on the NATO Standing Group. He retired from the Royal Navy in 1959.

Captain Manson: Yes, yes, that's the way it's happening, isn't it? Then another thing about Roskill was his—well, I suppose he was a strong family man and lived at home there with his wife in Cambridge. He was very attentive to detail. I find that so many of the people who achieve things are attentive to detail. By that I mean he would make certain that every kindness was given to me, where I was staying, what my schedule would be, and all that. He was just that kind of person.

Paul Stillwell: I don't know that you can draw that generalization. I mean, you've pointed out someone who was exactly the opposite, Carney, who achieved things but was not one who concentrated on details.

Captain Manson: Well, you're right, you're right. In a sense, yes, but Admiral Carney, if he were going to have a meeting with someone with equal rank or place in the world—he'd just depend on other people to make sure all the details were correct. He'd be thinking about what they were going to talk about. That's about the way he was. Yes, I guess that's right. I suppose I'll have to walk the cat back, because he certainly was an exception. Most of them are. But, again, though, I suppose if you spend too much time on that sort of thing, you've only got so much time.

Paul Stillwell: That's right.

Captain Manson: That, I suppose, is one of the reasons why the Navy has taken so much pains to free the officer corps from the mundane activities.

Paul Stillwell: And been criticized for it.

Captain Manson: Yes. But I found it very useful when I was on active duty. I thought it was very helpful.

Paul Stillwell: Well, let me ask you about that aspect. From your time in the Pentagon and public information, did you have to put up with that kind of criticism, the privileges that senior officers had?

Captain Manson: Well, yes. It seemed right after World War II, there was a strong feeling there. First of all, there was an anti-reserve sentiment in the regular Navy. Then beyond that, there was a feeling that officers had too much privilege, and too many of them had taken advantage of it, and it was something that didn't exist in civilian life. So the officers were criticized for it. If any officers ever were caught being excessive, it usually showed up in Drew Pearson's column or somewhere else. But no, there was a feeling that somehow this was not the way that things were done in the United States. This feeling was pretty fairly prevalent, and it still exists.

Paul Stillwell: How did you try to deal with that?

Captain Manson: Well, we tried always to show the human side of every senior officer. I'll use Admiral Carney as an example. He was tarred with that senior officer status. He played the guitar, and he could sing little ballads. They had a magazine in those days, I believe it was called the *American* magazine and one called *Redbook*. I'm not sure which magazine, it may have been *Redbook*, but I asked one of the editors if they would like to have a little story about Admiral Carney and his guitar playing. They thought that would be fine. So we got a little profile and a picture in this very popular magazine of that era, showing Admiral Carney with a red plaid shirt on, strumming his guitar. Well, this helped to humanize the admiral. Then we put out stories about his hunting and fishing and that sort of thing, and always tried to make stories available to the media that would humanize the people. That was one way we went about it.

A lot of the people would go out and make speeches and appear in community affairs, which would be helpful. I don't know, to me this whole business of discipline in the military is so essential to having a good military organization and yet at the same time, it's contradictory to a democratic type of society that we have. It is, totally. So you have to operate with that sort of a contradiction. From a public information viewpoint, it's a very difficult thing to humanize people who are exercising, and should exercise, command performances. You can't be very democratic when you're issuing commands.

Paul Stillwell: That's right.

Captain Manson: So your question is a difficult question, because in dealing with it, you have to do it—well, you can generalize to some extent. Now, Admiral Dan Gallery helped, because he used to write articles for the *Saturday Evening Post* and *Collier's* magazine, little tales. He usually had somebody in the story who was commanding a garbage barge or in charge of something. Gallery's brother was a priest, by the way. But, anyway, he was different in a sense that he didn't have that problem as much as others. But, as you probably know, some of the officers were and remained aloof, and they never were any other way.

Paul Stillwell: One that I interviewed, he was one of the top ranking from that period was Mel Pride, a very unpretentious gentleman.[*] Did you meet him?

Captain Manson: Yes. Now, he was different, though, because he had been an enlisted man, and he had come up through the ranks. So he had a touch of humility that he'd gained at a very tender age, and he never lost that touch. I don't think that it's necessary for a person to completely lose their humility, even though they achieve the highest stations in life. I don't see the necessity for them not recognizing the time to be humble and a time not to be. But some people have trouble making that distinction.

Paul Stillwell: Well, his personality is very becoming.

Captain Manson: Yes. Oh, yes, absolutely. What you'd have to say is he's a refined gentleman.

---

[*] Vice Admiral Alfred M. Pride, USN, served as Commander Seventh Fleet from 1 December 1953 to 19 December 1955. The oral history of Pride, who retired as a four-star admiral, is in the Naval Institute collection.

Paul Stillwell: He is. Were there others that you had a lot harder time humanizing? Clark would strike me as one example.

Captain Manson: Well, now, Jocko Clark was—no, you couldn't do anything much to change him. He's a Cherokee Indian and had he been with the tribes back there before he became an admiral, I'm sure he'd have been chief of the Cherokees. But Jocko had one way to march, and that was forward, and he was kind of stomping as he went.

Paul Stillwell: And one speed and that was full. [Laughter]

Captain Manson: He had one speed, that's right. But I'll tell you this about Jocko Clark. I personally was very fond of him. When you got beneath that rough exterior, which is so frequently the case, he was one of the kindest men you'd ever want to know. But you had to work a long time to get beneath that exterior. Of course, it was always his decision whether or not this would ever happen. But Jocko told me stories, when we got to really know each other, about one or two admirals that he considered, well, in his words they were "yellow." He told me about the skipper, I think it was the *Lexington*, Pownall I believe his name was.*

Paul Stillwell: He was the admiral on board Clark's carrier in 1943.

Captain Manson: Yes. Well, he didn't have very much use for him, and he didn't have any use at all for Harrill, who was the task group commander.† He had tried to get Harrell to join with him and his task group. Clark was task group commander. He tried to get Harrell to join with him and they were both going to come back from the north. It was during the Battle of the Philippine Sea.‡ They were going to come down and try to

---
* In late 1943 and early 1944 Rear Admiral Charles A. Pownall, USN, was commander of the fast carrier task force in the Pacific. Captain Joseph J. Clark, USN, was then commanding officer of the carrier *Yorktown*. Because Pownall was perceived as not being sufficiently aggressive, Admiral Chester Nimitz replaced Pownall with Rear Admiral Marc A. Mitscher, USN, in early 1944. The oral history of Pownall is in the Naval Institute collection.
† Rear Admiral William K. Harrill, USN, Commander Task Group 58.4.
‡ The Battle of the Philippine Sea took place in conjunction with the U.S. invasion of the Mariana Islands in mid-June 1944.

catch or cut off the retreating force, and Harrill wouldn't do it. Jocko said he sensed that they could do that, that they could cut them off and sink the whole, the total, annihilate them. He went over there to talk to Harrell about that, and Harrell said, no, they had orders from Mitscher to protect Saipan and the invasion forces, and he wouldn't do it. So Jocko said, in his opinion, the man just didn't have the courage to do it.

But that's the sort of thing that Jocko would talk about, unhesitatingly, and he didn't care who heard it or anything about it. They tell me at night he'd walk out on the carrier when the planes were coming in after a tough night, tough strike, and he'd have Navy Crosses and Silver Stars hanging out of his pockets. He'd catch a young man, "Hey, young man, I want to give this to you," and he took one out of his pockets. He'd say, "Get the paperwork written up tomorrow or sometime, but I want you to have the medal tonight." He'd be out there in his pajamas handing out all kinds of medals, because he'd know which ones had done some good work up there, and he wanted to be sure he got the medals to them right away. I thought this was something.

Paul Stillwell: A nice leadership touch.

Captain Manson: It sure is. No, of all the attributes you might ascribe to Jocko, humility was not one of them.

Paul Stillwell: [Laughter] No. Well, have we about caught you up on some of these backlogged things on your tour in London?

Captain Manson: I think so. Just let me quickly glance here. One thing we did over there was we placed a marker to commemorate the battle of the *Bonhomme Richard* and the *Serapis* right off the coast.* I think this was up about midway of the British Isles, as I recall, that we placed this marker. I don't know if it's still there. But this we did in about 1959 or '60. I thought it was an excellent thing to do, so I joined in getting that done.

---

* The Battle of Flamborough Head took place in the North Sea off Yorkshire, England, on 23 September 1779. Captain John Paul Jones, flagship *Bonhomme Richard*, defeated the British ship *Serapis*.

We ran into some of the letters that John Paul Jones had written to at least one lady up there, and they were quite amorous letters. So I guess the tradition of the Navy starting with John Paul Jones has been that most naval officers have quite an attraction to the ladies or vice versa or something.

Paul Stillwell: Well, there's Lord Nelson and Lady Hamilton, for example.*

Captain Manson: Yes, yes, that's right. Maybe it's just because men go to sea, and that conditions them for shore leave, for shore duty. Anyway, that's one of the things we did over there. I guess that's about all I can remember.

One thing about the men, I took a little note here, many of them got married over there in London, while we're on the subject of women. These British women and English women, well, not just English, I guess Scottish and all. But, for instance, in my office, I had perhaps maybe 12 enlisted personnel, and I suppose about eight or nine of them married, and they usually didn't wait too long.

I had one case there where a young seaman named Golub came in and he wanted to marry this girl. I said, "Well, certainly you have my permission."

He said, "Yes, but the chaplain won't let us do it."

I said, "What's the problem?"

"Well," he said, "you'll have to talk to the chaplain."

So I checked with the girl first to see if she wanted to marry Golub. She did. She was a rather attractive little girl.

So I went to see the chaplain, and he wasn't in, but the chaplain's assistant was there. She was a British lady, and she said, "Well, I checked into this girl's reputation, and she was charged with shoplifting a few years ago."

I said, "Well, what did she shoplift?"

"Well, I don't know." She said she didn't know, but it was something on the order of a few shillings, I think on the order of 75 cents or something like that.

I said, "Well, yes, that's serious, all right."

---

* Emma Hamilton was the mistress of Lord Horatio Nelson, Britain's great naval hero of the late 18th century and early 19th. Hamilton was the mother of Nelson's daughter Horatia, born in 1801.

She said she didn't think anybody that had ever been charged with anything like that should be able to marry an American Navy type, a sailor. I said, "Yes, but the girl's pregnant."

She said, "I don't care if she is. Our position here is that we're not going to permit this."

I said, "Well, my position is that we're going to permit it. And furthermore, I'm going to authorize it as his commanding officer, and y'all can do what you please."

So I did, and they were married and they moved to the States. He became a topflight businessman, and they've had a number of children. They named their first child after our little daughter who was lost to cancer, and it's really been a good marriage. I know a number of the men that married British girls, they've had good marriages. So apparently it was a very worthwhile thing for them to be engaged in. Anyway, that's just a note. I don't if anybody will support my conclusions on this or not, but it was a rather happy hunting ground for young Navy types.

Paul Stillwell: Strikes me as a very sanctimonious position by the chaplain's office.

Captain Manson: Well, I couldn't understand that, and this man, the chaplain, later became Chief of Chaplains.

Paul Stillwell: Who is he?

Captain Manson: Frank Garrett.* He was a Protestant chaplain. I don't know whether Frank really knew about this himself or not, but they were trying their best to stop this.

Paul Stillwell: So that was more just an excuse than a real reason, it sounds like.

---

* Rear Admiral Francis L. Garrett, CHC, USN, was the Navy's Chief of Chaplains from July 1970 to June 1975.

Captain Manson: Exactly, exactly, that's right. They lectured to me on why this was not a good idea for these men to marry these British girls. I didn't agree and still don't agree. Anyway, that's the way that ended up.

For Britain, I think that's about all I can say at this point, unless you have a question about something.

Paul Stillwell: No. I think that it's an appropriate time to bring you back to the States and put you in the hot seat there in the Office of Information.

Captain Manson: Well, Admiral McCain's the one who brought me back.[*] He put me in a difficult position there, as I told you in the previous recording, of being sort of his deputy without being his deputy. This aggravated the situation.

Paul Stillwell: I guess the useful thing to put on the record is that back then, the Chief of Information was a line officer, and so the deputy was the top public affairs specialist.

Captain Manson: Yes, that's correct. In those days that's the way it was. The reason Admiral McCain, of course, wanted to use me, because he knew me. He knew what I knew, and that's why he put me in that position. But still, it was an untenable position.

Paul Stillwell: Who was the official deputy?

Captain Manson: Jim Dowdell, James Dowdell.[†] Jim didn't take kindly to this, because he was a proud man. His main interest in public information was in dealing with the personnel. He was sort of a personnel type, and he was interested in their careers, that everybody got jobs going up the line and so forth. He was interested in that kind of thing, more so than in programs. And, of course, McCain was interested in building a fleet. That's not exactly the same thing—not always, anyway—where your emphasis is.

---

[*] Rear Admiral John S. McCain, Jr., USN, was the Navy's Chief of Information from August 1962 to August 1963.
[†] Captain James S. Dowdell, USN.

I had difficulties from time to time with Dowdell. One day he and I were having a rather strenuous discussion about something. I told him there were two types of people you always had to stay close to, your friends and your enemies, and I was standing real close to him at that time.

During that period, first of all, I was called the plans officer, I believe, plans and policies. They wanted me to find out why junior officers were not being retained in the Navy. So I had to do a Navy-wide study on that subject, and I sent out hundreds of questionnaires to commanding officers. I made up an elaborate questionnaire and got their answers back and then tabulated it and wrote it up. As far as I know, the report or the study never did win any accolades, so I don't know whether it was ever very highly regarded or not. I remember an awful lot of people, though, had written in and given us their best on what we could do to attract young officers and keep them in the Navy.

Paul Stillwell: Why was it done by the Office of Information instead of the Bureau of Personnel?

Captain Manson: I suppose that they must have thought that if personnel could have done anything about it, they would have already done it.

Paul Stillwell: What were the findings of your study?

Captain Manson: I'd have to review that. One of the things I know that we put in there was that the junior officer had to be recognized by his seniors that his work was useful, that he had to have greater recognition, identification. Also, that the Navy had a future and therefore he had a future, the officer had a future in it. Actually, out of the thing, there were many, many recommendations, but I really don't recall the conclusions of that report.

Along about that time, I got brought into this multilateral force concept with Admiral Claude Ricketts.[*] Admiral McCain made me available to him to handle the PR

---

[*] Admiral Claude V. Ricketts, USN, served as Vice Chief of Naval Operations from 1 November 1961 until his death on 6 July 1964.

side of that. So that, along with my other duties there, sort of defused the situation in public information, because I was at least half or maybe more than half my time, probably more like two-thirds of it, was spent with the Vice Chief. I, of course, would write his speeches or draft them, anyway, and work out all his PR agenda. He put it all in my hands. We had a marvelous rapport and relationship.

Paul Stillwell: Tell me what kind of a guy he was. You've given me impressions of Burke and Carney. How about Ricketts?

Captain Manson: First of all, Ricketts had the big picture. He was not as aggressive in his manner as, say, Burke or—

Paul Stillwell: Few people are. [Laughter]

Captain Manson: Well, well, true. Well, Ricketts was less vociferous. He never went around chest thumping. He was a very religious man and mild-mannered and kind, courteous, generous. He had so many superior qualities as an individual. He came from humble beginnings out there in Missouri. But still, he was a fun-lover. He loved to play tennis and did a lot of it, right up until he died. But he told me a story one time. He lived on a farm in Missouri, and coming home, they had an old Ford car that he would drive and it had these pedals on it, three pedals, I think.

I don't know if he was alone or had one or two others in the car, but he decided what fun it would be to get down underneath the thing and make the car operate without anybody—you couldn't see any heads or anybody else in the car. So he came driving home one day and the car was empty. He said his mother was really fit to be tied when she saw the car drive up and nobody in it. But that's the sort of thing that Admiral Ricketts would do.

Paul Stillwell: Would you call him a warm person?

Captain Manson: He was warm, although he was quick to take control if things were getting out of hand or if something wasn't going the way he had planned for it to go. For example, one day he started sort of asking me about the white fleet, and this was not too long before he died.* I was sort of ignoring him. I'd say, "Oh, yes, well, that's something we tried."

"But what was it?"

I'd say, "Well, you know, it was an idea to use ships to fight poverty and disease and so forth."

He said, "Well, I've got to have more than that. I want you to prepare me a thorough memo on this." I thought, man, I've prepared so many memos on this, this is the last thing I need to do. So I really didn't do it.

I went on, we kept working on the multilateral force, and one day two or three weeks later, he said, "I don't have that report yet."

I said, "Oh, Admiral, you've got more things to do."

He said, "I want that report, and I want it soon."

I said, "All right." So, boy, I really got cracking and prepared him a ten-page report or whatever. I asked him if that was adequate.

"Yes, that's adequate." He didn't need any more. So he said, "Now I want you to get the OMB people down here to meet with me on this." That's Office of Management and Budget. He said, "I also want you to get some people here from around in the department to be there." Well, he was just about that vague.

I thought, "Gee." That's the way he'd tell you, just "Get them together, and I want to meet with them." So I said, "Fine."

So I called up OMB and told them that Admiral Ricketts wanted to have a meeting with a couple of them over there and told them what the subject was too. They said, "Fine," they'd be there.

So meanwhile, I looked up in the Pentagon phone book there of all the people I thought would probably be interested if we were really going to be serious about that, I mean from BuShips, OpNav, Bureau of Yards and Docks, Seabees, Public Health. I don't know, I lined up about 20 or 30.

---

* Admiral Ricketts died on 6 July 1964.

Paul Stillwell: Were you getting your hopes up again?

Captain Manson: Oh, well, to some extent. I thought evidently he really meant business; he was going to have all these people meet with OMB here. So it was noon, and we were going to have the meeting, I think, at 2:00 o'clock, and he came back to his office. I had that whole Pentagon E-ring lined up with people, Navy people—admirals, captains, commanders.

He called me in there and he said, "Frank, what are all these people doing here?"

I said, "Well, you told me to organize a group to meet with OMB this afternoon."

"Oh," he said, "I didn't mean all that many."

I said, "Well, I didn't know, Admiral. You said get a bunch of them together."

"Well," he said, "a bunch, I think maybe George Miller and yourself and one or two others will be enough. Tell the others to get going."

So I went back out in the hall, and I got all their attention and said, "Gentlemen, we're not going to have the meeting, or not this big, anyway, so I'll let you know. Right now we don't really need anyone here." Everybody shoved off, and I got George Miller's arm and held him. I thought that would be enough. Anyway, I thought he and I with Admiral Ricketts could handle that OMB crowd. But Admiral Ricketts was quick. He realized we might run into some—I didn't even know what he had in mind, didn't have any idea what he had in mind.

We got in there, and we got into a real battle with OMB, and OMB was taking the position that this is no way to use boats, as they called them. Of course, that irked Admiral Ricketts, the fact they kept referring to them as "boats." And that boats are the least effective way to give out aid of any kind. They didn't know anything about it, and it was quite apparent. Admiral Ricketts really did get upset with them, because they really didn't know what they were talking about, and yet they represented the money from the U.S. government.

So, anyway, Admiral Ricketts finally got disgusted and left the meeting. He said, "Captain Miller," Captain Miller or Admiral Miller, I forget which it was at that time, probably was Captain Miller. Anyway, he said we could carry on, there wasn't anything further to discuss, but he had other things to do and he left.

So the next move that Admiral Ricketts made on this thing, he didn't give up, you see. He wrote down to the Deputy Chief of Naval Operations, who was Admiral Ramage, and told him he wanted an op plan, a requirement for one ship, and so he got it.* What the ship would be, it was an LST or an LSD, I forget, but he was going to put a public health team and Seabees type of operation on this ship, and he was going to send it to Indonesia.†

Admiral Ricketts told me that he had talked to the CNO out there, and he wanted such a ship, so he knew what he was doing. That's all we ever talked about it. The requirement was written up, the op order was brought to Admiral Ricketts's office, and he died right then about that time. Admiral Rivero came in and found that in his incoming basket and sent that right back down to OP-03 where it was finished, ended.‡ Admiral Rivero was not interested in that sort of thing at all, and that's the end of the story.

Anyway, I might as well go ahead with Admiral Rivero while I'm talking about him. In the Washington scene there, as soon as Admiral Ricketts died, I think on that very day, Admiral Smith called me from Norfolk and asked if I wouldn't like to change duty.§ I said, "Yes, yes."

He said, "Well, I've got a spot for you down here to be chief of information for SACLant, the Allied Command. So if you want to come on down, I'll phone personnel."

I said, "By all means, do that."

Paul Stillwell: Wasn't that also triggered by the fact that your protector McCain had left as Chief of Information?

Captain Manson: That's right. If Admiral McCain had been there, of course, and I never did particularly like the fact that Admiral McCain sort of brought me in there under those

---
* Vice Admiral Lawson P. Ramage, USN, served as Deputy Chief of Naval Operations (Fleet Operations and Readiness) in 1963-64. Admiral Ramage's oral history is in the Naval Institute collection.
† The LST, tank landing ship, and LSD, dock landing ship, were types of amphibious warfare vessels.
‡ Admiral Horacio Rivero, USN, served as Vice Chief of Naval Operations from 31 July 1964 to 17 January 1968. His oral history is in the Naval Institute collection.
§ Admiral Harold Page Smith, USN, served as Supreme Allied Commander Atlantic, Commander in Chief Atlantic, and Commander in Chief Atlantic Fleet from 30 April 1963 to 30 April 1965.

conditions and then left me, abandoned me. He became ComPhibLant.* Well, he went out there, and, of course, there wasn't any way he could take me with him in a job like that. I had to have at least a fleet for the type of work we do in public information, my being a captain. Admiral McCain was always going to make me an admiral, but, of course, he was always going to make a lot of people admirals. Anyway, in this case, yes, the fact that he was gone, I was in a compromised situation.

Paul Stillwell: Before we get you there, could you talk also about Admiral Rivero and then about the MLF you were involved in?

Captain Manson: Oh, well, going back to the MLF.† The idea behind the MLF, as you are aware, was to put nuclear weapons aboard merchant ships that were in different configurations and different flags so that there'd be no way that spies in the sky or submarines or anyone else would know which ship had the nukes. That was the plan, and, really, there never was, as far as I know, ever any real answer to it.

But the criticism of it was that you could never get a bunch of different countries, different navies, to operate on these ships with any kind of coherence, cohesion, and unity of purpose, that they'd be going in different directions. Admiral Ricketts didn't believe that, so he was working on putting together a ship with a number of nations on it for an experiment. Of course, after he died, they did that.

Paul Stillwell: With a Navy ship.

Captain Manson: With a Navy ship, yes. I think they called it the *Claude Ricketts*.‡

Paul Stillwell: Right. It was originally the USS *Biddle*, and it was renamed in his honor.

---

* Vice Admiral John S. McCain, Jr., USN, served as Commander Amphibious Force Atlantic Fleet from 1963 to 1965.
† MLF – multi-lateral force.
‡ DDG-5, commissioned originally as the USS *Biddle* on 5 May 1962, was renamed *Claude V. Ricketts* on 28 July 1964. For pictorial coverage of the multinational experiment, though without nuclear weapons, see "The Mixed-Manning Demonstration," *U.S. Naval Institute Proceedings*, July 1965, pages 87-103. The issue has a painting of the USS *Claude V. Ricketts* on the cover.

Captain Manson: Oh, that's right. I remember now. Yes, that's what they did. So, anyway, Admiral Ricketts was getting a lot of static from different countries in Europe and from Great Britain, so he sent me over there on a trip to talk to people I'd dealt with for the four years I'd been over there, people like Stephen Roskill and Desmond Wettern and Noel Barber, Chapman Pincher of the *Sunday Express*.*

Likewise in Germany, where I had people that I thought might influence their thinking on this thing, to lay out to them what this really was, and to sort of allay their anxiety about the ship. So I did, and whether I really had a lot of success with these people or not, I never was able to measure that. But, of course, Admiral Ward was in charge of our program.†

Paul Stillwell: This was the fellow you tangled with in Scotland.

Captain Manson: Yes, right, and who was now my friend. But he knew now that my plan was a good one, the one that we had tried out over there, so he was very much in my corner.

Paul Stillwell: Well, not only that, because you were trying to sell his program.

Captain Manson: Well, of course, that's exactly why we had to do it the way we did it. I think as he thought it over, he realized that his approach might have been a little bit too fast and maybe too heavy for the Europeans and for the British. I think he must have thought about that a while. When he saw how smoothly it worked, though, why, he was all in favor of my working on the MLF program. Of course, he was doing an outstanding job for Admiral Ricketts, putting together the actual concept for this operation, drawing up the plans, working with different countries. It was a big job, this MLF thing. I guess Kennedy was President at that time.

---

* Harry Chapman Pincher, born in India in 1914, joined the staff of the *Daily Express* in 1946 as science and defence correspondent. He later wrote on the subject of espionage.
Desmond Wettern and his wife Gillian became close friends of the Manson family. The Desmond Wettern Media award goes annually to the person who has done the most to raise awareness of British maritime issues. He is known for his book *The Decline of British Seapower* (London: Jane's, 1982).
† For details on the multilateral nuclear force, see the Naval Institute oral history of Rear Admiral Norvell G. Ward, USN (Ret.). Ward recalled that the program died when Kennedy died.

Paul Stillwell: Yes, he was.

Captain Manson: So Kennedy was in favor of it, and Ricketts was in favor of it.

Paul Stillwell: I got the idea from Admiral Ward that it came from Kennedy's initiative.

Captain Manson: Well, it may have, it may very well. Admiral Ricketts never told me where the initiative originated. But Kennedy would be the type that could think of something like that. He had quite an imagination. Whether he thought of it or not, he would have someone on his staff, because he had a lot of idea men around him. But I never knew; I never heard just where that idea did originate.

But I thought the idea had merit, because it would give many nations participation in a nuclear response, but it wouldn't give them actually a trigger finger. The United States would still hold, in this concept, the trigger under any circumstances. There's no way that it would ever be relinquished. But at the same time, it would place the Soviets in a position where they never could be sure that they'd knocked out all these ships because they wouldn't even know which ones they were, or where they were.

So I think the idea did have a lot of merit, plus it brought participation. It brought something into NATO and into our treaties and alliances that was very much needed, something very much needed now. Unless you infuse these treaties every now and again with something that's positive and constructive, they tend to dissipate, fall apart. So the MLF gave the whole treaty alliance concept sort of something to think about. Even if they weren't for it, it gave them something to oppose, which was good because it got their adrenaline going.

It reminds me of Field Marshal Montgomery; his great strength in any kind of an international conference was to try to make everybody angry right off. Admiral Carney was telling me one time, the field marshal came into a meeting and said, "Tell me, Nick, what can I say real quick to make everybody mad?" The admiral gave him an idea, and he said, "Fine. I need something, because unless you get them mad, they won't think."

Paul Stillwell: Well, Admiral Rickover used that tactic also, but he didn't need any advice on how to get people mad.

Captain Manson: No. Admiral Rickover had a built-in cabinet full of ideas. He used to get me upset right off. If he couldn't think of anything else, he would question my choice of words, that I'd used the wrong word. This was a sure thing to get you ticked off when you say something was excellent, "Boy, you sure do have a loose language there, using the word excellent," or whatever.

But, anyway, on the MLF concept, my opinion is that if Admiral Ricketts had lived and if President Kennedy had lived, that we would have had an MLF program, and I also think that the three nations would have been much better off for it. It's a shame that this thing—and the experiment with *Claude V. Ricketts*, although they had problems. But I went aboard that ship a number of times and saw the international crews at work there, and they were doing their job. Now, true, they did have problems, as much as anything, with different pay scales, because Americans were being paid a lot more than the other navies. But at the same time, these things were all anticipated, and they could have been worked out.

It's one of those things, whether it will ever be revived again, I don't know. Now that we're on the downhill slide with nuclear weapons, I don't know when it will stop.[*] Maybe it will be zero pretty soon, but it's something we ought to keep in our hip pocket, though.

Paul Stillwell: Well, I think one outgrowth of that, an issue that remained is the Standing Naval Force Atlantic composed of ships of different nations.

Captain Manson: Well, that was the thing that Admiral Colbert and I worked out when he and I arrived at SACLant headquarters together.

Paul Stillwell: Well, maybe that's a good point to pick up the narrative about SACLant.

---

[*] On 27 September 1991, a few years after this interview, President George H. W. Bush announced a unilateral initiative to cease deployment of tactical nuclear weapons on board U.S. Navy surface ships, attack submarines, and land-based aircraft during "normal circumstances."

Captain Manson: Yes, right. It was a tremendous boost to my morale when I found out that Admiral Dick Colbert was assigned there as readiness officer; I believe that was his title. He was sort of the number-three admiral down there. We only had three. He was the one that had the imagination. When he was a captain over at the State Department there, he had called me in one time and asked me if I would permit the CIA to take over this white fleet idea. I told him I thought the word would probably get out and then it would defeat the whole idea, and so we didn't do it. In hindsight, I thought I made a mistake on that, a terrible mistake, because I think it would have been better to let the CIA do it than to not ever do it. Anyway, Admiral Colbert, Dick Colbert, was the one that called me in and said he thought this thing would work under CIA. Anyway, he and I had worked together before.

Paul Stillwell: You said Admiral Smith called you to see if you'd be interested in joining his staff.

Captain Manson: Smith was there first, then Moorer, then Holmes.

Paul Stillwell: What year was that?

Captain Manson: That would have been in '64. I'm pretty sure Dick Colbert was there. We came, it seems like, about the same time. But, anyway, both of us were looking for something that we could promote, because we thought that NATO was, if not on its last legs, at least on shorter legs. If we didn't do something, that the thing was going to die. The headquarters down there was just about as dead as anything you could ever run into, nothing much going on.

Paul Stillwell: What did the command do? I mean, there had to be some justification for existence.

Captain Manson: Well, they had an annual exercise and that kept them busy, getting ready for that exercise. Then they had a briefing team, and that sort of kept them going around the country. Sometimes they'd take that briefing overseas. Then they had paper exercises, quite a few of those command post exercises. So about all you could do, except for that one major exercise which was done with a tremendous amount of planning and international planning, but aside from that, that's about all they did.

They celebrated all the national days there, and that kept everybody busy hoisting flags with some punctuality and aplomb. Oh, another thing they had down there was foreign guests. Somebody was always coming with some kind of rank or prestige that required a certain amount of planning. I remember the King of Norway came. I suppose it must have been Olav.* I don't remember what King it was; that sure is something. It's certainly a blemish on my memory not to remember what the King's name was, particularly after Vice Admiral Bill Ellis had given all of the staff there about two or three weeks' training on how we were supposed to deal with a King.† I guess some of the people had never been around royalty or anything, so I guess Admiral Ellis was afraid that somebody might slap him on the back, or I don't know what he thought we might do.

Paul Stillwell: This is sort of like the Jocko Clark sword training.

Captain Manson: Exactly. So he'd call us together and give us this sword training on what we were supposed to do about the toast and this and that and every detail. Then he issued written instructions.

So the day came that we had the big luncheon, and the King was there. The King was really a thoroughgoing man, a gentleman, and all that stuff just went out the window. He was just a normal person that had to put his trousers on one leg at a time, and that's the kind of a man he was. Of course, he was dignified person, but you would have thought from all the planning and prepping that we got, that we were going to meet some kind of a super person from outer space. So to tell the truth, I think most of us were kind of let down when we found out that this guy was just a normal person, not any dumber or any brighter than the rest of us.

---

* Olav V was King of Norway from 21 September 1957 until his death on 17 January 1991.
† Vice Admiral William E. Ellis, USN, was then chief of staff to the Supreme Allied Commander Atlantic. He had previously commanded the Sixth Fleet from June 1964 to September 1966.

But, anyway, it was fun if you could look at it from a distance, to see some of the planning that went into these visits. But that was, of course, one of the things that the headquarters did, was to carry the NATO flag. We didn't have an awful lot of connections with the Pentagon.

Paul Stillwell: Please tell me more about your work with Admiral Colbert.

Captain Manson: When he and I got together for the first time there, we were both thinking about what could be done to sort of stimulate NATO, to stimulate the thinking, to bring the countries closer together, to encourage the idea of mutual defense. The first idea that—and I don't remember, it just came as a result of our talking. We used to get together two or three or four times a week, just the two of us. We were trying to figure out something that wouldn't cost anything, because we didn't have any money, the budget, and something that was pretty likely to succeed. So this standing naval force really came out of our conversations. I'd say it evolved from both of us trying to figure out something we could do with ships where you wouldn't have to have more ships put on active duty, where you wouldn't diminish the fleet strength—some of the navies didn't have very much fleet strength to diminish—and something that would be acceptable.

So, anyway, the standing naval force was one idea that evolved from those discussions. Of course, the other one was Iberian Command Atlantic. Now he, Dick Colbert, is the one that really thought of Iberian Command Atlantic, and then I was all for it when he told me he thought this was something we might be able to put across.

Paul Stillwell: What advantages did you see from that?

Captain Manson: Well, the first advantage was that it would give NATO a greater sort of defense capability, having a command post right out on the very edge of the Iberian peninsula there. It would have defense advantages that we didn't otherwise enjoy. It would have its greatest distance from the Soviet Union on that peninsula. It was geographically located where it could give NATO the very best possible coverage from a point of view of radar and actually directing forces from over on the continent. It was really an ideal spot from an operational viewpoint. The only problem was that Portugal was not enthusiastic about anything big, and we didn't have any money. So, again, we were working from just almost nothing.

But once he started, Admiral Colbert started thinking up ways of putting this thing across, and he made a trip around all the NATO countries explaining to each Chief of Staff and Minister of Defense in NATO why this thing would give NATO a stronger military posture. And it might have a little influence on the Warsaw Pact. We didn't know about that, we couldn't evaluate that. But, anyway, it would certainly cause the Warsaw Pact nations to know that NATO was still alive, in any case. So that was good, that was an advantage other than geographic, the influence it would have vis-à-vis the Soviet forces.

Anyway, the concept for a command headquarters over there finally got down to a farmhouse. There was sort of a colonial-type structure over there that had just been built, and no one was living in it. I suppose it had about six rooms in it or eight, and it looked very much like a colonial-type house you'd see here in Annapolis or something, stucco finish, but new. Well, anyway, that was good enough, and we put some radios in there and put a few offices and two or three officers, not many. There might have been as many as seven; it was really a sparse staff.

But we had one of the biggest opening ceremonies I think I've ever participated in.* It was probably not as big as Holy Loch, but I'll tell you right now, we had a big one inviting the press from all nations around and inviting all the military dignitaries. Airports were crowded with military planes coming in. Then they set up a big tent out there to make—I think I still have some of the photographs of the opening ceremonies. But talk about pomp and circumstance, I'll tell you, that one really had it and had a lot of speeches and so forth.

Admiral Moorer was the supreme commander by the time we got around to putting the thing in force.† I can remember every now and again Admiral Moorer would

---

* The Iberian Atlantic Command began operation in 1967.
† Admiral Thomas H. Moorer, USN, served as Supreme Allied Commander Atlantic, Commander in Chief Atlantic, and Commander in Chief Atlantic Fleet from 30 April 1965 to 17 June 1967. His oral history is in the Naval Institute collection.

caution me when he'd hear something Dick Colbert and I were cooking up. He'd say, "You guys better go easy on that for a while." He'd tell us to soft-pedal something or other.

Paul Stillwell: Why?

Captain Manson: Well, I remember one time he told us that the political situation was not right for whatever it was we were trying to do, and I wish I could specify just what we were trying to do at that time. But he used to send us around. I had to go over to see the First Sea Lord, the place outside of London where he was.

Paul Stillwell: Northwood?

Captain Manson: Yes, I had to go out to Northwood. This would be in about '67, and Admiral Moorer wanted me to go there and tell the British admiral why we had to get this standing naval force going and so forth. I wish I could think of his name, but, anyway, he told Admiral Moorer he wanted him to get me off his back.[*]

So Admiral Moorer was laughing when I came home, and he said, "Boy, you must have done a job on [whatever his name was]."

I said, "How so?"

He said, "Well, he called me and said 'Get this guy off my back. I'll do it.'"

But the two of us together, Colbert and I, were a little bit dangerous because I didn't mind trying something new, and neither did he. Several years later, when he got to be CinCSouth, he wanted me to come over there and join him.[†] I already was out of the Navy, but he wanted me to come back. He said he thought we could get some projects going, but I didn't want to go back.

Paul Stillwell: Was Admiral Colbert a really imaginative person?

---

[*] Admiral Sir Varyl C. Begg, RN, served as Great Britain's First Sea Lord and Chief of Naval Staff from 1966 to 1968.
[†] Admiral Richard G. Colbert, USN, served as Commander in Chief Allied Forces Southern Europe from May 1972 to November 1973.

Captain Manson: Yes. Admiral Colbert was the type of fellow that almost every day he came up with new ideas. He'd try them out, different ones, and then maybe he could expand it or pull back. But his mind was very nimble and he was quick. Beyond that, he was really a classy fellow, a classy individual. He just had a lot of class. His background and all I really don't know anything about, how he got to be the way he was. I believe he'd had some background with Admiral Conolly. This may not be true, but it seems like that's where he'd had a lot of high command experience.

Paul Stillwell: What do you mean when you say, "the way he was?"

Captain Manson: By "the way he was," he was a big thinker. He thought of concepts, he was a conceptual thinker. He thought in terms of change if things were static or if things were going the wrong way. He was innovative and sharp. I mean, he knew that a new word, just one new word, could make a speech on it if he could think of one new word. Just like Clare Booth Luce said that one time, "Give me a new word and I'll make a speech."* But, anyway, that was the way Dick Colbert was.

Paul Stillwell: How well did he interact with the representatives from the other countries?

Captain Manson: He was liked and respected. They were, I think, at times a little mystified by Admiral Colbert, because he was so unlike most European officers.

Paul Stillwell: In what ways?

Captain Manson: This is a generalization, but they tend to be less innovative than American officers. Not only do you have here in Colbert an innovative type, but one of the most innovative and imaginative. The European-type officers tend to accept things as they are, and if it gets any worse, well, that's too bad, but we'll just have to accept it. But

---

* Clare Boothe Luce was a playwright and author. She served as U.S. ambassador to Italy, 1953-56. He was the wife of *Time-Life* magnate Henry R. Luce.

they don't move out into the political realm and try to build an environment that will enable them to expand their forces or increase their responsibilities. That just doesn't exist in the European countries, even in Britain. They don't do that.

Paul Stillwell: It's also a factor of resources. They saw this big, rich United States and looked to us for leadership.

Captain Manson: Exactly, they did, they did. I mean, I don't know about how things are as of 1988 in terms of comparable resources, but in those days the United States had so much more to offer in industrial capacity, in military experience.

At that time in the '60s, we had a high number of officers that had been through World War II still on active duty, and European people had a very high regard for these people. So it was military experience, economic strength, and, of course, the United States is just sort of an adventurous and innovative place that doesn't exist elsewhere. So Colbert was looked up to, but at the same time I'm not sure they fully understood him. I never did talk to any of the officers.

Now, once we got the standing naval force going, they were for it. But while we were trying to get it going, we had quite a lot of opposition from the foreign representatives, because they were already set and they didn't have any extra ships. They thought they were going to have to let those ships be gone too long, and this and that, you know. There are always reasons why you shouldn't do something.

Paul Stillwell: The Vietnam War was heating up in that period. Was that a distraction in any way, or did it affect your command?

Captain Manson: Not a lot, although it affected me personally. The Navy was trying to determine what mistakes had been made out there, what lessons had been learned, and they didn't know. So Admiral Bill Martin, said, "Well, you've got the perfect officer down there in Norfolk to come up here and do a quick work on this and he'll let us know what the lessons are and so forth," and that was me.*

I guess he called me and said he'd put my name in the hopper there with Admiral Rivero to come up to Washington for a couple of months and do a quick study on lessons we'd learned, what we were doing right, what we were doing wrong, and give it to them, because they were in a quandary as to why they were doing so poorly, why it was such a quagmire, and hoped that I could be helpful. So the admiral—it was either Smith or Moorer—said, "Sure, go right on up there and do it," and they would have somebody cover for me while I was gone.

So I was detached there for, I suppose, about maybe two months, and I sat in on all the briefings when CinCPac would come in or if we had the Seventh Fleet Commander. I had access to all the dispatches. They just cut me right in on what was going on and then gave me access to all the reports and all.

But I hadn't been there any time at all until I could see the problem. The central problem was that the Navy wasn't involved in the war. It was a land war, and our forces were simply not able to do the work offshore there and in the rivers that needed to be done. It was just so obvious that there was this tremendous gap, and yet the admirals, and I heard them say this, the Vice Chief, fleet commander, and different ones saying they wanted to stay in the blue water. This was a phrase they used—let's just keep the forces out there because, well, they weren't going to run into any mines, that's one thing. I don't know for sure what they thought. Well, they might run into some ground fire if they got in. I don't know what the story was. It was just a mess, and they didn't want to get in it.

So I wrote up a quite a paper, and amongst the recommendations that I included was that this was too big a job for the Coast Guard out there to try to prevent the offshore infiltration that was taking place and the river transport of supplies and troops, the Coast Guard was sort of being relied on at that point to do all that work. I said, "This is something that the Navy's got to do, and there's plenty of historical precedent for the Navy being involved in rivers. Go back to the Civil War, the Revolutionary War." In the

---

* Rear Admiral William I. Martin, USN, served as Assistant CNO (Air) from 1964 to 1967. The oral history of Martin, who retired as a vice admiral, is in the Naval Institute collection.

Civil War, the Mississippi, Mobile Bay, and all around, we had forces that were fighting in very close coordination with ground actions. But, anyway, of course, even in World War II we'd gotten involved in river action over in North Africa, for example. I don't know how many examples I picked up from history, but quite a number where the Navy had been very useful.

So I said, "We simply have got to become involved in the war that's going along inshore, close inshore, and the riverine warfare." Well, that went over like a lead balloon in the Vice Chief's office. Admiral Rivero didn't like that at all. He called me in and said that he didn't like the sound of this, that it was contrary and opposite of what they had already decided they were going to do. He said he didn't want me to talk about this, he didn't want me to mention it, and that soon I would be returned to Norfolk, and I could resume my duties. But mainly he didn't want me discussing anything about my report to anyone, and those were his personal orders.

So I was staying at the time with Congressman Ed Edmondson, an old friend who lived out just two or three blocks from the Naval Observatory.* I frequently stayed with him, because we were childhood friends. So one night we were sitting there at the dinner table, and he got up and called Lyndon Johnson to talk to him about this.† Lyndon Johnson was pleading for ideas at this point. Anybody with any ideas, maybe to come directly to Congress, I don't know how.

But, anyway, Ed Edmondson called the President, and I don't know if got him on the phone or not, but he came back to the dinner table in a little while and he said, "Frank, they want you down at the White House in the morning to explain this fleet idea." Now, he'd been a sponsor of the fleet idea in the Congress, so he knew I was prepared to do it. The white fleet, I'm talking about now. So he said, "Will you go?"

I said, "Well, I'd certainly like to clear this with Admiral Rivero, because he's my boss, and you don't go to the White House without clearing it with your boss."

He said, "All right, I'll clear it with Rivero. He's a good friend of mine, anyway."

I said, "Well, fine, if you'll do that, then I'll happy to go down there and brief the White House people."

---

* Edmond E. Edmondson, a Democrat from Oklahoma, served in the House of Representatives from 3 January 1953 to 3 January 1973.
† Lyndon B. Johnson served as President of the United States from 22 November 1963 to 20 January 1969.

He says, "Well, the President wants you to do this."

I said, "Well, sure, I will. But at the same time I'd like to have this all cleared."

Well, anyway, Edmondson started trying to get in touch with Rivero right after we finished dessert. Rivero was out at a diplomatic party and would not take the phone. He was there, but the aides kept saying, "The admiral has a practice of not talking on the phone when he's at receptions and parties." I guess he was probably drinking a little bit and didn't trust himself. I don't know why his policy was as it was, but it was, so he wouldn't talk to the congressman. So, boy, that put me in a real bind. Here I was with a 9:00 o'clock, already agreed to go providing they got it cleared with Rivero, and yet it wasn't cleared at 9:00 o'clock.

So I went to the White House. I thought, "Well, to hell with it, if that's the way it is." I couldn't get in touch with Admiral Rivero the next morning, which I tried to do. So, of course, when the Navy Department started operating the next day, Admiral Rivero was trying to find out what this congressman wanted to talk to him about. When he found out what it was, he called the congressman and the congressman told him, of course. Then Rivero started trying to find me, which he did. He found me up at the White House, and I was in conference at that time. And here I had got the admiral on the phone, and I was busy explaining this thing.

The first thing right out of the box, the admiral said, "I thought I told you not to discuss that river warfare, inshore warfare to anyone at any time at any place." That's what he thought I was up there talking about when he'd actually forbidden me.

I said, "Admiral, you did, that's right, you did, and I haven't."

"You haven't?"

I said, "No."

He said, "What are you up there for? What are you at the White House for?"

I said, "Well, I'm discussing an idea for the constructive use of ships to use in times of emergency and for technical assistance and that sort of thing," I summarized for him.

He said, "Did you ever hear of AID?"* That's just the way he measured those words. Now, mind you, the White House staff was listening to this too.

---

* AID – Agency for International Development.

I said, yes, that I had heard of AID and I thought they were doing a good job, but that there evidently was room for improvement or maybe other ways of doing it or whatever.

He says, "This is not the Navy's job or the Navy's work, and my suggestion to you is that you kind of cut there. Exercise your best judgment."

I said, "Well, Admiral, you can be sure I will." And that was the end of that conversation.

So after I was over at the White House, Jim Jones, who was the chief of staff for Lyndon Johnson, said, "Admiral Rivero?"[*]

I said, "Yes."

He said, "Don't worry about it, I'll take care of him. I know him, so don't worry at all about him."

So I said, "Well, yeah, but I'm going back down there right now."

So I went back down, and the aide to Admiral Rivero was Jerry Miller.[†] So he said, "Frank, the admiral is pretty unhappy with what you've done here."

I said, "Well, I'm not surprised, I'm not at all surprised. There was very little I could do about it. I was staying at Congressman Edmondson's," and I went over the whole litany.

He said, "Yeah, but the admiral is still very, very unhappy. I don't know what they're going to do. He's down there talking with the Secretary of the Navy. The Secretary of the Navy is unhappy too."

I said, "The only thing I can tell you is that they told me over at the White House that if there's anybody unhappy down here, they'd like to know their names and serial numbers, and that's all I know. That's all I can tell you. So if there is anybody unhappy, I guess I'd better go make a phone call."

He said, "No, no, wait a minute." So Jerry went inside, and what went on, I don't know, but he came back out and he said, "Nobody's unhappy."

I said, "Not the Secretary?"

---

[*] James R. Jones was de facto White House chief of staff while serving as appointments secretary from 27 April 1968 to 20 January 1969.
[†] Captain Gerald E. Miller, USN. The oral history of Miller, who retired as a vice admiral, is in the Naval Institute collection.

"No, not the Secretary."

"Not the Vice Chief?"

"No, no, nobody is unhappy."

"Well, I suppose if nobody is unhappy, then there's no problem."

He said, "No, no problem. And he said, "Do you want to come to the admiral's birthday party? They're going to have cake in there in a few minutes."[*]

I said, "Sure, I'd like to come to the party."

So we went in there, and I was really up to no good, because I didn't care. I knew everything was all right at this point. Still at the same time, I walked up and sat down next to Admiral Rivero at the party, and I sort of whispered to him, I said, "Admiral, I hope everything is working out on this trip over at the White House." And he wouldn't answer. He wouldn't say anything. And from that day to this, Admiral Rivero has never spoken to me.

Now, about two or three months later after I'd gone back to Norfolk, I'd been invited back up to Washington to some kind of a big shindig at the Statler Hotel, and Admiral Rivero was there. I walked up to him and held out my hand to talk with him, and he just turned and walked away. I never talked with him again.

But, anyway, you asked about the Vietnam War. I didn't discuss it with anyone, but I did give Admiral George Miller a synopsis of the paper and he, in turn, went to Wally Greene, who was Commandant of the Marine Corps.[†] The two of them took that paper, and they expanded on it and thus was born riverine warfare, the concept and the forces. But that's the way that happened.

Paul Stillwell: You said that Admiral Martin had initiated this. Did you have any further contact with him?

Captain Manson: No, no. The only thing, he just laughed and said, "Well, Frank, . . ." By the way, he supported the white fleet always, and he and I were good friends from back when he was a commander and I was a lieutenant commander. But, anyway, he

---

[*] Rivero was born 16 May 1910.
[†] Rear Admiral George H. Miller, USN; General Wallace M. Greene, Jr., USMC, served as Commandant of the Marine Corps from 1 January 1964 to 31 December 1967.

laughed when I had told him what had happened up there. Later he came down to CinCLant. He came down there as chief of staff as a three-star admiral.* He was in the Sixth Fleet for a while too.†

Paul Stillwell: He was Commander Sixth Fleet.

Captain Manson: He was Commander Sixth Fleet, and he and I used to write. He and I would write back and forth on whatever was on our minds. But I always had a profound regard. So when he came back down as CinCLantFlt chief of staff, why, then he and I would compare notes, as people do who are friends, on lots of things. But I don't remember anything specific that we were doing between myself and Bill Martin except that we were seeing each other, and socially we saw each other, too. But we didn't have any projects.

Paul Stillwell: What are your recollections of the two commanders down there at Norfolk, Admiral Moorer and Admiral Holmes?‡

Captain Manson: Well, Admiral Moorer was the best-qualified officer for a fleet command. He'd worked up, he'd sort of been pre-selected, and they had sent him to the Seventh Fleet, and they sent him to CinCPac, and then he came in as CinCLantFlt and SACLant. So he had in his mind a concept of running a fleet at a fleet level, fleet command level, that was far superior, I would say, to most any officer and certainly more so than Admiral Holmes, who hadn't had that kind of fleet training or fleet background.

Admiral Holmes was much more reserved, much more conservative. I'll give you an example I think will cover it pretty well. This happened with Admiral Holmes now, what I'm about to tell you. But if had had happened with Admiral Moorer, I'll tell you how I think Admiral Moorer would have reacted and how Admiral Holmes reacted. What was that fellow's name from *The New York Times* who was down there at the

---

* Vice Admiral Martin served August 1968 to January 1971 as deputy and chief of staff to Commander in Chief Atlantic Fleet
† Martin commanded the Sixth Fleet from 10 April 1967 to 14 August 1968.
‡ Admiral Ephraim P. Holmes, USN, served as Supreme Allied Commander Atlantic, Commander in Chief Atlantic, and Commander in Chief Atlantic Fleet from 17 June 1967 to 30 September 1970.

headquarters and he's now head of the bureau at the *Minneapolis Tribune*, I believe? A very well-known reporter, excellent reporter, but he was with *The New York Times* at that time.* Maybe his name will come to me and maybe it won't. But anyway, he was just sort of nosing around down there looking for anything to write about, but he didn't come to Norfolk. I think this is maybe the only time he ever came down there. So I said, "Well, we'll go in and we'll talk to the chief of staff." This is after Admiral Holmes had taken command of CinCLant and SACLant. Bill Ellis was still the deputy for Allied Command Atlantic. Did you know Bill Ellis?

Paul Stillwell: No.

Captain Manson: Well, he was a pretty straightforward, straight-talking kind of guy. So he figured there was no point of having a reporter in here unless you gave him something to write about. So he was telling what was going on with the Soviets, and then he said, "Well, it's like that aircraft carrier they've got over there." I've forgotten what the status of it was, but I believe it was already operating at this point, but it hadn't been released at all in the States. I didn't even know about it myself. But Bill Ellis was just telling what kind of an aircraft carrier it was, helicopters mainly.

Paul Stillwell: *Moskva*, I believe.†

Captain Manson: Yes, that's the ship. So, anyway, I knew right then, boy, the cat was out of the bag, because you can't tell a reporter from *The New York Times* something like that, I didn't think. But I didn't realize until we walked out of the room that he wasn't as sharp as I thought he was. Anyway, in conversation, Bill Ellis gave him another little something. It was about naval personnel, or I don't remember because it so dwarfed anything else in the conversation to me. I paid very little attention to what else he said.

We got outside the room there, and we were walking over to see Admiral Holmes, and I said, "Well, [I think the guy's name was Bill], "I suppose you realize that you've

---

* The reporter was William M. Beecher.
† *Moskva* was a Soviet cruiser with a stern flight deck for antisubmarine helicopters. She began operating on sea trials in July 1967 and was commissioned 25 December 1967.

got one of the best stories of your lifetime and maybe of anybody else's lifetime in a military way."

He said, "You mean about that NATO Iberian Command or whatever it was?"

I said, "No, I don't mean that."

He said, "Well, what?"

I said, "Well, that new Soviet aircraft carrier."

His eyes just got big and round and practically popped out. He said, "You mean to tell me that—?"

I said, "No, that's never been told, written about. I didn't know it myself. Of course, I know it now, and so do you. But evidently there's no harm in it, because Admiral Ellis was telling us all about it."

So we got over to Admiral Holmes, and all this guy wanted to talk about was that aircraft carrier, and Holmes was looking at me, and then he'd look back to him, expecting me to do something. I said, "Well, Admiral Holmes, the story is already out, I mean, Admiral Ellis has already told him."

"Oh, well, I don't think—" Everything Admiral Holmes said: the displacement, the footage, about as much as we knew about it. So Admiral Holmes really did lay it on, and, gee, the next day *The New York Times* had a big front-page story of this new Soviet aircraft carrier.* Dispatches started flying in from Washington, the Pentagon, and they were really getting after Admiral Holmes for releasing this information. I was of the opinion at that time and, frankly, I always have been of the opinion that when the Soviets have something that's out in public display like that, that the only people we're keeping it a secret from are in the United States. The Soviets had this ship out there, and all the Soviets knew about it, and yet nobody over in this part of the world knew about it. So I didn't see how there was any great security involved. There wasn't any security involved, in my judgment.

So Admiral Holmes called me over, and he was absolutely sweating blood. He said, "Frank, you never should have let them do this to me. You never should have."

---

* William Beecher, "Russians Building Aircraft Carrier; Policy Shift Seen," *The New York Times,* 23 October 1967, page 1.

I said, "I didn't let them do it to you, Admiral. Admiral Ellis told them about it before he ever saw you."

"Yes, but it's the command, it's everything. We're terribly embarrassed, and I'm being severely criticized and I may lose my command." He thought he would. So, anyway, Admiral Ellis was kind of walking around like a Cheshire cat. He didn't realize, I don't think, that it wasn't public knowledge either. I don't know whether he did or not.

But some time after that, Admiral Ellis, we were having a frank chat with each other, as we frequently did. He said, "Well, I'll tell you one thing. Holmes thinks you could have kept that story under wraps. He holds that against you."

I said, "Well, I don't know, Admiral, I don't see how I could. You told him about it."

He said, "Yes, I did. I don't think you could have, but Holmes thinks you could have in some way or another kept him from printing that story."

I said, "Well, I'm sorry he feels that way."

Anyway, now, how would Admiral Moorer have reacted to that? Admiral Moorer, in my own judgment, would have said, "By gosh, I've been wanting that thing out ever since I've known about it, and now I've got a clear shot at it, and I'm really going to zing it." He would have embellished it. That's my judgment of how Admiral Moorer would have reacted to that. Then afterwards, he would have called me in and said, "Frank, I want to commend you. You've done a great thing for the country." If he thought I had any part of it, he'd have commended me for it.

And that's the way sort of those two fellows were. Now, Moorer was more an operational type, in a way, having been an active flier and fleet commander, much more so than Holmes. Holmes was more of, I would say, a planner. He liked to work with papers. He was not as imaginative, either, as Moorer. Now, I don't mean to say that Holmes was a dummy by any manner or means; he wasn't. He was a very bright guy, but he was up against an exceptional person in Thomas Moorer. Those kind don't come along very often, not the Moorers. Well, Burke is someone like Moorer. They have many things in common—guts, especially.

I'll give you another example with Moorer that shows something in Holmes. I don't know how Holmes would have reacted, but I guess I can tell you more about these two guys by talking about examples. The Telstar satellite was already launched, and it was in orbit.* We were going to send the first message from Allied Command Atlantic to Allied Command Europe, the first from Telstar, and it was going to be a short message. We were having a hard time of trying to figure out how we were going to get press coverage on this thing. So I suggested that maybe we ought to build a mock-up. I went to various people around in the Norfolk area, and finally found somebody that thought they could build one that would look about like it, paint it grey, the antenna and all those things.

So we called in the press and had this mock-up. The communications officer we had in Norfolk at that time was a straight-laced guy named Baker. I don't remember his first name, but he was straight-laced. But he knew that sometimes you had to bend a little if it came down to it. So I said, "Admiral Moorer, you know there's a chance that that message, may not go through. Suppose we can't contact that satellite."

Moorer looked straight at me and said, "Frank, the message will go through."

I said, "Yes, I think it will. I think we'll be able to do this."

He said, "Well, I thought we could."

So we had the big press conference, and Admiral Moorer got on the phone, and the words he put out, I don't recall. They were not very long, but he sent to SACEur a message from SACLant. This is first message direct by satellite and so on and so on. Then the press, boy, they had their story and everybody wrote down "First message by Telstar has gone out," and etc., etc.

Then I called Baker and said, "Did we get that message through?"

He said, "I don't know."

I said, "Why don't you know?"

He says, "Well, I just don't know. I haven't heard anything."

So I said, "Well, what's the real story?"

He says, "I don't know what the real story is."

I said, "You don't know whether the message got through?"

"No."

I said, "Did you send the message?"

---

* The communication satellite Telstar 1 was launched 10 July 1962; Telstar 2 was launched 7 May 1963.

"Yes, I sent the message."

I said, "Well, the message got through."

"Well, yeah, I guess it did."

So the press conference had gone, and we'd already announced that we'd gotten the message. It just didn't worry Admiral Moorer one bit. I don't know if we ever did get a reply, to tell you the truth. Whether we did get it and did reply or didn't get it, I don't even know this myself. But I just know this, that we sent the message. That's the way Moorer is. He's kind of a gung-ho guy when it comes right down to saying whatever he has to say, and he's proved that since he was Chairman of the Joint Chiefs.[*]

Now, if I had said to Holmes, "Suppose the message doesn't go through," I think he would have said, "Maybe we'd better cancel the press conference." That would probably have been his reaction, but it wouldn't have been "go ahead with it," because he would have seen that there was a possibility that we wouldn't get through or they wouldn't answer us or whatever. It's like launching a missile. When you send a radio message up in a satellite, you don't know if it's going to be on frequency or what. But those are the two guys, Holmes and Moorer.

Paul Stillwell: Do you have any more recollections about Ellis?

Captain Manson: Well, he's the one that instructed us on how to deal with the King. He never minced words; he was very straight. He never worried about the diplomatic side of things. It was a little unusual to have him in sort of a diplomatic post there at Allied Command. He'd been a former Sixth Fleet Commander, as well. But my opinion of the man is he's a very straight shooter, very direct, incisive, but he didn't particularly enjoy public relations or public functions.

Paul Stillwell: You've already made the point that a lot of senior officers didn't. Well, at least media relations.

---

[*] Admiral Thomas H. Moorer, USN, served as Chairman of the Joint Chiefs of Staff from 3 July 1970 to 30 June 1974. His oral history is in the Naval Institute collection.

Captain Manson: No, he didn't. Yes, that's true, a lot didn't. Most of them saw a risk there; it was not necessary or unacceptable. I think he probably viewed it that way. But I had a high regard for Bill Ellis.

Paul Stillwell: Well, it's curious that if that was his approach, that he would be so open with this reporter.

Captain Manson: That's right. Now, there's a contradiction for you. It's a real paradox. I don't know, it just seemed like that morning he was in a very talkative mood, and he was going to hold forth. I guess maybe he hadn't been talking to anybody lately, because it was a rather quiet job he had over there, you know. Normally I'd never take anybody to him, but I'd take them to the Deputy Supreme Allied Commander, who was usually a British officer.

So our American deputy there didn't get an awful lot of time, because you wanted to give them the allied flavor and all that. And usually the British type would like to talk anyway. Anyway, that morning—you never know how these things, you almost think that this is the way it was meant to be, that that story needed to be out, because otherwise how in the world did it happen? Here was a deputy who said they've got one, and the supreme commander rather hesitatingly says yes, they do have one, and to a *New York Times* reporter. What better way? Why this met such hostility at the Pentagon with the Secretary of Defense, I'll never know. I suppose it goes back to budgets.

Paul Stillwell: Well, maybe also they had the view that it should come out from Washington when it came out.

Captain Manson: Yes, of course. Yes. I'm sure that was part of it; it must have been. But when they'd planned to do it, maybe next year, maybe the following year, nobody knows because the ship was already operational.

Paul Stillwell: It's interesting. I was in the fleet at that time, and I was seeing classified intelligence publications. I would see reports on that carrier classified secret, and at the same time I'd see them in *Time* magazine.

Captain Manson: Oh, well, then you probably were as puzzled as I was when I heard about it the first time, because I didn't know. I had said I don't know how many times, publicly, that I thought the Soviets were perfectly capable of building an aircraft carrier. I believed that, but I didn't dream they'd done it. Then here's Bill Ellis, just right out on the table. But I can see why you would have been surprised.

Paul Stillwell: Well, this is later than you're talking about. I mean, this was after *Time* had gotten it, obviously.

Captain Manson: Well, *The New York Times* first.

Paul Stillwell: Some time had passed.

Captain Manson: I've often thought I would call the reporter up one of these days and ask him if he'd ever gotten a better story than that one, because I don't think he ever did. He was so surprised himself when I said, "You've got the best story you'll ever have, certainly the best one you've ever had."

Paul Stillwell: What effect, if any, did the Israeli attack on the *Liberty* have on your command?[*]

Captain Manson: Well, I guess the best words I could think of would be disappointment and sadness that something like this could happen. Most of us didn't know for sure

---

[*] On 8 June 1967, during the Six-Day War between Israel and Egypt, Israeli aircraft and torpedo boats made a number of attacks on the U.S. communications intelligence ship *Liberty* (AGTR-5). Of the ship's crew of 297, 34 were killed and 171 wounded. Israel claimed that the attack on the *Liberty* was a case of mistaken identity and apologized. Many in the ship's crew were skeptical of the claim.

whether it was an intentional attack or whether it wasn't, but we assumed it was, and then we couldn't understand it. I tell you right now, I still don't understand it.

Paul Stillwell: Yes. Did Admiral Moorer talk about it?

Captain Manson: No. I don't recall that he ever brought it up when I was in the audience with him. I believe I'd remember that, too, because I'm still looking for answers on that one, I am. Do you know the answer? I mean, do you know why the Israelis did that? Because it was out there getting intelligence on them and they decided to bomb it?

Paul Stillwell: Presumably it could report on their intentions.

Captain Manson: It already had reported, I think. But I'm surprised they would attack a U.S. Navy ship.

Paul Stillwell: Well, you have to go beyond that to a presumption that we would tell the other side and try to affect things.

Captain Manson: Yes, that's what they presumed. It's what the Israelis, I guess, presumed and that's why they thought they had to sink the ship. There's someone that was on that ship that still talks about it. Every now and again I see something public on it.

Paul Stillwell: A guy named James Ennes wrote a book, and Moorer is sympathetic to this group of *Liberty* survivors.*

Captain Manson: Moorer is?

Paul Stillwell: Yes.

---

* James M. Ennes, Jr., *Assault on the Liberty: the True Story of the Israeli Attack on an American Intelligence Ship* (New York: Random House, 1979).

Captain Manson: He kept that pretty close because it was so delicate. I'm sure if I had brought it up, he would have discussed it with me, because we had that kind of relationship. But I don't recall bringing it up with him, and it wasn't exactly in our area of responsibility. So I don't think he ever discussed it, not then, anyway.

Paul Stillwell: Are there any other things from that tour of duty that should be put on the record?

Captain Manson: Well, I think we probably should discuss what I regard as one of the most comprehensive NATO exercises that we ever conducted, certainly the PR side of it, because I was in charge of the command information bureau. I had had it for three years sort of as a result of being in London. I had been sort of the link between the U.S. forces and whoever was in charge of that thing. Like when Admiral McCain was over there, I think twice, and I think Red Yeager was over once as head of the command information bureau as admirals.

Then when my time came, Admiral Smith said, "Well, Frank, you're going to be in charge, and I want you to wear my four stars liberally." I think I ought to really be going. It's getting kind of late here, and I wouldn't have quite time to tell you how I planned that operation or what went on with it, but it was one of the most thorough—it was almost a textbook type of PR plan where I had a fallback position. We had people fanned out over the whole continent of Europe. I'd rather I think do that probably the next time and might end it up with the next time too.

Paul Stillwell: All right, look forward to it then. Thank you, sir.

Interview Number 6 with Captain Frank Manson, U.S. Navy (Retired)
Place: U.S. Naval Institute, Annapolis, Maryland
Date: Thursday, 28 April 1988
Interviewer: Paul Stillwell

Paul Stillwell: Captain, typically we've begun these sessions with a little catch-up. So what do you want to catch up on this time?

Captain Manson: Well, of course I knew Admiral (CNO) McDonald pretty well and worked for him for a very brief time in London and in a kind of a way when I was working for Admiral Ricketts later, because Admiral Ricketts was Vice Chief and McDonald was CNO.[*]

But going back to that period when he was in London for a brief time, coming from the Sixth Fleet in transition to CNO, really, of course, I knew that was what he was going to do, and so did he. He had a very good friend named John Connally, who was Secretary of the Navy.[†]

Paul Stillwell: Not at that time he wasn't.

Captain Manson: Well, he had been, and had seen to it, I think, that Admiral McDonald probably became the Sixth Fleet commander or at least helped him a little, because they had formerly been in some combat information center aboard a carrier, I believe, during World War II.[‡]

Paul Stillwell: Right.

---

[*] Admiral David L. McDonald, USN, served as Chief of Naval Operations from 1 August 1963 to 1 August 1967. His oral history is in the Naval Institute collection. As a vice admiral he had commanded the Sixth Fleet from 13 July 1961 to 18 March 1963. He was to Sixth Fleet when Connally was SecNav.
[†] John B. Connally Jr., served as Secretary of the Navy from 25 January 1961 to 20 December 1961.
[‡] Commander McDonald was executive officer of the aircraft carrier *Essex* (CV-9) during World War II, and Connally, a Naval Reserve officer, was fighter director officer.

Captain Manson: But, in any case, Admiral McDonald wanted to talk to me about some of the problems facing CNO, because he knew I had served there for a considerable length of time under different CNOs. He was talking about the aircraft carrier as a weapon system that he would have to defend as CNO. I won't forget that he told me that, "If I do anything at all while I'm CNO, I'm going to make that aircraft carrier an inch shorter." He took his fingers, and he measured an inch shorter than it is. In other words, he didn't want to get the thing any larger than it was. He said if he had anything in his mind that he intended to do, it was to make that carrier one inch shorter.

Paul Stillwell: Why did he say that?

Captain Manson: Well, I believe in the back of mind was the fact that the carriers were getting too expensive, and it was very hard to justify an increase in the size of them. He didn't really justify in his mind, except we were talking about the fact that the carriers were becoming a very expensive item in the budget, and they were increasingly difficult to win congressional approval.

Actually, my memory is that we had been talking about the possibility of building somewhat smaller carriers and building more of them, which I have always been a proponent of. I've always thought that we'd be better off to have more parts of the world covered with some form of competitive sea power than to have only a few areas covered in the most sophisticated manner. I've thought that having forces on the spot, available and ready, would serve as a deterrent in case something happens and a corrective force in case you have to use them, if they're there and available on the first few hours or the few first few moments of a problem, rather than waiting for the thing to fester and then burst into warfare and require heavy involvement.

But, anyway, that was generally the discussion we were having, and that's when he said, well, he thought if he didn't accomplish anything else, he was going to make them a little smaller. I don't know that this ever happened under his leadership. I wasn't able to keep track of the link that long after he got there. Ike Kidd might remember whether or not that ever happened, or the admiral himself might remember.*

Paul Stillwell: Well, it would be easy enough to look up.†

Captain Manson: Yes, it would. You can check it out. But that's the main point that he had on his mind.

Paul Stillwell: What kind of person was Admiral McDonald to work for?

Captain Manson: Admiral McDonald is an easygoing type.‡ He's a cool cat, in a way. I don't know if "a cool cat" is a good way to talk about an admiral, but he didn't get upset or excited about things. He was a staff man in the sense that he relied heavily on staff to do the work, and then when decision time came, why, of course, he would do it. He's a very refined person and gentle in his attitude toward his fellow beings, but he was not what I would call an incisive thinker, and a very cautious man. He wasn't the type of person that you would want if you were, say, going to build a Navy or that sort of thing.

I was there with Admiral Ricketts, I suppose, over a year, and I would say that Admiral Ricketts was performing more as a CNO. Admiral McDonald was happy to let Admiral Ricketts fly the airplane from the second seat. One day, Admiral Ricketts was overburdened with problems, small ones and large ones and all the rest of it, and he was pressed.

I said, "You know, Admiral, it seems to me that your job here, that you've got a rather heavy share of the decision-making on your shoulders."

He said, "Yes, I guess that would be a pretty good observation."

I said, "What's it like, trying to fly an airplane from the second seat?"

He said, "Yes, that would be a good analogy."

---

* Admiral Isaac C. Kidd Jr., USN (Ret.). In the early 1960s, as a captain, he was executive assistant to the Chief of Naval Operations.
† The keel for the *John F. Kennedy* (CVA-67), the Navy's last conventionally powered aircraft carrier, was laid 22 October 1964 at Newport News Shipbuilding and Dry Dock Company. McDonald was then Chief of Naval Operations. She was 1,067 feet, 6 inches long. The next aircraft carrier was the nuclear-powered *Nimitz* CVAN-68), authorized by Congress in the fiscal year 1967 budget. She is 1,092 feet long.
‡ Admiral McDonald died on 16 December 1997, several years after this interview.

Paul Stillwell: How do you mean that? In what sense do you mean that?

Captain Manson: Well, I mean the pilot, the number-one pilot is saying, "Claude, take it and carry on."

Paul Stillwell: Do you have examples of the kind of things on which he would do that?

Captain Manson: Well, the multilateral force is an excellent example of something that was coming right directly from the White House, and yet Admiral McDonald took very little interest in it. I mean, I'm sure that from time to time Admiral Ricketts would sort of bring him up to date, but as nearly as I could tell, it was not a hands-on policy, the way the two of them operated.

Now, I also know that Captain Ike Kidd, who was administrative assistant in that time frame to Admiral McDonald, was an extremely able man. My impression of the way things happened was that if Ike Kidd couldn't get it done, then he usually would probably go to the Vice Chief. In other words, it was minimizing the work that the CNO was doing in terms of the substantive decisions with regard to shipbuilding, budgets. Of course, the Vice Chief, I suppose, is charged with the responsibility of taking all programs and policies and getting them pretty much decided and staffed out before going to the CNO. But the CNO's office itself was not anything like as busy under Admiral McDonald.

Another thing, which I'm not sure which one is correct on this, but Admiral McDonald was a golfer and he did like to go off, when the weather was nice, and get a game in. His wife liked to play as well. So he was never embarrassed on a good day to go and have a game. This was something that Admiral Burke never did, Admiral Denfeld never did. Admiral Carney, when he was off on a trip, would go fishing or hunting if he could work in two or three hours. Admiral McDonald never told me this, but I just think that he thought as long as he had these hundreds of officers in there, that he might as well let them do some work, and he let them work. [Chuckle]

Paul Stillwell: Do you think the situation changed after Admiral Ricketts died and Admiral Rivero took over?

Captain Manson: Admiral Rivero carried a heavy part, much more—well, no, I don't think it changed a great deal, although the problems that the Navy was dealing with changed to some extent, because Admiral Rivero did not continue with the same agenda that Admiral Ricketts had. MLF is a good example. But it's a question of degree and shading as to just what substantive matters that Admiral Rivero took less interest in, let's say, than Admiral Ricketts, because this does, in the final analysis, become a matter of what the individual is most interested in. What does he want to emphasize, and what does he want to press and pressure for? Not having been there except for that time when I was studying the lessons of the Vietnam War for Admiral Rivero, I never did really see his agenda as Vice Chief, and I don't know the relationship between the two.

But I just know that when Admiral Ricketts was there, and I found out especially because I wrote the speeches, or drafted them, rather, for Admiral Ricketts, and he was the person doing most of the speech-making and a good deal of the testifying on the Hill—in other words, he carried a lot of weight.

Paul Stillwell: Well, part of it could be that Admiral McDonald never really sought the office in the first place. He was thrust into that when Admiral Anderson was fired.[*]

Captain Manson: You know, that's a good point, Paul. As I say, he wasn't a competitive person like so many of the others, and he really didn't. He wasn't a person that was aggressive about the CNO job. I'm sure he never would have minded at all if he never had been CNO. I don't think he would have minded.

I'll give you another example the caution that Admiral McDonald exercised as a person and as a commander. This was during the Panama Canal battle. This was after I'd already retired from the Navy. I went up one night—I believe they call it the Order of

---

[*] The Chief of Naval Operations, Admiral George W. Anderson, Jr., USN, disagreed openly with Secretary of Defense Robert McNamara about disposition of U.S. ships during the Cuban Missile Crisis in 1962. For that reason and others, Anderson's tenure as CNO was cut short in August 1963, after one two-year term. For Anderson's side of the story, see his Naval Institute oral history.

the Cincinnati on Connecticut Avenue.[*] Admiral McCain was having a bash up there and had invited quite a number of congressmen, senators, and Admiral Carney was there. Of course, Admiral Carney and I gravitate to the same point usually when we're in the same meeting, or we did in those days. This would have been in the late 1970s. Admiral Carney and I were discussing the sort of tactical battle that we were in to try to retain the Panama Canal for the United States.[†]

In the midst of discussing tactics, we were trying to think if there was anything the admirals, like Carney and others, could do. I remember we sat down on a trunk there in one of the big rooms, and Admiral Carney was leaning over against the wall there. He said that he thought that if we could get a really strong letter written up and have as many former CNOs as possible to sign that letter, he thought that might have some influence. I agreed with him and said, well, I'd be willing to draft the letter. Then he could take it and revise it as we had done with his speeches and back and forth until we got what he thought he and I were happy with. Then we'd go to the other CNOs with it. And it was agreed that we would do that.

So then I went shortly thereafter to Captain Miles DuVal, who usually came to my office at least once a day.[‡] He spent his entire life on the Panama Canal issue and wrote two books, actually three, but I don't know if the third one was ever published. In any case, Captain DuVal was active on the canal issue at the time on the Hill. He said, yes, that he thought this would be a good idea. So he had some ideas about the letter, and I drafted up a letter for the CNOs to sign.

Well, Admiral Carney and I sent it back and forth to each other until we had it honed to where we thought it would be acceptable and would be a powerful instrument to send to President Carter.[§] Then we began checking out the CNOs, and Admiral Moorer said absolutely he'd sign it, sight unseen. Admiral Burke said, well, he didn't need any

---

[*] The Society of the Cincinnati is the country's oldest patriotic organization, founded in 1783.
[†] On 7 September 1977, President Omar Torrijos of Panama and President Jimmy Carter of the United States signed a new Panama Canal Treaty. It specified that the United States would transfer full control of the canal to Panama on 31 December 1999. The treaty did away with the Panama Canal Company, the Canal Zone, and its government as of 1 October 1979. The Panama Canal Commission then operated the canal during the 20-year transition period that began with the treaty.
[‡] Captain Miles P. DuVal, USN (Ret.).
[§] James E. Carter, Jr., who had graduated from the Naval Academy in the class of 1947, served as President of the United States from 20 January 1977 to 20 January 1981.

more letters to sign just yet, besides he was getting ready to go to Europe and he was very busy, and he'd want to postpone that. I went down to see Admiral Anderson. He was living down at Watergate and had been on the Intelligence Committee there at the White House for quite a while. Anyway, he and I had a little chat about it, and he said, yes, he would sign the letter.

So we had four lined up, and I was hoping for five, so I called Admiral McDonald, who was down in Florida. He said, "Well, Frank, you know I've been out of Washington for a while, and I don't know all the details and nuances of this battle that's going on there."

I said, "Yes, I realize, but Admirals Carney, Burke, Anderson, and Moorer are going to sign it."

He said, "Well, that's well and good, but I just don't think I will. If I were up there, and if I knew all of the details of it, why, it would be a different situation. But since I'm down here and I'm remote from what's actually taking place, I just don't think I'll sign it." Now, there was a man of caution, in a retired status, you see. I urged him a little bit, but it didn't do any good.

Paul Stillwell: Did you go to Admiral Zumwalt?

Captain Manson: No, no, I didn't go to Admiral Zumwalt. I don't know which side he would have been on, anyway. There's no telling. I think he would have taken the politically attractive course, and at that time he was pretty much a Democrat because he either had run or was going to run for the Senate against Byrd.*

Paul Stillwell: He had already run and been beaten.

---

* Admiral Elmo R. Zumwalt Jr., USN, served as Chief of Naval Operations from 1 July 1970 to 29 June 1974. In 1976 he ran unsuccessfully for the U.S. Senate.

Captain Manson: Well, anyway, I had no idea about Zumwalt's inclinations. I had known him for a short time as a captain and as a vice admiral when he was out in Vietnam.* But, no, I didn't ask him, and neither did Admiral Carney want me to.

Paul Stillwell: Do you have any recollections of Admiral Zumwalt from your contacts with him?

Captain Manson: Well, Admiral Zumwalt, the problem I had with him was I never quite knew the set of his sail. By that, I never knew just what his goals were, what you might call the central motivating theme of his life was. I remember one time, this was after he had retired as CNO, and he and I happened to be sitting side by side in some sort of a big conference there in Washington. I said to him, "Well, Admiral, what are you doing these days?"

He said, "Well, I'm taking every opportunity to [blank] on Henry Kissinger. Yeah, that's where I'm spending most of my time. I'm really trying to do him in."† The phrase he used there left no doubt that that's what his prime objective was. At that time I think I did know where some of the differences were that he had had with Henry Kissinger, but at that point in his life that's what he was involved in.

But going back to when Zumwalt was CNO, I talked, of course, with people at all levels in the Navy—from admirals, vice admirals, rear admirals, captains, all the way down to the enlisted ratings—about Zumwalt, and I found that a large number of the enlisted personnel liked Admiral Zumwalt. They liked those Z-grams that came out, that were aimed directly at the enlisted, bypassing the whole rank structure in the Navy.‡ I think Admiral Zumwalt's purpose was to go directly to the forces in much the way that I guess a labor boss goes to workers in the unions.

---

* Vice Admiral Elmo R. Zumwalt, Jr., USN, served as Commander Naval Forces Vietnam/Chief of Naval Advisory Group Vietnam from 30 September 1968 to 14 May 1970. His oral history is in the Naval Institute collection.
† Henry A. Kissinger was the President's national security adviser, 1969-73 and later served as Secretary of State, 1973-77.
‡ Z-grams were consecutively numbered policy directives from Chief of Naval Operations Zumwalt that attempted to deal with such issues as enlisted rights and privileges, equal opportunity, and Navy families. Junior personnel viewed them much more favorably than did their seniors. See *U.S. Naval Institute Proceedings*, May 1971, pages 293-298.

But I found that the admirals, by and large, were disappointed, very disappointed, in the way that Zumwalt was running of the Office of Chief of Naval Operations. I don't know, really, down deep in Zumwalt's heart whether he was disappointed in the leadership of the Navy, whether he thought they were outmoded and dated in their outlook and so forth. But such things as uniform and wearing of the hair and, oh, so many details that have to do with morale and tradition, it just seemed to me like that Zumwalt was unhampered with tradition, like the Air Force motto, "unhampered by tradition." He saw tradition as more or less an obstacle rather than an asset.

Now, when he was CNO, I was down there at a NATO job, and so I wasn't actually directly able to gauge the pulse, but I did talk with sufficient number of senior people that I knew that they were highly disappointed in the manner in which he was conducting the Office of CNO, very disappointed. When Zumwalt was a captain, I found him an imaginative person, highly articulate. When I was out in Vietnam, I saw him out there in charge of the naval forces and riverine forces, as they were called at that time. I got the impression that he was on top of the job, that he was intensely interested in prosecuting the war and in being aggressive, and knew the status of his forces, he knew their state of readiness, and, in general, my own evaluation of his performance out there in Vietnam was high.

Paul Stillwell: What was your contact with him when he was a captain?

Captain Manson: He was working in the Secretary of the Navy's office, and at that time I'm pretty sure I was with Admiral Ricketts. Well, in Chinfo, too, but spending an awful lot of time with Admiral Ricketts.

My recollection is that one of the most lengthy conversations I had with him was when Admiral Ricketts used to invite the captains who were operating at policy level to his home for dinner. He might have as many as 20 or 30, and he used to invite me rather frequently with my dinner partner, and in one instance it was Zumwalt, who was then a captain. We were talking over the problems that faced the Navy, chitchat, as you do, one on one, same level, and we were at approximately the same rank. I don't recall exactly the subjects that we brought up—of course, that many years ago—but I do recall that my impression of him was that he was sharp. I didn't see, even then, any thrust to his thinking.

In other words, I'm like Captain McCain, let's say. You couldn't talk with him five minutes until you knew exactly what he was thinking as a captain, a commander, or whatever. And most of the people that you talk to, after a little while, you get an idea of their direction, what it is they're trying to get done in their career, other than just get promoted, because most of them share that.

So I was a little surprised that Zumwalt suddenly blossomed into a rear admiral and then to a vice admiral and then CNO. I can only conclude that Paul Nitze had a favorable impression, a highly favorable impression, of Captain Zumwalt.[*] Then he had sort of his own PIO there, who was Bill Thompson, and apparently Bill Thompson and Zumwalt got along quite well, because they were both on the Secretary's staff.[†] So I thought that it probably made a pretty good team there. It's possible in the Navy, that anyone in the Navy ranks, in the military, that is, uniformed Navy, that if the Secretary of the Navy takes a—I don't know if this is true today, but it certainly was true then—if he takes a strong liking or dislike, either one, whichever way, he can influence that officer's career.

Paul Stillwell: Well, I have a feeling that's still true.

Captain Manson: You do?

Paul Stillwell: Yes.

Captain Manson: Well, it was certainly true then. I know one time the Secretary of the Navy, it was Francis Patrick Matthews, ordered Captain Burke's name off the promotion list for rear admiral and had a captain on his staff named Glass, Richard Glass, put on. My boss at that time, Captain Walter Karig, got hold of the list and spread it around

---

[*] Paul H. Nitze served as Secretary of the Navy from 29 November 1963 to 30 June 1967. During part of that time Captain Zumwalt was his executive assistant.
[†] Commander William Thompson, USN, a public affairs specialist, was on Nitze's staff. Later, as a rear admiral, he served as the Navy's Chief of Information from July 1971 to February 1975.

Washington. There was much flurry, gnashing of teeth for a little while. But Admiral Forrest Sherman was then the new CNO, and he and the Secretary of the Navy apparently decided, after much discussion, that the best thing to do would be to restore Admiral Burke's name to the list and also to keep Glass on there, which is what they did.[*]

But Admiral Burke told me that the Secretary of the Navy subsequently apologized to him for taking his name off the list. Admiral Burke, as a rear admiral, told me that he had done this, that he had seen the work he was doing out there in Korea at NavFE headquarters and was so well impressed with the way Admiral Burke had tightened that command up and improved the general command situation, that he said he could see that he was a man that should have been a flag officer and was delighted that he was.[†]

But, anyway, as far as Zumwalt is concerned, I never did have a very close relationship with him, not like with the other admirals, although I didn't want to see him in the Senate when he ran against Harry Byrd, simply because I thought that he was so very liberal in his views that I didn't know what his attitude would be toward the Navy or toward the military in general, going back again to where I just don't know where he's coming from and I don't know where he's going. I don't know who knows that, but I certainly don't.

Paul Stillwell: Any more to say about Admiral Zumwalt?

Captain Manson: No, I don't think of any details.

Paul Stillwell: I know another topic that you wanted to address in this session was the fleet exercise you were working on when you were on the SACLant staff.

Captain Manson: Yes. Every year, the NATO forces hold an exercise, and it is usually a very large exercise with combatant ships, with international fleets, with merchant ships, and they exercise on everything from penetrating the land mass of Europe, thrusting air

---

[*] Rear Admiral Richard P. Glass, USN.
[†] NavFE – U.S. Naval Forces Far East.

power ashore, to convoy of merchant ships, to antisubmarine exercises, minesweeping. The whole spectrum of naval warfare usually passes in review at these exercises.

I had worked with the command information bureau for three years when I was in London. It was sort of like it was all happening in my backyard, because I had close ties with the media in England especially, but also in other countries, as well. The admirals that came over there relied on me pretty heavily to run that thing, to help them out.

So when it came time when I was at SACLant to do that thing, Admiral Page Smith called me in and he said, "Well, I'm not going to send an admiral over there. I'm going to send you, and I want you to select the very best people you can to help you." So I sent word up to Washington that I was going to run it, and I would appreciate the best help I could get.

Jim Dowdell was not always a friendly person for me to deal with, because he and I were sort of rivals, and that creates a competitive situation that's not always conducive to the most cordial relations.* Anyway, Jim thought this was good, that we would take the best that we had in the reserve, and he asked me to come up and help select them.

Paul Stillwell: Do you know what year that was?

Captain Manson: That was in 1964. It was Teamwork, and I'm sure it was '64, because I hadn't been down there very long.† Anyway, I got up to Washington, and they had pulled from files just the very top reserve public information people in the United States. So Jim had them all laid out there on the desk and he said, "Okay, Frank, they're going to be yours, so you go over them and tell me which ones you want." I had told him that basically I wanted people who were good writers; that would be one thing. I wanted to have people who were technically competent in the use of cameras and movie cameras. I wanted people who could do magazine stuff and people generally who were able to function in some of the specialized ways. In other words, I wanted a high degree of competence.

---
* Captain James S. Dowdell, USN.
† The exercise was in September and October 1964.

So he said, "Sure, let's go through them on that basis," and we did. So I remember I found a fellow named Charles Trishman, who came from up around Michigan, I believe. He had done some films, he had produced some films, and I thought he would be a good man to put in charge of television and that sort of thing. I found Bob Garrick out on the West Coast, and Ferd Mendenhall was another one.* He owned a group of newspapers out there on the West Coast. I guess Robert Garrick and Ferd Mendenhall had worked together quite a lot. So I thought it wouldn't be a bad idea to have a person who owned some newspapers. I was pretty sure we'd get some coverage at least in those.

Then up in the Northwest sector there was Donald Brazier, who was a captain and was the editor of the *Seattle Times*.† It was sort of a family-owned newspaper, as I recall. It was plain from reading his fitness reports that not only was he a good editor, but he was a good writer, and I thought he would be an outstanding person as the exercise unfolded to send on special missions. So he became my special missions man.

Trishman, Garrick—actually, at this point, I don't recall the entire team that we brought together for this operation, but I remember there were about 20 highly qualified officers, maybe more than that. It might have been closer to 30, I don't recall. But, anyway, we got over there in London. First, they gave us a special aircraft to fly the whole team over there, and I'll never forget before the plane had taken off, Bob Garrick and Ferd Mendenhall had gotten themselves into bright orange flight suits, and I could see they were a couple of clowns, amongst other things. So that made the trip rather pleasant for a lot of us, because we saw that we had some fun-makers as well as serious people there along with us.

Paul Stillwell: On the other hand, you had a real challenge to be able to channel and use all this talent you've got.

Captain Manson: Well, I knew that we were going to have to work very quickly. I had to get each person imbued with what he had to do. So we had a meeting as soon as we

---

* Commander Robert M. Garrick, USNR; Captain Ferdinand Mendenhall, USNR.
† Captain Donald G. Brazier, USNR, who had served on board a destroyer in World War II.

landed and got everybody together at the officers' club in London. I reserved a room up there, and we went up for a morning session. I gave them my concept of how we were going to run this operation, and I gave each one of them his assignment. We had a discussion about the assignment, and I told them why I had assigned them the way I had, why I'd read their fitness reports and their background, and I knew what their jobs were in the United States right now, that I thought that these assignments were jobs that they could perform well.

The general concept of the operation was that we would, every day while this exercise was taking place, even prior to the time it started, we were going to have daily briefings at London headquarters. We were going to brief the international press, on, first of all, what we planned to do, and then we were going to brief them on what we were doing. Bob Garrick wanted to be the briefer. He said he'd volunteer for that, and he turned out to be a good man for that. So every day they could expect to have him.

Anyway, the concept of the operation was, first of all, the forces were going to be involved in carrier operations up off the Norwegian coast. They were going to be involved in ASW operations across the GI-UK gap.[*] That's the gap we were going to try to put some submarines through there and see if we could intercept and so forth. Then we were going to run some convoys off through the Bay of Biscay. We had some minesweeping operations that were also scheduled in the channel. Channel Command had some work that they were going to do inside the channel, and I don't recall exactly what those—in addition to minesweeping.[†] Perhaps amphibious, but I don't recall exactly.

Anyway, this was a big exercise. It was, in a way, tantamount to a major invasion force, is what it really came down to. My own concept of how to get the maximum coverage out of this exercise, since they'd been doing it for years, was, first of all, we would brief every morning at 10:00 o'clock on operations that were going to follow that day. Then along about 4:00 o'clock or 5:00, we would put out a summary through the wire services for general distribution, on just what did happen that day. Then our third and fallback situation was that we were going to send correspondents to every ship in the

---

[*] ASW – antisubmarine warfare; G.I.-U.K. Gap – the sea area between Greenland, Iceland, and the United Kingdom.
[†] Channel Command was part of the Royal Navy.

fleet that looked as if they were having anything that was at all exciting or interesting. We'd transfer them back and forth by helicopter or whatever means we could.

We were going to send as many as 40 or 50 correspondents from these NATO nations. I remember we had four from Iceland, from Denmark, Germany, France, Italy. We had correspondents that were keen on doing this thing. So then we had to send sort of a Father Superior out there; we'd put a public information officer with each of these people. I tried to select people for these jobs who had had considerable experience in dealing with international media as much as possible. These people then would write their stories from the fleet, and they'd be flown every night on a COD aircraft to our headquarters there or to an airfield that wasn't socked in wherever.[*] Sometimes we had a little trouble getting the plane in from the fleet. But every day we would load up with pictures or film—that is, raw film—and with footage, whatever we had, and fly that information in and then make it available the following morning. So that was the routine that we set up.

It was my only chance in my naval career to do something exactly the way I wanted to do it and without anybody standing over me and saying, "You can't do this," or, "You can't do that," or something.

Admiral Smith had told me when I walked out of his office, "Frank, you wear my rank over there, and I think you can do that."

I said, "Thanks, Admiral," and, of course that was, I think, part of the reason why it was successful.

So I remember one Sunday—this is a minor detail, but we got bags that were bright orange so that they couldn't be lost with other supplies or other materials. Those bright orange bags were going to be the bags with the hot news in them so that everybody in the fleet knew what these bags were, and we had plenty of them, so they wouldn't get lost. One Sunday afternoon, Soviet aircraft had been out mixing it up with our aircraft, and we knew that. So I was hoping that we'd have some photographs of this. Our offices were over in Whitehall at the Admiralty, and on Sunday the photo labs were closed down; everything was closed down. But I had a chief photographer that I'd brought from

---

[*] COD – carrier on-board delivery, an aircraft configured for carrier takeoffs and landings, dedicated to transporting personnel and cargo between ship and shore.

Norfolk, and I said, "Chief, these photographs may be very worthwhile. You know the Soviet aircraft have been out today."

He said, "Yes."

I said, "Is there anyway you can develop these things without being in a photo lab?"

"Yes," he said, "have you got some wastebaskets around?"

We went around to some of those admiralty offices and gathered up some wastebaskets that didn't leak. We went into the men's room, and he made up his solutions, and, sure enough, we found just exactly what we'd hoped we would find, and that was we had an F-4 right directly underneath the belly of a Bear.[*] There was no question about which one had tactical control of the other one. That Navy fighter could do anything with that bomber because he was right under him. So I said, "Man, that's about the best one I've ever seen," and everybody agreed. I said, "Chief, get that thing ready." So he started producing that photograph for us, and I bet we got 50 of them out.

Paul Stillwell: All in the men's room?

Captain Manson: In the men's room there, yes, and I don't know where he put them up to dry. I don't recall how he did it, but he did all that operation in about two to three hours.

So we had those pictures. I guess the package got in maybe about 2:30 or 3:00, and along about 5:00 o'clock we were calling everybody in town saying, "We've got the best photograph over here you'll ever see." Of course, the British just love that.

The next day, of course, this picture was all over the London press and all over the world and on television. It really did just zing around, and that picture, to this day, I still see it on all the time on television, and it turned out to be a classic. But I just think because we were rigged for that kind of an operation and because we were able to get it out so quickly, and fired such a clean shot.

---

[*] The McDonnell Douglas F-4 Phantom II was the Navy's primary carrier-based jet fighter of the period. "Bear" was the Allied designation for the Soviet Tu-95 strategic bomber, a missile platform and maritime reconnaissance aircraft.

Paul Stillwell: You must have gotten into a darkroom at some point, because men's rooms don't come with enlargers.

Captain Manson: I don't know. Now, he may have taken an enlarger. He may have had that with him. But I know that whatever the photographic lab that he was using over there at Whitehall, he didn't have, so he had to substitute. Now, I'm sure he brought a lot of things with him to operate from the seat of his pants or whatever. I just know that that Sunday he got those photographs, got the film developed, got the prints made, and we got them out.

Paul Stillwell: Do you remember any other big events from that exercise?

Captain Manson: I recall it seemed like we had a submarine lost, a nuclear submarine lost out there for maybe 24 hours, maybe longer than that, I don't recall. But the submarine wasn't really lost; it just wasn't communicating. But it seems like maybe we threw some apples or something off of one of the ships. A Soviet trawler was trailing pretty close behind one of the ships, and they threw some things over for them to pick up and they did, like fruits and vegetables, probably fruits, I think it was.

Paul Stillwell: What was the point of that?

Captain Manson: Oh, just an act of—I don't know. You can't figure out why Americans do what they do.

Paul Stillwell: Well, sometimes you can.

Captain Manson: Well, I don't know in this case why they were throwing that. I suppose they'd heard that maybe the Soviets were short on citrus fruits. I don't know what caused them to do that, and I don't recall whether we got any coverage out of that or not.

I remember one detail, I'll tell you one little specific of it, but I couldn't figure out when we were making the initial release on this—you know, you always like to have the first of something or other. The first exercise, the first time so many ships are involved, the first time this or that. I believe that we had perhaps more merchant ships involved in this one than in previous NATO exercises.

But I said, and was quoted around the world, that this was the most comprehensive NATO exercise yet. So with the word "comprehensive" I figured I could hide behind any amount of camouflage if I had to. So that was the thing that caught on, "comprehensive," one word.

When I would hear that there was a rather exciting exercise taking place and we weren't getting the coverage on it, I would send Don Brazier out from the Seattle paper. He had been writing features for many years, and he would come back with the bacon. He would fish out what about that particular phase of the exercise was newsworthy, and he would come back with enough that we could then lay it on heavy. Besides having a real good story that he'd write, we'd spread it out to the entire media. So I remember that he performed his role. I also recall that many of the photographs were high quality, whether it was a movie or film. But I don't recall that we had any serious accidents during the exercise, didn't lose any correspondents. We didn't have of them bitching about getting plenty of action.

Paul Stillwell: Were there any political objectives in your program?

Captain Manson: The main political objective in the entire effort was laid out to me by Admiral Smith before I left. He said that he wanted the small nations and those with smaller navies to get some of the ink. He said, "I just think that the small countries, in terms of the effort that they put out, ought to have better coverage than they've been getting." So this was a political objective, to try to bring countries into it.

I had one press officer there named Hank Bax on the command information bureau. He was from the Netherlands, an outstanding man, and he was the number-two information officer in his country, really.

Actually, at that particular time, there weren't many NATO officers that really had much of a public information background. There were far more of them that were skilled operationally. But in terms of dealing with the media, they didn't have that kind of background at all, just weren't accustomed to it. So many of them, the King or somebody up in high level, sort of put out an edict on what was going to happen, and that's what happened.

But, anyway, that was a political objective and, of course, to emphasize during all of the releases and commentaries, to always keep as many nations as we could actively participating. I mean keep their interest up, even to the point where I finally, after it was all over, put together a book on that exercise. We sent probably even as many as five copies to each head of government so that they could distribute them around and see what their participation and their coverage had been. I thought this was a good move, and since so many of them had been covered, it turned out to be a great thing. Of course, as a result of that, Admiral Smith gave me a commendation for that operation, and then we won the Silver Anvil for that operation, as well—the first time that had ever happened in a NATO operation and, I suppose, the last time.*

Paul Stillwell: Well, you had a lot of good people to help support you.

Captain Manson: Oh, of course, that was the secret to it. I mean, had I gone over there alone with a chief petty officer or a whole bunch of people who didn't know what they were doing, the result would have been zilch. But I had all the talent I needed, and I had all the authority from seniors that I needed, and the elements were there. And the elements are usually there in a naval operation, usually exciting. You've got so many things happening with a naval operation that if you'll just think about it, let a little imagination drift in once in a while, you can figure out things that are tremendously interesting. Because after all, it isn't every day that you've got a whole household floating out there at sea, doing everything that you do on shore, except that you've got the water, too, and all that.

Paul Stillwell: How much cooperation did you get from CinCUSNavEur that year?

---

* The Silver Anvil award is presented annually but the Public Relations Society of America.

Captain Manson: Well, certainly it was all that we needed. I didn't really need it, because I'd been over there just a year or two before. I did use their facilities of CinCUSNavEur to call my command. I'd go over to their headquarters. I remember when I wanted to send a dispatch, sometimes Bob Mereness would give me a little static, but he wouldn't have been Bob Mereness if he didn't give me a little static.*

Paul Stillwell: I'm surprised you could get a word in edgewise talking with him.

Captain Manson: Well, that was one of the things I had to work around. He ultimately would send the dispatch, but it would take a while.

Paul Stillwell: He's a very loquacious gent.

Captain Manson: Oh, yes, I think a lot of Bob. He was tremendously excited when I would walk in the door over there with something that we needed to do. I think Bob, as public affairs officer for CinCUSNavEur, was very pleased with the amount of coverage that we had.

The only one problem that I really got into, I guess I should tell you about it, was over the release of that photograph without clearing it with the intelligence section of the operation. I didn't even check it with them. I just thought it was too good to hold, and I thought I had the authority, and I did have, to release it.

The next day I heard rumors going around, particularly in the British side of things, that they thought maybe we had violated security by releasing information about the Soviets and the forces being in this close contact, and that we may have violated security. So I just ignored it. I thought, "Well, if they call me on the carpet, of course, I'll go."

Sure enough, about 11:00 o'clock, the morning after the release, I was on the carpet with one of the top Royal Navy intelligence persons. He started out the conversation by expressing his concern that this photograph had been released without clearance. I told him, yes, but it was Sunday, and there were no intelligence officers

---

* Captain Robert H. Mereness, USN, a public affairs specialist.

around. I couldn't see why it would embarrass or violate the security since everybody knew we were having this exercise, and everybody knew the possibility the Soviets would come out and see about it.

"Yes," he said, "but our procedures in the Royal Navy and in the British military are that you clear these pictures. The public information branch always clears them for security before releasing."

I told him I thought that was a good policy and as a general rule that I would agree with that, but in the case of NATO that we didn't have any such policy, because I was in charge of it, and I didn't have that requirement. He was absolutely puzzled that I would tell him that NATO didn't have the requirement that the British had. I said I could understand from a national point of view why he would hold such an opinion. And I said, "Do you see anything about those photographs that you think violate security?" He had to admit that he didn't. I said, "Well, since you're in charge here and since I'm in charge with SecNav, I don't see where we've got a problem." That was the end of it, never heard any more, not from any of the intelligence forces of any of the countries. The fact is, they were all pleased.

Paul Stillwell: Were there any media people that you particularly remember from that exercise?

Captain Manson: Well, I had Jack Norris from the Washington Post.[*] He was a Navy captain, also, so he came over in both capacities. I had Ed Prina, who he was a Navy captain, retired, who also was representing the *Evening Star* from Washington.[†] Let's see. Who were some of the reporters? Of course, we had Desmond Wettern going out from the *Sunday Telegraph*. I have a list of a good many of those. Desmond Clough, I think, was one. It was really American correspondents that were over there. It's hard for me to separate them from being one place or another. I just remember that Jack Norris was there because he was getting in some reserve time as well as doing his paper a favor.

---

[*] Captain John G. Norris, USNR.
[†] Captain L. Edgar Prince, USNR (Ret.), worked for the Copley News Service.

As far as the British correspondents, I remember there were four from Iceland, that I remember because they got a little upset, I remember, before we got things under way. They were a little bit worried that they weren't going to get the same opportunities that all the others were getting because they came from such a small country. But when they found out that they were going to be given an opportunity to go aboard all the ships and so forth, they were happy.

No, it's hard for me to remember. If I could find that Teamwork book, and I think it's over at the Naval History Division right now in Washington, it would have the full coverage of this thing. That coverage, in terms of reporting on an operation, is the most comprehensive I've ever seen, and in that book it's all there. So somewhere it does exist. We could find it if somebody wants to.

So anyway, that's about the extent, although I might as well tell you another thing. When I got back to Norfolk, Admiral Smith was just absolutely delighted with the way things had gone. But Admiral Hogle was upset.* He was the chief of staff. He called me in one day and he said that he didn't entirely agree with the way I had run that operation. I said, "Well, let's have the details. Like what?"

He said, "Well, for one thing, you called Admiral Smith directly from London. I was here. You could have called me and I could have saved you that trouble."

I said, "Yes, that's true, Admiral. But I did try to call you and you weren't here, and so I just had to go straight through to Admiral Smith."

Well, he said I could have waited until the next day if it wasn't anything too urgent. He thought I'd been a little bit too quick to sort of cut him out of the pattern, and he felt a little upset about that. He picked out two or three things that he was really picking at me about. I'd been through this type of exercise so many times in my life that I was getting a little aggravated myself. The fact is, I was really aggravated. So I said, "Admiral, do you have any real objection for me to call my wife on your telephone?"

"Oh, no, no," he said. He hadn't quite got through eating me out.

So I called my wife and I said, "Would you have any real objection if I retired, say, today, from the Navy? I've got my time in. I'm down here involved in something that I don't particularly enjoy, and I'm fed up with this kind of thing."

---

* Rear Admiral Reynold D. Hogle, USN.

She said, "No, if you think it's all right, go right ahead."

So I just put the phone down and told Admiral Hogle that I just checked it with my wife, and she didn't mind if I retired. I said, "The truth of the matter is, Admiral, that I've had to put up with what I think is too much of this kind of thing. You obviously don't have anything serious to talk about, and all this nibbling and nabbling about when we've got a great thing going here, and for us to be sitting here with this kind of thing, I can't put up with it. So I'm going to retire."

He said, "Oh, Frank, I didn't mean anything like this."

I said, "Well, I know you didn't, but I'll just tell you right now, Admiral, I think both of us are too long in the tooth to be standing around here with this kind of nitpicking discussion, and I'm not going to put up with it, so I'll just retire."

"Oh, no, no, no, I'm not going to permit it."

I said, "Well, I don't want any more criticism."

He said, "Well, you're not going to get any more."

So then he rushed over and told Admiral Smith that we'd had this little discussion. So I didn't hear anything about it for, oh, maybe a month. Admiral Smith was laughing one day—he and I were frequently laughing about something or other—and he said, "Say, Frank, I heard you and Toby had a little discussion." His name was Toby Hogle. Toby Hogle was a good friend of Admiral Smith, as well as I was. He said, "I hear you and Toby had a little discussion about that exercise."

I laughed and I said, "Yes, I'm afraid we did."

He says, "Oh, Toby was really upset about that. He didn't mean to upset you."

I said, "Well, no, I'm sure he didn't. He's a nice admiral." And that was the end of that.

Paul Stillwell: You stayed on in that job several more years. Any other things to recall from that period?

Captain Manson: Well, the main operation there was to try and get any way we could to enhance, or rather to make it look like that NATO was an ongoing rather than a down-going international set-up. So we really did try to think of things, to create things, that would give the public the impression.

For example, the NATO briefing team, I used to schedule that. This was about seven officers from seven countries would go around the United States, and once or twice we sent them over to Europe. It took a lot of money to send them to Europe. But around the United States we'd get a Navy aircraft and they'd send these people. It had quite a fascination to Americans to see seven different nations represented in a presentation. One of them would give the Soviet threat, and one of them would give the capabilities and another in another. It was a good presentation. In a way, it was sort of an international sea power presentation. This thing would get us a lot of coverage like in Houston or some big city or in Chicago.

Anyway, I've got to tell you one more Hogle story. Usually we'd have a vice admiral to lead this briefing team, and it would ordinarily be the American, but sometimes the British admiral would lead the team and give the introduction remarks and introduce the speakers. But we'd gone down to Texas, and we were giving a pretty good—had a number of different cities we were attending, and Houston was one. We got down there in a press conference in Houston. I remember it was in the morning, about six or seven members of the press there. Admiral Hogle was getting ready to hold forth, and one of the press fellows right off said, "Well, Admiral, why have you done this? Why have you come here with this NATO briefing team?"

You know, sometimes they say you either react with fright or warmly, a lot of us react one of two ways, either favorably toward the thing or you're afraid. Well, Admiral Hogle reacted out of fear. The way he answered the question was that it was really a waste of time for us to be there and that we really didn't have much of a purpose. The answer just didn't come out at all, so then the press didn't ask any more questions. They just saw that if we didn't know exactly why we'd come, that they certainly didn't care why we'd come, and one of them said, "Thank you very much, Admiral," and that was the end of it.

We were on the airplane after that, going to Tulsa, to a big crowd assembled there, the oil capital of the world. I was talking to the admiral about having a press conference as soon as we arrive.

He said, "Well, at that press conference they didn't ask much, did they?"

I said, "No, they really didn't seem to be very interested."

He thought a little bit, and I said, "You know, Admiral, when we get there, they're liable to ask you why we've come to Tulsa."

The admiral nodded and said, "Yes. Frank, why are we going to Tulsa?"

I said, "Well, Admiral, I'm sure glad you asked me." So I gave him a few points such as educating the American people on the purpose of NATO and what our commitments were and so forth.

He said, "Yeah, that sounds like a good answer. I'll use that." And sure enough, he did.

But you can imagine my shock when we were airborne there and almost ready to land, and he said, "Why are we going?" And yet now he was going to make the introductory remarks, too, you see, but that was all memorized. I don't know whether he just had a lapse of memory or what. I never will know.

Paul Stillwell: It sounds like he wasn't all that interested in what he was doing.

Captain Manson: Well, I think maybe that was it. He just sort of saw it as—frequently I found a lot of U.S. naval officers, that when they were on shore duty, and if the command itself wasn't too actively involved, as SACLant wasn't, that they did sort of lose interest. But you give them a fleet and their interest picks up, and they get very excited. Life begins again, and they start living, and the juices flow. But you get them ashore again, and, oh, man, they start thinking about horse races and girls or anything to distract them.

Paul Stillwell: Suspended animation.

Captain Manson: Exactly, yes. But I won't forget that question.

In that job it was tough. We had command exercises every year, and sometimes we would do a movie of the command exercise and try to peddle that. Then down in Norfolk we had a little radio station, and every week we would put out a five-minute radio program, interviews with anybody we could interview and put any sounds in there we could think of and send it out to about 400 stations. The response was good. It was all free; the stations didn't have to pay a thing. So that was a pretty good device for a fairly continuous story line of what was happening.

But so many times there wasn't a lot going on. That's why Admiral Colbert and I had to dig deep to come up with Iberian Command and the standing naval force, which it turns out, both of them, as far as I know, are still in operation.

Paul Stillwell: Yes, they are. Did you have any interaction with Congress?

Captain Manson: Well, we did. I remember that from time to time we would have senators or congressmen come down. Once a year we had an international group of legislators come. That was just a one-shot thing a year, and then we'd brief them and let them visit around headquarters and so forth.

But I remember we had individual senators. I remember Henry "Scoop" Jackson coming down.[*] I'd known him personally for many years. He came down and brought two or three of his staff and held a press conference and told how he valued NATO and what NATO was doing to preserve peace, that as long as we'd had it, we hadn't had any wars and so forth. But from time to time we had other congressmen that would visit. About all we could do for them there would be to give them a briefing and then let them talk to whomever they pleased. Frequently, too, they'd want to see something of CinCLant while they were down in that area, and we tried to arrange that as often as possible.

Then every year we had the Azalea Festival. This was the main problem, or I don't know if you'd call it a problem, but it certainly had to be a carefully thought-out diplomatic choice for the queen, or princess, I guess it was. If the President had a daughter, that made it easy. She had to be about the right age, 17, 18, 19, or 20, somewhere along there, and it helped if she was pretty. So it would usually turn out that in looking over 15 countries, we'd go to the maritime countries for this queen. It

---

[*] Henry M. Jackson, a Democrat from the state of Washington, served in the House of Representatives from 1941 to 1953 and then in the Senate from 1953 until his death in 1983. He was chairman of the Senate Armed Services Committee and a strong proponent of nuclear-powered warships. The ballistic missile submarine *Henry M. Jackson* (SSBN-730) was named in his honor.

wouldn't be good to bring someone in who wasn't a maritime power, really, or didn't have maritime interests.

But this thing would result in a banquet and a parade and a ceremony. It was festive. The Tidewater area thought highly of it, but it was pretty much local. I remember we had Luci Johnson when LBJ was president.* I can't remember all the girls. But every year, why, that was something that required quite a little bit of planning and got everybody involved.

There was a lot of socializing in this allied command. It was a little bit like each country, the senior officer would entertain the others, and this kept going around and around. I think they had 27 U.S. admirals in the Norfolk area, and by the time they entertained twice, each one of them during the year, it kept them busy every week just going around from somebody's quarters to another. It might have been 29. I think it was 27.

Well, anyway, they had the same thing in the NATO set-up, and what people enjoyed about the fact was they'd always serve the food of their native country, or try to. The Norwegians, for example, would always have that herring and sour cream for hors d'oeuvres, whatever else was fashionable from Norway. So it really was a fascinating method of socializing.

We did have at times a little bit of conflict between the officers for one reason or another. I had very little trouble, although the Canadian captain down there named Steele used to try to—every now and again, he'd get a little bit tired of not having anything to do. He was in charge of security, amongst other things, and personnel. Particularly if we had a U.S. political problem, he would usually not be sympathetic at all.

Going back to Scoop Jackson again, we had a case where they wanted me to take a young man from the state of Washington into my office. He was serving somewhere in Norfolk, or it might have even been in our command, I don't know. But he was being used as a mailman, to put up the mail and so forth. He had his master's degree in journalism, as I recall. His name was Bailey. I'm almost sure of the name.

But I had a number of calls from Senator Jackson, because Senator Jackson had been a law partner of this young man's father. So I went to Captain Steele and told him

---

* Lyndon B. Johnson served as President of the United States from 22 November 1963 to 20 January 1969.

that we had this problem, this young man's talents were not being properly utilized, and if he didn't have any objections, I'd be most happy to take him into our program and give him some writing jobs.

"Well," he said, "I don't need any advice from you on how to handle personnel; that's the first thing. The second point is that I don't have any interest in U.S. political problems, that's not part of the NATO set-up. The third thing is, I don't intend to do it."

I said, "Well, Captain, I wish you wouldn't come down too hard on this. I mean, I hope you'll keep an open mind on it."

"Well, I just don't see how. Suppose we did this for all the countries."

I said, "Yes, but the man's talents, I could probably use him, and there wouldn't be any unhappiness, and I don't know that the mail people would miss him."

Well, he said he was sure he wasn't going to do it. But as political pressure intensified from Washington, and instead of coming to me directly it was coming through the supreme commander before long and the chief of staff, and everybody was aware of it. When the pressure got sufficiently intense, he had to transfer the young man to my office, but he held this against me then. He thought that I had been meddling in his affairs. So he was just waiting to figure out something that he could figure where I was in Dutch.

We had security there in the wings, the way that headquarters was built in Norfolk. It had separate wings, and I had a wing of one of the buildings. So the door at all times was supposed to be kept locked. He had his security people come by and find the door unlocked, and he saw some of my people, instead of coming around back to the main hall and going out through the front entrance, were sometimes coming and going from that door. So he put in my division for violating security.

I don't recall at what level we had to go to deal with this problem, but something above us, anyway. The chief of staff, I suppose. So I had to assure him that we'd keep that door locked at all times and that we'd be careful.

Well, anyway, it wasn't very long after that until we had a large group of people from the chamber of commerce wanting to come out to visit the command, and they wanted their picture taken out by the sundial.

Well, also, the sundial goes right in front of the building and the flags and made a beautiful picture. But the sundial was considerably soiled; so many pigeons had visited the place over a period of time that it was in a disheveled state, to say the least. So I realized then that I had my answer to Captain Steele and that I would at least get even with his problem with my door.

So I prepared, on the most official stationery I had, a complaint that he wasn't keeping the facilities clean, that while the floors seemed to be adequately swept, that the sundial was in a terrible state and that the command had been really embarrassed when we had all these people from the chamber of commerce out there, businessmen and so forth, and they had seen this thing in an absolute disreputable situation, and I would like to have this corrected at once.

I got a brief note back from him saying that there are a lot of things he was in charge of, but the one thing he didn't have any say so was where the pigeons defecated, and, in short, he wasn't going to do anything to make it better. I don't recall how this was resolved. Whether he ever did, I don't know, but I know one thing, his face turned red every time he saw me for about a month.

But that's the sort of thing that when you're an operation that requires total effort, men's minds will get off into a lot of channels and sometimes they don't have a lot to do with anything important.

Paul Stillwell: Sounds like a lot of time wasting.

Captain Manson: Well, it is, absolutely. One day I remember we were in a conference down there, and we were talking about budget. Everybody was figuring out how we could spend a lot more money, and I knew perfectly well we were not going to budget, from the U.S. point of view, any more money to NATO at that time. So I just said, point blank, "I'd like to ask this staff here, where do you think money comes from. Do you think it grows on trees?"

I used those very words, and they were all highly incensed that I would be so primitive. But at the same time I think I did get the point across, that the United States was not an open treasury for everybody's ideas, and that unless the idea really did merit the use of funds, then we shouldn't do it. So, anyway, I frequently got involved with that kind of discussion.

Paul Stillwell: After you had that discussion with Admiral Hogle about your retirement that wasn't a retirement, you went on, but that wasn't obviously the end of your career. Where did you go after SACLant?

Captain Manson: One other thing I had done down there at SACLant was that I had built a marina and had built a seafood restaurant, and my wife was operating it. The reason I had built this marina was I thought that during my naval career that I simply hadn't been close enough to as many ships as I would like to have been. I thought, boy, if I have a marina, I'll have them around me all the time, and I'll have boats that I can control. They'll just be boats, but there will be a lot of them. And I thought it was something the family would enjoy as the children grew up. So I built this marina, dredged the creek, Knitting Mill Creek, built these piers and places, moorings and so forth.

Well, anyway, I just wanted to mention one thing about that seafood restaurant. Amongst other things that we had there, we featured various kinds of crab delicacies. But in order to do this, we had to have lots of crabs, so I had a crab fleet, three or four boats. The first day we started out, my son sank the first boat. But, later on, it got necessary to have a lot of crab pots to run the crab fleet. I had 100 crab pots made up at a little school nearby where the marina had been built. These people were handicapped, but they could still build crab pots. So I was quite a hero up there, every time the captain came in, everybody stopped building crab pots to visit with me.

But amongst other things, the thing I couldn't find was a rubber band about 12 inches long to tie the lid on the crab pot so that the crabs couldn't get out, but you could open it. About the only thing we could find would be a strip of inner tube.

So I went around to all the filling stations and whatnot, couldn't find anything. And I had to go out to the city dump to look for these things, and I had to negotiate with the man in charge of the city dump to let me look over the trash. I thought, boy, if anybody ever found a Navy captain out here negotiating at the city dump for a used inner tube, I'd be in deep trouble. Fortunately, I never was found out.

Barney Solomon, who was the information chief over at CinCLant, wanted to come down and be my bartender at the restaurant.* But because Barney had some proclivities toward imbibing sometimes, I thought he wouldn't be such a good fellow to run the bar, and decided I wouldn't make it totally an information deal down there.

I guess the biggest thing that came out of that was one afternoon I just had to have some fish to bait the crab pots so the crab fleet could go out. Down near the shore there in Norfolk, there was a man that would clean fish. People would go out and bring all the fish to him, and he'd clean them, and then you'd get the heads and the insides and all that. I thought that would make absolutely wonderful crab bait. So one day I went down to try to see if I could negotiate with him about getting some of his waste. He said, no, he didn't want to do that. He said, "What's your business?"

I said, "Well, a seafood restaurant."

He said, "Do you have any crabs?"

I said, "Oh, yeah, sure."

He said, "If you bring me a bushel of steamed crabs, I'll give you everything I've got."

So I said, "Well, that's a deal."

So I went down there with my bushel of crabs one Sunday. I was usually there on Sunday. That was my day that I could closely observe the business. And who do you think would be there but a skipper of an aircraft carrier. And I wish I could recall his name. But here he was, he'd brought in just a tremendous amount of fish that he wanted cleaned.

At the same time I was standing there at this table trying to bargain with this guy for these fish heads, I mean to tell you, if he had known that I was a Navy captain, again it would have been a laugh that would have gone through Norfolk and perhaps around the Navy. But fortunately he didn't know who I was. I knew him, but he didn't know me, and so it worked out all right.

But, anyway, getting back to your question, what did I do? I wanted to wind up my career with magazines and books. Pickett Lumpkin was the deputy chief of

---

* Captain Bernard S. Solomon, USNR.

information.* So I called Pickett one day and said, "You know, Pickett, the job I'd like to wind up my career with is I'd like to be head of magazines and books for the Department of Defense." Captain Karig had been head of magazines and books for the Navy way back when I started in Washington. I was interested in books more than anything.

So he said, "Well, Frank, if that's what you want, that's what you'll get." So I was ordered in there and was having really a ball, just doing the very thing I loved to do and was getting acquainted with all the publishers and renewing my relationship with Naval Institute and everybody. New York, I was getting back with the Rineharts. Well, one of the Rineharts was still alive, Ted. And with different ones, with *Reader's Digest* and *National Geographic* and all the people that I wanted to work with for the rest of my life.

But I found in that job that there were also some very difficult political problems associated at times with it. One of them had to do with how did the Vietnam War get started. One of our destroyers was reportedly fired on in the Gulf on Tonkin. The question that kept coming up, if not every day, certainly every week as long as I was there, from somebody, was whether that attack actually took place in the Gulf of Tonkin.†

Paul Stillwell: It was the *Maddox* and the *Turner Joy*.

Captain Manson: That's right. Those were the two. Johnson was Commander Seventh Fleet at that time.‡ Well, Paul Trahan was out there, an information officer who was a very close friend.§ So I asked Paul about that. I said, "You know, I need help on this thing. I don't know the answer."

He said, "Well, neither do I, and I was there."

---

* Captain Pickett Lumpkin, USN.
† On 2 August 1964, North Vietnamese patrol boats in the Tonkin Gulf attacked the destroyer *Maddox* (DD-731) in international waters during daytime. On the night of 4 August the *Maddox* and the destroyer *Turner Joy* (DD-951) reported being attacked by North Vietnamese craft. The question of whether the second attack occurred has never been completely resolved, but it is unlikely that it happened. The reports of the two attacks led to the congressional Gulf of Tonkin Resolution, which provided the legal basis for the commitment of U.S. armed forces in Vietnam.
‡ Vice Admiral Roy L. Johnson, USN, served as Commander Seventh Fleet from 11 June 1964 to 1 March 1965. The oral history of Johnson, who retired as a four-star admiral, is in the Naval Institute collection.
§ Commander Paul K. Trahan, USN.

So then I asked Admiral Moorer about it later, and he couldn't give me a straight answer on that. So you can see how difficult when people, they're looking you straight in the eye in pursuit of truth, and you can't tell them whether something really happened or whether the President of the United States sort of dished it out and made it happen.

Paul Stillwell: It still hasn't been resolved.

Captain Manson: Is that a fact?

Paul Stillwell: I heard a session about that over at the Naval Historical Center a couple of weeks ago, and there's no sure answer.

Captain Manson: Well, this aggravated me to no end, because I wanted to be straightforward about it. Do you know, I went to every source and, as you say, well, there's still no answer so I don't know. Maybe LBJ knows, and if so, he'll never tell.

Paul Stillwell: What were some of the other issues that you remember dealing with when you were in that OSD job?

Captain Manson: Another serious problem during that time was the accidental poison-gas episode out in—I know it was in the sheep country and I don't recall where exactly where all the sheep died, but it had to be North Dakota or South Dakota or in that area out there somewhere, where we had a very serious accident and, of course, there were all kinds of questions that were coming in about how come all these sheep died quickly. It's sort of like trying to find out how the Vietnam War got started. I simply couldn't get the responsible people to tell me how this happened, nor did I ever get them to tell me.

So it made me look a little bit stupid, to have people asking me rather frequently how this terrible accident could occur, and you know perfectly well that all those sheep just can't stand out there and fall dead. I never was able to get to the bottom of it, although my deputy there, who was an Army colonel, one time he sort of hinted to me that he thought he knew what happened, that one of the Air Force officers had accidentally discharged one of the tanks that he was carrying. I mean, he accidentally fired it, hadn't meant to. I thought what on earth was he carrying the stuff for in the first place, if that was the case. I'm sure that is the case, but I don't know even at this date and time, but it caused me a lot of grief.

Of course, one of the other problems I had there in that job was an awful lot of people didn't appreciate the importance of magazines and books. They thought that the newspaper or the television or something else, some other forms of media, were far more important than magazines and books. I continually had to assure everybody and reassure them, that in the long stream of history, that it would be the magazines and books that they would cherish the most and that would mean the most to the military, but it was not an easy thing to achieve, because there was just a feeling that it was sort of a extraneous thing that didn't matter all that much. Not very many people write books or write magazine articles, and so you're dealing with a very small percentage of people, not like the press or not like people who read every day.

Paul Stillwell: What were your functions in that job, to provide information?

Captain Manson: Yes. You had a two-way street. Your job was to, first of all, know what the publishers wanted. So the way I handled that is I went to New York and visited with a number of publishers to find out what sort of military stories they were looking for. Then I sent out invitations for them to come and see me, which they did. Then from the other side, I had from all the services, manuscripts, ideas coming in, wanting to write things, books and articles. So if I already knew things that were wanted, I could be pretty authoritative and help them, but a lot of times they were things that we just had to search, see if we could find markets for.

Paul Stillwell: So did you act as authors' agent?

Captain Manson: Sort of authors' agent, yes, we were and we had some. Now, like Malcolm Cagle, came to me, and he said, "Frank, how about it. You got any need for any books that I can write?"

I said, "Well, I've got about three military books here that no one seems to be interested in tackling," and I told him what they were.

He said, "Oh, well, I think I can do all those," and sure enough, he did. I don't recall exactly the subjects that he took, but they were fairly complex and difficult, I do remember that, but that never bothered Malcolm Cagle. So he did the books.

But I had other authors who would get my ideas on what I thought they could write about and so forth. It was a fun, really a fun job. I had a Navy section, an Air Force, Army section. Now, the Marines had their own section, so I didn't have the Marines, but I did deal with the Marines.

Paul Stillwell: How much dealing did you have with the Naval Institute in that period?

Captain Manson: Not much. The Naval Institute—now, that would have been in '68, and the Naval Institute in those days was not anything comparable to what it is now. They were still pretty much of a professional organization, mostly concentrated on the *Proceedings* at that point. Books, of course, yes, they would publish books, but it wasn't anything like it is now.

Oh, yes, we would discuss things from time to time. I would call up and ask them if they would be interested in a certain type of book or whatever, but I don't recall that we ever did connect on a book. We did connect on some articles that people had written. I still find that it was the most fascinating job of my career.

One day I'll never forget, I had an unusual visitor step in, his name was John Eisenhower. He was then a lieutenant colonel on two weeks' active duty. He, of course, is a West Point graduate, and came in and asked me if I could make a space for him in my shop. I said, "Well, I probably could," but I wanted to know what on earth he wanted a job in my shop for. Well, he was writing this book called *Bitter Woods*, and he just wanted to get better acquainted with the publishing field.[*] In a sense, he sort of had the same interests that I had. I said, "Well, Colonel, sure, there's no question I can bring you

---

[*] John S. D. Eisenhower, *Bitter Woods: the Dramatic Story, Told at All Echelons, from Supreme Commander to Squad leader, of the Crisis that Shook the Western Coalition: Hitler's Surprise Ardennes Offensive* (New York: Putnam, 1969). The author, who was the son of President Dwight D. Eisenhower, resigned his active commission in 1963 and entered the Army Reserve, from which he eventually retired in 1975 as a brigadier general.

in here. But my question to you is, why would you want to come here now when it looks to me from I sit that your son is going to be the son-in-law of the President of the United States very shortly?" This was in '68, just before Nixon was elected.*

He said, "I don't have any assurance. If I knew that to be a fact, then I suppose I wouldn't be so interested in it." But he said, "You know, I stopped out to help my dad with his book and his memoirs when I had 19 years in the Army, and I missed out on that 20-year retirement. I just simply don't see my way clear—I need that 20-year retirement from the reserve."

So I said, "Well, I know one book you could certainly write right away, and that would be your memories of your relationship with your father."

He said, "No, I could never write a book about that."

I said, "Well, why not?"

He said, "I didn't know my father that well. My relationships with him were few and far between. He was always usually so busy with what he was doing that he never really had time to talk to me. I simply don't have enough of my own personal memories to write a book." And he said, also, the only time that he'd really ever had a close time with his father was just right after V-E Day and he had three weeks.† He said he was with his dad every day and they talked and they just really had a wonderful sort of union and reunion and all the rest of it, but he said that wouldn't be really enough. Of course, he could have written a book about those three weeks. But in thinking back he said, no, he just didn't think he could.

Well, anyway, the way we left it was I said, "Well, I think if I read the tea leaves correctly, you'll be getting an ambassador's post somewhere. Nixon is going to win this election, and I'm sure he's going to offer you something."

Well, he said he thought he would.

I said, "Well, my suggestion to you is you just wait another few months before you come back. Presumably I'll still be here, and the job will still be here if you want to come here. Why don't you see whether he doesn't win this election?"

---

* John Eisenhower's son David married Julie Nixon, daughter of future President Richard M. Nixon on 22 December 1968. Nixon had been elected the month before but had not yet taken office. David was then a Naval Reserve officer.
† V-E Day – Victory in Europe Day, 8 May 1945, when the German surrender was ratified in Berlin. His father, a five-star Army general, was then Supreme Commander Allied Expeditionary Force.

He said, well, maybe he would.

That's sort of the way he left it. It was sort of an iffy thing that if Nixon did not win, that he would come back. But he didn't come back, because Nixon won and he became ambassador to Belgium.* So I've never seen John again. Well, I thought it was interesting that he didn't think that he had enough sufficient memory of his relationship with his father to do a book.

Paul Stillwell: What were the differences for you in that job having all the services instead of just the Navy?

Captain Manson: Well, certainly I had to approach life and my philosophy of life, my philosophy of the military, with, in a way, the same attitude that I think the Chairman of the Joint Chiefs or the Secretary of Defense, or anyone who has responsibility for all the services. I felt, in a way, that I had responsibility for all the services to see to it that they were properly represented, that they were fairly represented, and that they were represented. In other words, I felt it my duty to see to it that the infantry and the Signal Corps had the same shot at the public as the destroyer forces or whatever.

In other words, all the elements of the military—now, of course, I suppose I had my own ideas about what parts of the military that I thought were a little bit useless. I had that in the Navy, so it didn't change when I got into it. But generally speaking, my attitude was that if it's a good story, then it should be told, if it has all the elements. I didn't necessarily feel that the story had to be good. Sometimes stories that aren't good help too.

Paul Stillwell: What do you mean by good, favorable?

Captain Manson: Well, favorable, yes. I mean maybe somebody is writing a book about some procurement policies or contracts are excessive, and money is being wasted and that sort of thing. In other words, I didn't feel that I had to sit in judgment on proposals. A lot of times civilians were coming to my office and me with stories that weren't too

---
* Eisenhower was U.S. ambassador to Belgium, 1969-71.

happy. But at the same time, that's they way freedom works, that's the way democracy works. Again it goes back, I guess, to some of the training I received from Walter Karig.

I won't forget, one time Shirley Temple was in the naval hospital in Bethesda. She had a baby, and she had some infection develop shortly afterwards. The doctor, her obstetrician, had something more interesting to do than to watch out for Shirley Temple, so he went off to a cocktail party or something like that. I know it made the news, but it made the news because Captain Karig said he didn't think this kind of a story should be kept from the public. It was an obvious case where the doctor had ignored his duty, and, of course, it was Shirley Temple too.[*]

So when there were stories, I mean, for example, say the loss of the *Thresher* or a submarine or whatever, it seemed to me that the most important thing when I was head of all the armed forces and this sort of thing, was that the truth be known.[†] Let the public know the truth. That's where I come from and where I came from in that job. As a matter of fact, that's the way I feel right now.

Paul Stillwell: What other specific stories do you remember? The *Scorpion* was lost in '68.[‡]

Captain Manson: Yes, there were a lot of questions about the *Scorpion*'s loss as to just what did really happen. You know, when they finally gathered up from the sea bottom some of the pipes, my recollection is that they determined that some of the pipes had either eroded or had some weaknesses in them.

Paul Stillwell: I thought that was the *Thresher* that had that problem.

Captain Manson: Maybe that was the *Thresher*.

---

[*] Shirley Temple was a famous child movie star of the 1930s. She married Army Air Forces Sergeant John Agar in September 1945, and their daughter Linda was born 30 January 1948.
[†] The nuclear-powered attack submarine *Thresher* (SSN-593) was lost with all hands on 10 April 1963 while operating east of Cape Cod. The presumed cause was a reactor shutdown during a dive.
[‡] The submarine *Scorpion* (SSN-589) was lost with all hands while en route from the Mediterranean to Norfolk. She was last heard from on 21 May 1968. On 27 May she was reported overdue and on 5 June presumed lost with her entire crew of 99 officers and men. The wreckage was located on 30 October of that year. No definitive conclusion as to cause has been made public.

Paul Stillwell: What about the *Pueblo* incident?* Did you get a lot of inquiries on that?

Captain Manson: I got a lot inquiries, yes, I did, but I certainly didn't have many answers. My initial impression of that story really never did change. My impression was, having written about how things happened in Korea and having been out there and seen the way, it was hard for me to see how a group of small boats could come in and surround and capture a ship the size of the *Pueblo*, unless there'd been some lookouts and some failure to respond to a situation that was obviously developing. In other words, I thought we were, our side, our command out there, it has to be the skipper, of course, but I thought there was some dereliction of duty right from the start. That was my impression, and I still feel that way.

Paul Stillwell: That was the official view, certainly.†

You said dealing with books and magazines was your most fascinating job. Why do you describe it that way?

Captain Manson: I describe it that way because I see the world of books and magazines as a world of ideas. It's where ideas can be, where you can imagine, you can magnify—not just historical books, but books of all types, books probing the future. But to me, the best way to have a perpetuation of the human process in the stream of history is through books.

Now, TV may be a very good method coming on here, on line, and I was thinking of talking to you about these interviews. Perhaps you might ought to have a camera working when you're doing these interviews because you can run two or three hours without ever doing a thing with them. Because the video aspect of it might have some utility to you later on and you might think about it for the future.

---

* USS *Pueblo* (AGER-2), an electronic intelligence ship, was seized on 23 January 1968 in the Sea of Japan by North Korean naval forces. The ship's crew members were held as prisoners until 23 December of that year. Of the 83 officers and men on board, 28 were intelligence specialists.
† Commander Lloyd M. Bucher, USN, was commanding officer of the *Pueblo* at the time of her seizure. A court of inquiry in 1969 recommended that he be court-martialed for loss of the ship, but Secretary of the Navy John Chafee decided not to carry out the recommendation, saying that Bucher had suffered enough. See also Paul Stillwell, "Bucher and the *Pueblo*," *Naval History*, April 2009, page 2.

Paul Stillwell: We've looked into that and it's very, very expensive.

Captain Manson: Oh, is it?

Paul Stillwell: Yes.

Captain Manson: Oh, well, I didn't realize that would be that expensive.

Paul Stillwell: To do it well, it is.

Captain Manson: Oh well, then you wouldn't want to do it. We frequently will go rent a camera and take it to a family occasion and just set the camera over in the corner and let her roll, like we're doing here, and three hours or two hours later, we just go take it out. Of course, nobody ever looks at it because it's not all that exciting to look at. But we still have it.

Anyway, my idea on books was that my respect for them as a means of continuing the human process, it's the best form of recording. That's why I liked the job, because it was possible to bring people of ideas together, and I always have cherished the opportunity to deal with people with ideas. So that's why. And of course, I have found writers to be fascinating individuals. Usually their minds are stirring all the time. You never know for sure what they may come down on as a subject for a book or an article. So that was fascinating, just the people that I'd be associated with. But I've always found people in the publishing world, the writing world, to be the world that I felt the most comfortable in. So that's why I wanted that job, and still regard it.

I think I made a real mistake in my life when I left that job after having only been there about a year to become director of national security and foreign policy for the VFW.* And I had to be talked into doing it. But I went to two of the admirals that I had the most respect for at that time on active duty: Admiral Moorer, who was Chief of Naval Operations at that time, and Admiral McCain, who was Commander in Chief

---

* VFW – Veterans of Foreign Wars.

Pacific.* I talked to both of them about whether I should do this or not, that I was in a key position there to get some good stories out for the military and for the Navy and so forth. I didn't know getting in this position with a veterans' group, just whether I would be able to serve—whether the mission—and they said, "Listen, you'll be in the field of foreign policy. You'll be able to help shape foreign policy in some areas where we might be weak. You'll have a greater potential in that job so our suggestion." Both of them said, "Yes, by all means, take that job."

So I did, I went into that. And altogether in my retired years, I spent seven years in charge of foreign policy. I was two years with the VFW, and then I went with the American Legion, and I was five years there. I did have a lot to do with shaping foreign policy, not so much national security, because those were areas that were pretty much on track. I also found too, in those jobs, that the services, particularly the Navy, didn't seem to be all that keen on working with veterans' organizations, so I didn't hear too much from the services. The Army more so, much more interested.

Paul Stillwell: Why would you say that is?

Captain Manson: I believe it's because they didn't understand the interface between civilian organizations and justification for a Navy. I don't think they realized that, and I'm not sure they do today either. But I tried a few times to talk to various ones about it, but I was just so very busy, dealing in many cases with the heads of state and with secretaries of state and the foreign ministers.

One of my purposes in this whole thing was to shape a much stronger orientation toward America—Latin America, Central America—so that the United States, because we had the land continuity, would build up Latin America, build up its development, its production, its economy, all the nations, so that we didn't have to look across the Atlantic Ocean for so much, or across the Pacific, but rather in our own hemisphere.

---

* Admiral Thomas H. Moorer, USN, served as Chief of Naval Operations from 1 August 1967 to 1 July 1970. His oral history is in the Naval Institute collection. Admiral John S. McCain, Jr., USN, served as Commander in Chief Pacific from 31 July 1968 to 1 September 1972. His oral history is in the Naval Institute collection.

So when I first went in that job, I went to Dante B. Fascell, who was head of foreign relations for the House of Representatives, he was the chairman of that committee, and told him what I was thinking.* He said, in his judgment, I was absolutely, 100% on the beam, and that I should try to encourage an improvement in our relations with Argentina, for example, Mexico, Canada. There was much room for improving trade.

I'd seen from particularly when I was in the NATO commands, how things could fall apart real quickly, and the building of bridges, particularly trade bridges between our countries. To interweave our economies so we could—well, it would take many, many years for the United States if we just really went at it in earnest, to really build thriving economies in the Western Hemisphere.

So, anyway, that was one of my objectives and, of course, I wanted to keep NATO strong, vibrant, and our relationship with Japan and so forth. So I found here, in these jobs, a tremendous challenge to go on, as Admiral Moorer and Admiral McCain had suggested that I ought to and pursue, with all the force I could, improving the relationships between the United States and other countries. So that's what I did, and I've done most of that in my retirement.

Paul Stillwell: Any notable successes that you would point to?

Captain Manson: Well, I was making some progress with Mexico. I was able to get resolutions favoring increased ties with Argentina, with Chile, with Mexico, with Canada. Now understand, these resolutions that we got through with these veterans' organizations, there were none like them and this had some influence on the State Department. They'd call me in, of course, and want to discuss these things.

In the case of South Africa, I hadn't been there, so I organized an expedition. A group of us went down to South Africa and we stayed about four or five weeks. We went to a number of countries. We spent most of the time, though, in South Africa itself, but we went to Namibia, Transkei, and got to the borders of Angola, Swaziland. I even took

---

* Dante B. Fascell, a Democrat from Florida, served in the House of Representatives from 3 January 1955 to 3 January 1993.

my wife in a car, and we drove all the way to Swaziland from Johannesburg, just the two of us. I had an invitation from the King to come over and visit their government.

I tried as best I could to show the leaders of the United States that it was in the United States' interest to work cooperatively with South Africa, and that in time, the apartheid system would be greatly improved, and it might even be completely eliminated, with the economy of the United States interwoven with South Africa. They wanted to buy aircraft from us in the worst way. They had bought a lot of Boeing aircraft already, but they wanted to buy 16 P-3 Orion aircraft.* And they've wanted other things that we had that would have really affected our economy quite an amount.

What is more important, South Africa had the cash, they had the diamonds, they had the gold, they had the uranium. They had the greatest mineral resources. Beyond that, it was very important strategically for the United States to understand that if South Africa and the Soviet Union ever combined their minerals and resources, we were in deep kimchi. So we had to keep some sort of a special relationship until we are bosom buddies with the Soviet Union, and I don't know when that's going to be.

But we have a very vital security interest here, and I've thought this, my head's been bloodied so many times that I can't remember on this issue, but nevertheless, I got resolutions through these veterans' organizations to support cooperative measures between the United States. I didn't think that the Southern political advantages, which is, in effect, what we've tried to do, it to cater to sort of a Southern political strategy in our relationships with South Africa. I didn't think that these outweighed our strategic urgencies, still don't, and I regret very much that the trend hasn't been completely successful. I turned the trend, I shifted it a little, I think, just from my own efforts. But not enough.†

---

* The Lockheed P-3 Orion is a high-performance, propeller-driven, land-based patrol plane. It first entered operational squadrons in August 1962.
† Conditions in The Republic of South Africa changed dramatically subsequent to this 1988 interview. In 1990 the government lifted its ban on the black African National Congress party. In February 1991, President F. W. de Klerk announced the end of all apartheid laws that directed racial segregation. In 1994 Nelson Mandela of the ANC because South Africa's President.

I'll never forget, I was talking one day with Ian Smith, who was the Prime Minister of Rhodesia, now Zimbabwe.* Using old Navy parlance, I said, "You're not going to let this ship sink here, Mr. Prime Minister."

"Oh, no."

I said, "So you are going to hold the line?"

"Yes, I'm going to hold the line," but a few years later he was gone.

Paul Stillwell: Any overall thoughts that you'd like to put on the record about your naval career, Captain?

Captain Manson: Well, I think that, to me, I started out in life thinking I wanted to be a U.S. Senator. My early life in Oklahoma, I was planning. I was sending Christmas cards out when I was in college to as many as 300 and 400 people every year. I was building a political base to run for Congress. Then as I sort of progressed along, I thought, well, I wouldn't mind, too much, I think, of being some sort of an international representative. If I could be an ambassador, say, to a major country, that might be a worthwhile goal in life. So I sort of shifted from being a senator to an ambassador.

I saw, as I kept on staying in the Navy, that I had an opportunity to do and pursue all these things, things that senators did, things that ambassadors did. I had the opportunity to do these things and to work with the senators and the ambassadors. But I had a different constituency; I had the Navy. Sometimes it was just the Navy, sometimes it was NATO. But at the same time, I had a feeling all along that I was representing a broad constituency. So it gave me an idea to dream and to visualize, and this is really all I wanted, anyway.

As I grew older, I found out that the closer you get to some of these key jobs, the less opportunity you have to really dream dreams. You're so worked down with personnel problems usually, that you don't have time get much beyond that. So I really think, though, that I believed from the first time I saw a carrier force, strike force—now this, believe you me, was the biggest thing I'd ever seen in my life. When I moved out in

---

* Ian D. Smith served as Prime Minister of Rhodesia from 13 April 1964 to 1 June 1979. Zimbabwe became independent in 1980.

the Pacific aboard the *Laffey* and looked out across that horizon and there were ships as far as we could see, and I looked on the radar scope and they went way, way beyond that, that was the first time that I ever realized what tremendous power there was in a Navy task force.

So I guess you'd have to say that I've spent the remainder of my life trying to tell other people the kind of power that can be projected from the sea—the power to destroy, the power to build. The spectrum goes from the extreme humanitarian to the most destructive. But the whole idea is that those oceans are out there to be used. They're there to buoy the ships. Rising tide lifts all ships. I've never seen why the United States is a maritime nation, with the great coastal areas that we do have, why it's been so difficult for us to project ourselves in a maritime manner and still be as difficult. Although I know why this is so, because most people, most of our citizens don't understand how you can use the oceans to advantage. Some of our top leaders don't understand it. I would have to say that I think my time has been well spent, because I didn't change it all, but I certainly helped hold the line.

Paul Stillwell: Well, and more people are informed of that power as a result of your efforts.

Captain Manson: Yes, yes, I would say. And I still feel this central thrust in my life. I even feel it right now. But unlike, I was talking earlier about Admiral Zumwalt, I'm not real sure he feels this. I don't know too many people that do. I know a few that do, that are still around, but I've seen some admirals that have told me right out in front that, "I really don't know what I believe in." I've had that happen. I've had some that disappointed me when they told me, under very frank conditions, and not conditions that ought to be—that the confidentiality of it would not be advantageous to anyone but I've just had that happen. But that doesn't mean they were not good operators or that they were not good warriors, because they were or they wouldn't have been admirals. In my own life, I've seen very few people who were chosen for flag rank whom I thought were absolutely incompetent, very few. And that, I think, speaks fairly highly of our selection board, our system.

Paul Stillwell: You've spent a career informing people about the Navy, and now you've spent these hours on your oral history doing exactly the same thing, and so I'm going to express my thanks and those of the Naval Institute for what you've accomplished here.

Captain Manson: Well, I appreciate that. Thank you.

Paul Stillwell: Thank you.

Launched in 1969, the U.S. Naval Institute's award-winning oral history program is among the oldest in the country. Used in combination with documentary sources, oral histories offer a richer understanding of naval history through candid recollections and explanations rarely entered into contemporary records. In addition, they help depict the atmosphere of a particular event or era in a manner not available in official documents.

The nonprofit Naval Institute accomplishes its history projects through contributed funds and gratefully accepts tax-deductible gifts of all sizes for this purpose. This support allows the Institute to preserve the life experiences of today's service men and women so they may enlighten and inspire future generations.

For information about opportunities to underwrite Naval Institute oral history projects, please contact the Naval Institute Foundation at 291 Wood Road, Annapolis, Maryland 21402; by phone at (410) 295-1054; or by e-mail at foundation@usni.org.

Index to the Oral History of
Captain Frank A. Manson, U.S. Navy (Retired)

Acheson, Dean
As Secretary of State in January 1950, made a speech in which he suggested the United States was not interested in Korean security, 152-153

Agadir, Morocco
Site of a devastating earthquake in February 1960, 253-254

Air Force, U.S.
Role in the inter-service unification squabbles in the late 1940s, 28-30, 203

Air Reconnaissance Squadron Two (VQ-2)
A VW-2 Super Constellation from the squadron crashed in Germany in May 1962 with the loss of all 26 crew members, 214-216

Air Warfare
Effect of U.S. aircraft during the early stages of the Korean Warfare, 53, 63-64

Alcohol
Distribution of whiskey to crew members of the destroyer *Laffey* (DD-724) during a kamikaze attack in 1945, 18
Drinking on board the aircraft carrier *Philippine Sea* (CV-47) during the Korean War, 63-64

All Hands
Magazine published in the mid-1950s by the Bureau of Naval Personnel, 103-104

Almond, Lieutenant General Edward Mallory, USA
Commanded the Army's X Corps during the early stages of the Korean War, 56-57

Amen, Lieutenant Commander William T., USN
Commanded Fighter Squadron 111 (VF-111) during the Korean War, shot down a MiG, 64

American Legion
Cultivated in the mid-1950s by the OpNav Office of Progress Analysis, 170
Manson's post-Navy activities on behalf of the organization in the area of foreign relations, 355-359

Amphibious Warfare
Successful United Nations amphibious assault on Inchon, Korea, in September 1950, 49, 53-54

Anderson, Admiral George W. Jr. USN (Ret.) (USNA, 1927)
In the late 1970s was part of a group of senior officers who sought to retain the Panama Canal for the United States, 321-322

Anderson, Jack
Journalist who assisted muckraking columnist Drew Pearson in the late 1940s, 205-206

Anderson, Robert B.
As Deputy Secretary of Defense in the mid-1950s, reviewed a speech to be delivered by Chief of Naval Operations Robert Carney, 112-113

Army, U.S.
Role in the early stages of the Korean War, 56-57

Attlee, Earl Clement R.
British politician who discussed Manson's "White Fleet" concept with him in the early 1960s, 256-257

Aurand, Captain Evan P., USN (USNA, 1938)
Served as President Dwight Eisenhower's naval aide from 1957 to 1961, 74, 140, 192

Awards, Naval
During World War II Rear Admiral Jocko Clark handed out medals soon after successful operations, 281
Paucity of medals for U.S. Navy personnel in the early stages of the Korean War, 53-56

Baldwin, Hanson W. (USNA, 1924)
Served for many years as military editor for *The New York Times*, 207, 210

***Barb*, USS (SS-220)**
In 1949 was the subject of an article in *The Saturday Evening Post*, 33-34

Bates, Rear Admiral Richard W., USN (Ret.) (USNA, 1915)
Served as chief of staff to Vice Admiral Jesse Oldendorf in the Philippine campaign in 1945, 198-199
Did analytical work at the Naval War College in the late 1950s, 198

Bates, William H.
As a member of the House of Representatives in the late 1950s, advocated Manson's "White Fleet" concept, 188, 191, 195

Battle Report
A series of commercial books published in the 1940s and 1950s on the U.S. Navy's role in World War II and the Korean War, 31-41, 50-70

Bay of Pigs
Vice Admiral Claude V. Ricketts, as Commander Second Fleet, was disappointed that the U.S. Navy did not intervene in the April 1961 invasion, 269-270

Becton, Commander F. Julian, USN (USNA, 1931)
Commanded the destroyer *Laffey* (DD-724) in 1944-45, 7-25, 40
Combat operations in the Pacific in 1944-45, 8, 12-25, 40

Beecher, Rear Admiral William G., USN (USNA, 1925)
Served 1954-55 as the Navy's Chief of Information, 115-116

Beecher, William M.
New York Times reporter who broke the story in October 1967 that the Soviet Navy was operating its first helicopter carrier, the *Moskva*, 307-309, 312-313

Bergen, Rear Admiral John J., USNR
In 1957 was part of a barnstorming tour to promote the Navy League and sea power, 157-158

Bertrand, General Rene, French Army
In the early 1950s served as a special assistant to CinCSouth, the commander in chief of NATO's Allied Forces Southern Europe, 71-73

Boston Navy Yard
During World War II, Destroyer Force, Atlantic Fleet had a representative in Boston to prepare ships for combat service, 4-9
Pre-deployment service to the destroyer *Laffey* (DD-724) in 1944, 9-10

Bradley, General of the Army Omar N., USA (USMA, 1915)
Served 1949-53 as Chairman of the Joint Chiefs of Staff, 45-46, 82, 119-120

Brazier, Captain Donald G., USNR
Reserve officer who was recalled to active duty to provide public information support for the 1964 NATO Exercise Team Work, 328, 333

Bright, Captain Cooper B., USN
Served as commanding officer of the ammunition ship *Wrangell* (AE-12) from 1956 to 1958, 146
In the late 1950s served in OP-09D, the Office of Progress Analysis, on the OpNav staff, 147-149
Tried unsuccessfully to sell the idea of inflatable rubber airplanes, 148-149

Briscoe, Vice Admiral Robert P., USN (USNA, 1919)
   Served 1954-56 as OP-03, Deputy Chief of Naval Operations (Operations and Readiness), 115, 122-123

Brown, Vice Admiral Charles R., USN (USNA, 1921)
   Enjoyed action while commanding the Sixth Fleet, 1956-58, 145-146

Bruce, David E. K.
   As U.S. ambassador to Great Britain in the early 1960s, was involved with a dinner to promote Manson's "White Fleet" concept, 272-275

Burke, Admiral Arleigh A., USN (Ret.) (USNA, 1923)
   Wife Roberta, 122, 129-131
   Recalled anecdote from his junior officer duty in a battleship, 142
   Service with Vice Admiral Marc Mitscher in 1944, 133-134
   In 1949 headed OP-23, which was a pro-Navy organization in the unification battle against the other U.S. armed services, 29, 210-211
   In the late 1940s was originally left off the promotion list for rear admiral, later restored, 325-326
   In the early part of the Korean War was on the staff of Commander U.S. Naval Forces Far East, 65-67
   In the early 1950s Chief of Naval Operations Robert Carney considered him as a possible successor, 115, 127
   Served as Chief of Naval Operations from 1955 to 1961, 95, 100-102, 106-109, 113-119, 121-133, 135-150, 159, 164-164, 173, 190-191, 226, 243
   Delivered a fake reprimand to Captain John McCain for exceeding authority, 164-165
   In the late 1970s was part of a group of senior officers who sought to retain the Panama Canal for the United States, 321-322

Caine Mutiny, The
   World War II Navy novel that was made into a movie in the 1950s, 25-26, 38

Cagle, Commander Malcolm W., USN (USNA, 1941)
   In the 1950s coauthored books on the U.S. Navy's role in the Korean War, 41, 50-51, 69-70, 78, 98, 150-157
   In the mid-1950s was speechwriter for Secretary of the Navy Charles Thomas, 78, 97-98, 103, 171
   In the early 1960s was stationed in Europe, 220
   Writing projects in the 1960s, 350

Carney, Admiral Robert B., USN (Ret.) (USNA, 1916)
   Wife Grace, 72, 99, 129
   As a midshipman in the 1910s, 79
   Personality, including his wit and intelligence, 23, 78-79, 84, 113, 116-119

In 1944-45 was chief of staff to Admiral William F. Halsey, Commander Third Fleet, 74-75, 79-80

Served as Commander in Chief Allied Forces Southern Europe, 1951-53, 70-75, 84-90, 292

In Manson's view would have been excellent as Chairman of the Joint Chiefs of Staff, 73-74, 117

As Chief of Naval Operations, 1953-55, 75-79, 95-100, 103-105, 110-121, 126-128, 132, 141, 143, 155-156, 277-278, 319

In the early 1950s, as CNO, supported nuclear power for U.S. surface warships, 75-77

In the late 1970s was part of a group of senior officers who sought to retain the Panama Canal for the United States, 321-323

Central Intelligence Agency
Rejected as a possible source of support for Manson's "White Fleet" concept in the early 1960s, 197, 294

Chaplains
In the early 1960s the chaplain's office at CinCNELM in London tried to forbid the marriage of a U.S. enlisted man to a young British woman, 282

China, People's Republic of
In 1950 sent troops into North Korea as part of the Korean War, 57

Chippendale, Captain Burton W., USN (USNA, 1915)
During World War II commanded the Cornell Naval Training School, Ithaca, New York, 3-4

Churchill, Sir Winston S.
Clement Attlee's joke in the early 1960s about how Churchill would react to Manson's "White Fleet" proposal, 256-257

CinCNELM (Commander in Chief U.S. Naval Forces Eastern Atlantic and Mediterranean)
In the early 1960s the commander in chief, Admiral Harold Page Smith, received a gag order from Defense Department officials, 167-168

In the early 1960s the chaplain's office at CinCNELM in London tried to forbid the marriage of a U.S. enlisted man to a young British woman, 282-283

A VW-2 Super Constellation crashed in Germany in May 1962 with the loss of all 26 crew members, 214-216

Concern with naval events in the European theater in the late 1950s-early 1960s, 167-168, 214-259

Events at CinCNELM headquarters in London while the Cuban Missile Crisis was taking place in October 1962, 266-269

Relationship with NATO on annual exercises in the 1960s, 257

CinCSouth
  Formation of NATO's Allied Forces Southern Europe, 1951-53, 70-73, 84-90

Clark, Admiral Joseph J., USN (Ret.) (USNA, 1918)
  Hard-charging personality, 280
  As an aircraft carrier task group commander in 1944-45, 280-281
  In 1948 was in charge of swordsmen for a Navy wedding, 261-263
  In 1957 was part of a barnstorming tour to promote the Navy League and sea power, 157-158

***Claude V. Ricketts*, USS (DDG-5)**
  Destroyer originally renamed *Biddle*, used for multi-national manning experiment, 290-293

Clifton, Lieutenant Colonel Chester V. Jr., USA
  Around 1950 tried unsuccessfully to persuade Manson to collaborate on an article for *Reader's Digest*, 45-46

Close, Commander Robert H., USN (USNA, 1934)
  Commanded the destroyer *Collett* (DD-730) during the Korean War, 55

Colbert, Rear Admiral Richard G., USN (USNA, 1937)
  In the mid-1960s worked on concepts such as the Standing Naval Force Atlantic and the Iberian Atlantic Command while on the staff of SACLant, 197, 293-300, 341
  In the early 1970s, as CinCSouth, asked Manson to return to active duty, 298

***Collett*, USS (DD-730)**
  Supported the September 1950 landing at Inchon, Korea, 55

Combs, Vice Admiral Thomas S., USN (USNA, 1920)
  Served 1956-58 as Deputy Chief of Naval Operations (Operations and Readiness), 148-149, 190

Communications
  In the mid-1960s NATO's Supreme Allied Commander Atlantic sent the first message via the new Telstar satellite, 309-311

Congress, U.S.
  Role in the late 1940s in the inter-service battles over unification, 30
  Congressional hearings in 1946 on the Japanese attack on Pearl Harbor, 36-37
  Messy scandal involving a Navy liaison officer to Congress, 1948, 261-266
  Support for the Navy's nuclear power program in the 1950s, 106-107
  Cultivated in the mid-1950s by the OpNav Office of Progress Analysis, 162-164, 179-180
  In the late 1950s, several congressmen advocated Manson's "White Fleet" concept, 162, 185, 187, 191-192, 195, 273, 302-303

In the mid-1960s congressmen visited the SACLant and CinCLantFlt headquarters in Norfolk, 341-343

In the early 1970s Representative Dante Fascell urged Manson to pursue inter-American relations, 357

Connally, John B. Jr.
Served as Secretary of the Navy through most of 1961, 316

Conolly, Admiral Richard L., USN (USNA, 1914)
In 1949 declined to be considered as a replacement for Admiral Louis Denfeld as CNO, 82

In 1950 was downgraded from four stars to three when he became president of the Naval War College, 44-45

***Consolation* (AH-15)**
Former Navy hospital ship that became the centerpiece of Project Hope, founded in 1958, 193-194, 274

Cornell Naval Training School, Ithaca, New York
Provided training for new Naval Reserve officers in 1942, 3-4, 25

Counihan, Captain John L. Jr., USN (USNA, 1932)
Served as Commander Naval Activities, Port Luaytey, Morocco, from 1957 to 1961, 243-245, 254

Crommelin, Commander John G., Jr., USN (USNA, 1923)
Had outstanding skills as an aviator, 145-146

Contact with the CNO's office in the late 1940s, 202

Crommelin, Captain Quentin C., USN (USNA, 1941)
In the mid-1950s was aide to the Chief of Naval Personnel, 103

Cuba
Vice Admiral Claude V. Ricketts, as Commander Second Fleet, was disappointed that the U.S. Navy did not intervene in the April 1961 invasion at the Bay of Pigs, 269-270

Cuban Missile Crisis
Events at CinCNELM headquarters in London while the crisis was taking place in October 1962, 266-269

Cullinane, Leo P.
New York Herald Tribune reporter with whom Manson tangled in the late 1940s, 211-212

Darnell, Lieutenant (junior grade) Matthew C., Medical Corps, USNR
Served on board the destroyer *Laffey* (DD-724) in World War II, 15, 18

Deacon, Commander Edward T., USN
Commanded Fighter Squadron 114 (VF-114) during the Korean War, 63

Defense Department
In the early 1960s, as Assistant Secretary of Defense (Public Affairs), issued a gag order to Admiral Harold Page Smith, 167-168
In 1968 Manson headed the book and magazine section of the office of the Deputy Secretary of Defense (Public Affairs), 346-355

Denfeld, Admiral Louis E., USN (USNA, 1912)
Wife, 129
Served as Chief of Naval Operations from 1947 until 1949, when he was fired by Secretary of the Navy Francis Matthews, 30-31, 41-42, 44, 46-48, 50, 82-83, 129, 204, 260-261, 266

Dennison, Admiral Robert L., USN (USNA, 1923)
Served in 1959-60 as Commander in Chief Allied Forces Eastern Atlantic and Mediterranean (CinCNELM), 193, 225-227, 242, 244, 255-256
After retirement talked to Manson about a possible book on the Cuban Missile Crisis, 269

Destroyer Force, Atlantic Fleet
During World War II had a representative in Boston to prepare ships for combat service, 4-9

Dowdell, Captain James S., USN
In the early 1960s served as deputy to the Navy's Chief of Information (Chinfo), 284-285, 327

Doyle, Vice Admiral Austin K., USN (USNA, 1920)
Served 1954-57 as Chief of Naval Air Training, 133

Doyle, Rear Admiral James H., USN (USNA, 1920)
Amphibious commander during the early stages of the Korean War, 53-56

Dulles, John Foster
Controversy in the mid-1950s over a speech made by Chief of Naval Operations Robert Carney, 110-111

Duncan, Admiral Donald B., USN (USNA, 1917)
In the early 1950s, as Vice Chief of Naval Operations, opposed nuclear power for U.S. surface warships, 75-77

Concern in the mid-1950s about the reluctance of the Naval History Division to make records available for research, 155-156

Dunoon, Scotland
Shopping and liberty location for crew members of Polaris missile submarines deployed to Holy Loch in 1961, 236-237

Durgin, Commander Calvin T. Jr., USN (USNA, 1941)
In the 1956 argued for Navy seaplanes, to the detriment of his career, 42, 132

DuVal, Captain Miles P. Jr., USN (Ret.) (USNA, 1919)
In the late 1970s was part of a group of senior officers who sought to retain the Panama Canal for the United States, 321-322

Eccles, Rear Admiral Henry E., USN (Ret.) (USNA, 1922)
Taught logistics at the Naval War College in the 1950s, 198

Edmondson, Edmond E.
As a member of the House of Representatives in the 1950s and 1960s, advocated Manson's "White Fleet" concept, 187-188, 191, 302-304

Eisenhower, President Dwight D. (USMA, 1915)
In the early 1950s was NATO's Supreme Allied Commander Europe, 73, 93
Served as President from 1953 to 1961, 73-74, 111-112, 192, 214

Eisenhower, Lieutenant Colonel John S. D., USAR (USMA, 1944)
In the late 1960s wrote a book titled *Bitter Woods* about the Battle of the Bulge, later became ambassador to Belgium, 350-352
Son David married Julie Nixon, daughter of future President Richard Nixon, 351-352

***Eldorado*, USS (AGC-11)**
As flagship for Vice Admiral Richmond Kelly Turner, was the site of a press conference for Manson in April 1945, 19-21

Elizabeth II, Queen
In the early 1960s hosted a garden party in London that Manson and his wife attended, 270-272

Ellis, Vice Admiral William E., USN (USNA, 1930)
In the mid-1960s served as chief of staff to NATO's Supreme Allied Commander Atlantic, 295, 307-309, 312-313
In October 1967 told a reporter that the Soviet Navy was operating its first helicopter carrier, the *Moskva*, 307-309, 312-313

Enlisted Personnel
Crew members of the destroyer *Laffey* (DD-724) in World War II, 12-13, 18

In 1959 a young U.S. sailor in London had a very young wife, 225
In the late 1950s and early 1960s a number of U.S. enlisted men married British women, 282-283

F-4 Phantom II
Photo of an American F-4 fighter shadowing a Soviet Bear reconnaissance aircraft was released to the media as part of the 1964 NATO Exercise Team Work, 330-332, 335-336

Fairbanks, Captain Douglas E. Jr., USNR
Actor who introduced Manson and his wife to Princess Margaret and her husband at a garden party in London in the early 1960s, 271-272

Fascell, Representative Dante B.
In the early 1970s urged Manson to pursue inter-American relations, 357

Fechteler, Admiral William M., USN (USNA, 1916)
Served as Chief of Naval Operations, 1951-53, 26, 49-50

Felt, Admiral Harry Don, USN (USNA, 1923)
In the 1950s strongly favored carrier aircraft over seaplanes, 42, 132, 173
Intimidating personality as Vice Chief of Naval Operations, 1956-58, 171-173

Flatley, Vice Admiral James H., Jr., USN (USNA, 1929)
In the mid-1950s described his leadership techniques in commanding aircraft carriers, 143-144

Fleck, Lieutenant Commander Richard W., USN
Commanded Attack Squadron 115 (VA-115) during the Korean War, 63

Fluckey, Commander Eugene B., USN (USNA, 1935)
In the late 1940s provided material for an article in *The Saturday Evening Post*, 33-34

Food
Adjustments by the Manson family to food available in London in the late 1950s-early 1960s, 216-220

France
In the early 1950s contributed members to the staff of CinCSouth, NATO's Allied Forces Southern Europe, 92
Question in 1954 on whether the United States should support the French military effort in Indochina, 114. 141-142
In the early 1960s, as U.S. ambassador to France, Lieutenant General James Galvin tried to persuade the U.S. Navy to provide nuclear power technology to France, 93-95

Franke, William B.
  Served as Secretary of the Navy, 1959-61, 183-184

Gallery, Rear Admiral Daniel V. Jr., USN (USNA, 1921)
  In the late 1940 headed the Navy's guided missile program, 42, 200
  Was the author of humorous stories with Navy themes, 39, 279

Garrick Commander Robert M., USNR
  Reserve officer who was recalled to active duty to provide public information support for the 1964 NATO Exercise Team Work, 327-328

Gates, Thomas S. Jr.
  Served as Secretary of the Navy, 1957-59, 182-183

Gavin, Lieutenant General James M., USA (Ret.) (USMA, 1929)
  In the early 1950s served as chief of staff to Commander in Chief, NATO's Allied Forces Southern Europe (CinCSouth), 93
  In the early 1960s, as U.S. ambassador to France, tried to persuade the U.S. Navy to provide nuclear power technology to France, 93-95

Great Britain
  Adjustments by the Manson family to living conditions in London in the late 1950s-early 1960s, 216-224
  In the late 1950s the U.S. Navy placed a marker in Yorkshire, England, to commemorate John Paul Jones's victory over the British in the 1779 Battle of Flamborough Head, 281-282
  In the late 1950s and early 1960s a number of U.S. enlisted men married British women, 282-283
  In 1961 the Navy deployed opened a support base for deployed Polaris submarines at Holy Loch, Scotland, 227-242
  Impact on the British defense program when the Skybolt missile was cancelled in 1962, 242
  Decline of the Royal Navy in the early 1960s, 250-251
  Use of U.S. Marines as extras on British television in the early 1960s, 251-253
  During the Cuban Missile Crisis in October 1962, 267-269
  In the early 1960s Queen Elizabeth II hosted a garden party in London that Manson and his wife attended, 270-272
  Unsuccessful discussions in the early 1960s on turning an American ship over to the British to implement Manson's "White Fleet" concept, 272
  Headquarters in London for the NATO Exercise Team Work in the autumn of 1964, 327-336

Greece
  In the early 1950s contributed members to the staff of CinCSouth, NATO's Allied Forces Southern Europe, 73, 84-85, 87-88, 91-92

Groves, Major General Leslie R., USA
  In the late 1940s had a dismissive view of naval power because of nuclear weapons, 203

Gunnery-Naval
  Effect of U.S. naval gunfire support of troops in Korea in 1950, 67-68

Halsey, Admiral William F. Jr., USN (USNA, 1904)
  As Commander Third Fleet in 1944-45, valued having Rear Admiral Robert Carney as his chief of staff, 74-75, 79-80, 114-115

Harlow, Bryce N.
  In the late 1940s was on the staff of the House Armed Services Committee, 30
  In the 1950s was a speechwriter for President Dwight Eisenhower, 111

Harrill, Rear Admiral William K., USN (USNA, 1914)
  As Commander Task Group 58.4 in June 1944, was criticized by Rear Admiral Jocko Clark for lack of aggressiveness, 280-281

Harris, Lieutenant Commander Russell L., USNR
  In the late 1940s was a coauthor of part of the *Battle Report* series on World War II, 35, 37, 261
  In 1948 was one of the swordsmen at a Navy wedding in New York, 261-263

Heffernan, Rear Admiral John B., USN (Ret.) (USNA, 1917)
  Served as Director of Naval History from 1946 to 1956, 151, 154-155

Hogle, Rear Admiral Reynold D., USN (USNA, 1929)
  In the mid-1960s was chief of staff to NATO's Supreme Allied Commander Atlantic, 337-340

Holloway, Vice Admiral James L., Jr., USN (USNA, 1919)
  Served from 1953 to 1958 as Chief of Naval Personnel, 103-103, 181-182

Holovak, Lieutenant Charles, USN (USNA, 1939)
  Served as executive officer of the destroyer *Laffey* (DD-724) in World War II, 10-11

Holy Loch, Scotland
  In 1961 the Navy opened a support base for Polaris submarines at Holy Loch, 227-237
  During the Cuban Missile Crisis in October 1962, 267-269

Holmes, Admiral Ephraim P., USN (USNA, 1930)
  Served from 1967 to 1970 as NATO's Supreme Allied Commander Atlantic, 306-311

Hope, SS
    Former Navy hospital ship *Consolation* (AH-15) that in 1958 became the centerpiece of a humanitarian organization, Project Hope, 193-194, 274

Hughes, USS (DD-410)
    Badly damaged by a kamikaze hit in the Philippines in December 1944, 13-14

Huie, William Bradford
    In the late 1940s wrote pro-Air Force, anti-Navy magazine articles and an anti-Navy book, 28-29, 203-204, 210

Humphrey, Hubert H.
    As a senator in the late 1950s and early 1960s, advocated Manson's "White Fleet" concept, 162, 185, 187, 191, 273

Iberian-Atlantic Command (IberLant)
    Established in Portugal in 1967 as part of NATO, 296-298

Inchon, South Korea
    Site of a successful United Nations amphibious assault in September 1950, 49, 53-54

Indochina, French
    Question in 1954 on whether the United States should support the French military effort in Indochina, 114, 141-142

Information, Navy Office of (Chinfo)
    Activities in 1963-64, 284-286

Ingersoll, Vice Admiral Stuart H., USN (USNA, 1921)
    While president of the Naval War College in the late 1950s, declined to present a medal to Manson, 199

Italy
    In the early 1950s contributed members to the staff of CinCSouth, NATO's Allied Forces Southern Europe, 73, 84-85, 87-92
    Naples as the site of the headquarters for NATO's Allied Forces Southern Europe in the early 1950s, 70-73, 84-92

Jackson, Senator Henry M.
    In the mid-1960s arranged for the son of his law partner to work on the staff of NATO's Supreme Allied Commander Atlantic in Norfolk, 341-343

Japan
    Kamikaze attacks on U.S. warships in 1944-45, 8, 12-16
    U.S. Naval Forces Far East had headquarters in Tokyo during the Korean War, 65-66
    Supplied commercial minesweepers to support U.S. efforts in Korea in 1950, 69

Jones, Captain John Paul, Continental Navy
In the late 1950s the U.S. Navy placed a marker in Yorkshire, England, to commemorate Jones's victory over the British in the 1779 Battle of Flamborough Head, 281-282

Joy, Vice Admiral C. Turner, USN (USNA, 1916)
Served as Commander U.S. Naval Forces Far East during the early stages of the Korean War, 65-66
Negotiations with North Koreans, 66-67

Kamikazes
Attacks on U.S. warships in 1944-45, 8, 13-20

Karig, Captain Walter, USNR
In the 1940s and 1950s wrote about naval history and worked in Navy public relations, 25, 28, 29-34, 39-40, 44, 50-51, 82, 121-123, 166, 200, 208-209, 260-261, 325-326, 347, 353

Kennedy, President John F.
During his administration in the early 1960s favored the idea of a multi-lateral naval force, 291-293
Establishment of the Peace Corps by his administration, 257
During the Cuban Missile Crisis in 1962, 266-269

Kerama Retto
Group of islands used as an anchorage and logistics base during the Okinawa campaign in 1945, 19-20

Kidd, Captain Isaac C. Jr., USN (USNA, 1942)
Capable officer who was executive assistant to Chief of Naval Operations David McDonald in the early 1960s, 317-319

Kimmel, Rear Admiral Husband E., USN (Ret.) (USNA, 1904)
At the 1946 congressional hearings about the Japanese attack on Pearl Harbor in 1941, 36-37

Kinkaid, Vice Admiral Thomas C., USN (USNA, 1908)
Post-World War II discontent on Admiral William Halsey's role in the 1944 Battle of Leyte Gulf, 35, 80

Kirkpatrick, Rear Admiral Charles C., USN (USNA, 1931)
Headed the Navy's Office of Information in the late 1950s, 164, 190-191, 256

Korea, North
Manson's assessment of it as an untrustworthy nation, 52-53
U.S. minesweeping operations at Wonsan in 1950, 59, 68-69, 154

United Nations armistice negotiations with North Koreans in 1950, 66-67

Korean War
    As Secretary of State in January 1950, Dean Acheson made a speech in which he suggested the United States was not interested in Korean security, 152-153
    Successful United Nations amphibious assault on Inchon, Korea, in September 1950, 49, 53-54
    Paucity of medals for U.S. Navy personnel in the early stages of the war, 53-56
    Role of the U.S. Army in the early stages of the Korean War, 56-57
    Effect of U.S. aircraft during the early stages of the Korean War, 53, 63-64
    Effect of naval gunfire support in 1950, 67-68
    U.S. minesweeping operations at Wonsan in 1950, 59, 68-69, 154
    Books published in the 1950s on the U.S. Navy's role in the war, 41, 50-70, 150-157

Kuczma, Julius E.
    In the mid-1950s served as labor relations advisor on the staff of the Office of Naval Material, 160

Labor Unions
    Cultivated in the mid-1950s by the OpNav Office of Progress Analysis, 160-162

***Laffey*, USS (DD-724)**
    Pre-deployment preparations and training in 1944, 7-12
    Combat operations in the Pacific in 1944-45, 8, 12-23
    Enlisted crew members in World War II, 12-13, 18
    In November 1944, rescued a Japanese pilot from the ocean, and Manson interrogated him, 15-16
    Survived a heavy attack by kamikazes in April 1945, 16-20
    Post-attack repairs in Seattle in the summer of 1945, 22-23

Laning, Captain Richard B., USN (USNA, 1940)
    Commanded the submarine tender *Proteus* (AS-19), which deployed to Holy Loch, Scotland, in 1961, 227-237

Latta-Lawrence, Captain Harold A. L., USNR
    Staff officer for congressional liaison for Chief of Naval Operations Louis Denfeld in 1948, 260-261, 266
    Involved in messy marriage and divorce, 1948-50, 261-266

Lederer, Captain William J., Jr., USN (USNA, 1936)
    Navy public information officer who coauthored the influential 1958 book *The Ugly American*, 186-187

Leo, Stephen F.
    Served as the first public relations director for the newly formed Air Force in the late 1940s, 28, 205

Libby, Rear Admiral Ruthven E., USN (USNA, 1922)
In the early 1950s Chief of Naval Operations Robert Carney considered him as a possible successor, 115, 127

***Liberty*, USS (AGTR-5)**
Controversial attack on the ship by Israeli forces in June 1967, 313-315

***Life* Magazine**
In July 1959, promoted Manson's "White Fleet" concept in a cover story, 187-194, 217, 272

London, England
Adjustments by the Manson family to living conditions in the city in the late 1950s-early 1960s, 216-224
In the early 1960s Queen Elizabeth II hosted a garden party in London that Manson and his wife attended, 270-272
Headquarters in London for the NATO Exercise Team Work in the autumn of 1964, 327-336

Long, Commander Robert L. J., USN (USNA, 1944)
In 1961 commanded the ballistic missile submarine *Patrick Henry* (SSBN-599) deployed to Holy Loch, Scotland, 233, 237-240

Lucas, Jim G.
Scripps-Howard newspaper reporter who wrote about Navy topics in the late 1940s, 200, 210-211

Lumpkin, Captain Pickett, USN
In 1968, as the Navy's Deputy Chief of Information, arranged for Manson to get a billet in the book and magazine section of the office of the Deputy Secretary of Defense (Public Affairs), 346-347

MacArthur, General of the Army Douglas, USA (USMA, 1903)
Commanded the successful United Nations amphibious assault on Inchon, Korea, in September 1950, 49, 57

Manson, Captain Frank A. USN (Ret.)
Parents, 1
Wife Lee, 33, 63, 217-219, 221, 261, 263, 270-272, 337-338, 345
Children, 63, 130, 157-158, 169, 174, 201-202, 217-219, 221, 258, 345
Boyhood in Oklahoma in the 1920s and 1930, 1
Graduated from Northeastern State Teachers' College in Oklahoma in 1941 and began his civilian employment, 1-2
Joined the Naval Reserve in 1942 and went through the naval training school at Ithaca, New York, 2-3

In 1943-44 was part of the staff of the Boston Representative of Commander Destroyers Atlantic Fleet, 4-7

Served in the crew of the destroyer *Laffey* (DD-724) in 1944-45, 7-25

Shortly after World War II was selected as a public information specialist and augmented into the regular Navy, 39-40

Served in the late 1940s on the Secretary of the Navy's Committee on Research on Reorganization (SCOROR) and participated in the writing of volumes of *Battle Report* about the Navy's combat operations in World War II, 27-38

In the late 1940s-early 1950s served as speechwriter to CNOs Louis Denfeld and Forrest Sherman, 38, 44-50, 56, 82-84, 200-211, 260-266

From 1951 to 1953 was historian at the foundation of NATO's Allied Forces Southern Europe (CinCSouth), 70-75, 84-95

From 1953 to 1956 served as speechwriter for two Chiefs of Naval Operations, Robert Carney and Arleigh Burke, 75-80, 95-110, 171-173

Served from 1956 to 1958 as head of Plans and Policies Analysis, Office of Progress Analysis, in OpNav, 107, 147-148, 157-165, 169-170, 173-184

Coauthor, with Commander Malcolm Cagle of the 1957 book *The Sea War in Korea*, 38, 150-157

As a student at the Naval War College, 1958-59, 149, 184-190

In 1959 *Life* magazine published a cover story on his "White Fleet" concept, 187-194, 217, 272

From 1959 to 1963 served as public information officer for CinCNELM in London, 167-168, 214-259, 266-284

In 1963-64 served in the Navy's Office of Information (Chinfo), 284-293

Served 1964-68 as public affairs officer for NATO's Supreme Allied Commander Atlantic (SACLant), 166-167, 293-330

In the 1960s operated a marina and seafood restaurant in the Norfolk area, 345-346

In 1968 headed the book and magazine section of the office of the Deputy Secretary of Defense (Public Affairs), 346-355

Post-retirement activities in the foreign relations field on behalf of the American Legion and Veterans of Foreign Wars, 355-359

Margaret, HRH Princess

Recently married and pregnant, the British princess met the Mansons at a garden party in London in the early 1960s, 271-272

Marine Corps, U.S.

Use of U.S. Marines as extras on British television in the early 1960s, 251-253

Maritime Commission, U.S.

In the early 1960s argued against turning an American ship over to Britain to implement Manson's "white fleet" concept, 273-274

Martin, Vice Admiral William I., USN (USNA, 1934)

In 1956-57 served as CNO Arleigh Burke's executive assistant, 140

From 1964 to 1967, while on the OpNav staff, asked Manson to come to Washington to evaluate the Navy's role in the Vietnam War, 300-301
Served 1967-70 as Deputy Commander in Chief Atlantic Fleet, 305-306

Matthews, Francis P.
Served as Secretary of the Navy 1949-51, fired CNO Louis Denfeld, 31, 82-83, 183, 325-326

McCain, Admiral John S. Jr., USN (Ret.) (USNA, 1931)
Wife Roberta, 174-175
Working style and personality, 127, 173-182, 325
From 1955 to 1957 headed the Office of Progress Analysis in OpNav, OP-09D, 140, 157, 159-164, 169-170, 173-184
In 1957 was part of a barnstorming tour to promote the Navy League and sea power, 157-158
Received a fake reprimand from CNO Arleigh Burke for exceeding authority, 164
Attention-getting outfit when he played tennis in England in the early 1960s, 258-259
Served 1962-63 as the Navy's Chief of Information, 284-290
In the late 1960s advised Manson to work for the Veterans of Foreign Wars, 355-356
In the late 1970 hosted a group of senior officers who sought to retain the Panama Canal for the United States, 320-321

McDonald, Admiral David L., USN (Ret.) (USNA, 1928)
Working style and priorities during his tenure as Chief of Naval Operations from 1963 to 1967, 316-320
In the late 1970s, after he was retired, declined to sign a letter in favor of keeping the Panama Canal for the United States, 320-322

McLean, Rear Admiral Heber H., USN (USNA, 1921)
Unpleasant encounter with Vice Admiral Arthur D. Struble while serving in OP-03 in the late 1940s, 58

Medical Problems
Methods of combating venereal disease on board aircraft carriers in the 1950s, 143-145
Former child movie star Shirley Temple had an infection following the delivery of her baby in the naval hospital in Bethesda, Maryland, in the late 1940s, 353

Mehle, Captain Roger W., Jr., USN (USNA, 1937)
Fiery individual who was deputy to CinCNELM in London in the early 1960s, 245-246

Mendenhall, Captain Ferdinand, USNR
Reserve officer who was recalled to active duty to provide public information support for the 1964 NATO Exercise Team Work, 327

Menocal, Captain George L., USN (USNA, 1922)
   In 1943-44 served as Administrative Commander Destroyer Squadron 27/Boston Representative of Commander Destroyers Atlantic Fleet, 4-7, 27

Mereness, Captain Robert H., USN
   In the mid-1960s served as public affairs officer for Commander in Chief U.S. Naval Forces Europe, 335

Middle East Force, U.S.
   Token U.S. presence in the Persian Gulf in the early 1960s, 224-225

Miller, Rear Admiral George H., USN (USNA, 1933)
   In the 1950s and 1960s was involved in strategic planning on the OpNav staff, 75-77, 103, 140, 180, 305

Miller, Captain Gerald E., USN (USNA, 1942)
   Served in the mid-1960s as executive assistant to Vice Chief of Naval Operations Horacio Rivero, 304-305

Miller, Captain Henry L., USN (USNA, 1934)
   In 1957 was part of a barnstorming tour to promote the Navy League and sea power, 157
   Delivered modified sea power presentations in the mid-1950s, 165, 184

Mine Warfare
   U.S. minesweeping operations at Wonsan, North Korea, in 1950, 59, 68-69, 154

Missiles
   The decision to support the Polaris ballistic missile program in the mid-1950s killed the Regulus program and delayed the development of cruise missiles in the U.S. Navy, 101-103

***Missouri*, USS (BB-63)**
   Served as flagship for Commander Seventh Fleet during the early stages of the Korean War, 54-55, 61-62

Mitscher, Vice Admiral Marc A., USN (USNA, 1910)
   Commanded Task Force 58 in the Pacific in 1944-45, 133-134

Mohammed V
   Moroccan King's interaction with Americans in the early 1960s, 254

Momsen, Rear Admiral Charles B., USN (USNA, 1920)
   In the late 1940s, as Assistant Chief of Naval Operations for Submarine Warfare, dealt with the news media, 201

Montgomery, Field Marshal Sir Bernard L. British Army
NATO Deputy Supreme Allied Commander Europe in the early 1950s, 71-72, 292

Montgomery, Robert
Movie actor and Naval Reservist who did publicity work on behalf of the Navy in the late 1940s, 210-211

Moorer, Admiral Thomas H., USN (Ret.) (USNA, 1933)
Served from 1965 to 1967 as NATO's Supreme Allied Commander Atlantic (SACLant), 297-298, 306-310, 313-315, 348
In the late 1960s advised Manson to work for the Veterans of Foreign Wars, 355-356
In the late 1970s was part of a group of senior officers who sought to retain the Panama Canal for the United States, 321-322

Morison, Rear Admiral Samuel Eliot, USNR (Ret.)
Supervised the writing of the 15-volume *History of United States Naval Operations in World War II*, 6, 37-39

Morocco
Interaction between the U.S. Navy and Moroccans at Port Lyautey in the early 1960s, 242-243, 254-255
Agadir was the site of a devastating earthquake in February 1960, 253-254

***Moskva* (Soviet Cruiser)**
Reporter William Beecher broke the story in October 1967 that the Soviet Navy was operating its first helicopter carrier, the *Moskva*, 307-309, 312-313

Mountbatten, Admiral of the Fleet, Lord Louis, Royal Navy
In the mid-1950s avoided taking a ride in a P6M seaplane while visiting CNO Arleigh Burke, 131-132

***Mount McKinley* (AGC-7)**
Flagship of Rear Admiral James Doyle in 1950, during the Korean War, 53-54

Multi-Lateral Force
Concept that evolved in the 1960s from widespread distribution of nuclear weapons to mixed-nation manning of ships, 290-293

Murrow, Edward R.
As head of the U.S. Information Agency in the early 1960s, was interested in Manson's "White Fleet" concept, 274

Naples, Italy
Site of the headquarters for NATO's Allied Forces Southern Europe in the early 1950s, 70-73, 84-90

National Naval Medical Center, Bethesda, Maryland
Former child movie star Shirley Temple had an infection following the delivery of her baby in the hospital in the late 1940s, 353

National Security Council
Limited role in the mid-1950s, 116

Naval Forces Far East, U.S.
Commanded U.S. naval forces in the Korean War from headquarters in Tokyo, Japan, 65-66

Naval History Division, Washington, D.C.
Reluctant to make historical documents available to authors in the mid-1950s, 151-155

Naval Institute, U.S.
In 1957 published the Cagle-Manson book *Sea War in Korea*, 151-157

Naval Reserve, U.S.
In 1964 a number of reserve officers were recalled to active duty to provide public information support for NATO Exercise Team Work, 327-338

Naval War College, Newport, Rhode Island
Admiral Richard L. Conolly in 1950 was downgraded from four stars to three when he became president of the college, 44-45
Manson spent his year there, 1958-59, developing his concept of a peaceful "White Fleet," 184-194
Curriculum for students in the late 1950s, 195-199

Navy League
In the early 1950s Chief of Naval Operations Robert Carney challenged the organization to take a more active role in supporting the Navy, 120
In 1957 several senior officers made a barnstorming tour to promote the Navy League and sea power, 157-158
Cultivated in the mid-1950s by the OpNav Office of Progress Analysis, 163

News Media
The amphibious force flagship *Eldorado* (AGC-11) was the site of a press conference for Manson in April 1945, 19-20
In the late 1940s journalist William Bradford Huie wrote pro-Air Force, anti-Navy works, 28-29, 203, 210
In the late 1940s various newspapers covered the controversial marriage of Naval Reserve Captain Harold Latta-Lawrence, 262-263
Story in *The Washington Post* in 1950 about Admiral Richard Conolly changing duty to become president of the Naval War College, 44-45

Coverage in the mid-1950s by *The New York Times* of a speech by Chief of Naval Operations Robert Carney, 110-111

In 1955 *Collier's* magazine published a cover story on new CNO Arleigh Burke, 121-124

Manson's relationships with media representatives over the years, 121-124, 165-169, 187-190, 200-216, 227-237, 251-253, 264, 267-269, 278-279, 291, 307-309, 329-330

In July 1959, *Life* magazine promoted Manson's "White Fleet" concept in a cover story, 187-194, 217, 272

Around 1966 planned NATO athletic events in the Norfolk area were cancelled because of a reporter's story that claimed falsely there would be racial segregation, 166-167

Reporter William Beecher of *The New York Times* broke the story in October 1967 that the Soviet Navy was operating its first helicopter carrier, the *Moskva*, 307-309, 312-313

Coverage of the 1964 NATO Exercise Team Work, 329-338

New York Times, The

Hanson W. Baldwin served for many years as military editor for the newspaper, 207

In 1948 covered the society wedding of Captain Harold A. L. Latta-Lawrence, 262

In 1958 published material on humanitarian Project Hope, 193

Reporter William Beecher broke the story in October 1967 that the Soviet Navy was operating its first helicopter carrier, the *Moskva*, 307-309, 312-313

Nimitz, Fleet Admiral Chester W., USN (USNA, 1905)

As Chief of Naval Operations after World War II, provided guidance to Manson on the writing of the *Battle Report* books about the war, 34-35

Advice to Manson on the staying power of the Navy, 176

Norfolk, Virginia

Site of the annual Azalea Festival in the 1960s, 341-342

Around 1966 planned NATO athletic events in the Norfolk area were cancelled because of a reporter's story that claimed falsely there would be racial segregation, 166-167

Socializing in the mid-1960s among senior officers stationed in the area, 342

In the 1960s Manson and his family operated a marina and seafood restaurant in the Norfolk area, 345-346

Norman, Lloyd

Washington Times-Herald and *Chicago Tribune* reporter whom Manson found he had to be wary of when discussing Navy business in the late 1940s, 211, 264

Norris, Captain John G., USNR

Washington Post reporter who also provided public affairs support for the 1964 NATO Exercise Team Work, 336

North Atlantic Treaty Organization (NATO)
Formation of NATO's Allied Forces Southern Europe, 1951-53, 70-72, 84-90
Annual exercises in the 1960s, 257-258, 294-297, 326-338
The multi-lateral force concept evolved in the 1960s from widespread distribution of nuclear weapons to mixed-nation manning of ships, 290-293

Nuclear Propulsion
In the early 1950s Chief of Naval Operations Robert Carney and Vice Chief Donald Duncan differed on the issue of nuclear power for U.S. surface warships, 75-76, 103
Plan in the mid-1950s to equip the P6M SeaMaster seaplane with nuclear power, 100-101
Relationship in the 1950s between individuals in the nuclear power program and the Chiefs of Naval Operations, 105-109
In the early 1960s Vice Admiral Hyman Rickover balked at providing nuclear power technology to France, 93-95
Reactor events on board the ballistic missile submarine *Patrick Henry* (SSBN-599) in 1961, 239-241

Nuclear Weapons
In the late 1940s Major General Leslie Groves had a dismissive view of naval power because of nuclear weapons, 203
Debate in 1954 on whether the United States should support the French in Indochina with nuclear weapons, 114
Lieutenant Commander Marsden Perry made films in the mid-1950s on behalf of the OpNav Office of Progress Analysis, but they couldn't be shown because of nuclear weapons content, 177-178
In 1961 the Navy opened a support base for deployed Polaris missile submarines at Holy Loch, Scotland, 227-230
During the Cuban Missile Crisis in October 1962, 267-269
The Multi-Lateral Force concept evolved in the 1960s from widespread distribution of nuclear weapons to mixed-nation manning of ships, 290-291

Nunn, Rear Admiral Ira H., USN (USNA, 1924)
In the mid-1950s headed the Navy's office of legislative liaison, 164

Office of Management and Budget (OMB)
Lackluster reception in the mid-1960s to Manson's "White Fleet" concept, 287-288

Okinawa
The destroyer *Laffey* (DD-724) survived a heavy attack by kamikazes in April 1945, 16-20

Olav V, King
Norwegian monarch who visited the SACLant headquarters in Norfolk in the mid-1960s, 295

OP-09D (Office of Progress Analysis in OpNav)
Promotion of the Navy and sea power in the mid-1950s, 157-165, 169-182

OP-23 (Assistant CNO for Operational Research and Policy)
Role in the late 1940s in the inter-service battles over unification, 29-32, 210-211

Ormoc Bay, Philippine Islands
Kamikaze attacks on U.S. warships in December 1944, 8-9, 13, 58

P6M SeaMaster
Plan in the 1950s to equip this seaplane with nuclear power, 100-101
In 1955 the prototype crashed not long after Admiral Arleigh Burke and Admiral of the Fleet Louis Mountbatten avoided taking a flight, 131

Panama Canal
Debates in the late 1970s on whether to turn the canal over to the nation of Panama, 320-322

***Patrick Henry*, USS (SSBN-599)**
In March 1961 became the first Polaris missile submarine to deploy to Holy Loch, Scotland, 233, 235, 237-241

Pearl Harbor, Oahu, Hawaii
Congressional hearings in 1946 on the 1941 Japanese attack on Pearl Harbor, 33-34

Pearson, Andrew
Muckraking newspaper columnist in the late 1940s, 205-206, 274

Peet, Commander Raymond E., USN (USNA, 1943)
In the late 1950s served as aide to Chief of Naval Operations Arleigh Burke, 109, 117, 190

Perry, Lieutenant Commander Marsden J., USNR
Made films in the mid-1950s on behalf of the OpNav Office of Progress Analysis, but they couldn't be shown because of nuclear weapons content, 177-178

Philippine Islands
Kamikaze attacks on U.S. warships 1944, 8, 13-14

***Philippine Sea*, USS (CV-47)**
Launched air strikes in 1950, during the Korean War, 63-64
Deck crash and fire in December 1950, 64

Phillips, Robert H.
In 1955 shot photos of new CNO Arleigh Burke for a cover story in Collier's magazine, 121-124

Photography
In 1955 *Collier's* magazine published a cover photograph of new CNO Arleigh Burke, 121-124

Photo of an American F-4 fighter shadowing a Soviet Bear reconnaissance aircraft was released to the media as part of the 1964 NATO Exercise Team Work, 330-332, 335-336

Pickett, Captain Ben B., USN (USNA, 1938)
Involvement in setting up a specified command in connection with CinCNELM in London in the early 1960s, 247-248

Pillsbury, Commander John D., USNR
In the late 1950s headed the public information program at CinCNELM in London, 225-226

Pineau, Lieutenant Roger, USNR
Was involved in the research and writing of the 15-volume *History of United States Naval Operations in World War II*, 38-39

Polaris Missile Program
The decision to support the Polaris ballistic missile program in the mid-1950s killed the Regulus program and delayed the development of cruise missiles in the U.S. Navy, 103

In 1961 the Navy opened a support base for deployed Polaris submarines at Holy Loch, Scotland, 227-237

Submarines at Holy Loch during the Cuban Missile Crisis in October 1962, 267-269

Port Lyautey, Morocco, Naval Air Station
Operations in the early 1960s, 224, 242-243

Portugal
NATO established the Iberian-Atlantic Command (IberLant) in 1967, 296-298

Pride, Admiral Alfred Melville, USN (Ret.)
Personality of this genial former enlisted man who became a flag officer, 279

Prisoners of War
In November 1944, the destroyer *Laffey* (DD-724) rescued a Japanese pilot from the ocean, and Manson interrogated him, 15-16

Project Hope
Founded in 1958 with a former Navy hospital ship, *Consolation* (AH-15), 193-194

Proteus, USS (AS-19)
Submarine tender that deployed to Holy Loch Scotland, in 1961 to support Polaris missile submarines, 227-237

During the Cuban Missile Crisis in October 1962, 267-269

Public Relations
Shortly after World War II the Navy created a new restricted line specialty, the public information officer, 42-43
Promotion of the Navy and sea power in the mid-1950s by the OpNav Office of Progress Analysis, 107, 147-148, 157-165, 169-170, 173-182
In 1957 several senior officers made a barnstorming tour to promote the Navy League and sea power, 157-158
On behalf of CinCNELM in London in the early 1960s, 249-253
The Navy provided media access and releases to the news media during the 1964 NATO Exercise Team Work, 329-336

Pueblo, **USS (AGER-2)**
Intelligence ship seized by North Korea in 1968, 354

Raborn, Rear Admiral William F., Jr., USN (USNA, 1928)
Headed the Polaris ballistic missile program in the 1950s, 106

Racial Issues
Around 1966 planned NATO athletic events in the Norfolk area were cancelled because of a reporter's story that claimed falsely there would be racial segregation, 166-167

Radford, Admiral Arthur W., USN (USNA, 1916)
Served 1953-57 as Chairman of the Joint Chiefs of Staff, 73-74, 97, 111, 114-115, 128

Reck, Lieutenant Henry D., USNR
Was involved in the research and writing of the 15-volume *History of United States Naval Operations in World War II*, 6, 39

Regulus Missiles
The decision to support the Polaris ballistic missile program in the mid-1950s killed the Regulus program and delayed the development of cruise missiles in the U.S. Navy, 103

Rhodesia
In the 1970s Manson visited the nation to try to further its relations with the United States, 359

Ricketts, Admiral Claude V., USN (USNA, 1929)
Personality, 286-287
As Commander Second Fleet in April 1961, was disappointed that the U.S. Navy did not intervene in the invasion of the Bay of Pigs, Cuba, 269-270
Served 1961 to 1964 as Vice Chief of Naval Operations, 285-293, 318-320, 324

Rickover, Vice Admiral Hyman G., USN (USNA, 1922)
    Sparse eating habits, 105-106
    Relationship with CNOs Robert Carney and Arleigh Burke in the 1950s, 105-108
    In the early 1960s balked at providing nuclear power technology to France, 93-94
    In 1957 got Lieutenant Commander George Steele to be detached from the OpNav Office of Progress Analysis in one day, 162

Rivero, Admiral Horacio Jr., USN (USNA, 1931)
    Served 1964-68 as Vice Chief of Naval Operations, 289-290, 301-305, 320

Rogers, Edith Nourse
    Congresswoman who was wrongly accused in the late 1940s of being involved in a messy marriage scandal, 261-263

Roskill, Captain Stephen W., Royal Navy (Ret.)
    Respected British historian whom Manson met in the early 1960s, 250, 275-277, 291

Royal Navy
    Decline of in the early 1960s, 250-251
    Participation in the 1954 NATO Exercise Team Work, 329-336

Runk, Lieutenant Theodore W., USNR
    Service on board the destroyer *Laffey* (DD-724) in World War II, 20-21

Russell, Rear Admiral James S., USN (USNA, 1926)
    In the mid-1950s, as Chief of the Bureau of Aeronautics, opposed nuclear-powered seaplanes, 101

Saloman, Lieutenant Commander Henry, USNR
    Was involved in the research and writing of the 15-volume *History of United States Naval Operations in World War II*, 38-39

Satellites
    In the mid-1960s NATO's Supreme Allied Commander Atlantic sent the first message via the new Telstar satellite, 309-310

SCOROR
    Role of the Secretary's Committee on Research on Reorganization during the inter-service unification squabbles in the late 1940s, 27-33
    Later became OP-23, 29

Scotland
    In 1961 the Navy opened a support base for deployed Polaris submarines at Holy Loch, 227-237
    Dunoon was a shopping and liberty location for crew members of Polaris missile submarines deployed to Holy Loch in 1961, 236-237

Events at Holy Loch during the Cuban Missile Crisis in October 1962, 267-269

Shaw, Commander James C., USN (USNA, 1936)
Was involved in the research and writing of the 15-volume *History of United States Naval Operations in World War II*, 38-39, 154-156

Shear, Commander Harold E., USN (USNA, 1942)
In 1961 commanded the ballistic missile submarine *Patrick Henry* (SSBN-599) deployed to Holy Loch, Scotland, 233, 237-238

Sheets, Ensign Jerome B., USNR
Service on board the destroyer *Laffey* (DD-724) in World War II, 10

Shepley, James R.
In 1959, as head of *Time* magazine's Washington bureau, spearheaded the publication of Manson's "White Fleet" concept in *Life* magazine, 188-194

Sherman, Admiral Forrest P., USN (USNA, 1918)
Demonstrated intellectual brilliance while serving as Chief of Naval Operations from 1949 until his death in 1951, 44-50, 56, 83-84, 326

Sherrod, Robert L.
Journalist who covered inter-service battles in the late 1940s and later wrote a book about Marine aviation in World War II, 207-209

Shetler, Dwight
Engineer who advocated ballistic missiles for the Navy in the mid-1950s, 102

Ship Handling
On board the destroyer *Laffey* (DD-724) in the Pacific in 1944-45, 8, 16

Skybolt Missile
Impact on the British defense program when the missile was cancelled in 1962, 242

Smedberg, William R. III, Rear Admiral, USN (USNA, 1926)
Served from 1953 to 1956 as director of the Politico-Military Policy Division of OpNav, 133, 136-137

Smith, Admiral Harold Page, USN (Ret.) (USNA, 1924)
Served as CinCNELM in London, 1960-63, 167-169, 228-231, 242-248, 254-256, 266-269, 271
In the early 1960s was the recipient of a gag order from the Assistant Secretary of Defense (Public Affairs), 167-169
At CinCNELM headquarters in London while the crisis was taking place in October 1962, 266-269

Served 1963-65 as NATO's Supreme Allied Commander Atlantic (SACLant), 315, 327, 330, 333-334, 338

Solomon, Captain Bernard S., USNR
In the mid-1960s was public affairs officer for Commander in Chief Atlantic Fleet, 346

South Africa, Republic of
In the 1970s Manson visited the nation to try to further its relations with the United States, 357-358

Soviet Navy
New York Times reporter William Beecher broke the story in October 1967 that the Soviet Navy was operating its first helicopter carrier, the *Moskva*, 307-309, 312-313
A Soviet trawler shadowed American ships during the 1964 NATO Exercise Team Work, 332

Soviet Union
Frequent topic of speeches by Chief of Naval Operations Robert Carney in the early 1950s, 105
Photo of an American F-4 fighter shadowing a Soviet Bear reconnaissance aircraft was released to the media as part of the 1964 NATO Exercise Team Work, 330-332, 335-336

Spaak, Paul-Henri
Served 1957-61 as Secretary General of the North Atlantic Treaty Organization, 91, 194, 256

Spain
Relationship with CinCNELM in the early 1960s, 255

Sparrow, Colonel Herbert G., USA (USMA, 1933)
In the early 1950s was a secretary of staff for NATO's Allied Forces Southern Europe, 92-93

Stark, Admiral Harold R., USN (Ret.) (USNA, 1903)
At the 1946 congressional hearings about the Japanese attack on Pearl Harbor in 1941, 36-37

State Department
Controversy in the mid-1950s over a speech made by Chief of Naval Operations Robert Carney, 110-111

Steele, Lieutenant Commander George P. II, USN (USNA, 1945)
In 1957 served briefly in the Office of Progress Analysis, in OpNav, 107, 162

Struble, Vice Admiral Arthur D., USN (USNA, 1915)
    Amphibious command in the Philippines in 1944, 58
    Served as Deputy Chief of Naval Operations (Operations), OP-03, 1948-50, 58
    Commanded the Seventh Fleet during the early stages of the Korean War, 54-59, 69

Stump, Admiral Felix B., USN (USNA, 1917)
    Served as Commander in Chief and Commander in Chief Pacific Fleet from 1953 to 1958, 141

Sullivan, John L.
    Resigned as Secretary of the Navy in 1949 during the inter-service unification squabble, 30-31, 129

Supreme Allied Command Atlantic (SACLant)
    Imaginative ideas in the mid-1960s from Rear Admiral Richard Colbert, a member of the staff, 293-294
    Held annual exercises in the mid-1960s, 294-295
    Ran the Wide-ranging NATO operational exercise Team Work in Western Europe and adjacent waters in the autumn of 1964, 326-338
    Around 1966 planned NATO athletic events were cancelled because of a reporter's story that claimed falsely there would be racial segregation, 166-167
    Public relations promotion of the command in the mid-1960s, 339-341
    Various activities in the mid-1960s, 339-345

Sylvester, Arthur J.
    In the early 1960s, as Assistant Secretary of Defense (Public Affairs), issued a gag order to Admiral Harold Page Smith, 167-168

Symington, W. Stuart
    As Secretary of the Air Force, role in the late 1940s inter-service unification squabble, 28-30, 183, 205

Tu-95 Bear (Soviet Bomber)
    Photo of an American F-4 fighter shadowing a Soviet Bear reconnaissance aircraft was released to the media as part of the 1964 NATO Exercise Team Work, 330-332, 335-336

Team Work, Exercise
    Wide-ranging NATO operational exercise in Western Europe and adjacent waters in the autumn of 1964, 326-338

Telstar
    In the mid-1960s NATO's Supreme Allied Commander Atlantic sent the first message via the new Telstar satellite, 309-311

Temple, Shirley
  Former child movie star had an infection following the delivery of her baby in the naval hospital in Bethesda, Maryland, in the late 1940s, 353

Thach, Captain John S., USN (USNA, 1927)
  Commanded the escort carrier *Sicily* (CVE-118) during the early stages of the Korean War, 60-61

Thomas, Charles S.
  As Secretary of the Navy in 1955, selected Admiral Arleigh Burke as the new Chief of Naval Operations, rather than reappointing Admiral Robert Carney, 78-79, 95, 97-100, 111-112, 128
  In the mid-1950s favored the idea of a nuclear-powered seaplane, 100

Tokyo, Japan
  U.S. Naval Forces Far East had headquarters in Tokyo during the Korean War, 65-66

Tonkin Gulf Incident
  Controversy about attacks on U.S. destroyers in Tonkin Gulf in August 1964, 347-348

Trahan, Commander Paul K.
  Served as Seventh Fleet public affairs officer in the mid-1960s, 347-348

Turkey
  In the early 1950s contributed members to the staff of CinCSouth, NATO's Allied Forces Southern Europe, 73, 84-85, 91-92

Turner, Vice Admiral Richmond K., USN (USNA, 1908)
  Commanded amphibious forces during the invasion of Okinawa in 1945, 19-21

Turner, Lieutenant Stansfield, USN (USNA, 1947)
  In the mid-1950s provided advice to CNO Arleigh Burke and his staff about junior officers, 133

Unification
  Inter-service battles in the late 1940s on the unification of the U.S. armed services, 27-33

VW-2Q Super Constellation
  Crashed in Germany with the loss of all 26 crew members on 22 May 1962, 214-216

Venereal Disease
  Methods of combating VD on board aircraft carriers in the 1950s, 143-145

Veterans of Foreign Wars
    Manson's post-Navy activities on behalf of the organization in the area of foreign relations, 355-359

Vietnam War
    Controversy about attacks on U.S. destroyers in the Gulf of Tonkin in August 1964, 347-348
    In the mid-1960s, while on temporary duty in Washington, Manson evaluated the Navy's role in the ongoing war, 300-305
    Controversy about attacks on U.S. destroyers in Tonkin Gulf in August 1964, 347-348

Walley, Commander David M., USN
    Aeronautical engineering duty officer who in the 1950s sought to equip the P6M SeaMaster seaplane with nuclear power, 100-101

Walsh, Dr. William
    Civilian doctor who founded Project Hope in 1958 and persuaded the Navy to donate a hospital ship, 193-194, 274

Ward, Rear Admiral Norvell G., USN (USNA, 1935)
    In the early 1960s commanded Submarine Squadron 14, the first with Polaris submarines, 230-237
    In the mid-1960s worked on the proposal for a multi-lateral nuclear force, 291-292

War Games
    At the Naval War College in the late 1950s, 196

Waters, Commander Odale D., Jr., USN (USNA, 1932)
    Commanded the destroyer *Laffey* (DD-724) in 1945-46, 22-23

Watson, Mark
    Baltimore Sun reporter who in the early 1960s asked fellow newsmen not to reveal that Admiral Harold Page Smith was under a gag order, 167-169, 200

Weschler, Commander Thomas R., USN (USNA, 1939)
    In the mid-1950s served as personal aide to the Chief of Naval Operations, Admiral Arleigh Burke, 102, 109, 121-124, 131

Wettern, Desmond
    British naval journalist who became a friend of the Manson family in the late 1950s-early 1960s, 291, 336

"White Fleet" Concept
    In his year at the Naval War College, 1958-59, Manson developed the idea of using a separate group of Navy ships for humanitarian purposes, 184-190

In July 1959, *Life* magazine promoted the idea in a cover story, 187-194, 217, 272
Ongoing interest after the article appeared, 197, 255-256, 272-273, 287-289, 294, 302-304
Unsuccessful discussions in the early 1960s on turning an American ship over to the British to implement Manson's concept, 272
Manson's work with Vice Chief of Naval Operations Claude Ricketts in 1963-64 to try to bring the concept into being, 287-289
Manson rejected the Central Intelligence Agency as a possible source of support for the "White Fleet" concept in the early 1960s, 197, 294

Wilkinson, J. Burke
In the mid-1950s served as Deputy Assistant Secretary of State, 110-111

Williams, Commander Ralph E., Supply Corps, USN
In the mid-1950s served as speechwriter for Chief of Naval Operations Arleigh Burke, 159

Wonsan, North Korea
Site of U.S. minesweeping operations in 1950, 59, 68-69, 154

Wouk, Herman
Wrote the Navy novel *The Caine Mutiny*, published in 1951 and made into a movie in 1954, 25-26

***Wrangell*, USS (AE-12)**
Hijinks on board when Cooper Bright commanded the ship, 1956-58, 146

***Yamato* (Japanese Battleship)**
Sunk by U.S. aircraft during her sortie toward Okinawa in April 1945, 24

Yeager, Rear Admiral Howard A., USN (USNA, 1927)
Served in the late 1940s as administrative aide to Chief of Naval Operations Louis Denfeld, 82, 261
In the early 1960s was involved in annual NATO exercises, 257-258

Zumwalt, Admiral Elmo R. Jr., USN (Ret.) (USNA, 1943)
Manson's assessments of over various facets of Zumwalt's career, 322-326, 360

MY MOST DANGEROUS JOB IN WW II

By Frank A. Manson

Captain USN (Retired)

Each soldier, sailor, airman and marine has his own eye witness memories of "what happened to me" during World War II. My story started when my destroyer skipper, Commander F. Julian Becton, called me to Laffey's bridge to ask if I had read a dispatch which he held in his hand. It was what the Navy called an ALNAV, meaning it had been sent to all the Navy's ships and stations around the world.

I quickly glanced at the ALNAV and confirmed I had read it. In fact I had almost memorized it. When it first arrived in the radio shack where all our radio traffic was received, I realized PR had become important to Navy high command.

The ALNAV had ordered each ship and station to designate one officer as it's Public Relations Officer. That officer would be responsible for providing information to the Navy Department concerning newsworthy events.

Without a moment's hesitation I confirmed I had read the ALNAV.

"You have read it?" the Captain confirmed as his binoculars scanned the skies for bogies (incoming Japanese aircraft). Our ship was then operating off the coast of Japan. We were serving as an early warning radar picket.

"Do you understand what they want?" the skipper asked still

keeping his binoculars on the horizon.

"Yes sir, I do," I said.

Momentarily lowering his binoculars from his eyes he said, "Well, you're it. Do the best you can." He handed me the ALNAV and once more placed his binoculars so he could scan the horizon. Operating so near the Japanese coast was an open invitation to Kamikaze.

As I left the bridge and went below to my stateroom I fully realized there wasn't one person aboard the Laffey with whom I could exchange ideas about my new public relations assignment.

So I went to the Executive Officer, LCDR Charles Holovak, to ask for a part time typist, someone who could help me canvas the crew for human interest stories and type up whatever we found.

The "Exec" chuckled when he read the ALNAV.

"What do they think we're runnin out here?" he said, "Some sort of publicity show."

"Beats me," I said. "But I must get a brief bio on each crew member. I must know each person's hometown and the name of his local newspaper."

"Good luck," said the Exec, "but don't conduct interviews when we're at General Quarters." I had no idea how I could fit PR into my primary duties and watch standing.

However, I got the Exec's drift. He thought the ALNAV was a dumb idea, added paperwork for the overworked destroyers. Our ship's office was already stretched to the limits trying to keep up with ship's logs and other paper work required by the squadron commander, the type commander, the fleet commander and the Navy Department. Beyond that the Laffey had to send in action reports after each engagement, plus dozens of other reports with deadlines, deadlines, deadlines.

"You can use Herb Rick," said the Exec, "but don't take him away from the important stuff." Nor would I overlook my own primary duties.

While the Exec was less than enthusiastic about my new PR duties he also knew the Navy Department wasn't kidding - - and that we had to make an effort - - however feeble it might be.

I was secretly pleased with the extra duty assignment. I thought the public needed to know more about what our ships were doing in far away places. I had requested P.R. duty when I first applied for commissioned service.

In fact PR duty was the one thing I knew how to do. In college I had worked as a sports reporter, building up the self esteem of our local athletes. I had been editor-in-chief of my law school paper. I had done radio announcing, entered radio and speech contests. I had coached and taught others how to write editorials, speeches, news reports and radio scripts. So I felt comfortable with my new assignment, much more so than when I was on Laffey's bridge as officer-of-the-deck and received orders to change stations in the destroyer protection screen.

Most of my duties on Laffey's bridge made me nervous, for example, I was never sure how the ship's rudders were responding to my orders. The bow moved ever so slowly when coming to a new course

- - and unless I looked at the compass, I could not be sure the bow was changing it's direction at all. It was the same with changing speed. I could crank on a few extra turns of our twin screws, or slow the screws a few turns and then I just had to wait and see what happened. Maneuvering a destroyer wasn't at all like running a motor boat back home in Oklahoma on the Illinois River.

Herbert Rick with the rating of Yeoman Second Class turned out to be an ideal assistant PR. He had exceptional intelligence and he was sensitive to our circumstances. We both knew PR was not exactly essential to manning the guns, or dropping depth charges.

We were given a PR office about 3'x 4' in a space just after amidships. I think the space had been intended as an ammunition storage for 20mm or perhaps as a small spud locker. It would have made an excellent broom closet.

For starters my PR job was a contradiction. The Navy Department requested newsworthy stories. Yet, all our combat experiences were secret. In all our personal letters to friends and relatives we could not write about any ships, their locations or combat experiences. Now, the Navy Department had requested I send it newsworthy events. And we did have many newsworthy events.

For example, if we could have written up the story of Laffey saving the battle damaged destroyer Hughes (DD410) from her certain grounding and destruction on the shore of Mindinao, we could have made news. This drama would have been of national interest with the wire services and radio networks. Certainly all of Laffey's crew members could have been written up in their local papers.

Especially interesting would have been the fact Mindinao still had it's share of cannibals and headhunters.

Yet, saving the Hughes from certain destruction was a secret operation. Her boiler room had been exploded by a direct hit from a Japanese kamikaze. About 20 of the Hughes crew had been steamed until their faces were beyond recognition. They were brought aboard Laffey to die. This was a dramatic story. Yet, no one in the U.S. even knew the Japanese were using kamikaze (suicide pilots) to attack our ships. Nor did anyone know the effectiveness of the suiciders, not even the Japanese.

If I could have written a story about the Japanese bomber pilot Laffey crew members rescued off the east coast of Luzon, it would have been newsworthy. If I could have told U.S. newspapers what that pilot told me while Dr. Matthew Darnell sewed up his numerous wounds we could have put Laffey's name in the national spotlight. Americans didn't know four Japanese carriers had been recently sunk.

To tell the Japanese pilot's story would have revealed for the first time that his aircraft carrier, SHOKAKU, had been sunk as had the three remaining Japanese aircraft carriers in their Navy. This story would have compromised U.S. intelligence. The Japanese knew they had lost all their carriers, but Americans did not know. I have never agreed with WW II policies of keeping our good news away from the American public.

Herb and I decided about the best we could do was write up vague summary statements on Laffey operations and forward them along with a photo of each crew member to his hometown newspaper. We did not know the Navy Department had already established a hometown news service out of Chicago Great Lakes Training Center.

Had Herb and I known this center existed we could have sent only one summarized story with the photos of each crew member and their addresses and we would have splashed Laffey publicity far and wide.

Meanwhile Herb and I worked in the sub tropical heat in our small PR office. We had no air conditioning, not even a fan. But we plodded along setting up individual PR files on each crew member. We had about 300 crew members and 22 officers. Since we could only work at the PR job when we were not at General Quarters, which was most of the time, and when our primary jobs would permit. Actually, we didn't do much PR duty. It was slow going.

I remember that awful heat. I remember Herb and I mopping the perspiration from our heads and necks as we put those home town news service files together. Crew members were mildly interested although they never understood why we were working so hard at it. Only a few of them it seemed had ever had any publicity and they didn't see much value in it.

The ship's office, run by Chief Pierce V. Doyle and Yeoman Earl Kennedy thought we were engaged in a worthless, time consuming job. Laffey's officers never questioned my PR assignment. I assume they also thought it was an impossible mission and a waste of time. But at times the war itself seemed such a waste, lacking any constructive purpose.

Frankly I didn't put much faith, or future in my destroyer PR job. If I had been PR for a Task Force or for the Pacific Fleet I could get the Navy some needed publicity. Furthermore I could prove to Washington's Navy Department that I was a "can do" PR type. And further that the Navy could use me as one of it's PR pioneers. At this point of time the Navy was still feeling it's way with PR. Most Admirals regarded PR as "non essential" to put it discretely.

Captain Becton never asked me how I was doing in the PR department. He knew we had so many restrictions on what we could tell that it was difficult, if not impossible, to send anything of value or interest to the Navy Department. But the Skipper was too busy fighting the war to worry about telling the world what, where and how we were doing it.

Since becoming Laffey's PR we had been sent as a radar picket destroyer to protect the fast carriers striking the Japanese homeland, bombing military targets as well as fleet anchorages, airfields and navy yards. At times Laffey steamed less than 100 miles off the Japanese coastline. The fleet's job was to isolate Iwo Jima while the U.S. Marines conquered the island.

My special assignment during the "Tokyo strikes" was to report incoming Japanese aircraft picked up by radar. I would give range and bearing of all bogies so our pilots could intercept them in time to protect the carriers, battle ships and cruisers.

During those Navy air strikes the seas were grey and heavy, clouds were dense. We didn't report many Japanese aircraft. Still, Herb and I had to concentrate on battle stations. We had no time to send out home town news stories. We did have 322 stories ready for mailing except for the photos.

From my press training I did know if we did not get our stories out in a timely manner they would not be used by local editors - - or that is what I thought anyway.

It seemed the ship's photographer, Ensign Jim Fravel, later killed in action, was too busy to take individual photos. Also the Laffey was either in combat or preparing for combat about 90% of the time. If we had anytime left Herb, Jim and I wanted to go with our shipmates to one of the Ulithi Islands for rest and recreation (R and R). We surely did not want to use such precious time in our non-ventilated PR office preparing individual homtowners, particularly since we didn't have much happening that we could write about.

I wanted to write a profile on our skipper Commander Becton. He had fought all over the South Pacific. He was a true hero and yet, in his hometown of Hot Springs, Arkansas, I doubted if many knew his name. The citizens would have been proud of him had they known what he had done in combat.

But when the skipper and I had time to talk he preferred to reminisce about our trips to the horse track in Boston or tell jokes, or sometimes he would tell me about a letter from one of his girlfriends. He never seemed interested in talking about the Battle of Guadalcanal or Savo Island - - or <u>Iron Bottom Bay</u> where so many U.S. ships and shipmates were buried.

So all in all it was fair to say my PR job aboard Laffey was not advancing my career as a Navy PR officer. To put it bluntly, I was a failure. Our results were zilch. Herb and I had not mailed one envelope or sent one message to the Navy Department.

We did have 322 mimeographed pages ready to send. Except for adding the names, addresses and photos of each crew member we were ready to do our first mailing.

That was our PR situation the day Laffey received orders to proceed to Okinawa as part of the U.S. invasion armada.

So much was happening at Okinawa that Herb and I never went near our PR office. One day Laffey was exploding mines off Okinawa's east coast. The next day she was shooting enemy tanks dug in near the front lines of our troops. Next we were in formation as the number two destroyer to make a torpedo attack on Japan's one remaining battleship, the YAMATO. Now that one chilled our blood. Fortunately, Navy flyers, nearly 400 of them reached YAMATO before we did and our planned torpedo attacks could be canceled.

U.S. destroyer type ships were being sunk and damaged sometimes four or five each day, by Japanese kamikaze pilots. It was plain to me that U.S. surface ships were no match for Japan's kamikaze pilots. ~~Surface ships of World War II vintage were no match for suicide pil~~ots. The fleet commander, Admiral Raymond Spruance would later tell me in his judgement the Japanese could have wiped out our fleet and sent our invasion forces packing if they had struck our fleets en masse at dusk.

But I've jumped ahead of my PR story. At Okinawa I was simply too busy to think about PR. Our first job aboard ship was to destroy our targets and survive if possible.

All these matters would come into question on April 12, 1945. Laffey received orders that day to proceed to Roger Peter one, (radar picket station one). We would be part of a ring of 16 destroyers surrounding Okinawa to report incoming Japanese suicide aircraft.

Our ship would be placed on a direct flight path between Japan's southernmost island of Kyushu and Okinawa. Our job was to send out U.S. fighter planes to intercept the attackers.

Altogether five destroyers had been sent to Roger Peter One since April 1, 1945 invasion day at Okinawa. It was now April 12. None of the five destroyers sent to Roger Peter One had survived. All had been sunk or sufficiently damaged to become useless in combat.

The Japanese kamikazes made it clear to us on the morning of April 16 they had Laffey targeted for the "graveyard" as Tokyo Rose put it. At 7:44 a.m. The first VAL (a dive bomber) flew toward us. By 8:20 a large formation, 50 or more, was headed our way. U.S. fighter planes and Laffey's guns tangled with the suicide armada. Twenty-two kamikazes attacked. Eight were shot down. Seven missed and seven hit us killing 32 and wounding about 60, nearly one third of our complement. Five of the seven kamikazes made damaging hits putting holes in the ships hull and keel.

As the damaged Laffey was being towed stern first to Okinawa for our picket station the skipper called me to the bridge.

"Son," said Commander Becton, "do you have a pretty good idea of what happened this morning?"

"Yes," I said, "I surely do remember what I saw. I am not sure how many planes came in or how many we shot down, but I can make a close estimate."

"As soon as they tow us to our anchorage I want you to go to Admiral Richmond Kelly Turner's flagship and tell his staff what happened to us. If it will help you Lt. Bob Storm and I will meet with you before you go so you can have the benefit of how we saw it."

"Yes Captain," I said, "I'm prepared to go, but I would appreciate anything you and Bob can tell me about the way you saw it."

A few hours later the skipper called Bob and I to his sea cabin on the bridge.

The skipper took a pencil and a piece of blank paper and sketched out the incoming kamikaze attacks.

"You will remember," the Captain said, "the first four came in from the bow and two split off - - our five inchers pounded away."

"Yes," said Bob, "and the very first one veered off - Then those four flew directly toward us, they straffed us a few times."

"Then we took our first hits from 2 planes coming in from the stern," I said, "and we took our first casualties then also, they systematically wiped out many of our guns, our firepower and superstructure, including our PR office."

As we talked the skipper sketched the flight path of each attacking Japanese aircraft.

After an hour or so I told the skipper I was ready to go. I stuffed his sketch in my pocket and was off to the flagship in someone's motor whale boat. I don't recall it being ours. I'm not sure our boat was seaworthy.

I arrived at the Flagship, the Eldorado, before dark, about 16:30 on April 17th. That's 4:30 p.m. I went directly to the flagship PR office when a red-headed, freckle faced commander by the name of Paul Smith welcomed me. In civilian life Commander Smith was editor and General Manager to the San Francisco Chronicle.

"We heard you had a little excitement on the picket line." Smith said in understatement.

"That is true." I said.

"We heard you guys on our voice radio," Smith continued. "you put up quite a fight."

"We tried," I said, "but there were too many planes."

Smith smiled sympathetically.

"Yes, we know," he said.

"Do you have what happened on the tip of your tongue?" Smith asked.

"Yes sir, I'm ready." I said.

"I'm calling a press conference within the hour," said Smith. They all want to hear the story - as do the Admirals and Generals as well as our staff".

"So just take it easy around here for awhile, collect your thoughts and I'll let you know when we're ready."

Our ace gunnery officer was named Paul Smith too, but I had

heard of this PR Paul Smith during my Washington tour of duty. I had heard he had a verbal skirmish with the Chief of Naval Operations, Admiral Ernest King, following a press conference. According to the story, Smith had suggested that Admiral King inform the press on some ships we had lost in a battle. At the very least, Smith thought, King should admit some of the losses the U.S. had suffered in our defeat at Savo Island. In fact, we had lost three cruisers, including Chicago. King had refused to admit our losses. He had become irritated with Smith's suggestion. As the two returned to their offices following the press conference King turned abruptly to Smith and asked, "By the way Smith what do you do between wars?" Smith replied just as abruptly, "I run a newspaper Admiral. By the way what do you do?"

Not surprisingly I would later learn Commander Smith had departed the Navy to become a combat officer in the Marine Corps. Following his fighting on Guam he had returned to reclaim his Navy commission. And the reason Smith could move from the Navy to the Marine Corps and back to the Navy were the orders of his close personal friend, Frank Knox, Secretary of the Navy and a powerful figure during World War II.

Although I was in the office of the fabled Paul Smith, I made no connection between him and Admiral King and Secretary Knox. In any case it is doubtful I would have had the temerity to ask Commander Smith if the story was true. In those days to me a full commander was a powerful person.

A full commander might have considered me presumptuous to

inquire about any of his personal experiences.

While Commander Smith was probably in his late 30's or early 40's I regarded him as a much older person, the same as with my skipper, Commander Becton. I was 24 and Commanders reaching for 40 were getting old I thought. They deserved my respect. My father had taught me to address all my seniors as Mr. so and so or to use the word sir. So Navy regs requiring that I say sir to seniors did not change what I had been taught from early childhood.

Aboard Admiral Turner's flagship I felt relaxed and safe, more so than aboard Laffey. After all our picket line terror, our ship was now anchored close aboard an ammunition ship. If hit an exploding ammo ship would blow every ship out of the harbor, including of course the flagship. But the flagship was anchored further from the ammo ship than the Laffey. I never considered what the crew of the ammo ship might be thinking. Perhaps they had become accustomed to their danger.

During my time alone before the news conference I kept thinking of all the tragic and heroic scenes I had witnessed during the action hoping I could remember most of the details.

I knew this was my one moment as a PR officer to put my ship into the history books for all time. I did not know at that time that Laffey had fought off the most intensive and concentrated kamikaze attack against a single ship during World War II. Yet, she had. Nor that one day, years later, Laffey would be enshrined as a National Historical monument at Patriots Point, SC. I only knew what I had seen and what the skipper and Bob Storm had seen.

"O.K. Lieutenant," said Smith, "our press conference is ready. Come with me."

We entered what I believed to be the officers wardroom. The room was dimly lit. I could barely see faces. It was filled with people somewhere between 100 and 150 faces. I would guess about half press and half staff including Admiral Turner himself.

"We have brought you Lt. Frank Manson of the destroyer Laffey for tonight's briefing," said Commander Smith. Turning to me he said, "Lieutenant it's all yours."

I began by telling the group what was going on every day at Roger Peter One. We had been out there for four days and we had been under attack each day - Some days were worse than others. We had pulled kamikaze pilots bodies from the water and I had recovered code books from one pilot.

Before my briefing was half finished and before I had started telling about the dawn of our longest day, the air raid sirens of the flagship went off. Flash Red . . . Flash Red came over the intercom. Nearby ships were told to make smoke, offering camouflage and cover to all ships in the anchorage. As I talked we were in the midst of another kamikaze attack.

Smoke permeated each passageway and room of the flagship. It soon became impossible for me to see the far side of the wardroom and I could only see the faces of those seated near me. I heard no anti-aircraft firing. The ships were now covered with smoke. A few Japanese pilots flew low over our masts but they could not see us and they made no suicide dives in our area.

Despite the air attack plus the sputtering, choking and coughing from my audience I told the Laffey's story as best I could remember. It was a rare moment for a PR officer. Here I had the wire services, the networks, many large city newspapers and the top flag officers at Okinawa, all listening, all at once. I had nothing to read from, no script, but I needed no notes. I talked about the attacks, the seven hits, our gunners accuracy, the U.S. Marine Corsair pilots who helped us and our casualties, and our damage. I told how Laffey's rudder had jammed hard left.

When I completed the briefing newsmen and flag officers asked numerous questions.

The one question which caused me to pause and think deeply was about the Skipper's words. Had he said anything during the action that I could remember. At first I paused and said I would have to think about that.

Then I recalled our brief conversation, just the two of us, about whether or not we should abandon ship. At that point the stern had sunk beneath the water about 2 feet or so and the bow was riding high in the air. I said it looked as if we might be forced to abandon ship.

The captain replied firmly, "I would never abandon ship as long as a gun will fire."

I thought, well that sure sounds like our skipper alright and he's absolutely correct. But I never thought I would be asked to recall what he said, or that his words in time would become legend alongside the immortal words of such Navy greats as John Paul Jones, "I have not yet begun to fight." David Farragut's, "Damn the torpedoes, full speed ahead."

When the press conference ended Commander Smith asked me back to his office.

"What did I plan to do after the war?" he asked.

"Write editorials for a newspaper," I said, "or maybe finish law school," I said.

"I'll return to running the newspaper in San Francisco," said Commander Smith, "if you ever want a job in the editorial department of my newspaper, you've got it," said Smith. "Just give me a call."

I assumed by Commander Smith's offer that my briefing had his approval.

After returning to the Laffey I briefed the Captain on what happened. I had no idea how far our story would go.

The next day our ship being repaired with soft patches was visited by a few reporters. They talked to the captain and as many of the crew as they wished.

At that point we had not buried the dead and we were still in the process of searching for bodies. The press did not ask many questions during their brief visit. The atmosphere was somber. It just wasn't appropriate to ask questions under the circumstances.

Neither the Captain nor I had any idea what impact my briefing at the flagship would have on the press. Nor would we know until we got back to Seattle, Washington where we would go into dry dock for permanent repairs.

It was 7 weeks after we left Okinawa that we learned what had happened. After reading the press reports and after reading the Captains action reports the Navy Department had decided to open the Laffey to full press converge and to invite the public aboard to see what the kamikaze war was all about.

The Laffey was swamped by the national and local press for a few days in Seattle. Most all my shipmates were asked to give their accounts of what happened. Where were they during the action. What did they see. How did they react and so on. The Laffey story was featured in Life and Time Magazine, in books and newsreels. We were page one nationwide.

Although this all happened fifty years ago, I had achieved my secret wish. I had wanted to be a PR officer in that war. Thanks to the actions of my ship and brave shipmates I was given a boost in that direction.

Largely because of that briefing, I was asked to co-author the history of World War II, plus I was given PR assignments I could never have imagined.

www.ingramcontent.com/pod-product-compliance
Lightning Source LLC
Chambersburg PA
CBHW080622170426
43209CB00007B/1497